CW01658581

INSIGHT GU

Provence
& the Côte d'Azur

Discovery CHANNEL

APA PUBLICATIONS
Part of the Langenscheidt Publishing Group

INSIGHT GUIDE
PROVENCE
& THE CÔTE D'AZUR

ABOUT THIS BOOK

Editorial
Project Editor
Clare Peel
Editorial Director
Brian Bell

Distribution
UK & Ireland
GeoCenter International Ltd
The Viables Centre, Harrow Way
Basingstoke, Hants RG22 4BJ
Fax: (44) 1256-817988
United States
Langenscheidt Publishers, Inc.
46–35 54th Road, Maspeth, NY 11378
Fax: (1) 718 784-0640
Canada
Thomas Allen & Son Ltd
390 Steelcase Road East
Markham, Ontario L34 1G2
Fax: (1) 905 475 6747
Australia
Universal Press
1 Waterloo Road
Macquarie Park, NSW 2113
Fax: (61) 2 9888 9074
New Zealand
Hema Maps New Zealand Ltd (HNZ)
Unit D, 24 Ra ORA Drive
East Tamaki, Auckland
Fax: (64) 9 273 6479
Worldwide
Apa Publications GmbH & Co. Verlag KG (Singapore branch)
38 Joo Koon Road, Singapore 628990
Tel: (65) 865-1600. Fax: (65) 861-6438

Printing
Insight Print Services (Pte) Ltd
38 Joo Koon Road, Singapore 628990
Tel: (65) 865-1600. Fax: (65) 861-6438

First Edition 1989
Fourth Edition 2001

CONTACTING THE EDITORS
We would appreciate it if readers would alert us to errors or outdated information by writing to:
Insight Guides, P.O. Box 7910, London SE1 1WE, England.
Fax: (44) 20 7403-0290.
insight@apaguide.demon.co.uk

www.insightguides.com

This guidebook combines the interests and enthusiasms of two of the world's best-known information providers: Insight Guides, whose titles have set the standard for visual travel guides since 1970, and Discovery Channel, the world's premier source of nonfiction television programming.

The editors of Insight Guides provide both practical advice and general understanding about a destination's history, culture and people. Discovery Channel and its website, www.discovery.com, help millions of viewers to explore their world from the comfort of their home and encourage them to explore it first-hand.

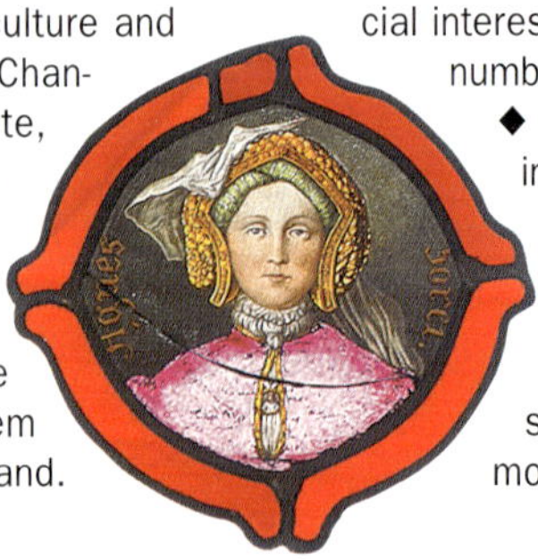

This fully updated edition of *Insight Guide: Provence & the Côte d'Azur* is structured to convey a rich understanding of this region and its culture as well as to guide readers through its sights and activities:

- The **Features** section covers Provence's history, people and culture in a series of informative essays.
- The main **Places** section is a complete guide to all the sights and areas worth visiting. Places of special interest are coordinated by number with the maps.
- The **Travel Tips** listings at the back of the book provide a handy point of reference for information on travel, hotels, shops, restaurants and more. An index to this

EXPLORE YOUR WORLD
Discovery CHANNEL

section appears on the back flap, which also serves as a bookmark.

The contributors

The revision of this edition of *Insight Guide: Provence & the Côte d'Azur* was managed by **Clare Peel** at Insight's editorial headquarters in London. Peel wrote the new chapter on the Cannes Film Festival and revamped the Revolution to World War and Côte d'Azur chapters.

Playing indispensable roles in this new edition were two French-based contributors with wide experience both of their adoptive home country and of travel writing: **Ingrida Rogal** and **Rosemary Bailey**. Rogal updated most of the History and Features sections, while Bailey, an Insight veteran and project editor of several other French guides in the series, updated the majority of the Places section and the travel tips. Bailey also wrote the new chapter on Fine Art, a new feature on Provençal champion Frédéric Mistral and the original feature on perfume.

The current edition builds on the excellent foundations created by the editors and writers of the original edition of the book. Of particular note is **Anne Sanders Roston**, editor of, and main contributor to, the original *Insight Guide: Provence*.

Other contributors to the original version of the book include Riviera-based journalist **David Ward-Perkins** (Cuisine), folklorist **Caroline Roston** (Folk Art) and Grasse-based **Peter Robinson** (The Vaucluse and The Camargue). Francophile and former Toulon-resident **Peter Capella** wrote the chapter on the Alpes-Maritimes and the feature on Marseille's underworld, while Paris-born freelance writer **Mary Deschamps** provided features on Christian Lacroix and the bikini. French graduate and London-based journalist **Caroline Wheal** penned the chapter on The Var.

Most of the images in this guide are by the American travel photographer **Catherine Karnow**, a Francophile who has worked at *Paris Match*, *Le Point* and Magnum's Paris office. Karnow has photographed many Insight Guides, including those to France, Los Angeles and Washington DC.

Another veteran Insight Guides photographer, **Bill Wassman**, was our main source of new pictures for this latest edition.

Penny Phenix proofread and indexed the book, **Cathy Muscat** provided in-house editorial back-up, and **Helen Stallion** was unfailingly helpful on the ground in Provence.

Map Legend

- International Boundary
- *Département* Boundary
- Border Crossing
- National Park/Reserve
- Ferry Route
- Métro
- Airport: International/ Regional
- Bus Station
- Tourist Information
- Post Office
- Church/Ruins
- Monastery
- Mosque
- Synagogue
- Castle/Ruins
- Mansion/Stately home
- Archaeological Site
- Cave
- Statue/Monument
- Place of Interest

The main places of interest in the Places section are coordinated by number with a full-colour map (e.g. ❶), and a symbol at the top of every right-hand page tells you where to find the map.

INSIGHT GUIDE
Provence & the Côte d'Azur

CONTENTS

Maps

Introduction

History

Features

Bormes-les-Mimosas, a hill-town in the Var.

Information panels

Travel Tips

◆ **Full Travel Tips index is on page 289**

Places

MA 433394
MA706667
Sun Speed S

VISITE DES CALANQUES
LCA
MA 596483
481205
A 308 197
MA 263 603

BIENVENUE

Provence has many riches, from lavender fields, remote villages and culture to France's second city and chic coastal resorts

Located in the sunny southeastern corner of France, Provence has a history as rich as its soil. Prehistoric Ligurians, Classical Greeks and Augustan Romans all left their mark here. Later invaders included the warring Arabs and the medieval lords of Baux, famed for their "Courts of Love". It wasn't until the 15th century that the Gauls claimed Provence for their own.

Mary Magdalene is said to have spent her last years in the Var, and several popes made Avignon their home during the 14th century. In the 19th century the Impressionist painter Paul Cézanne was born and worked in the Bouches-du-Rhône, the same *département* in which Vincent van Gogh was driven to madness; by the end of that century even Queen Victoria was holidaying on the Côte d'Azur. Twentieth-century arrivals included the painters Raoul Dufy, Pablo Picasso, Henri Matisse and Marc Chagall and writers such as F. Scott Fitzgerald and Graham Greene. Today, retired statesmen, film stars and the European aristocracy continue to seek out second homes in Provence, in turn encouraging some of France's best-known chefs to open restaurants in the region.

The attractions across Provence's six *départements* (the Vaucluse, Bouches-du-Rhône, Var, Alpes-de-Haute-Provence, Alpes-Maritimes and the Hautes-Alpes – the last is not featured in this book, as this alpine area is generally covered under guides to the Alps) and its two subregions (the Camargue and the Côte d'Azur) are very diverse. No single element is responsible for the region's enduring appeal. Perhaps it's the dazzling light that bathes this intoxicating land of black cypress and crooked olive trees. Or it could be the sweet-smelling lavender that sprawls endlessly across its fields and hill-sides, and the mouthwatering melons and tomatoes produced by its sun-rich soil. Perhaps it's the attraction of the glamorous lifestyle enjoyed along the Côte d'Azur. Or it might be Provence's strategic position between the Mediterranean Sea, the great River Rhône, the Alps and the Italian border.

Even as members of the younger generation increasingly leave the tiny villages where their grandparents herded sheep, mined ochre or grew vegetables to try their luck instead in cities such as Avignon, Marseille and Nice, they bring with them a deep-rooted apprecia-tion of the land and its traditions. ❑

PRECEDING PAGES: shutters and colourful façades; medieval fountain in Séguret; hiker and friend; harbour in Cassis.
LEFT: decorative well.

THE LAND

The varied and complex geography of Provence – a region where the earth is all – is central to the area's history, economy and character

The southeastern corner of France was covered by the sea until around 200 million years ago, when a rock continent called Tyrrhenia began to emerge in strata of limestone, shale and clay. Tyrrhenia was followed, 150 million years later, by a second land mass slightly further "inland"; the latter would become what we now know as Provence.

Submarine forces pressed the Provençal land mass up from below the sea and into the high folds running east–west above the modern coastline, forming mounts Ste-Victoire, Ste-Baume and Ventoux, the Alpille Ridges and the Lubéron and Baronnies mountain ranges. This new earth continued to develop next to Tyrrhenia, until the latter fell back into the sea about 2 million years ago. All that is left of Tyrrhenia is Cap Canaille, the Esterel Massif and some Mediterranean islands, including Sicily and Corsica.

Provence has remained geographically more or less constant since then, although certain natural changes occurred over time and are still slowly taking place. The Val du Rhône (Rhône Valley) began to hollow out, and the Rhône was rerouted from its original seaward path, via the Durance east of the Alpilles and down through the plateau de la Crau (Crau Plain), to its current position flowing directly south to the sea from Avignon. Over the centuries, under the gradual process of erosion, some of the oldest coastline was covered by the sea, and a little more land is reclaimed each year by the Mediterranean.

Structure of the region

Today Provence forms part of the administrative region Provence-Alpes-Côte d'Azur, which splits into six *départements:* the Bouches-du-Rhône, Vaucluse, Var, Alpes-de-Haute-Provence, Haute-Alpes and Alpes-Maritimes. Provence's natural boundaries are the Rhône (to the west), the Mediterranean (south), Italy (east) and the Baronnies and alpine mountain ranges (north).

Popularly, however, Provence is less clearly defined. Parts of Languedoc-Roussillon, including Nîmes and the Pont du Gard aqueduct, and the Rhône-Alpes region are often included in descriptions of the area, and inhabitants of the western areas such as the Vaucluse and the Bouches-du-Rhône often exclude the Alpes-

Maritimes when discussing eastern Provence. Although the Côte d'Azur (popularly known as the French Riviera) is technically part of Provence, it usually stands as an area in its own right; this book therefore features a separate chapter on that region.

The Bouches-du-Rhône

The Bouches-du-Rhône is generally considered to be the oldest part of Provence, as the earliest civilized settlements were centred on its shores. Set in the lower half of the western area of Provence, the *département* is marked by the Rhône to the west, the River Durance to the north, the sea to the south and the Massif de

PRECEDING PAGES: vineyard village of Gigondas.
LEFT: Provençal cherries.
RIGHT: the Grand Canyon de Verdon.

Ste-Baume to the east. Geographically the Bouches-du-Rhône is so varied that it can be taken as a microcosm for the rest of Provence.

The western part of the *département* is characterised by plains filled with alluvial deposits. To the north are plains cut off from the rest of the area by the ragged Alpilles chain. To the south lies the Crau, a vast plain of smooth pebbles polished by the river that once ran through it. South of that, along the coastline and to the extreme west, are the wet plains of the Rhône Delta, commonly known as the Camargue and often referred to as a geographical region in its own right.

The eastern section of the Bouches-du-Rhône is more mountainous, alternating with synclinal basins. The Ste-Victoire mountain range is separated from the Etoile chain by the Val de l'Arc. Beneath them, the Val de l'Huveaune and the Marseille Basin lean against the Ste-Baume mountain range. Most of this area's cliffs are limestone and some peaks reach over 1,000 metres (3,280 ft). Along the coast, these mountains create narrow valleys penetrated by the sea, which are called *calanques*.

Overall, the *département* is dry and rugged, with vegetation ranging from cypress trees and Norwegian pines to low shrubs and heathland; over 100,000 hectares (256,000 acres) are under forest. Abundant sun and mineral-rich soil have helped to make the Bouches-du-Rhône France's top producer of fruit and vegetables. Olive groves, almond trees and wheat fields dominate massive portions of the 180,000 hectares (445,000 acres) of cultivated land. Market goods include garlic, tomatoes, courgettes (zucchini) and asparagus.

The Vaucluse

The Vaucluse bears a certain resemblance to the Bouches-du-Rhône. It also lies along the Rhône to the west and is bordered on the south side by the Durance. Much of its land is flat plain, called the Comtat-Venaisson, and it boasts a wide valley, the Vallée du Coulon, to the south. However, to mark the Vaucluse out from its southern neighbour, the bulk of its area is consumed by the Plateau de Vaucluse, which is hemmed in by the imposing Ventoux Massif to the north. At 1,909 metres (6,263 ft), Mont Ventoux is the highest peak in the region.

The Plateau de Vaucluse merges into the Plateau d'Albion to the north. The latter is speckled with miscellaneous fissures that lead down to a vast network of caves. Rainwater spills down through these holes, collects in the caves, then runs off into an underground network of rivers. These rivers flow beneath the

permeable limestone that composes the plateau, emerging in springs such as the Fontaine de Vaucluse *(see page 137).*

These springs are not all that set the Vaucluse apart from the Bouches-du-Rhône. Overall, its land is more fertile than that of the latter and luxury produce such as melons, wine, lavender and strawberries are grown here.

FOREST FIRES

The fires that annually destroy vast areas of forest are mostly human induced – typically accidental fires caused by permanent inhabitants, rather than tourists. The dry shrub land makes excellent tinder.

The Var

Much of the land in the Var is acutely dry, and summer droughts and forest fires are a big annual threat. Wedged in between the Mediterranean, the Bouches-du-Rhône to the west and alpine foothills to the north and northeast, the Var is largely occupied by the deep forests of the Massif des Maures. With over 50 percent of its area under forest, the Var is the second most heavily wooded French *département*. Each year thousands of acres of pine forests are scorched by fierce fires, which are fuelled by winds often in excess of 80 kph (50 mph), and hundreds of families have to be evacuated from their summer homes.

LEFT: vineyards in the Vaucluse.
ABOVE: Marseille's Vieux Port.

Shrubby grasslands climb rocky slopes in some parts, making the Var a fine spot for raising goats and sheep. By the coast, the Massif pushes up against the sea creating a natural *corniche* where many of the hilltowns of the French Mediterranean waterfront are perched. Offshore are a number of islands included within the Iles d'Hyères.

The alpine regions

To the north of the Var, in between the Vaucluse to the west and the Alpes-Maritimes to the east, is the Alpes-de-Haute-Provence, home to one of Provence's greatest natural wonders, the vast Grand Canyon de Verdon. Although many of the same products are grown in the Alpes-de-Haute-Provence as in the rest of Provence, this *département* is dominated to the south by the Plateau de Valensole and it possesses an unmistakably alpine feeling of physical remoteness. The further north you go, the more alpine the land becomes.

The Alpes-Maritimes vary between the rocky plateaux of the Var and the ridges of the Alpes-de-Haute-Provence. On the eastern side, the region is influenced by the mellowing Italian Alps. Like the residents of the Var, those of the Alpes-Maritimes live in constant fear of fire.

Embracing Provence

One thing that all the *départements* share is dazzling light from a potent sun. Farmers delight in the long growing season, and painters revel in the magical glow that surrounds the land. Another unifying characteristic is the infamous mistral. This wild, indefatigable northern wind, whose name fittingly comes from the Provençal word *mestre* (master) sweeps across almost the entire region between late autumn and early spring, although the western and central sections are generally the worst hit. Its violent, chilling gales are created whenever a depression develops over the Mediterranean. Areas of forest that have been burnt away in summer fires are especially susceptible to erosion from the mistral.

The geography within Provence is varied and complex and this variety is one of the many reasons why the region has always been – and remains – so enduringly attractive. ❑

PROVINCIA.
La Provence.
LANGE
DOC.
DAVLPHI
CONTE DE
VE
NAN
CIN
CONTE DE
SAULT
LE BERONMON
Montauban
Monvoillon
Samllac
Sault
Les Omergu
Bedoin
Revest
Carpentra
Masan
Verague
Requemaure
Ville neufve
Avignon
Perne
S. Didier
Aramon
Valebergus
Cabrieres
Rustaret
Iocas
Apt
Bubon
Laurade
La Castelet
Beaucaire
Nismes
Castelet
Fourques
S. Gillis
Lamote
Durance
S. Remy
Orgon
Les Bauls
Aiguines
Launs
Vitrole
Manosque
Ancons
Pertuis
Ragues
Petrolls
Allon
S. Canat
S. Mare
Sambuc
Merveiles
Grans
S. Martin
Istre
Aix
Rognac
Bove
Magnan
Tour d. Para
FOS
Les penes
Fuveaus
Tres
Grvol
Sauvereael
Trois Maries
Fo. d. belua
Marseille
Tucis
S. Marcel
Massielle veivo
Planier
Espoholen
Rieulx
Cassidaine
Bendor
Gras d'orgon
Gras de Pau
Paulet
Gras grant
Gras dengi
Roque de Dour
Gras de Passon
Les Tignes
MARIS MEDITERRANEI
La Plamase
Petrus Kærius Cælavit
43 Occidens
42
25
26

28
29
Embrun
Gap
Roßet
Durance flu.
Vars
Maurin
Theus
Tallert
Les Huermis
S. Paol
Lausier
Bacillone
Huvade
Pontis
Antraygne
Breses
Peivepove
Laup
Sambuc
CONTE DE BVEIL
S. Dalmas
Pors
S. Esteve
Lieusole
Peona
Pieri
Bueil
Floma
S. Salvat.
CONTE DE NICE
La Roquette
Aspremont
Fallicon
43
Oriens.
42
Montreau
Laragne
Vastavon
Estoin
Melve
Valernes
Nibles
S. Martin
Miolans
Gigas
Anset
Collobrious
Barles
Chanole
Tora
Guillumes
Aste
Peonie
Lamote
Toare
Villose
Chantorci
Aimac
Digné
Archal
Lagromuse
Mesel
Lesmees
S. Legiar
Autvare
Annot
Glandeves
Gars
Mornes
Val clause
Nevoiles
S. Iolhian
Senes
Beines
Bras
Lapel
Tervans
Castelane
S. Crois
Rias
Demdes
La pene
Le Cor
Gillete
Les Erres
Lebore
Vence
Soleis
Evals
Le biose
Oinguion
Aiguine
Comps
Leborguet
Lebar
Mons
Braudmar
Artignosa
Beudveil
S. Cesari
Grasse
Antibo
Cagne
Barnoul
Enjous
Erapus
Benconte
Canes
Chauvert
Sillans
LE
Callas
Bagnels
Lanapole
Montfort
Trans
Draguignan
TER EL
Frenuls
S. Maxemin
Brignole
Torenet
Lemvy
La Grenille
C. Garaupe
S. Marguerite
S. Honorat
de Teule
C. Rouls
P. Dagat
PARS.
Camp
Cabasse
Roquebrune
Grimault
S. Vincent
Pignans
Cogolin
Cuers
Turris
Laverne
Romatuelle
La Molle
Gassin
C. de Helbe
C. de Portes
C. Taliar
C. Lardier
Les Isles D'or Stecades
Titan
Milliaria Gallica Communia
Milliaria Germanica commu
2
4
6

Decisive Dates

PRE-ROMAN AND GALLO-ROMAN ERA

***circa* 1 million BC** Earliest evidence of humans in Provence in the Vallée des Merveilles, Monaco.
1000 BC Ligurians occupy the Mediterranean coast.
600 BC Marseille is founded by Greek traders.
121 BC The Romans conquer southern Gaul and establish Aquae-Sextiae (Aix-en-Provence).
102 BC The Romans defeat invading Germans.
58–51 BC Subjugation of Gaul by Julius Caesar.
27 BC–AD 14 Reign of Caesar Augustus. Provence begins to flourish.

AD 12 Romans occupy the settlement at Vaison.
AD 19 Construction of the Pont du Gard.
AD 3rd–5th centuries Christianity spreads.
395 Arles becomes the administrative capital of the western provinces (Gaul).
476 Fall of the Western Roman Empire. Vandals, Visigoths, Burgundians, Ostrogoths and Franks invade the coastal zones.

THE MIDDLE AGES

8th–10th centuries Provence becomes part of the Carolingian Empire. Arabs from the Iberian peninsula invade and settle by the coast, staying for 200 years until expelled by Guillaume le Libérateur.
1096–99 The First Crusade.
1032 Provence is annexed to the Holy Roman Empire.
***circa* 1125** Troubador poetry flourishes.
1152 St-Trophime church is consecrated in Arles.
1178 Frederick I (Barbarossa) is crowned king of Provence in Arles.
1209–29 The Albigensian Wars.
1246 Provence becomes part of the Angevin dynasty through marriage.
1248 Louis IX embarks on the Seventh Crusade.
1274 The Comtat Venaisson (east of Avignon) is ceded to the Pope.

THE RENAISSANCE

1308 The Genoese Grimaldi family acquires Monaco.
1309 Clement V of France is given the papal crown.
1316 Pope John XXII moves the papacy to Avignon.
1320 Carpentras is made capital of the region.
1348 Pope Clement VI buys Avignon. Plague strikes.
1377 The papacy returns to Rome.
1388 The eastern part of Provence (the Comté de Nice) falls under the rule of the House of Savoy (Italy).
1409 The University of Aix is founded.
1471 "Good" King René (1434–80) moves to Aix.
1486 Charles du Maine hands Provence over to the king of France.
1501 The founding of the parliament in Aix.
1503 Nostradamus is born in St-Rémy-de-Provence.
1535 Massacre of the Vaudois.
1539 French replaces Provençal, the *langue d'oc*, as the official language.
1545 Destruction of Protestant villages in the Lubéron during the Wars of Religion.
1598 Under the Edict of Nantes, the Huguenots are granted the right to worship in freedom, ending the Wars of Religion.
1577 The first soap factory is founded in Marseille.
1685 The Edict of Nantes is revoked, and thousands of Huguenots emigrate.
1691 The French conquer Nice, but the town is handed back to Savoy in 1715 after the Spanish War of Succession.
1718 Nice becomes part of Sardinia.
1720 Plague spreads from Marseille into Provence and more than 100,000 people die.

THE REVOLUTION AND NAPOLEON BONAPARTE

1789 The storming of the Bastille.
1790 Provence is divided into three *départements:* Basse-Alpes, Bouches-du-Rhône and Var.
1791 France annexes both Avignon and the Comtat Venaisson.
1793 End of the siege of Toulon, which sparks Napoleon Bonaparte's rise to glory.

THE BELLE ÉPOQUE TO THE EARLY 20TH CENTURY

1815 The end of the Napoleonic Wars; the English aristocracy begins to winter in the south of France.
1830 Frédéric Mistral, Provençal champion and poet laureate (1904), is born at Maillane near Avignon.
1834 Lord Brougham settles in Cannes and the south French coast becomes the preferred winter residence of the English nobility.
1839 Cézanne is born in Aix-en-Provence.
1854 Mistral founds the Félibrige, a cultural school intended to advance the Provençal language.
1860 Nice is returned to France.
1861 Impoverished Monaco is forced to sell Menton and Roquebrune to France.
1863 Monte Carlo casino opens its doors.
1869 Publication of Daudet's *Lettres de Mon Moulin.* The Suez Canal opens, and Marseille gains in importance as a Mediterranean port.
1887 The term Côte d'Azur is coined by the writer Stephen Liégeard.
1888 Van Gogh settles in Arles.
1892 Paul Signac moves to St-Tropez.
1906 Renoir arrives to live in Cagnes.
1924 F. Scott and Zelda Fitzgerald visit the Riviera.
1925 The writer Colette moves to St-Tropez. Coco Chanel visits the Côte d'Azur.
1928 Jean Médécin becomes mayor of Nice. The Médécin dynasty rule Nice for 62 years.
1929 Monaco holds it first Grand Prix.
1936 Introduction of the paid holiday in France.

FROM WORLD WAR II TO THE PRESENT DAY

1939 The Cannes Film Festival is inaugurated but the onset of World War II causes the first festival to be delayed until 1946.
1940 Italians occupy Alpes Maritimes.
1942 German troops occupy southern France.
1944 The Allies land on the beaches of Pampelonne towards the end of World War II.
From 1945 Mass tourism. The coastal strip is no longer a playground for the rich and famous only.
1946 First Cannes Film Festival. Picasso in Antibes.
1952 Le Corbusier's now iconic housing block, the so-called "Cité Radieuse" is built in Marseille.
1956 Fairytale marriage of the American film star Grace Kelly to Prince Rainier III of Monaco. Brigitte Bardot hits St-Tropez, starring in the film *And God Created Woman.*

PREDEDING PAGES: Provence under the Romans.
LEFT: triptych detail, Cathédrale St-Sauveur, Aix.
RIGHT: commemorating Napoleon's 1815 landing, Golfe-Juan.

1960 Opening of the dam at Serre-Ponçon.
1962 Many French Algerians settle in Provence after the Algerian war of independence.
1964 The Fondation Maeght art gallery opens.
1966 Jacques Médécin succeeds his father as mayor of Nice.
1969 Sophia Antipolis Science Park is founded.
1972 The Provence-Alpes-Côte d'Azur region is cre ated with the reorganisation of local government.
1975 Opening of the dam at Sainte-Croix.
1982 Princess Grace of Monaco dies in a car crash.
1990 Nice's Musée d'Art Moderne et Contemporain opens. Jacques Médecin, Mayor of Nice for 25 years, flees to Uruguay to avoid trial for corruption.

1992 Floods in Vaison cause havoc.
1994 Jacques Médecin returns to face trial. He is sentenced to imprisonment for three and a half years but is released after two years. In 1998 he dies of a heart attack in Uruguay.
1998 France wins the World Cup.
1999 The Front National is split by internal feuding between Jean Marie Le Pen and his sacked deputy, Bruno Mégret. An extreme-right breakaway party is formed.
2000 The TGV extension is planned along coast to Nice; local protest continues.
2001 The renovated TGV terminal opens in Marseille.
2002 From 30 June the euro replaces the franc as the main form of currency in France. ❑

PREHISTORY TO THE MIDDLE AGES

Provence's location and climate have always been appealing – especially to conquerors such as the Ligurians, Greeks, Romans and Arabs

Provence's strategic position along the Mediterranean, giving the northern Europeans access to the sea and the southern Europeans, Africans and Middle Easterners access to northern Europe, brought age after age of new colonisation and settlement before France became the stable entity it is today. Ligurians, Celts, Greeks, Romans, Teutons, Cimbrians, Visigoths, Franks, Arabs – they all had their day under the warm Provençal sun.

The Rhône, which snakes down through Provence and tumbles out into the Mediterranean, offered added incentive to settlers. The Greeks supposedly used the river as a trade route to tin-producing Cornwall; the Romans were quick to recognise its value as a means of communication between their numerous conquests. Not until the invention of the railway did the Rhône's attraction to traders and travellers diminish.

Prehistoric farmers

Even in prehistoric times the area was popular. Archaeological sites within the Bouches-du-Rhône (at Châteauneuf-les-Martigues and the Baume Longue) link Provence with Mesolithic development. Pottery from the middle Neolithic period (5th millennium BC) has been found at the coastal sites of Ile Maire and Ile Riou.

Although most Stone-Age sites were submerged in the post-glacial rise in sea level, making it difficult to determine what the material culture in Provence of that time was like, scientists agree on two facts. Firstly, that the early Provençals, like their descendants, were as involved in growing cereals as they were in hunting. (All the elements of an agricultural economy were in place by 5000 BC, although it was probably not until 4000 BC that agriculture became the firm subsistence base.) Secondly, that communications between settlements across the area were fluid. Most Stone-Age settlements were found in the arable lands of the Provençal basins and on the coastal Languedoc plain, but caves discovered inland that were probably employed as transit sites suggest that there was a well-spread economic system. Evidence of early human habitation in the form of rock carvings and skeletons has been discovered in the region, dating back more than 250,000 years.

LEFT: detail of the interior of the crypt in the Cathédrale St-Victor, Marseille.
RIGHT: prehistoric graffiti in the Mercantour.

PREHISTORIC ART

Thousands of prehistoric cave paintings and engravings are accessible at sites across Provence. Perhaps the most notable of these are the Bronze-Age rock carvings at Mont Bégo in the Vallée des Merveilles. Tourists can also visit the lagoon-surrounded spot of St-Blaise, near Martigues, where some traces of human occupation date back more than 7,000 years, and excavations have revealed a parade of inhabitants who occupied the area sporadically between 700 and 50 BC. For those less inclined to wander around half-ruined spots in the sun, in July and August the museum in Sault *(see page 135)* offers a fine collection of Stone-Age artefacts.

The Ligurians

Between 1800 and 800 BC the land in Provence was inhabited and cultivated by the Ligurians. (Ligurian is a term that usually refers to anyone living around the Mediterranean as the Neolithic Age spilled over into the Iron Age. Some people believe that all Ligurians were descended from Spain's Iberians; others insist that only some Ligurians were linked to the Iberians.) The Provençal Ligurians lived in small, disparate village settlements and gleaned whatever they could from the rocky land around them. Early cultural bonds between the various Ligurian outposts, which stretched from Catalonia through Provence to the base of the Swiss Alps, can be whittled down to a propensity for flat burial graves and a particular skill with razor design. Eventually, the Ligurians were "Celticised", although genetically they were related to neither the Gauls nor the Celts.

Even if the shape of their heads may elude historians, we do know that these later Ligurians were an extremely tough people whose taste for piracy annoyed the Romans. Posidonius, the 2nd-century BC historian, said of them: "…daily hardships are such that life is truly difficult for these people whose bodies, as a result, are skinny and shrivelled. It sometimes happens that a woman gives birth to her child in the fields, covers the little one with leaves, and then returns to her work so that a day will not be lost."

One thing the Ligurians did enjoy was a considerable degree of anonymity from outside influences. The Phocaean Greeks would change that, however, in the 6th century BC.

The arrival of civilisation

Marseille, it might be plausibly argued, was the birthplace of Western civilisation on the European continent. It was to this marshy bay that Ionian Greeks from Phocaea set sail during the early 6th century BC.

THE FOUNDATION OF MARSEILLE

Ici
Vers L'An 600 Avant J.C.
Des Marins Grecs Ont Abordés
Venant De Phocée
Ils Fonderent Marseille
D'Où Rayonna En Occident
La Civilisation

A plaque on Marseille's quai des Belges bears the above inscription, which roughly translates as:
On this spot, In around 600 BC, Greek sailors landed from Phocaea. They founded Marseille, from whence civilization spread across the West.

According to legend, the Phocaeans cemented their interest in what was to become Marseille with a marriage. Gyptis, the daughter of the local Ligurian king, was in the process of choosing a husband when they arrived. A gathering of hopeful suitors waited as she decided to whom she would give the cup of wine that indicated her choice. When Protis, the captain of the Greek sailing party, stepped forward, she handed him the chalice.

The Phocaeans formed a happy alliance with the locals. They had come for economic purposes, not battle, and quickly set up a successful trading post. Their new colony, Massalia, soon became the most important commercial centre along the coast and a flourishing republican city-state in its own right. During its heyday in the mid-4th century BC, the Phocaean presence spread throughout the area. Some of the cities founded were Nikaia (Nice), Antipolis (Antibes), Citharista (la Ciotat), Olbia (Hyères) and Athenopolis (St-Tropez).

In the 4th century BC, Massalia was still very much a Greek city, although independent in nature. Pytheas, the Greek responsible for our modern method of measuring latitude and for explaining the tides, was actually a 4th-century Massalian. He expanded the Phocaean world view by visiting the British Isles and the Baltic. Another Massalian navigator, Euthymenius, explored the west coast of Africa *circa* 350 BC.

Provincia Romana

During the late 3rd century BC, however, the ties with Greece were weakened, as a budding relationship with Rome began to develop. When the legendary Carthaginean general Hannibal, on his way northeast from Spain towards the Alps, appeared on the plains of Provence with his elephants and his army of 40,000 men, the Phocaeans were quick to join forces with the already outraged Romans. This alliance grew steadily, to the point where, in 212 BC, Massalia switched from the Greek form of municipal government to the Roman one.

The friendship with Rome initially proved beneficial. The northern and warlike Celts, Ligurians and Celto-Ligurians had been watching the prosperous Phocaeans with envy for quite some time and banded together in 125 BC to seize the Massalian riches. Overwhelmed, the Phocaeans turned to the Romans for help, and, in response, the warrior Caius Sextius Calvinius brought in an entire Roman army. Although a bloody three-year war ensued, the Romans nonetheless prevailed. At the end of the war, Caius Sextius Calvinius decided that he liked the area and established the city of Aquae Sextiae (Aix-en-Provence), near to the site of Entremont, a Celto-Ligurian capital that the Romans had already enslaved.

As a sign of generosity, the Romans decided not to disturb the Massalian control of the coastal strip that stretched from the Rhône to what is now the Principality of Monaco. They increased their own interest in the region, however, and in 102 BC, led by ancient Provençal hero Caius Marius, went on to defeat even more northern barbarians, the wild Teutons and the savage Cimbrians.

Before long, the Romans had replaced the Phocaeans as lords of the region, which they called "Provincia Romana" and from which the modern name "Provence" is derived. Massalia, however, continued to thrive and to operate with a fairly high degree of autonomy. Now no longer just a trading post, the city became famous as an intellectual centre, with universities rivalling those of Athens.

LEFT: Ligurian and Roman ruins at Glanum.
RIGHT: Musée des Docks Romains, Marseille.

The rise of Arles

The good times were not to last, however. Massalia made the fatal error of siding with Pompey against Caesar during Rome's civil war. After Caesar's victory, in 49 BC, the emperor punished the city by making it a Roman vassal. He further crushed the colony by strengthening the port of Arelate (Arles) and using its inhabitants to besiege Massalia.

Arles was not a new town, having been originally founded in the 6th century BC by the Greeks. During the 2nd century BC, Marius had built a canal that connected Arles's position on the Rhône to the Fos Gulf, making the city a convenient river-and-maritime port. The waterway had helped exploit the Arlesians' talent for building rafts supported by goat bladders. To add to its fortunes, this city was situated beside the Roman Aurelian Way, the highway that linked Italy with Spain.

With the fall of Massalia, Arles became established as the most important city in the area. Rome converted the entire south of France into a Roman province and made Arles its capital, with a secondary city at Cimiez, located just to the north of Nice.

The Romans would remain in Provence for an additional 600 years, most of which were

Roman Remains

Among the most visually stunning remains of Roman Provence is the Pont du Gard *(see page 123)*, a marvel of 1st century AD engineering – the aqueduct was sealed against leaks using a bizarre (and, presumably, pungent) cocktail of lime, wine, pork fat and extract of fig. The acqueduct, which spans the River Gard and is believed to have been constructed by Agrippa, has three layers and measures 49 metres (160 ft) high and 275 metres (900 ft) long. The great edifice carried water from springs in Uzès along to Nîmes. The ancient city of Vaison-la-Romaine *(see page 129)* is another monumental Roman site, where visitors can meander through streets that have changed little since Roman times and take stock of Roman baths, theatres, statues and residential buildings. The Roman arches at Orange and at Carpentras betray the agony of the conquered Gauls, who were forced to chisel depictions of their vanquishers' triumph into the stone façades. Other Roman sites to inspire the imagination include the Musée des Docks Romains (Dock Museum) in Marseille *(see page 150)*, the Musée de l'Arles Antique (Museum of Antiquity), Arles *(see page 172)*, the remains of the ancient city of Glanum, just outside St-Rémy-de-Provence *(see page 182)*, and the perfectly proportioned Maison Carrée in Nîmes *(see page 125)*.

times of peace and prosperity. Great temples, bridges, acqueducts, baths and theatres were constructed across the region *(see panel on facing page)*, much to the delight of modern-day tourists.

During the reign of Augustus in the second half of the 1st century, culture and the arts expanded considerably, as did trade. Slowly, principally due to their firm control and imposing political machine, the Romans united what had once been a scramble of disparate trading posts. One sign of this growing unity was the growth of a regional language, Provençal, which was derived from Latin and is still widely spoken in the region today *(see page 180)*.

ST-TROPHIME

The holy man after whom this church in Arles is named is carved on its northeastern pillar. Other biblical scenes appear throughout the church, which is a fine example of Romanesque architecture.

The spread of Christianity

According to legend, it was also during the 1st century AD that "the Word" arrived in the northern Mediterranean. Many people believe that it was to these shores that Mary Magdalene and Martha, along with Martha's miraculously resurrected brother Lazarus, Mary Jacoby, sister to the Virgin Mary, Mary Salome, mother to the apostles James and John, saints Maximinius and Sidonius, and the servant Sarah, fled after the crucifixion of Jesus Christ.

Buffeted by the waves, without sail or oar, this saintly company landed on the shores of a town that is now called Stes-Maries-de-la-Mer. Supposedly, the voyagers erected a small chapel to the Virgin, before leaving the town and going their separate ways. Mary Magdalene found a cave up in the hills of Ste-Baume where she lived as a hermit until her death 30 years later.

Whether or not St Trophime was among this group is up for debate; he is, however, widely credited with the introduction of Christianity to the North. The saintly man headed for Arles, where he was made third bishop of the town and constructed the first Christian church in Gaul: St-Trophime *(see page 171)*, which is still standing today.

Medieval Provence

By the time the Roman Empire fell in AD 476, Roman civilization had left a permanent mark on Provence. The entire region had been Chris-

LEFT: the Pont du Gard.
ABOVE: portal detail, St-Trophime, Arles.

tianised and consequently imbued with the principles of that faith. The frugal and industrious streaks that are considered typical of the Provençal character today are widely accredited to their Roman ancestry. The Romans' predecessors, the Phocaeans, and more specifically the Massalians *(see pages 28–9)*, were enthusiasts for the joys of the flesh. The Romans, however, were much more attentive to cultivating the hard dry soil and building up sufficient fortifications – something that was

THE VISIGOTHS

Belonging to the western branch of the Goths (*visi* may mean "west", whereas *ostro* means "east"), the Visigoths invaded Rome's Empire in 410, establishing their rule in what is now Spain and Southern France.

their Provençal conquests to the Ostrogoths from Italy, who also appropriated all the Burgundian lands for themselves.

The Franks did not agree that the Ostrogoths deserved Burgundy and in 534 they succeeded in conquering that part of the country for themselves. The Ostrogoths incurred further problems by alienating the Byzantine Empire. In return for Frankish neutrality, these early Italians had no choice but to hand over their Provençal territory in 536.

probably central to their long and impressive reign in the region.

Goths, Burgundians and Franks

The fall did come, however, heralded by the Visigoths. Their interest in Arles came as no surprise, since they had been routinely attacking the city since the early 5th century AD. They quickly assumed all of the area south of the Durance River, while the Burgundians took over to the north.

The Visigoths did little for the region, however, and their rule was short-lived. In 507, they were firmly trodden upon by the Franks; to escape these northern strongmen, they ceded

The Franks now had a large amount of land to supervise – too much for one authority alone to manage. They decided to divide up the territory, uniting northern Provence with Arles, Toulon and Nice with Burgundy, but handing the strip including Marseille, Avignon and much of the coast over to the kings of Austrasia. The last ruled over the eastern part of the kingdom of the Merovingian Franks that now incorporates northeastern France, western Germany and the whole of Belgium.

Representatives, known as *patrices*, were appointed in each region by the central Frankish ministry. The *patrices*, however, proved much more interested in promoting their own independence than working for the good of the united region and were quick to bond with foreign elements if that meant protecting their own autonomy.

One such group were the Arabs. For the first couple of centuries under Frankish rule, Provence had fared pretty well commercially. Nonetheless, their integration with the rest of France was minimal at best, and when the Arabs arrived in Provence in 732, not all of the natives complained.

First Arab invaders

In 732, two Arab armies besieged and took Arles. Encouraged by their victory, they continued north until they encountered the French hero Charles Martel (grandfather of Charlemagne), in Poitiers. Although Martel expelled these Islamic intruders from Provence in 739, he was less than happy with the Provençal ambivalence towards them. Throughout the battle against the Arabs, he treated the region almost with as much hostility as he did the - enemy. Between his armies and those of the Arabs, great numbers of Provençals were slaughtered and whole cities were destroyed. The city of Avignon was virtually wiped out.

The Carolingian dynasty

Martel's son, Pepin the Short succeeded Charles, reigning from 751 until 768, and founding the Carolingian dynasty. Pepin's son, the mighty Charlemagne, went on to reign as king of the Franks from 768 until 814. Although both leaders were careful to keep Provence under strict Frankish rule, this did not prevent the return of the Arabs in 813. The Arabs' new tactic was to approach the area by sea rather than over land via Spain – a strategy that proved to be highly effective for around two further centuries.

Meanwhile, in the North, Charlemagne had established the Holy Roman Empire. With the Treaty of Verdun in 843, Provence was turned over to Charlemagne's grandson, Lothair I, as part of the "Middle Realm". When Lothair died, the region was labelled a separate kingdom and subsequently passed through the hands of several rather unremarkable rulers: Lothair's son Charles; the emperor Louis II, ruler of Italy; Charles the Bald; Boso, ruler of the Viennois; Boso's son Louis, who eventually went on to become king of Italy in 900; and, finally, Hugh of Arles, who handed Provence over to Rudolf II of Jurane Burgundy in the mid-10th century.

Norman invasion and Arab exit

All these kingships and dukedoms did very little to secure the area, however, and soon the Provençals had to deal with the Normans, who set out from Scandinavia, in 859, to stake a

claim in the south. They levelled Arles, Nîmes and much of the countryside, before the fierce opposition of Gérard de Roussillon made them decide to head back to Scandinavia.

The departure of the Normans gave the region little respite, however, as the highly persistent Arabs were soon to return. During the last part of the 9th century, their hold in Provence reached its apogee, as the entire coastal area fell to Arab powers and these invaders marauded right up into the Alps. Not until 1032 did Guillaume le Libérateur – abetted by an unusually conveniently timed outbreak of plague – eliminate the Arab menace from Provence once and for all. ❑

LEFT: the French hero Charles Martel quashes the Arab army.

RIGHT: Charlemagne, King of the Franks from 768 until 814.

FEUDING AND PAPAL AVIGNON

During the late Middle Ages internal feuding proved more of a threat than external invasion. Troubadours sang and the Popes moved in

Although contained within the Holy Roman Empire, Provence was a fairly independent entity by the year 1000. Threats from invaders subsided, giving Arles and Avignon a chance to smooth their feathers and the entire region the opportunity to cultivate an identity.

The departure of the Arabs and Normans also left the Provençals with time and energy for internal squabbles. When Boso, Count of Arles in the mid-10th century, died, he left Provence to his sons, Rotbald and Guillaume. The former was Count of Arles and the latter Count of Avignon, and they ruled over the region from their respective seats. By 1040, however, Rotbald's male line was extinct, and his inheritance moved over to the female side of the family. This was the start of a long, unfortunate pattern.

Power games

When Bertrand of Arles died in 1093, the last direct male heirs from the line of Boso stopped with him. Gerberge of Arles, sister of Bertrand, stepped forward to claim control, followed by Alix, heiress of Avignon. They were joined by Raymond IV, grandson to Emma of Toulouse (the daughter of Rotbald, Count of Arles, and wife of Guillaume III of Toulouse).

The countship of Provence fell into turmoil. The countship of Forcalquier was carved out of the region and given to Alix. In 1112, Gerberge handed her rights to her daughter Douce, who complicated matters further by marrying the Catalan Ramón Berenguer III, Count of Barcelona. Within a year, Ramón had changed his name to the more Gallic Raymond Berengar and taken the title of Count-Marquis to Provence. The Toulousians, outraged at his usurpation, contested his claim. They were soon joined by the house of Baux, whose own Raymond had married Douce's younger sister, Stephanie.

The Baux family was no insignificant enemy. Not known for their modesty, they traced their genealogy back to Balthazar, the Magi king, and implanted the star of Bethlehem on their arms. In the 11th century, before they attempted to claim control of Provence, the Baux had already subjugated some 80 towns and villages. As their power increased, they gathered up such titles as Prince of Orange, Viscount of Marseille, Count of Avellinoad and Duke of Andria.

LEFT: St-Gilles, a 12th-century church in the Camargue.
RIGHT: fresco from the Palais des Papes, Avignon.

THE HORRORS OF THE BAUX FAMILY

The history of the Baux family is a catalogue of savagery. One prince massacred the entire town of Courthézon; another was carved up in prison by his wife; a third besieged the castle of his pregnant niece so that he could violate her bedchambers. Perhaps the most famed member of the family, however, was the husband of Berangère des Baux, who slew the poet Guillem de Cabestanh and gave his heart and a goblet of his blood to his unknowing wife for dinner. After discovering the source of the meal, she declared that it was so lovely that no other meat or drink would defile her lips again – and she threw herself off the top of les Baux.

The Language of the Troubadours

Provençal is a Romance language derived from the Latin of the 1st-century BC Roman conquerors. The staying power of the language reflects the deep cultural effect of the Romans. Centuries after they had faded from power and been replaced by varied Germanic invasions, then by the Franks, the Provençal language clung to its Latin attributes. Hardly any of the Germanic traits evident in French can be found in Provençal.

The feudal organisation of the Midi during the Middle Ages resulted in the fragmentation of Provençal into a variety of related but individual dialects. Nonetheless, a unified literary language, "Classical Provençal", was recognised from the 11th to 15th centuries. It was in this language that the poems of the troubadours were written.

The oldest piece of Provençal verse still extant is a 10th-century refrain attached to a Latin poem in a Vatican manuscript. The earliest complete work to have survived is a set of poems by Guillaume IX, Duke of Aquitaine. These poems consist of 11 pieces, each written in stanzas and intended to be sung.

It is almost certain that Guillaume did not pioneer such work. More likely, his noble rank helped preserve his poetry when that of his predecessors and contemporaries fell into oblivion. The true creators of the troubadour style of literature were probably of much more modest social standing.

It is widely believed that the troubadours developed from a lowly class of jugglers, who combined poetry with their acts. This group evolved into a more refined circle of court residents, who composed and recited their poetry unaccompanied by tricks. These poets were encouraged by the lonely wives of their noble patrons to develop the love songs that became the mark of the troubadour, and they eventually created the medieval convention of "courtly" love *(see panel on facing page)*.

By the late 11th century, the troubadours had become a vital institution of a much higher status than their ignoble predecessors. Among the most famous were Bernart de Ventadour, patronised by Eleanor of Aquitaine; Jaufre Rudel de Blaye, poet of the *amor de lonh*, or "love from afar"; Giraut de Borneil, creator of the *trobar clus*, or "closed" style; Folquet de Marseille, a troubadour who became a monk, then an abbot and was finally elevated to the status of bishop of Toulouse; Bertran de Born; and Peire d'Alvernhae. In total, the works of over 460 troubadours have been preserved.

With the rooting out of the Cathares during the early 13th century came the rise of the French Crown's control over Provence and the fall of the feudal lords. The troubadours were no longer able to make a happy living from their music, and the use of Provençal as a literary language drastically declined as a result.

Over the next few centuries, a handful of valiant artists continued to write in Provençal, and the literature experienced a mild revival during the 16th century in what is generally referred to as the Provençal Renaissance. Nothing, however, could compare with the glory of the medieval period.

Nothing, that is, until the advent of the society of the Félibrige, founded by the poet Frédéric Mistral and other concerned Provençal writers during the mid-19th century *(see page 180)*. Mistral was strongly influenced by the schoolmaster and poet Joseph Roumanille – a native of St-Rémy, who turned to composing in his dialect so that his mother would be able to read his work – and he dedicated his enormous talent towards "stirring this noble race to a renewed awareness of its glory". Mistral's devotion was rewarded in 1905 with a Nobel Prize for literature. ❑

LEFT: an example of early written Provençal.

At the height of its splendour, the airy perch of the Baux fortress, which rises from a bare rock spar at 200 metres (650 ft), was famed for its "Court of Love". Here, as many as 6,000 troubadours composed passionate poems in praise of well-bred ladies. In return, the poets would receive a peacock's feather and a kiss. However, being hosts to the Court of Love didn't stop the Baux from being the bloodiest, cruellest group in the region *(see box, page 35)*. Although no-one wanted to parley with them, the Barcelonians and Toulousians signed an amicable treaty among themselves in 1125. This agreement gave everything south of the Durance River to the former and everything north of the river to the latter, with Avignon, Sorgues, Caumont and Le Thor to be shared. They seemed content with this solution, but the Baux continued to challenge the Barcelonians.

A complex line of Raymonds from Barcelona, Toulouse and Provence, plus an Alfonso from Spain, traded the countship of Provence during the 12th century. Eventually, the three claimant parties decided to divide up the region once and for all. Toulouse became Languedoc, Barcelona was named Catalonia, and Forcalquier evolved into a new, smaller Provence.

Throughout this period, the German kings, the true rulers of Provence, did not know who they should recognise as vassal for the region. The main evidence still visible of the era's rampant instability are the many isolated *villages perchés* dating from that time. The lack of stern central authority promoted the rise of the feudal system. Grandiose castles were built, and the arts found patronage within the various courts.

The arts were not all that flourished at this time, however. Towns such as Arles, Avignon, Nice, Tarascon and Marseille were reorganised as communal regimes under consular government and became independent forces in their

ABOVE: St-Michel's 12th-century tympanum, Salon.

THE TROUBADOURS AND THE ARTS

The troubadours *(see feature, left)* emerged as a direct result of feudalism, when wealthy heiresses – usually the daughters of territorial lords – were married off for economic, political and territorial reasons rather than for those of love or lust. Once wed, these noble ladies were left mostly to their own devices, and many of them welcomed the attentions of the troubadours, their husband's courtiers. The singing poets' ballads of love and admiration were usually offered in the most respectful manner, and their attentions were considered harmless and innocent – sometimes even convenient – by the men of the court.

own right. As a result of the Crusades, which began at the end of the 11th century, the Levant had opened up as a trade route and a source of refined cultural influence. This, together with the elimination of the Arab threat by Guillaume le Libérateur *(see page 33)*, sparked a commercial revival that added to the area's well-being.

The Albigensians

In 1209 a huge French army stormed south to rout out the Albigensians (or Cathares), an ill-fated people who supported a radical departure from traditional Christian dogma and were seen as dangerous heretics. The Albigensians owned a number of coveted treasures, and although the group was based in the Languedoc, the Toulousian link to Provence, especially Avignon, caused that city to be besieged and belittled by Louis IX of France in 1226.

The Angevin dynasty

After the Albigensian episode, the Toulousians were eager to get back on the good side of the French kingdom. In 1229 Raymond VII of Toulouse married his daughter to Louis IX's brother, Alphonse of Poitier. To further placate Louis, the Toulousian territories, including the Comtat-Venaisson region north of the Durance in Provence, were also passed to the French.

Unlike the area under Toulousian control, the one under Provençal countship had a greater taste of authority under Raymond Berengar VII. A strong ruler, Berenger also begat a bevy of daughters, all of whom made brilliant matches. The eldest, Marguerite, became queen of France after marrying Louis IX, the future St Louis. The second, Eleanor, married King Henry III of England. The third, Sancie, wed Richard, Duke of Cornwall, who later became the Germanic emperor. This left Beatrice, the youngest.

Although her three older sisters must have had ample charm to marry as they did (some credit must be given to the stature of their

homeland, Provence, at the time), Beatrice was considered to be the sweetest and most beautiful of all. Crowned suitors flocked to her side, yet eventually she chose Charles of Anjou, brother to the French king, to be her husband.

Raymond VII bequeathed Provence to Beatrice, and in 1246 her husband was named Count Charles I of Provence. Beatrice's sisters ridiculed her unadorned pate – until 1265, that is, when Charles was crowned king of Naples and Sicily. He was also made king of Jerusalem. The sisters were no longer laughing. Even less pleased were Charles's new subjects, who considered him a foreigner – ever a dirty word in Provençal. When he wasn't embarking on

Crusades, Charles concentrated on squashing rebellions, with Marseille the first to go.

Marseille had prospered during the Crusades. Its citizens had set up new trading centres in Asia Minor and North Africa that brought in money, and St Louis's departure in 1248 on his seventh Crusade had bolstered the economic activity back home. Charles' triumph in 1257 marked the end of this era of quasi-autonomy.

The new French dynasty provided long-absent stability. Charles's involvement with Naples and Sicily also heralded a revived link with Italy. Most of the succeeding noble families set up house in Italy and appointed administrators to lord over the state in their stead. In 1271, Philip III of France turned over the Comtat-Venaisson – inherited after the Albigensian Crusades – to the Rome-based Holy See. And Charles II, who took over in 1285, instigated many legal reforms based on Italian models. His successor, Robert, King of Naples and Count of Provence from 1309 to 1343, installed *syndicats* or municipal councils.

When Robert died in 1343, his grand-daughter Jeanne took over *(see panel, page 40)*. Jeanne, however, never produced a male heir. Her cousin Charles of Durazzo became the logical successor but a deep-rooted dislike for him caused Jeanne to adopt Louis of Anjou, brother to King Charles V of France, and name him as her heir instead. This created new possibilities for internal strife and finally incited Charles of Durazzo to have Jeanne kidnapped to a lonely castle in the Apennines in 1382, where she was tied to her bedposts and strangled. Another war for control of the dukedom ensued.

Meanwhile, the region was in the process of recovering from an invasion by Languedoc armies, who took Tarascon and besieged Arles and Aix before Neapolitan forces overcame them. To pay for these wars – and some say to be pardoned for killing her first husband – Jeanne had had to sell Avignon to the Holy See in 1348 *(see page 40)*. Avignon had already been the seat of the papacy for some 40 years.

Avignon as papal seat

Meantime, in the early 14th century Rome had been undergoing turmoil at the hands of warring local aristocrats. In 1309 Pope Clement V, a native Frenchman, decided that he had had enough of the anarchy in Rome, and when King Philip the Fair of France invited him to return home, he gathered his robes and headed for safety of the Comtat-Venaisson on the lower Rhône. The papacy was eventually removed to Avignon, six more popes were to follow, and a period called the "second Babylonian captivity of the church" began.

The third Provençal pope, Benedict XII, was criticised for being avaricious, egotistical, prejudiced and uncharitable. He instigated the erection of the vast Palais des Papes, supposedly to

LEFT: St Louis leaves for the Crusades from Aigues-Mortes.
RIGHT: Petrarch found love in Provence.

PETRARCH IN PROVENCE

The Italian poet Francesco Petrarca (1304–74) moved to Avignon in 1312. After studying in Bologna, he returned to Provence in 1326. In 1327 he met Laura, wife of Hugo de Sade, ancestor of the Marquis de Sade, in a church in Noves. Athough devoted to her family and the mother of 11 children, Laura was Petrarch's lifelong muse. From 1337 the poet lived in Fontaine de Vaucluse, where he wrote the 366 poems and sonnets of the *Canzonière*, inspired by his unrequited love. He was crowned Poet Laureate by the Senate of Rome in 1341. A few years later Laura died of the plague, and Petrarch turned his attentions to the cause of Italian unification. He returned to Italy in 1353.

exemplify the absolute power of the church. However, Benedict's successor, Clement VI, who had bought Avignon from Jeanne of Provence *(see panel below)*, for 80,000 gold florins, decided that it still did not properly represent the grandeur of the church. He added a more ornate section, bringing the total size up to 1 hectare (2.6 acres).

In 1376, the Florentines sent a Dominican sister from Siena (the future St Catherine) to intercede with the Pope in their favour, having perpetrated a failed attempt at annexing the papal territories. Catherine succeeded not only in gaining their pardon but also in convincing Gregory XI, last in this string of French popes, to return to Rome. Gregory agreed to the homecoming in the belief that reinhabiting Rome would improve negotiations with the Byzantine Church, thus increasing the possibility of holding on to the papal territories. He may have been right, although this did not mean that the Palais des Papes would remain empty for long.

JEANNE DE PROVENCE

Jeanne is alternately known as the "Good Queen" and the "Wicked Queen". She appears to have possessed some of that old Massallian attitude towards free love and to have exercised it liberally during her lifetime. Married first to Andrew of Hungary, it is believed she had him assassinated. She soon moved on from her second husband, Louis of Tarento, to wed the reportedly Adonis-like Jaime II of Mallorca. Eleven years her junior, Jaime was, however, mad – a result of having been imprisoned in an iron cage for 13 years. Jeanne's fourth spouse, Otto of Brunswick, seems to have enjoyed a far less turbulent relationship with her.

The next elected pope, Urban VI, an Italian, so displeased a large number of French cardinals that they decided to call for a new vote. In 1378 they selected a native of Geneva to be the new Pope, Clement VII. The next year, Clement VII retreated to Avignon, and the "Great Schism", lasting from 1378 to 1417, was born.

There were now two popes: one in Avignon and one in Rome. This situation continued for several bitter decades, although Avignon was not a papal seat for all of this time. Benedict XIII was driven out in 1403, and the city withdrew from controversy. Its heightened stature as the seat of the papal court, however, was retained.

"Good" King René to Louis XI

Meanwhile, the rest of Provence degenerated into a state of constant civil war. The area was already reeling from the arrival of the first great plague in 1348. A semblance of peace and order was restored only after the fortuitous murder of Charles of Durazzo and skilful manoeuvring in 1348 on the part of Louis of Anjou's widow, Marie of Blois, whose son, Louis II, proved to be a capable ruler. Louis fathered the most beloved count of Provence, René d'Anjou, popularly known as "Good" King René.

To this day, René is remembered fondly by the Provençals. A self-styled philosopher and humanist, he devoted himself to promoting the economic revival of Provence and its ports and to reinstating interest in the arts. He was a tolerant, amicable leader, whose steady control permitted cultural life to flourish. René, however, failed so miserably in battles that he was impelled to relinquish his right to designate his own heir and was forced by the crown to name his nephew, the Comte de Maine, Charles III as his successor. Charles, however, was an unlikely ruler, being a chronic invalid. He assumed the countship in 1480 but died in 1481. He was succeeded by Louis XI of France. ❑

LEFT: Pope Benedict XII, Palais des Papes, Avignon.
RIGHT: "Good" King René.

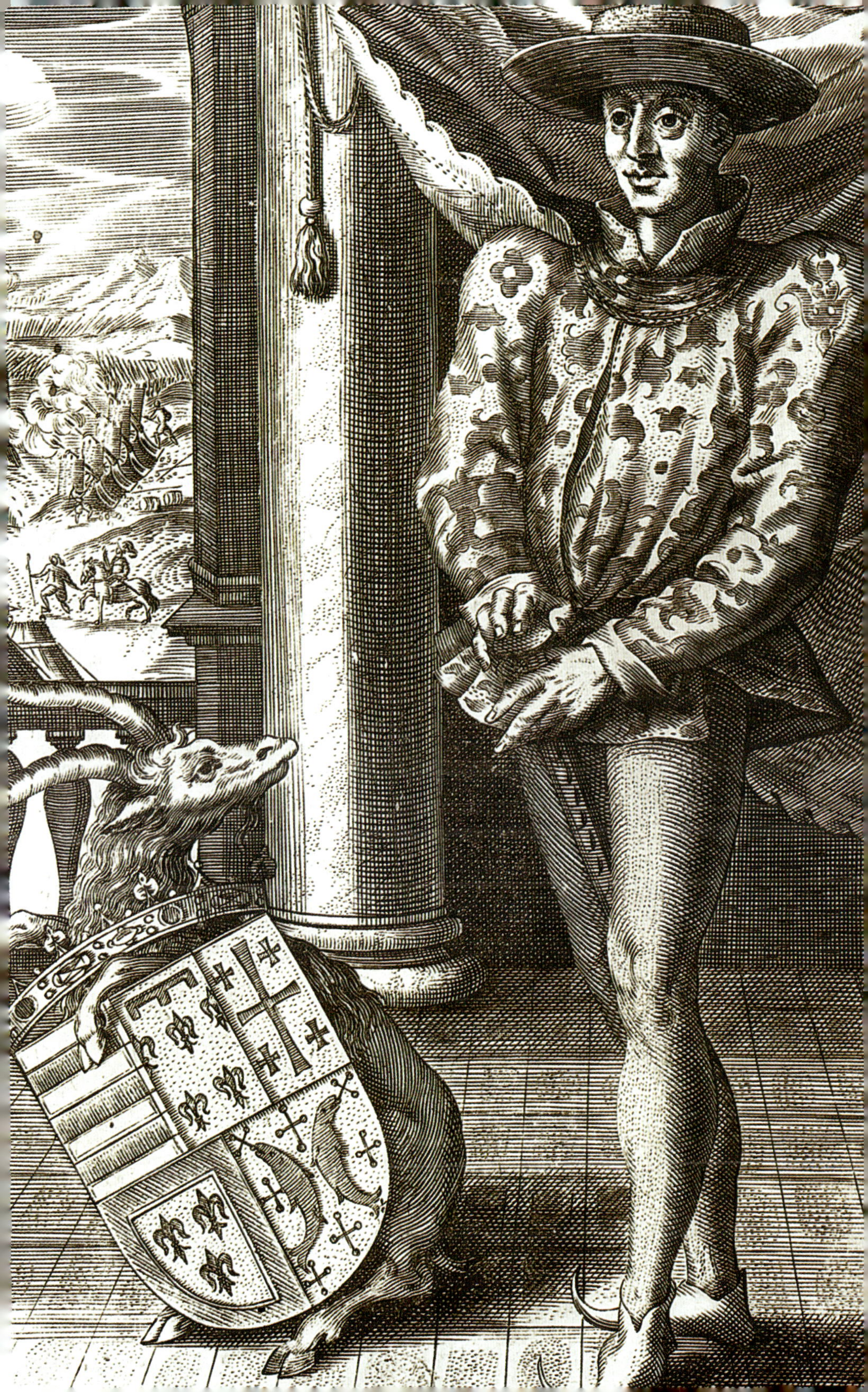

FRENCH PROVENCE

Unification with France in the late 15th century did little to ease the political strife across Provence. Wars of religion, plague and the Revolution followed

The first steps towards unification with France were taken when the three Estates of Provence (the Clergy, Nobility and Commoners) accepted Louis XI, King of France, as their ruler in 1482. Five years later, their union was cemented by a treaty designed to protect the autonomy of Provence. The constitutional equality of the countship and the kingdom was ratified, and the formerly independent state was allowed to retain a substantial number of individual liberties and traditional customs.

The rise of Aix-en-Provence

Marseille had its day under the Greeks, just as Arles had done under the Romans. With the advent of the counts of Provence and the papal residency, Avignon had sprung forth in glory. Under "Good" King René, however, Aix-en-Provence emerged as the star city of Provence. After losing Anjou to Louis XI, René and his second wife, Jeanne, retired to Aix, remaining there until Louis's death in 1480.

A metropolitan see since the beginning of Christianity and home to a venerable university, Aix did not diminish in importance with the passing of the "Good" King. The French chose to recognise its eminence and treated it as a capital. Not surprisingly, therefore, it was in Aix that the treaty of 1487 was signed.

It was also in Aix that Louis XII decided to establish a parliament, of French origin, in 1501. The Parlement de Provence was introduced as a supreme court of justice with limited political authority and as a place where all the estates would meet. Most of the native Provençals, however, felt that its real purpose was to impose stiff tax increases.

A repressed region

Although the affiliation with France may have brought a firm authoritarian command to the region, it did not usher in new-found peace. The martial escapades of Francis I engendered the invasion of Provence by the German Emperor

Charles V, both in 1524 and 1536. Meanwhile, annoyed by constant friction with Provence, Francis I further curtailed the region's independence. In 1535, he issued the Edict of Joinville, which severely limited the freedom of the Estates, quashed the Provençal-originated *conseil éminent* and strengthened the control of the hated Parlement over the local judiciaries.

In the end, Provence was left with more or less the same status as any other French province. But even this did not satisfy Francis: in 1539 he unfurled his Edict of Villers-Coterets, which introduced a new tactic in the suppression of Provence. This decree installed French as the language to be used in all administrative laws in Provence, supplanting the native Provençal dialect. Although the ancient dialect was not wiped out by this one action, the new law initiated its eventual decline.

NOSTRADAMUS

Michel de Notredame – now more commonly known as Nostradamus – was born in St-Rémy-de-Provence, in the Bouches-du-Rhône, in 1503. He studied medicine and, after extended travels, developed a successful remedy against the plague. He kept the cure a secret – a move that proved unpopular with his colleagues – and he was consequently expelled from the medical profession.

Nostradamus next turned to astrology. In 1555 he produced *Centuries*, a book filled with predictions on the future of the world, written in cryptic quatrains. These prophecies were banned by the Papal court, but Nostradamus gained widespread renown nonetheless. Interpreters claim that he foretold World War II and the holocaust, the assassination of President John F. Kennedy, the electronics revolution and the decay of the planet through global warming. Numerous other predictions, especially those relating to the end of the world, continue to tantalise his readers. Nostradamus died in Salon-de-Provence in 1566.

The Provençals fight back

Despite the repression by France during the early 16th century, individual families continued to thrive. Numerous châteaux were built, and small fortunes were amassed. Concerned that these wealthy inhabitants might try to rival the French nobility, the Parlement turned its Gallic eye towards their belittlement. Deciding that the châteaux, with their rounded corner towers, were potentially aggressive as well as presumptuous, they commanded that all towers be truncated to the level of the main roof. The stunted leftovers are still visible, dubbed *poivrières* ("pepper pots") by the locals.

The arts and intellectual life also continued to prosper. Although the troubadours had faded from eminence, in the 16th century there was a revival in native literature, mostly in the form of religious mystery plays; the period is hence sometimes called the "Provençal Renaissance".

Many such writers were scientific pioneers, notably the physician and astrologer Nostradamus, famous for his secret remedy against the first plague and his prophecies on the future *(see panel, above left)*. A less sensational Provençal was Adam de Craponne (1527–76). Born in Salon-de-Provence amid the dry plains of the Crau, de Craponne designed and oversaw the construction of the irrigation canal that diverts water from the Durance River through the Lamanon Gap, bringing water to the region.

The Vaudois

In the north, the French continued to devise ways to fetter Provençal activity. Not content to

LEFT: Adam de Craponne brought water to Crau.
RIGHT: Provençal astrologer and prophet Nostradamus.

concentrate on local legislation or suppressing the up-and-coming, Baron Megnier d'Oppède led one of the bloodiest campaigns in France's history against the religious sect of the Vaudois.

EDICT OF NANTES

This decree, issued in 1598, granted religious and civil liberties to French Protestants. The edict stood until 1685, when it was revoked by Louis XIV.

The Vaudois were descendants of the Waldensians, who had originally formed in protest against the growth of papal wealth and property under Pope Sylvester. Most controversial among Waldensian tenets were their beliefs that any layman could consecrate the sacrament and that the Roman Church was not the true Church

of Christ. Nonetheless, up until this point, the Vaudois had managed to escape the iron arm of the Church by living quietly and inaccessibly amidst the Lubéron mountains. The French did not let this deter their zeal, and the Vaudois were virtually decimated by the year 1545.

Religious wars and rebellion

The slaughter of the Vaudois was only a trial run for what was to come. The brutal Wars of Religion between the Catholics and the Protestants, brought on by the Reformation, lasted for most of the second half of the 16th century. Countless atrocities took place in the region, until, in 1582, a second bout of the plague caused the Provençal "heretics" to weaken; even the fiercely independent Marseille finally submitted to Henry IV of France.

With the Protestants under control, with many dead and with Marseille temporarily enfeebled, the 17th century rolled in on a more closely aligned Provence. Local authorities, however, displayed no sudden affinity for the Crown. Minor rebellions continued to flare up, often led by the bull-headed Marseillaises. Then, when in 1630 the French government tried to abolish the Estates' control over taxation, the Parlement de Provence at Aix simply refused.

Under the threat of overwhelming Gallic violence, the parliament voted in an extraordinary subsidy the following year. The Estates had already sounded their own death knell, however. After a particularly obstreperous showing in 1639, the Estates were simply no longer invited to attend the assemblies of parliament. Not until a century and a half later was their voice reinstated.

The Provençal Fronde

New dissension against the French emerged in the form of the Provençal Fronde. Unlike its northern brother, which pitted itself against royal absolutism from 1648 to 1653, the Provençal Fronde concentrated its venom on hostilities between the parliament and the governor. Only later did the struggle become one between the Sabreurs (adherents of the Rebel princes) and the Canivets (royalists).

The Provençal Fronde was suppressed in 1653, but discontent persisted in Marseille. The defiant city revolted in 1659, only to be stripped of all its remaining rights after its defeat the following year. To ensure his control over the uppity Marseillaises, Louis XIV personally ordered the construction of Fort St-Nicholas, from which both the town and port could be closely monitored. A year later, undaunted by their neighbour's lack of success, the citizens of Nice also took up arms. The town was subsequently occupied by the royal army as well.

In 1673, the beleaguered Louis XIV established the *généralité* of Aix, under a superintendent whose job it was to manage the province. From 1691 on, this office was united with that of the premier presidency of the parliament, giving the Crown effective legal control over the region.

The French king also continued his interest in Marseille, which, ironically, was to that city's ultimate benefit. He expanded the urban area threefold and encouraged the growth of seaborne trade by making it a free port. Marseillaise commerce continued to blossom during the 18th century, reaching its peak just before the French Revolution of 1789.

HEADS ROLL

The number of supposed Royalists decapitated in the city of Marseille during the French Revolution is believed to have been as great as the quota beheaded in Paris.

Plague strikes again

It is probably due to the greatly broadened status of the Marseille port that the third and deadliest of the plagues hit Provence in the early 1720s. The epidemic was brought by trading ships from the east, and over 100,000 people – 50,000 from Marseille alone – died. Whole towns disappeared. Traces of a vast wall built in the desperate effort to contain the disease can still be seen near Venasque in the Vaucluse.

The newly organised authority under the *généralité* led to improved relations between Provence and the French crown in the early 18th century. Invasions into the region by Austria and the Savoyards in 1707, and again in 1746, also helped push internal squabbles onto the back burner. Toulon and Nice suffered especially badly during the foreign incursions. Both ports were hardily ravaged by the Austro-Sardinian maritime forces before their final defeat in 1747.

By this time, the Crown was facing more serious upheaval than that provided by the arrogant Provençals. The discontent that would lead to the permanent removal of monarchical rule in France was brewing throughout the country.

The French Revolution

The people of Provence embraced the ensuing Revolution with open arms and an extraordinary excess of blood-letting, even for that violent era. Their interest in the new constitution stemmed not so much from a desire for social reform as from the hope that it might offer a chance to regain lost powers. Marseille was an especially enthusiastic adherent. Before long, a guillotine graced la Canebière, the city's main street, and the cobblestones ran red with spilt blood.

On 11 April 1789, the Société Patriotique des Amis de la Constitution was formed on the rue Thubaneau in Marseille, and it was there that Rouget de Lisle's *Le Chant des Marseilles* – now the bloody national anthem for all of France – was sung for the first time. It was from the small nearby town of Martigues that the *tricolore* (now France's national flag)

originated. Martigues consists of three boroughs, each with its own standard. Ferrieres's is blue, Ile St-Genest's white, and Jonquières's red. United, they form the red, white and blue flag adopted by the Revolutionaries.

The Revolution did not, however, restore the autonomy Provence had enjoyed in earlier centuries. Instead, the region lost what little independence it had been able to retain. The local government was completely dissolved in 1790, and the region was divided into three *départements*: the Bouches-du-Rhône, the Var and the Basse-Alpes. The Vaucluse was added three years later, after the French annexation of the papal territory in the Comtat-Venaisson. ❑

LEFT: protective clothing was worn to guard against the plague.
RIGHT: bust of "la Marseillaise".

REVOLUTION TO WORLD WAR

In the wake of the Revolution, Napoleon brought peace and the arts flourished. After a quiet century, glamour hit the region. Then war struck... twice

Among Provence's greatest contributions to the French Revolution was the young Corsican captain, Napoleon Bonaparte. The famed Napoleon first came to notice in Toulon, when he managed to wrest that important port city from an occupying Royalist-Spanish-British force in 1793. Three years later, as a commanding general at the age of 27, it was from Nice that Napoleon set off on his first glorious Italian campaign.

Emperor Bonaparte

Although the Provençals had embraced Napoleon the military genius, they were much less enthusiastic about Napoleon the Emperor. This same people, such eager participants in the early years of the Revolution, soon became staunch supporters of the returning Bourbon monarchy. Blood flowed again in the streets, as those suspected of being anti-Royalist were slaughtered with the same intensity as the anti-Revolutionaries had been under Jacobinism.

The Provençal antipathy towards Napoleon proved to be justified, for his ever-escalating wars finally resulted in the bequeathal of much of the eastern territory (including Nice and the land as far north as the Var River) to Sardinia during the Congress of Vienna in 1814–15, after Napoleon's defeat. It was not until 1860 that Napoleon II returned these lands to France.

The arts in the 19th century

Nonetheless, the 19th century was probably the most peaceful period Provence had ever experienced. The French revolutions of 1830 and 1848 and the new regimes heralded by each one roused little interest from the southern regions, and the Provençals concentrated on expanding their economic structure.

The martial lull also permitted the arts to flourish in a way that they had not since the days of "Good" King René *(see page 40)*. Poetry was rediscovered, and painters from colder climates became aware of the advantages of the Mediterranean environment. It was amidst this atmosphere that the Félibrige was established. This cultural and literary society was founded by the Nobel prize-winning Provençal poet Frédéric Mistral *(see page 180)* to encourage a revival of the dialect through the promotion of literary works written in the Provençal dialect rather than in French. It was at this time also that the novelist Emile Zola (1840–1902) was writing in Aix-en-Provence.

Creativity was not restricted to the written word. Painters flocked to the region, captivated by the long hours of bright, mediterranean light and the region's glorious landscapes *(see pages 77–82)*. Of particular note are Paul Cézanne (1839–1906), who was a schoolfriend of Zola, Dutch-born Vincent van Gogh (1853–90), Camille Corot (1796–1875), painting in Martigues, and, in Cassis, André Dérain (1880–1954), Maurice Vlaminck (1876–1958), Henri Matisse (1869– 1954) and Raoul Dufy (1877–1953).

LEFT: Emperor Bonaparte in coronation robes.
RIGHT: Nobel prize-winner Frédéric Mistral and wife.

Industry and tourism

Less artistic types were also busy. The industrial revolution, which came fairly late to France, did not leave Provence untouched. By the 1870s, industrialisation had carved a distinct foothold in the region. Between 1876 and 1880 alone, the primarily rural *département* of the Vaucluse lost some 20,000 inhabitants to the cities. Although still overwhelmingly agricultural in nature, the economy was changing.

The onslaught of phylloxera, which destroyed half the vineyards of the Ardèche and numerous orchards in the Rhône Valley in 1880, contributed to the imminent overhaul of local economies. New economic avenues were explored. By 1901, extensive mining for ochre in the cliffs of Haute Provence was underway and, by 1914, the Vaucluse was exporting 56,000 tons a year. This changed the population by encouraging the immigration of potential labourers, many of them Arabs.

Another new industry that encouraged, indeed thrived on, foreign interests was that of tourism. A scattered number of English aristocrats had begun wintering on the Côte d'Azur in the late 1700s, but not until Lord Brougham took a fancy to the town of Cannes did tourism become a profitable staple in the gross regional product *(see pages 50–51)*.

Nonetheless, agriculture remained the backbone of society. The size and distribution of fields changed little since the beginning of the 19th century and even today they closely resemble the patterns begun in the 1500s. Most farms are fairly small. Generally, one central tract circles a farmhouse while other fields are interspersed among the holdings of other farmers.

World War I and the Depression

World War I drained the countryside of its manpower, adding to the decay of the agricultural society. It also damaged the blossoming ochre-mining industry by immediately cutting off the Russian market. By 1917 all foreign markets had disintegrated, leaving the industry in trouble. After the war, bauxite and ochre mining returned to their former levels of production, then a new catastrophe hit: the Depression. Much of the ochre had been used for house paint, and the collapse of the construction industry meant that demand plummeted. The ochre industry never recovered. World War II closed off foreign markets again and, shortly after its conclusion, the US developed a synthetic ochre.

World War II

World War II destroyed more than the ochre industry. Although more men were killed in

World War I than World War II, Provence had remained physically untouched. During World War II the Provençals found themselves living on a battlefield for the first time in over 150 years.

On 21 June 1940, Mussolini struck out against the thin Alpine guard. Encouraged by the collapse of the French army under the Germans, the Italian dictator felt confident of victory, but the general armistice of 25 June cut short his onslaught. The region fell into an unoccupied zone during the ceasefire, but this semi-independence did not last. When the Allied North African landings were launched in the winter of 1942, the Germans marched on Toulon and Marseille. Eager to get in on the deal, the Italians took over the Côte d'Azur. After the collapse of the Italian regime ten months later, the Germans took possession of the entire area.

The Provençals were swept into the thick of things. Those who had not already been conscripted into the French army banded into fierce local Resistance groups. Particularly active in the mountainous regions, their guerrilla tactics brought relentless reprisals from the occupying forces. Meanwhile, the US Air Force began to mount counter-attacks against the Germans, causing additional damage to once-peaceful towns and destroying many historical monuments. While this went on, numerous innocent civilians lost their lives.

Finally, General de Lattre de Tassigny's 1st French and General Patch's 7th US armies landed on the Dramont beaches just east of St-Raphaël on 15 August 1944. By 15 September, most of Provence had been freed from the occupational armies and by April the following year, the enemy had been totally eliminated.

Economic recovery came quite rapidly after the end of the war. The coastal areas, in particular, enjoyed a new rush in tourism, brought on by the sun-starved years of the war. But the bitter emotional scars caused by the years of occupation and by the widespread loss of life and limb were not so quick to evaporate.

The Provençals had long become accustomed to their little niche in the southeastern corner of France and, even after losing all political autonomy, had felt fairly safe and separate from the crazy behaviour of the rest of the world. World War II shattered their sense of security and anonymity, resulting in a cynical lack of interest in the future that was similar to the response that the threat of nuclear war produced in many members of the next generation. ❑

LEFT: generals Diethelm, de Lattre de Tassigny and Cochet, Marseille-Toulon, August 1944.
ABOVE: the beach at Juan-les-Pins, 1944.

The French Riviera

Today, the Côte d'Azur conjures up images of luxury, pastel-coloured villas, exotic palm trees and dazzling blue skies – an idyllic place in which to live and the perfect holiday destination. Think of Monaco and you'll probably bring to mind the Grimaldis (Princess Stephanie et al), excess at the casinos and tax-reclusive, designer-clad, suntanned musicians, film stars and sporting types, complete with top-of-the-range sports cars and yachts.

However, the "French Riviera", as the Italians

affectionately dubbed this strip along the Mediterranean, was not always considered so glamorous. When the Scottish novelist Tobias Smollett (1721–71) came to Nice in 1764 to cure his bronchitis, he wrote that it was a land of little but rude peasants and persistent mosquitoes. Still, he admitted, the gentle climate was remarkable. This praise encouraged a few brave Brits to visit, but the French stayed away, preferring the fashionable spas of Normandy.

The region was more or less ignored until the advent of Napoleon I, several decades later, whose unsuccessful campaigns resulted in the annexation by the King of Sardinia of everything east of Nice and south of the Var River. However, his construction of the *grande corniche*, the coastal road linking Nice to Italy, would bring the area its biggest break. In 1834, Lord Brougham, the English Lord Chancellor, and his daughter were forced to wait in Cannes, while a bout of cholera spread through their favourite Italian winter playground. Although Brougham was at first less than thrilled by the detention, his displeasure was short-lived. Eight days after his arrival in the tiny fishing village, he bought land and ordered a villa to be constructed.

The rage had begun. Within a year, a small but extant winter colony had sprung up in Cannes. Within three years, 30 new villas had been built and, the following year, the harbourside avenue now called la Croisette was created. Five years later, the appropriately named Promenade des Anglais was constructed in Nice to facilitate the newcomers' morning constitutionals.

In the second half of the 19th century the Côte d'Azur went into full swing. Any halfway fashionable Briton wintered in Nice, Cannes, Menton or Beaulieu. The elaborate *Belle Époque* villas for which the Côte is still famous were built all along the coast.

Russian society joined the throng. In 1856, King Victor-Emmanuel of Sardinia, still ruler of Nice, invited Empress Alexandra for a visit. Her approval encouraged the Russian nobility to build villas along the coastline. The waterfront became so hectic that a municipal order was decreed in May 1856 forbidding anyone to bathe without underwear.

On 24 March 1860 the signing of the Treaty of Turin finally returned Savoy and the county of Nice to France. Although this made little difference culturally, it had a huge economic impact, as tourism in the region was fast becoming one of Provence's most profitable businesses.

Until this time, the Côte had been appreciated mostly for its therapeutic virtues – for "taking the waters". (This was long before Coco Chanel made sunbathing chic.) However, when Charles III of Monaco agreed in 1863 to inaugurate the now-infamous Monte-Carlo casino, this serenity disappeared for good.

The rigid morality of the Victorian Age proved to be no match against the Côte's seductive powers. Even the presence of Queen Victoria herself, who often vacationed here, didn't stop the mounting excesses of the wealthy Europeans who had made it their favourite home from home.

Stories of the era are legion. One night, for example, the Russian Princess Souvranoff won 150,000 gold francs at the Niçoise casino. To celebrate, she rented a villa for 7,000 francs, but when her invitees continued to party past the witching hour of 7am, she simply bought the house for an additional 120,000 francs.

It was not only the rich who made the Riviera their playground at the end of the 19th century. The Riviera's beautiful landscapes and long hours of Mediterranean light enticed painters including Paul Signac (1863–1935), Henri Matisse (1869–1954) and Auguste Renoir (1841–1919), who found inspiration on her shores.

They were not the first artists to come to the region: the composer Hector Berlioz (1803–69), the violinist Niccolò Paganini (1782– 1840) and the writer Guy de Maupassant (1850–93) had already discovered the delights of the sea air here.

The "Roaring Twenties" brought newly made US millionaires to the Côte, as well as the infamous writer Gertrude Stein (1874–1946) and the wild F. Scott Fitzgeralds. The arrival of the Americans marked another change in ambiance. Jazz clubs sprang up everywhere, and the coast's lively spirit encouraged painters such as Raoul Dufy (1877–1953) and Pierre Bonnard (1867–1947) to move in.

Perhaps the biggest revolution came in 1925 when the fashion designer Coco Chanel (1883–1971) hit the Côte and created three future mondial institutions: the tank-style bathing suit, her now-classic Chanel No.5 perfume, and the suntan. Until then, most people had come to winter on the Riviera. With Coco's help, summer tourism began.

When the stock market crashed in 1929, American tourists declined to holiday here, but the number of French visitors increased and the British remained faithful. The area thrived until World War II.

After the war, tourism picked up but things were never the same as in the glorious pre-war years. Chic artists and glamourous movie stars replaced aristocrats as the new lords of the Côte. The first official Cannes Film Festival was held in 1946; Picasso moved to Antibes in the following year. Between 1948 and 1951, Matisse decorated the Chapelle du Rosaire in Vence, and from 1957 to 1958 Jean Cocteau (1889–1963) worked on Menton's town hall. French starlet Brigitte Bardot (*b.*1934) made history when she appeared in the then-racy *And God Created Woman* in 1956, the year when Prince Rainier III of Monaco married the American film star Grace Kelly (1928–82).

Nowadays, only movie moguls, tax-reclusive stars and oil tycoons are able to afford the sky-high prices of the Riviera good life. However, a new element has appeared, along with dozens of unimpressive condominiums and modern hotels. The Côte has become a place for tourists from all walks of life. And come they do, in droves. ❑

LEFT: Grace Kelly – ever the epitome of elegance.
ABOVE: the *Belle Époque* Grand Hôtel, Nice.

PROVENCE SINCE WORLD WAR II

Not everyone wanted to modernise. But today tourism is strong, technology is developing, and the battles against crime and racism are being won

World War II heralded a new attitude across France, not just in Provence. What was once a boastfully agricultural country hardily embraced industrial expansion, investing in such advances as the Concorde supersonic aircraft and nuclear power. Even agriculture became industrial in practice, and farmers were encouraged to modernise their operations. On the coast, Provençal fishermen favouring traditional working methods struggled to compete with cheap foreign imports and stringent EU regulations.

Postwar agriculture

The change in attitude towards farming after the war had no small effect on the already poor region of Provence, which had historically centred its economy around agriculture. Suddenly, the people of the region discovered their pride, as well as their security, to be threatened. Some farmers tried to adapt, going into debt to buy new equipment. However, the new tools proved effective only for extensive farms and not the small, family farms that characterise Provence. The same farmers found themselves abandoned by the government, which was more interested in pumping funds into industrialisation then propping up small-scale Provençal agriculture. Some tried banding together in cooperatives, but their independent natures made it difficult for them to bear joint planning on a large scale.

In the 1960s several groups of hippies moved to the country. Most, however, became disillusioned and returned to their urban lives after a few years. With them went many of the dissatisfied offspring of farmers, hoping to find better lives in the cities. Although Provence remained agricultural at its core, for the next couple of decades that core struggled.

By the early 1980s only 10 percent of the natives worked the land, compared with 35 percent 40 years earlier. Nonetheless, the decade rejuvenated hope for the Provençal farmer. The mondial back-to-nature trend has filtered into the French mentality, and people have returned to using natural substances. Now, in the 21st century, importers around the world want pure high-quality goods that may be pricey but taste better and are healthier than extensively farmed or mass-manufactured food. Farmers' markets

display signs certifying organically produced vegetables, fruit and meats, which are all the more popular in the wake of the BSE crisis.

Vintners have always fared the best of all farmers, since no substitute has ever been found for the intensive human care required in winemaking. Now, the small Provençal farmer seems optimistic that demand for other "specialised" products – such as fresh-pressed olive oil and all-organic herbs – will rise.

Despite ongoing problems in several areas, Provence continues to be the top producer and exporter of fruit and vegetables in France – around 60 percent of the country's courgettes and 58 percent of its table grapes come from

LEFT: vineyards near Grambouis.
RIGHT: fishing is still a major industry in Marseille.

the Provence-Alpes-Côte d'Azur region. Animals are also raised locally – particularly sheep, whose high-quality wool is greatly prized. Although farmers in Provence have struggled as a result of changes in the industry since World War II, half of the region still subsists from activities linked to agriculture.

Coastal industries

Close to the farmer is the fisherman. Methods of fishing may have changed in some areas, but along the coast at dawn you will still see a large number of locals preparing their small boats for sail. Tragically, however, this age-old Provençal industry is being affected by overfishing and growing competition from imported products. The French are particularly concerned about Spanish fishing practices. Although the EU has imposed quotas and subsidies in an attempt to safeguard prices and control fishing zones, this move has been perceived somewhat cynically by fishermen affected by foreign poachers who tend to blatantly disregard such rules.

In spite of tussles over the southern French waters, the celebrated fish market of Marseille continues to convene each morning, and popular Mediterranean specialities such as sardines, tuna, eel and red gurnet are caught by large trawlers and small-time anglers alike.

Industrialisation

The coastline has also become extremely profitable in the areas of shipbuilding and oil refining. The last, which is centred around the wide Berre Lagoon, has in turn led to a large quantity of dependent petrochemical facilities in places including Fos-sur-Mer, Lavera and Mède.

Unfortunately, although industrial expansion in the Berre Lagoon area has gained for the locals a prosperity unknown to their inland brethren, this has been done at a price. Industrial estates consume the horizon here and the countryside in the area looks nothing like the rest of the region. To rub salt further into the

The Problem of Pollution

The issue of pollution is being tackled with vigour in the region of Provence-Alpes-Côte d'Azur – a result of the realisation that all the industrial development in the area was seriously affecting the vital, money-spinning tourist industry focusing around the Côte d'Azur. An exhaustive beach-cleaning programme was introduced by François Mitterrand's government during the 1980s, and by the end of the 20th century the majority of beaches along the southern strip of coast had been cleansed of their industrial sludge. Once free from pollution, the beaches were proudly allowed to sport the blue flags of cleanliness granted by the European Commission.

wounds, local critics claim that no new jobs were created by the expansion. Instead, they say, the jobs simply changed from the more traditional and appealing ones of the past, such as boat-building and fishing, to the more impersonal ones connected with big industrial plants.

Environmental ruin

The effect on the environment of this shift is unarguable. In 1965, you could happily swim or fish in two of the lagoons between the Berre Lagoon and Fos-sur-Mer: the Etang de Lavalduc and the Etang d'Engrenier. The waters of the Lavalduc Lagoon, which come from Manosque, were discovered to be extremely salty (60 percent). Profit-minded engineers drained its waters and placed them within the Engrenier Lagoon, from which they could produce liquid industrial salt more easily. Both lagoons were blocked off from the canal that linked them to the grand *étang*. Now, they are so polluted that you can see their filth from some distance away.

The industrialisation of Fos has brought the sea in about 2 km (1½ miles) closer. Meanwhile, even more ominous changes hang over this city. When Dutch engineers came down to help build the Port-de-Bouc they had to undertake massive dredging of the sea floor. While doing so, they discovered giant holes in it, and it is believed that the whole city will eventually and inevitably drop down into the sea.

The enormous Berre Lagoon itself has remained quite beautiful, but it is surrounded by ugly terraced houses and low-hanging smog. It has been France's principal petroleum port for the past 60 years, but the construction of a new port in Martigues and the South European Oil Pipeline during the 1960s even furthered its eminence. It now pumps more than 65 million tons of oil a year.

Of course, not all industrialisation in Provence has produced such dire results as those surrounding the Berre Lagoon. In 1952, the Donzère-Mondragon Power Station was inaugurated and, four years later, France's first nuclear reactor began operating in Marcoule. More power was created by the hydroelectric installations at Avignon, Caderousse and Vallabrègues along the Rhône, and St-Estève, Jouques, Mallemort, Slaôn and St-Chamas, along the Durance. Although solar energy production would seem a natural choice in an area of France that enjoys over 2,500 hours of

LEFT: nature and industry side by side in the Camargue.
ABOVE: nuclear research station, Cadarache, Alpes-de-Haute-Provence.

sunshine a year, advances in this area have been slow and as yet merely experimental.

Natural resources

Most of Provence's industrialisation makes use of local natural resources. Cork is gathered from the forests of the Massif des Maures, in the Var, and ochre and bauxite continue to be mined, although their contribution to the economy is less nowadays than it once was. In the Camargue and by Hyères, salt is pumped from seawater between March and September and, once crystallisation has been completed, the salt is gathered in September and October.

Crime and Corruption

The region of Provence has earned an unfortunate reputation as a hub of political corruption and mafia activity. Although episodes such as the mysterious assassination in 1994 of right-wing UDF politician Yann Piat, who was allegedly investigating corruption on the Côte d'Azur, and various underhand dealings during the late 1990s involving casino owners are the stuff of crime novels, they do very little for the area's political stability. The news is not all bad, however – Marseille's infamous role as a centre for gangster-style criminals and drug smugglers is now receding, and general crime rates in the area have fallen in recent years.

Olives are used not only in making martinis and salad oil, but also for lamp and oven fuel, soap and even fertiliser. The production of soap in France is still dominated by the *savonniers* of Marseille, although generally within large factories rather than in old-fashioned soap *ateliers*.

Lighter industries also depend on local raw materials. Almonds are used by the confectioners of Aix-en-Provence to make *calissons* (diamond-shaped speciality sweets made from almonds, sugar and preserved fruit). Fruits, especially berries, and vegetables from across Provence are canned. Sparkling Perrier mineral water is tapped from an underground spring near Nîmes.

Technology and tourism

Provence is also playing its part in the world's newest branch of industry – information technology. Over 20,000 people are employed within the hundreds of companies based at the Sophia-Antipolis Science Park. Hailed as Europe's equivalent of California's Silicon Valley, this international high-tech business and residential "village", located just north of Cannes, has been expanding steadily since its foundation in the 1970s and by 2001 it covered an area a quarter of the size of Paris.

Tourism continues to dominate the economy both of the Côte d'Azur region and that of some of the better-known cities such as Aix-en-Provence, Arles, Avignon and Orange. Since the 1990s, however, some smaller Provençal towns have begun to put more effort into wooing tourists as well.

The rural economy is experiencing a significant boost as a result of foreigners buying and renovating run-down farmhouses and other properties. Whole villages have been rejuvenated as a result of well-to-do British and German tourists buying holiday homes in the Provençal countryside. Unfortunately, visitors to Provence are annually warded away by the threat of forest fire. Despite advances in fire-fighting technology and methodology, the number and extent of fires every year is being reduced only slightly, and many tourist attractions, especially hiking trails, are closed off during certain high-risk periods. However, the EU is subsidising forest mapping as a measure to increase knowledge of potential fire-sites; the EU is also supporting research work into combating the long-term effects of forest fires.

Immigration and the Far Right

Meanwhile, as unskilled, factory-type jobs have grown in the region and discontent in North African countries has come to the fore, the number of foreign workers, including a proportion of illegal immigrants, has also swelled. Protectionism against these new foreigners reared its head in the form of Front National leader Jean-Marie Le Pen, who first became popular in the mid-1980s. Le Pen was not born in Provence, nor does he embody any particularly Provençal attributes. Nonetheless, this controversial political leader has found a remarkably large following in the region, especially in the area around Marseille.

LE PEN'S POLICIES

Jean-Marie Le Pen's policies, which are viewed by most people as outrageously bigoted, are centred around using so-called "foreign" elements in France as scapegoats.

In 1998, the steady rise of the Front National, was crowned by its greatest success yet, gaining a hefty 15.2 percent in the regional elections. However, since then, in the face of renewed anti-right wing sentiment and a general amelioration in the French national mood, support for Le Pen has dropped. His rival for leadership, Bruno Mégret, further diluted support for the Front National by splitting from the party in June 1999. That year, the total percentage of votes for Le Pen and Mégret together was only 9 percent. Numerous seats are still held on local councils in Provence, but interest in the extreme policies of the right-wing is waning.

France experienced its first ever mass influx of illegal immigrants when a ship carrying nearly 1,000 Kurdish refugees ran aground on the coast between Cannes and St-Raphael in February 2001. Hundreds of those on board disappeared into the Provençal hinterland and beyond, but some gave themselves up to claim asylum in France. Crises such as this are fuel for Le Pen's fire, which rages against France's growing multi-ethnic society.

A different kind of national sentiment has put the smile back on the faces of many a grim politician, however. In July 1998 France hosted and won the football World Cup, and the national team's star player was Zinedine Zidane, a Marseillais of Algerian origin. This is the kind of event that has symbolised the upswing in morale in evidence throughout the Provence area and the country as a whole.

LEFT: white-water rafting at Castellane.
RIGHT: Marseille's Zinedine Zidane, frontman for Adidas and a regional hero.

Into the 21st century

It has taken a while for this region, which for so long has been deep rooted in the agricultural life, to come to terms with modernisation. However, prosperity in the region is now growing, and unemployment continues to drop significantly each year – in 2000, among the region's population of just over 4½ million, around 260,000 people were

registered job seekers. Although the percentage of unemployed in Provence was above the national average, this figure was more than 50,000 lower than it had been in 1999. The European Fund for Regional Development is currently involved in supporting scores of minor rural enterprises and agricultural projects, which benefit the regional economy and help drive down unemployment figures.

Provence has become more optimistic in recent years and is learning to adapt to changes on its own terms. With the start of the new millennium the region is striding bravely into the future, proud of its contribution to the French state and of its distinctive identity within Europe. ❑

Haricot

PEOPLE AND TRADITIONS

To describe someone as a "true" Provençal is a great compliment in a region that has a strong awareness of tradition and respects local customs

There are many opinions as to what constitutes a "*vrai*" (or "true") Provençal. A Parisian whose grandparents are native to Provence may stake a claim to a Provençal heritage. Or perhaps the description is only applicable to someone who lives and works in the village where they were born and where their parents and their parents' parents were born, lived and died. To others, being Provençal may be an adopted concept, embracing all those whose families have come to live and work in the area and as a result speak with the regional dialect, and perhaps participate in local rural traditions.

Popular generalisations about the Provençals verge on contradiction: they are reputedly both suspicious of foreigners and the most warm-hearted of hosts; they are loyal Catholics but ardent upholders of ancient pagan rituals; local cuisine draws on the colourful informality of the land and is prepared using a few rudimentary ingredients, yet the area boasts some of France's most exclusive chefs and expensive restaurants; praise for the benevolent Provençal sun and its golden glow is matched by frightening tales of the chilling mistral wind.

Provençal characteristics

The people of Provence love to emphasise both the refined cultural life of their cities and the natural treasures of their countryside. The Provençals are overwhelmingly a rural people with enormous respect and love for the land on which they live. Even the region's city dwellers know how to cultivate an excellent garden and can sense the oncoming change of weather.

Certain variations in character also circulate within the region. The Avignonais are said to be different from the rest of the Provençals – more focused on their own world, prosperous, cosmopolitan. The people from the Alpilles are reputed to be both more conservative and more open than those from the Lubéron, due to their greater poverty and dependence on outside markets. The Marseillais are traditionally regarded as stubborn and outspoken – a notion demonstrated repeatedly throughout history. And those from the Alpes-Maritimes, even the Var... are they really Provençals at all?

PRECEDING PAGES: festival participants in traditional Provençal dress, Arles.
LEFT: farmer selling his produce, Vaison-la-Romaine.
RIGHT: young girl of North African descent.

A BUSY CALENDAR OF EVENTS

Merrymaking activities take place across Provence all year round, from celebrations marking the year's first batch of olive oil and festivals marking the wine harvest, to the Nice carnival. Major annual summer events include the Opera and Nuits d'Eté music festivals in Orange and the Festival d'Avignon, which has been running for over 50 years and has spawned the "Festival Off" fringe event. L'Eté de Nîmes is an eclectic mix of music, theatre and dance, and the festivals of opera, music and dance in Aix draw crowds from around the world. From February to September Nîmes, Arles and St-Rémy demonstrate their historical links to Spain with annual *ferias* and *corridas*.

Similarities can be found in their appearance. Provençals come in many guises, especially since today many are sun-seekers from the north or returned colonists from Algeria. For the most part, however, you can expect your average Provençal native to be on the small side, perhaps stocky, and darker than a typical northern Frenchman. They are, after all, Mediterraneans, and the many months of hot weather in Provence certainly give inhabitants a year-round, sun-kissed appearance.

If there is one thing, however, that really marks the Provençals, it is the richness of their traditions – and their pride in those traditions.

Centuries of complicated history, foreign invasions and determined independence from the rest of France have left their mark.

The regional dialect

Provence is one of only four areas in France to retain its own regional dialect. Not everyone speaks Provençal, but it is taught as an option in most schools, and in 1987, for the first time, a *faculté* (department) in the Provençal language and literature was created at the University of Aix-en-Provence. The push is on to preserve the language, begun by the determination of the Nobel Prize-winning native poet Frédéric Mistral in the late 19th century. The fashion for being able to speak the native tongue has even entered urban youth culture, with the appearance of pop song lyrics in Provençal.

Festivities

The most dedicated of Provençal families will don traditional clothing for annual festivities such as Christmas Eve. This "costume" recalls the style of the 18th-century bourgeois and is also worn for some of the numerous annual folkloric festivals. The colourful and lively festivals are a joy for the tourist trade, but Provençals are quick to state that the fêtes are not "shows" or "charades" put on for the entertainment of visitors but something that they take seriously.

Many festivals for which the Provençals are famous are connected to the earth around them: flower, olive and wine festivals, rites that beckon rain (such as the pilgrimage of St-Gens) or give thanks for the harvest. There are books on the mythology of the Provençal calendar.

Of course, not every Provençal cares for traditional costumes and gardens. After World War II, many young Provençals left their home towns, rejecting the lifestyle of their parents for

ABOVE: rice grower from the Camargue.
RIGHT: a former "Queen of Arles" in costume.

the ways of the big cities. In turn, they either lost interest in, purposefully shed, or simply forgot the old ways.

Traditions, costumes and festivals are far from specialised, however. The continuation of an independent regional life is a live issue among many Provençals. Groups are forming annually with the purpose of protecting the Provençal traditions. In Arles, a "queen" is chosen every three years on the basis of her ability to uphold these traditions (ie, speak the language) rather than specifically for her beauty or figure.

Religion

Religion plays a major role in the life of many Provençals, although at times it seems almost paganistic in interpretation. So strong are religious feelings across the region that belief in divine will and miraculous intervention can be found behind even the most mundane activities.

In most places, for example, the decision to build a bridge would be made by local elders. At Avignon, however, the 12th-century bridge spanning the Rhône – the *Pont d'Avignon* – was built after a shepherd-boy, Bénézet, claimed he had been commanded to do so by a voice he recognised as Christ's. Overcoming initial ecclesiastical hostility by singlehandedly lifting a stone big enough to form one of the bridge's piers, he set to the task. The structure was completed in a record eight years.

Harvest spirits and the beneficence of God, fairytale monsters and Christian saints walk hand-in-hand, often combined within the same legend or *fête*. Superstition also rages, even in the homes of the sophisticated. Never leave an iron out on the table of a Provençal hostess – it is believed to bring her bad luck.

There is a strong belief in the power of relics in the region, most of which are credited with miracle-working properties. The most powerful one of all, however, is the Holy Bit, made at the order of Helena, mother of the Emperor Constantine, out of two nails that are believed to have been extracted from the True Cross. It is reputed to drive out evil spirits and cure eye disease, neuralgia and haemorrhages. Now kept at the Cathédrale St-Siffrein (or Siegfried) in Carpentras, the Holy Bit is brought out on Good Friday and on 27 November.

CHRISTMAS IN PROVENCE

Nearly all Provençal homes still follow certain Christmas rituals that are unique to the area. Christmastime begins on 4 December with *le jour de St-Barbe*, derived from a pre-Christian Middle Eastern ritual. On this day, the children of each household plant a grain of wheat (or a lentil or chickpea) in a saucer. If it sprouts, this predicts good fortune for the coming year; if it doesn't, the household should prepare itself for a rocky time. Around the same time as the planting of the grain of wheat, the *crèches* and *santons* (small clay figures) are brought out of storage. These clay Christmas cribs are set up in a special corner, where they will remain for the rest of the season.

On Christmas Eve everyone in the family gathers around for the *cacho-fio* (roughly "hidden flame"). The oldest and youngest household members bless a log cut from a fruit tree, with a wine-soaked olive branch. The elder then lights it, reciting a traditional Provençal blessing. The way the log lights is considered a portent for the coming year. After the *cacho-fio* the family regroups for dinner by the *crèche*. The table is set with three cloths, commemorating Christ's birth, circumcision and Epiphany, and is lit by three candles, for the Holy Trinity. Traditional dishes are served, notably a 13-dish dessert for the 13 apostles. Before retiring, the adults put presents by the *crèche*, ready for the next day.

Pagan whispers

Despite all this piety, the visitor, chancing upon a local festival, may well notice some startlingly discordant elements. Why are masked and costumed mummers permitted to intrude on so solemn an occasion as a Corpus Christi procession? Isn't the noisy explosion of blunderbusses during the *bravades* (the typical saint's-day processions on the Côte d'Azur) reminiscent of the means used as far away as Africa and China to frighten away evil spirits?

The suspicion that one is witnessing something that owes little to orthodox Christianity becomes even stronger at feasts such as that of St Marcel at Barjols. Each 16 January the reliquary of this stern 4th-century pope is taken from the church to oversee celebrations that include the ritual blessing and slaughter of a garlanded ox. The animal's carcass is then paraded about the town before being roasted whole as the townsfolk dance round the fire to the sound of flutes, tambourines and, as at the *bravades*, volleys of shots.

These are survivals from a distant pre-Christian past that are found in innumerable Provençal folk customs. Take for example the practice of preserving half-burned logs from the bonfires lit on Midsummer Eve – itself a pagan tradition – as protection from lightning.

Or consider the custom of giving the newborn an egg, some salt, a piece of bread and a matchstick. The egg as a symbol of the continuity of life can be traced back to the ancient Middle East and survives both in the Jewish Passover meal and the Easter egg. The same archaic tradition regarded salt as the symbol of prosperity and bread as the staff of life. The matchstick, undoubtedly a later addition, is said to ensure that the infant grows straight.

Hints of a pagan heritage are often to be found mixed in with pious legend. St Martha, on reaching Tarascon, was taken for the goddess Diana, which provides good evidence that a cult to the pagan deity existed there. Another old story tells how St Trophime, who came to convert the town of Arles, consigned the goddess of love, Venus, to the nether regions.

Another prominent theme in traditional Provençal stories is that of the hero proving himself through supernatural strength, in particular by lifting a heavy stone. This is a deep-rooted pagan theme – it was by this means that Theseus asserted his right to the Athenian throne and how King Arthur proved his claim to the British one. The antiquity of this theme is proven by the fact that the Norse Odin underwent the same test and that something very like this is shown on a Hittite stone carving.

Celtic links

How did such patently foreign ideas originate? Perhaps more than any other region of France, Provence has always been a crossroads. From the 6th century BC, its first inhabitants, the Ligurians, played host to Greeks who crossed the Mediterranean to establish trading posts along the coast from Marseille to La Ciotat. Not long afterwards invading Celts swamped the Ligurians, and then in the 2nd century it was the turn of the Celts themselves to be invaded, this time by the legions of Rome.

Each visitor left a legacy. The bullfighting found here, as in Spain, may well have come from the Greeks. The ox sacrifice at the Feast of St Marcel suggests Mithraism, the Persian cult popular in the Roman army up to its conversion to Christianity.

Concrete evidence for this mixture of religious influences comes from excavation sites, such as that on the Glanum plateau, a short distance south of St-Rémy-de-Provence. Artefacts found there include the remains of temples, baths, a forum and a triumphal arch erected in the time of Caesar Augustus (31 BC to 14 AD) as well as a temple dedicated to the Phrygian Great Mother, Cybele, whose practices, which were forbidden to Roman citizens, included self-castration by her male devotees.

But, of all the very ancient pre-Christian peoples, those who left the most indelible paganistic footprints wherever they trod were the Celto-Ligurians. Their remains, too, have been found at Glanum. Among them is a lintel supported by pillars, which, as is typical of Celtic sacred places, lies close to a natural spring. Skull niches cut into the lintel itself are testimony to the custom of head-hunting. Similar discoveries have been made at other sites, such as Mouriès, Roquepertuse and St-Blaise. At Entremont, 15 male skulls have been uncovered, some retaining the nails by which they had been affixed.

Celtic traces found throughout Provence also include linguistic ones. For example, the word *aven*, used to describe the holes bored into the calcareous rock by rainwater, means a "well". The so-called *esprit fantastique* bears a striking resemblance to the British sprite "Puck" and to those mischievous fairies, the "sidhfolk", descendants of ancient gods, to be found in rural Ireland. But most Celtic of all is the very ability to absorb outside influences, Christian as well as pagan, and make them their own. ❑

LEFT: statuary to the Virgin Mary by Mt Ste-Victoire.
ABOVE: reliquary of Mary Magdalene, St-Maximin-la-Ste-Baume.

LE D'OLIVES
VIERGE
DES BARONNIES
47 F
FERME DE CLOSONNE
"Elevage au Grain"
26170 VERCOIRAN
75 28 13 42
HUILE D'OLIV
VIERGE
DES BARONNIES
47 F
1ère pression
à froid
100 cl
FERME DE CLOSON
"Elevage au Grain"
26170 VERCOIRAN
75 28 13 42

OILE D'OLIVES
VIERGE
DES BARONNIES
47F
FERME DE CLOSONNE
"Elevage au Grain"
26170 VERCOIRAN
75 28 13 42
ression
id

PROVENÇAL CUISINE

A two-hour lunch isn't unusual in Provence. Given the quality of the food across the region, that's perfectly understandable

The traveller to Provence is faced with a fine choice when looking for a restaurant. After eliminating the obvious tourist-traps, only two kinds of restaurant remain: either cheap and excellent, or out of this world.

If you are wondering how to recognise the former, just look for the paper tablecloths, hard wooden chairs and a rough-and-ready sign advertising the day's *menu*. Inland, towards Avignon or Sisteron, the soup will be vegetable, the fish will be trout, and the prices will be slightly cheaper than nearer the coast. Just about everywhere, however, the service should be warm and friendly, the portions generous and the meal will often be served on a sunny terrace, under the vines or in view of the sea.

Regional specialities

In selecting a meal, the first-time visitor to Provence should choose a dish containing tomatoes. If any vegetable or fruit symbolises Provençal cuisine, it is the tomato, the term for which, in Provençal, can be literally translated as "love apple". And if any method of cooking symbolises Provence, it is stuffing – look out for the word *farci*, which means "stuffed". Although the Provençals stuff meat, fish and fowl, their stuffed vegetables are particularly special. They stuff aubergines (eggplants) with onion and tomato, onions with garlic, and cabbages with sausage and parsley. A traditional recipe, adopted by the fashionable chefs of the *nouvelle cuisine*, is courgette (zucchini) flower, stuffed with the flesh of the courgette itself. Tomatoes are also often served stuffed.

The *farci* may be a fairly simple dish to prepare, but the *soupe de poisson* (fish soup) is not. The latter is a murky brown liquid, served in a big white tureen from which escapes the delicious, inimitable smell of myriad tasty sea creatures that go into its making. These are all the *poissons de roche* (literally "rock fish") that hide in the shadow of the indented Mediterranean coastline, including the ugly *rascasse*, the bony *girelle* and *rouquier*, crabs and eels. The fish are caught at night from the little wooden boats called *pointus,* and not even the fishermen know which of the 20 or so varieties they will bring to shore until dawn, when the nets are pulled in. In towns such as Beaulieu-sur-Mer, where the fishing fleet cater to at least a dozen restaurants, the competition is fierce. As the boats chug home around the headland, the restaurant chefs position themselves on the quays, to get the pick of the night's catch.

A first-rate *soupe de poisson* can take hours to prepare. In the traditional manner, the fish is crushed, then hung in linen sheets from the kitchen's rafters to squeeze out the rich juice. Nowadays, some cooks have replaced the sheet with a sieve that presses the juice out more efficiently. However, most fishermen's wives, the acknowledged experts, refuse to believe that the taste is the same when a sieve is used. They

PRECEDING PAGES: olive oil, a major Provençal export.
LEFT: M. Fonton, a celebrated *bouillabaisse* chef.
RIGHT: *herbes de Provence.*

prefer to stand on chairs in their kitchens twisting linen sheets rather than make changes to a recipe handed down through generations.

Another controversy is that of the *rouille*, a thick red spicy sauce whipped up into a kind of mayonnaise and served in most restaurants with *soupe de poisson*. You spread the *rouille* on the croutons that you float in the soup before sprinkling grated cheese on top. Most diners look forward to the *rouille* and consider it to be an integral part of the soup. However, the supporters of linen sheets claim that this sauce is a recent addition and clashes with the rich taste of the fish. In older recipes, they point out, you just rubbed a little garlic on the croutons to bring out the taste.

This may not seem of great importance to the traveller, but it is a subject of heated discussion in all the seaports of the French Mediterranean. Indeed, it is almost as heated as the rivalry between the supporters of *soupe de poisson*, as served in Nice and the eastern ports, and those of *bouillabaisse*, the speciality of the Marseille coast. The great difficulty in this comparison, however, is that *bouillabaisse* is not strictly speaking a soup. The fish are served whole on a side plate, and the liquid they were cooked in is placed in a dish in the centre of the table for all the diners to dip their hunks of bread into. (In some kitchens, however, the broth is ladled into each diner's bowl, then large pieces of fish are carved up and placed within the bowls.)

Bouillabaisse has always been served in the restaurants just off the old port of Marseille. Unfortunately, many of the restaurants of Pagnol's old port are slowly being turned into drycleaners or croissant-bars. Consequently, the modern visitor may have to go a little more out of his or her way, perhaps to one of the creeks or beaches – such as the Vallon des Auffes – where you can sit at a terrace, watch the boats and smell the sea while enjoying a good old-fashioned *bouillabaisse*.

THE OLIVE

The Phocaeans are believed to have brought the olive tree – a symbol of strength and peace – to Provence *circa* 600 BC, and harvesting and milling methods have changed little since then. Green olives are unripe, whereas black ones are mature. After been rinsed and soaked in lye, table olives are stored for up to a year prior to consumption. Whole ripe olives are milled and repeatedly pressed, producing about a litre (1¾ pints) of oil per 5kg (11lb) of fruit. Only the results of initial pressings may be called virgin oils. The cooking qualities and health benefits of this precious golden liquid have made it one of Provence's most prized exports.

Wherever these specialities are sampled, they don't come cheap. A good *bouillabaisse* or *soupe de poisson* is rarely billed at less than 12 euros a head, even in the simplest of cafés, and in Marseille you can easily pay 40–50 euros for a *Formule Marseillaise* (Marseille Menu) where *bouillabaisse* is the main dish. Most restaurants with bargain-priced all-inclusive menus buy the soup frozen from wholesalers in Toulon or Nice, who prepare it in the traditional way but on a large scale.

It takes a real connoisseur to tell the difference between the fresh and the mass-produced *bouillabaisse*. However, that little difference is the one that separates the cheap and excellent from the "out of this world". For the Provençal, the restaurant that serves frozen soup *manque de coeur* ("lacks heart"), a harsh criticism.

Simple, fresh ingredients

So, what makes a real Provençal dish? On one level, it's the choice of the ingredients: the best olive oil, from a first pressing of the olives; good firm cloves of garlic – preferably from the little heads that are purple ("like wine stains", as they say in the markets), not the white lumpy ones that look like potatoes; little tasty courgettes (zucchini) and tomatoes, not the big watery vegetables imported from the north. Then come the traditional *herbes de Provence*, which include thyme and rosemary in sprigs and fresh basil in season.

All this is prepared *avec coeur* (with heart), which means the willingness to take extra pains and work hard for little material reward. The cuisine explains something basic about Provençal life – about the precarious climate where the summer months may go by without a drop of rain and where an exceptionally cold winter may bring to nothing five generations of backbreaking labour. The people of Provençe are small-scale cultivators who fish and farm mostly in family units, and the produce of the land is valued tree by tree and row by row. When the Provençal family gathers around the table, the origin of each dish is known.

The purpose of Provençal cooking is not to disguise but to accentuate the flavours and to make the diners aware of each ingredient. Consequently, the cuisine includes none of the rich creamy sauces of central and northern France. The ultimate example of this emphasis upon freshness and simplicity is the Christmas meal that culminates in the *treize desserts*. The 13 desserts are actually 13 simple little side dishes,

CHEFS OF PROVENCE

Some of the biggest names in the culinary Eden of Provence include native Provençal tomato connoisseur, Christian Etienne, whose restaurant by the same name is to be found in Avignon, and Alain Ducasse, one of the most renowned chefs in the world and a man who combines rustic elegance with a youthful flamboyance at La Bastide de Moustiers (tel: 04 92 70 47 47), on the D952 just south of Moustiers-Ste-Marie. Ducasse, who also owns restaurants in Monte-Carlo (Bar et Boeuf, avenue Princess Grace, and Louis XV, Hôtel de Paris, place Casino) and Paris, trained with the affable Roger Vergé, whose Le Moulin de Mougins on the Côte d'Azur is one of Provence's most celebrated restaurants.

The cuisine of the infamously capricious Jacques Maximin can be found in Vence, and a new star of the Provence restaurant scene, Bruno Oger, is making his name at the Villa des Lys in Cannes. With menus in excess of 80 euros, dining at the table of a Maître Cuisinier de France has its price; however, it's very unlikely you'll go home disappointed – or hungry.

LEFT: the ubiquitous Provençal tomato.
RIGHT: *pompes à l'huile* from Marseille.

most composed of a single ingredient such as apples, figs, raisins, pears, almonds, walnuts, candied quinces or prunes *(see also page 63)*. To mix these ingredients, in the spirit of the English Christmas pudding, would be considered a kind of sacrilege in France.

The great chefs of southeastern France, such as Roger Vergé of Le Moulin de Mougins, return again and again to the simple side dishes of Provence. Vergé is aware of the influence of time and place on how a meal is received. "It is particularly important to serve the wine cool and abundantly," he says, "and to place the table in the shade of a large tree. The dish is already suffused with sunshine, leading to thoughts of a siesta."

Regional wines

The most famous wines of the region are the rich and peppery Châteauneuf-du-Pape reds. Less internationally esteemed but equally popular locally are the full-bodied Côtes du Ventoux and the lighter Côtes du Lubéron. Further south, Cassis produces perfumed whites and smooth reds, and a chilled glass of the fruity young Baux-de-Provence or crisp Côteaux d'Aix-en-Provence rosés provide the perfect accompaniment to the aromatic local

How to Choose a Restaurant

The casual tourist should be more than satisfied eating in moderately priced yet excellent restaurants close to the town centres: in Nice, on the sunny Cours Saleya; in the old town of Antibes; in the Suquet of Cannes, behind the port; in the back streets of St-Tropez; in Arles, in the quarter running west of the Roman Arena; in Avignon, south of the Palais des Papes; in Aix-en-Provence, on the place des Cardeurs or in front of the Hôtel de Ville. In the Provençal villages, if you see a restaurant where the tablecloths look clean, the waiters appear friendly and the menu is inviting, you should be guaranteed an honest meal, and often one than goes far beyond your expectations.

If you are more particular, or in search of something special, ask advice of the locals you meet. Talk to butchers and grocers, who know where fresh produce is served. Watch out for the restaurants that don't need to advertise – accessed through little doorways in shady streets and packed with local diners. Once you've found a spot, put yourselves in the hands of the waiter and defy him to produce a meal that will delight and surprise. Few waiters thus addressed will want to disappoint. They may even serve you dishes that are not on the menu. As elsewhere in France, restaurant management is not so much a means of livelihood as a profession of faith.

cuisine. Another famous Provençal tipple is *pastis* – a strong aniseed flavoured liqueur, which was created in Marseille in the 1930s. *Pastis* is served with ice and a carafe of water for mixing and is stereotypically enjoyed by elderly male *boules* players on hot Sunday afternoons.

RAVIOLI DE PROVENCE

Some readers may assume that *ravioli* is a typically Italian dish. Anyone in Provence will put you right: *au contraire*, it is a Provençal dish exported to Italy, originally called *ralhola*.

Départemental cuisine

There are, of course, variations in the dishes served across the region, with each *département* fiercely proud of its own cuisine and culinary representatives. One of the best-known personalities in Nice is probably "La Mère Barale". This *restauratrice extraordinaire* once threatened to stop serving the author of the Gault et Millau gastronomic guide if he continued to include her in the guide. "I am getting old," she said, "and I have enough customers." That year the honest critic took the risk and printed her name once again on his list of top recommendations. The chef has her own way nowadays; she no longer appears in the main dining guides and her restaurant still thrives.

Mme Barale even knows how to make a gourmet dish of stockfish (*estocaficada*, in dialect). This Niçois speciality is based on dried cod, soaked in water for several days, then cooked with onions, leeks and tomatoes. From an incompetent kitchen, it can smell of boiled manure and taste of glue. *Chez* Barale, it has a delicate flavour that sets off the taste of the vegetables.

Barale's other *spécialité de la maison* is ravioli. Provençal ravioli is stuffed with all manner of vegetables, meats and cheeses. The flavour will vary from town to town, subtly different according to the vegetables grown or the animals raised in each region. In the Camargue, the land of cowboys, you can find an excellent beef ravioli, served in a thick meaty sauce. In the rich plains between Nîmes and Aix-en-Provence, the stuffing is an assortment of vegetables. In St-Tropez, you can taste a *ravioli aux sardines*. As in Italy, the dishes of Provence are essentially local, reflecting the everyday reality of generations of farmers, traders and fishermen.

LEFT: asparagus on sale, Oppède-le-Vieux.
RIGHT: herbs and spices at market, Aix-en-Provence.

In the Alpes-de-Haute-Provence, on the high plateaux between Sisteron and Gap where the grass is frozen in winter and burnt away in summer, the shepherds drive their flocks across rocks and scree. The hardy sheep here have little in common with their fat complacent cousins in the lush valleys below. In taste, also, there is no comparison. An *agneau de Sisteron* has a spicy herby flavour and is never oily or heavy. A southern chef will choose no other kind of lamb for his *gigot de mouton à la*

Provençale, a leg of lamb that is boned, then stuffed with herbs, garlic and sausage, cooked in white wine, and served in a sauce made of tomatoes, aubergines and green peppers.

Variants of the *gigot* can be tasted at most of the better restaurants in the foothills of the Alps, such as the excellent Auberge de Reillanne. In the mountains, lamb tends to be served stuffed or in a garlic sauce. In the plains near Nîmes or Arles, it is more often cooked on a spit or in a stew with potatoes and parsley.

The truth is that the roots and emotional connotations are what make the Provençal cuisine. The landscape, the love, the struggle and the victory are all part of the recipe. ❑

FINE ART

Provence has intense light, inspirational landscapes, azure bays, tranquillity and glamour. No wonder so many artists have found it irresistible

Our image of Provence has been largely created by modern artists, and they in turn have given the history of modern art a distinctly Southern flavour. Familiar images include Cézanne's *Mont Ste-Victoire*, Van Gogh's tortured olive trees, Picasso's nymphs and sea urchins, the iron tracery of Matisse's balconies and Bonnard's red-tiled roofs and palm trees, seen through an open window.

Today Provence and the Côte d'Azur are among the best places in the world to see modern art in the setting in which it was created, to still enjoy the sensual pleasures and luminous light than inspired Cézanne, Van Gogh, Matisse and Picasso and also to see many of the masterpieces that resulted.

Van Gogh

Vincent van Gogh (1853–90) was one of the first artists to be inspired by the intense bleached light and brilliant colours of the South after the misty softness of the North. Although nowadays his image and work are ubiquitous in the region, adorning everything from wine bottles to ash trays, few people wanted to know him when he first arrived in Arles in 1888, at the age of 35.

However, his greatest painting was executed during his three years in the Midi, finding there a power and strength and vitality that inspired him almost beyond endurance. "The Midi fires the senses, your hand is more agile, your eye sharper, your brain clearer…" he wrote in one of his many letters to his brother, Theo, which provide a wonderful key to the artist's mind. Here he painted his sunflowers, chair, irises, night sky, train and the harvest scenes. "The olive trees look like silver, at times bluer, at times greener, bronze coloured, whitening on a soil which is yellow, purple or orange pink or even deep ochre red."

PRECEDING PAGES: *Ferme en Provence (Farmhouse in Provence)* by Van Gogh (*circa* 1888).
LEFT: Picasso and Françoise Gilot, Golfe-Juan, 1948.
RIGHT: bust of Van Gogh, Arles.

Van Gogh had only been painting for six years previously. He was born in the Netherlands, the son of a Protestant pastor, and although he began work as an art dealer, he became obsessed with evangelical Christianity. Determined to become a preacher, Van Gogh spent a year living in poverty in a mining community in Holland.

Slowly the inspiration to paint took over, and after training in Antwerp, Vincent followed Theo to Paris, where he was inspired by the work of the Impressionists. He went to Provence seeking light and colour and immediately began working furiously. He summoned his artistic comrades to Arles, declaring, "The whole future of art is to be found in the South of France." In preparation he rented the "Yellow House" in Arles as a studio and painted the sunflowers for his friend Gauguin's benefit. However, he was almost penniless, his heath was deteriorating, and he was drinking excessively. When Gauguin finally arrived he found Vincent impossible to tolerate and eventually they fell out. This was when Vincent sliced off part of his ear lobe (not the entire ear, as commonly believed) and, in a moment of anguished regret, gave it to a prostitute.

Van Gogh began to suffer from a series of mental breakdowns – he was not mad but suffering from epilepsy and syphilis, exacerbated by heavy drinking and a meagre diet. Finally he checked himself into the Asylum for the Alienated in St-Rémy de Provence, and although he suffered further breakdowns, he continued to paint, producing some of his best paintings from the depths of his suffering. He then went back to the North, to Auvers-sur-Oise (located around 30 km/19 miles from Paris) where he ended his life by shooting himself in the wheatfields.

The only original painting by Van Gogh to be seen in Provence is in Avignon, and none of his original subjects remain in Arles. However the landscape that inspired him remains unchanged, the starry nights, the harvest fields, the twisted olives, the bleached rocky hills, and experiencing this is the best way to appreciate this tormented artist.

Cézanne and Braque

The region became the focal point of key trends in modern painting. Paul Cézanne (1839–1906), a native Provençal who spent most of his life in Aix-en-Provence, inspired many followers. He was born in Aix in 1839 and educated at the local college, where he became friends with novelist Emile Zola. His father was a banker, and for a while Cézanne struggled to become his father's successor, despite his desire to paint. Eventually, however, his family realised that it would be better to allow him to pursue his painting and in 1863 he ventured north to join Zola in Paris. Once there, Cézanne's distaste for the "old school" soon led to his association with the revolutionary group of painters, now known as the Impressionists. However, he eventually also split from that group, believing that their work lacked an understanding of the "depth of reality".

In 1870 Cézanne returned to Aix, where he lived until his death in 1906. He painted the Provençal landscape, the gnarled olive trees and lavender terraces, and countless versions of his beloved Mont Ste-Victoire, determined to capture the structure of nature on canvas. "To paint a landscape well," he wrote, "I must first discover its geological characteristics."

ABOVE: Cézanne's *Maisons en Provence (Houses in Provence, circa* 1880).
RIGHT: Renoir's *Paysage autour de Cagnes (Landscape around Cagnes,* 1909–10).

You can tour around Mont Ste-Victoire, which was declared an international treasure by UNESCO in 1993 and, in Aix, visit Cézanne's *atelier* *(see page 162)* as well as the Musée Granet *(see page 159)*, which shows eight of his works including *Les Baigneurs (The Bathers)*.

Cézanne proved highly influential. He made several paintings of the bay and sea at l' Estaque, just outside Marseille, and these paintings inspired Georges Braque (1882–1963), who went to l' Estaque in homage to the master. It was at the same place that Braque painted his key Cubist painting *Les Maisons de l'Estaque (Houses at l'Estaque*, 1908), and although the port is now overwhelmed by industry the little houses that were transformed into revolutionary blocks and planes of colour can still be seen.

Renoir

The Impressionists came to Provence and the Côte d'Azur, fascinated by what Claude Monet (1840–1926) described as "the glaring festive light", which made colours so intense that he claimed no-one would believe that they were real. In 1883 Monet brought Pierre Auguste Renoir (1841–1919) on his first visit to the area; Renoir returned increasingly often to paint the filtered golden light, the olive trees and the

ARTIST COLONIES IN THE VAUCLUSE

The first artist colony in the Vaucluse dates back to the 14th century, when Petrarch informed his readers of an enclosed valley where "water sprang from the mountain". This valley is now known as the Fontaine de Vaucluse.

However, it was in the 1940s that the region underwent a cultural invasion. During World War II many artists took refuge in Provence, which offered beauty, peace and affordable housing. Consuelo de St-Exupéry, wife of the novelist Antoine and an exile from Paris, moved to Oppède, a small abandoned village, where she and other artists and architects turned ruins into studios. Gordes, abandoned in 1904 after an earthquake, was also being discovered by artists. In 1943 André Lhote moved to the town and tried to set up an art school there. A few years later, the painter Jean Deyrolles arrived, followed by Op-artist, Hungarian-born Victor Vasarely, who leased the château in Gordes, restored it and then transformed it into a museum.

The Lubéron continued to be a hotbed of inspiration long after the war. In the 1950s the surrealist painter Bernard Pfriem founded an art school in Lacoste; it is now affiliated to the Cleveland Institute of Art and over the years has attracted lecturers including Man Ray, Max Ernst and Henri Cartier-Bresson. Arles, Bonnieux and Lacoste are all now homes to schools of photography.

soft terracotta roofs that are characteristic of the Provençal villages.

Renoir finally settled in the South because of his arthritis, buying up a 500-year-old olive grove to save it from being destroyed by developers and building a house, les Colettes, there for his family. This proved the ideal setting for Renoir's final period; he had a glassed-in studio built among the olive trees, with curtains to control the light, providing a perfect solution to the choice between working from nature or in a studio. He even found the strength, with the help of an assistant, to sculpt. "Under this sun you have a desire to see marble or bronze Venuses among the foliage," he said. And here indeed among the olives you can still see his bronze *Venus Victrix*. Today les Colettes is a museum, surrounded by a magnificent olive grove that is a shady sanctuary on a hot day. Inside the house, you can see ten original paintings by Renoir as well as the master's studio, with chair, easel and palette just as he left them. Even his bath tub can still be inspected.

Picasso and his influence

Inevitably, however, the South of France is Pablo Picasso (1881–1973) country, and nowhere is his presence more palpable than the Musée Picasso *(see page 277)* in Antibes. Here, a glittering sea reflects strong sunlight into the windows of the château, providing a superb backdrop for the sculptures on the terrace.

Picasso's love affair with the Riviera began in 1920, when he spent the summer in Juan-les-Pins, and he was a frequent visitor to the coast over the following summers. When World War II broke out in 1939, Picasso was in Antibes, painting *Pêche de Nuit à Antibes (Night Fishing at Antibes)*, a luminous nocturnal seascape inspired by watching the fishermen and their boats illuminated by white acetylene lamps. The painter returned to Antibes in 1946 with Françoise Gilot, whom he had met in 1943, and was given the Grimaldi Palace to use as a studio.

After the grim war years in Paris, Picasso was inspired by the light, colour and antiquity of the Mediterranean; his nymphs, centaurs, goats, sea urchins and monumental women running on the beach have a pagan innocence that expresses the inspiration the painter derived from the hard shadows and bright colours of sea, beach and mountains. These paintings and drawings resulted in a major work, *Joie de Vivre (The Joy of Life)*, the gem of a collection

ABOVE: *Le Palais des Papes, Avignon* by Signac (1900).
RIGHT: *Place des Lices, St-Tropez* by Matisse (1904).

that includes paintings, drawings, sculpture, engravings and ceramics. The Musée Grimaldi also has the largest collection of work by Nicolas de Staël as well as works by César *(see page 82)*, Yves Klein and Joan Miró.

zwhere he single-handedly revived the town's pottery industry. Later in Cannes he painted the *Meninas* series (1957), after Velázquez's celebrated portrait. The pleasure he took in the environment is particularly evident in the wonderful dove paintings, *Els Colomins* (1957), which feature exuberant yellows and oranges with views of turquoise sea and black-and-purple palm trees.

Droves of painters followed in Picasso's footsteps, including Fernand Léger (1881–1955), whose interest in developing large architectural ceramic sculpture and murals attracted him to Biot *(see page 256)*, which, along with Vallauris, became the centre of a revival of ceramic art. Shortly before Léger died in 1955 he bought a plot of land just outside Biot on which to build a studio, and his wife subsequently created the Musée Nationale Fernand Léger *(see page 256)* on the site in his honour. It now houses his personal collection and is dominated by his massive, brilliantly coloured ceramic panels on the outside walls.

ST-TROPEZ

Although many of the ports and coastal towns beyond Marseille, such as Toulon, la Ciotat, Cassis and Hyères, became favoured destinations for artists, St-Tropez had the greatest pull. Paul Signac (1863–1935), a keen sailor, was one of the first artists to move here, although the place was then only accessible by sea. In 1892 he bought a villa just outside St-Tropez, which at that time was no more than a tiny fishing port. He invited many of his fellow artists, including Georges Seurat (1859–91), Maurice Utrillo (1883–1955), André Derain (1880–1954) and Raoul Dufy (1877–1953), who all painted the little harbour, the ochre cottages and the shimmering sea. Henri Matisse visited Signac in St-Tropez in 1904, resulting in his own experiment with pointillism – *Luxe, Calme et Volupté (Luxury, Calm and Delight)* – and the liberation from traditional techniques that led him to Fauvism. In 1909 Pierre Bonnard (1867–1947) also rented a villa in St-Tropez. He too was stunned: "Suddenly I was hit with a Thousand and One Nights; the sea, the yellow walls, the reflections which were as brightly coloured as the lights..."

The work of many of these artists, including Signac's *Saint Tropez au Soleil Couchant (Saint Tropez at Sunset)* and Matisse's *la Gitane (The Gypsy)* is on show at the Musée de l'Annonciade in St-Tropez *(see page 233)*.

Matisse

Henri Matisse (1869–1954) spent much of his life on the Côte d'Azur, eventually settling in Nice. He spent a year in the Hôtel Beau Rivage, painting the great sweeping bay of the Promenade des Anglais fringed with palm trees, and then bought an apartment on the Place Charles Félix, where he painted his famous *odalisques*, framed by shuttered windows and flowers, capturing forever the voluptuous ease of the Riviera.

One of the most moving examples of his work is the Chapelle du Rosaire, just outside Vence, an exquisite blue-and-white chapel, designed and decorated by Matisse at the end of his life, when he was very ill. The tiled roof, the blue-and-yellow stained glass, the appliquéd vestments, are all a poignant testimony to the artist's genius. He once observed that if there was a heaven, he would want it to be "a Paradise where I paint frescoes." In the Cimiez area of Nice is the Musée Matisse *(see page 280)*, which houses his personal collection. The museum has works from every period of Matisse's working life, as well as the vases, mask, pots, shell furniture, Moroccan wall hangings and even the giant cheese plant that he so often included in his paintings.

MATISSE ON NICE

"What made me stay are the great coloured reflections of January, the luminosity of daylight."

Chagall, Dufy and Cocteau

The Russian artist, Marc Chagall (1887–1985) also settled on the Côte d'Azur towards the end of his career, finding inspiration in the light and colour of the South. The Musée Chagall in Cimiez is home to the largest collection of Chagall's work; it was built to house his masterpiece *Message biblique (Biblical Message)*. Many local churches and chapels, including the cathedral in Vence, feature his mosaics.

Raoul Dufy (1877–1953) often came to the South of France, and his sensual paintings convey the delights of the region – the food, wine, palm trees and grand hotels – perhaps more than any other artist. Jean Cocteau (1889–1963) was also a frequent visitor, both to the grand villas of St-Jean-Cap-Ferrat and to the seedy sailors' bars of Villefranche-sur-Mer. In Villefranche, the candy-coloured Chapelle St-Pierre has an interior designed by Cocteau, and Menton has the Musée Jean Cocteau *(see page 287)*, which houses self-portraits, abstracts, tapestry and the *Inamorati (Lovers)* series of love paintings, and features mosaic flooring and tiling by Cocteau himself. Also in Menton is the Salle des Mariages, which Cocteau decorated with Art Nouveau murals, a seriously *recherché* wedding location.

Nouveaux Réalistes and beyond

In the 1950s Nice produced its own school of artists, the Nouveaux Réalistes. They are well represented at the Musée d'Art Moderne et D'Art Contemporain in Nice and include Yves Klein (1928–62), Arman (*b.* 1928), Martial Raysse (*b.* 1936), all from Nice, César (*b.* 1921), born in Marseille, and others such as Niki de Saint Phalle (*b.* 1930) and Daniel Spoerri (*b.* 1930).

These artists' fascination with everyday material surfaces, paint tubes, packaging and industrial waste, is evident in Arman's transparent containers packed with trash and flock of birds created from pliers. There are many works by Klein, who perhaps took the inspiration of the Riviera to its limit with his startling blue paint IKB (International Klein Blue). The Fluxus artist Ben (*b.* 1935; *see page 279*), whose 1985 piece *Il y a trop d'art (There is too much art)* is reproduced all over Nice, may have a point. ❑

LEFT: mosaic by Chagall, Vence.
RIGHT: César (1992).

5842 TD 83
CARRELAGE

FOLK ART

Miniature clay figures, brightly coloured textiles, decorative pottery and blown glass are just some of the local forms of folk art

Folk art remains a strong tradition across Provence, with many dedicated artisans preserving local crafts as well as finding new ways to interpret them. The result is a wealth of pottery, textiles and glass.

Christmas *santons*

One art form that reflects the importance of tradition in the region – perhaps doing so more strongly than any other Provençal art form – is the *santon* (literally "little saint"). *Santons* are symbolic clay figures displayed *crèches* in Catholic homes at Christmas to represent the Nativity. The figures are formed using plaster-cast moulds, which are baked, and their features and clothing are then painted on with acrylics. The figures generally range in size from less than 2 cm (¾ inch) to 13 cm (5 inches), and differently sized figures are commonly placed in the same *crèche* to create perspective.

The most important figures are the main characters from the Nativity: the infant Jesus, Mary, Joseph, the angel and the three wise men, who are all clothed in their Biblical costumes, plus the ox and ass. However, instead of Jerusalem, the Provençal *crèche* places the birth of Jesus in a typical and bustling 19th-century Provençal village. Clay models of stone houses are set up around the central stable. Moss and pebbles are used for the hillside; rosemary and thyme twigs act as trees.

A supporting cast of figures represents the tradesmen and society that one would typically have found in such a 19th-century Provençal town. The *santons* are painted as wearing traditional clothing of the period and carring a tool or product that symbolises their trade or social position; figures include: the garlic farmer; the fish merchant; women carrying newly drawn water; the gypsy; the coquette and the parish priest. In some *ateliers* (workshops), more than 100 subjects are produced.

LEFT: a tiled Jeep, made by a master-craftsman from Salernes.
RIGHT: Collet pottery from Vallauris.

Marseille, Aix-en-Provence and Aubagne are the main centres of *santon* production in the region. The great *Foire aux Santons* takes place in Marseille for two weeks each December. This fair has become an integral part of the Christmas festivities, and most towns in the Bouches-du-Rhône have their own annual smaller version.

Provençal textiles

Another traditional decoration that has kept a strong contemporary following are the printed cottons of Provence. Known as *indiennes* when they were first produced throughout France during the second half of the 17th century, they were made following the methods and designs of the imported *toiles peintes* (painted fabrics) of India. In 1686, the French royals declared a halt to the importation and production of the Indian fabric. However, as part of the Comtat-Venaissin, Provence was not on royal land. The industry, therefore, grew in this region throughout the 17th and 18th centuries, with factories in Orange, Avignon, Tarascon and Aix.

These fabrics, which formerly served as women's shawls and are now mostly used for interior decoration, are brilliantly multi-coloured prints in kaleidoscopic floral and geometric patterns. Originally, the dyes were obtained from natural materials and each colour in a design was applied with separate wood-block impressions.

Only one factory has survived the mechanisations of the textile industry: a company based in Tarascon and owned and operated by a member of its founding family, Charles Demery. It trades under the name of Souleiado – a Provençal term taken from the works of the poet Mistral and meaning "the rays of sun that pierce through clouds".

Decorative pottery

The region has produced earthenware since the days of the Romans. Pottery workshops complete with kilns dating from the 1st century AD have been excavated in la Butte des Carnes, near Marseille. Over the centuries, pottery continued to be made in individual workshops, both for domestic purposes and for international export through the Mediterranean seaports. Then, in the 19th century, factories began to open in answer to the ever-growing demand for thrown or moulded cookware and for building materials such as tiles and bricks. The 20th century's economic and martial turmoil and the advent of such materials as aluminium and plastic, however, led to the eventual closure of these factories.

In Aubagne – formerly a centre for earthenware manufacturing – one such factory (called Poterie Provençale) still produces the kind of handmade, mass-produced casseroles and coffee pots that were made during the 19th century. But in general, the days of utilitarian cookware production are over, and nowadays the majority of the pottery made is primarily for decorative purposes.

Three basic types of pottery are now produced. *Terre rouge*, the coarsest and humblest, is made principally from the red clay of the region. This type of pottery can be recognised by its reddish-brown colour (if it is covered with an opaque glaze, look at the underside of the base to see the material from which it is made), its rough texture and weight – this type of pottery is never thin and fine, as the clay cracks easily.

Objects such as unglazed moulded flower pots and tiles are still made in *terre rouge* for household use, while a wide variety of thrown forms such as jugs, bowls and mustard pots are sold as partly decorative, partly useful objects. Be sure, however, to check that the pots you buy are genuine handmade items. Roadside pottery stores, where they exist, are usually outlets for small family-run workshops. One such store is La Ceriseraie, in Fontvieille, a modest establishment where M. Monleau makes *la cuisinerie* (cookware) as well as *santons* out of *terre rouge*, and his daughter Chantal creates prize-winning *décoration*, or faïence.

Traditionally, if *terre rouge* was the poor man's pottery, faïence was the rich man's version. Faïence is made from the finest indigenous clays combined with various mineral elements to produce a greyish-white body that is formed in moulds, covered with an enamel shell (this is generally milky-white), decorated with engraved or painted designs and glazed. The decoration is wide-ranging, from entire hunting tableaux with garlanded rims to a simple initial.

Faïence, which was introduced to France by Italian ceramicists during the 16th century, was originally the unique province of aristocrats. By the 18th century it had become available to all as a popular form of decorative pottery. Elaborate tableware forms such as scalloped plates and platters, pierced bowls and tea infusers, which had been put into use by the aristocracy, joined figures as decorative pieces to be displayed on walls or mantlepieces.

Faïence can also be found in simple utilitarian forms, but you can always distinguish it from plain pottery by its enamel porcelain-like finish. Good collections of Provençal faïence are owned by the Musée Paul Arbaud *(see page 158–9)* in Aix-en-Provence, the Musée Cantini *(see page 151)* in Marseille and the Musée de la Faïence *(see page 213)* in Moustiers-Ste-Marie. The town of Moustiers-Ste-Marie, in the Alpes-de-Haute-Provence, has been a centre of faïence since the 16th century.

The "Moustiers-style", which is now made throughout Provence as well as in its namesake town, follows the patterns created by the grand 17th- and 18th-century masters who lived and worked in the small town. Perhaps the most distinctive motif of the "Moustiers-style" is the 18th-century *décor à grotesques* that represents fantastic monsters, donkey musicians, monkeys and plumed birds. You could visit the town's most celebrated *atelier*, Segriès, which is frequented by the fashion house of Hermès and members of the modern-day aristocracy.

The third type of pottery is *grès*, made out of grey clay from central France. Originally, artists introduced it to the region because its

LEFT: *gardians* from the Camargue, wearing shirts made of traditional Provençal fabric.
ABOVE: Biot glass.

hard consistency lends itself better than *terre rouge* to art pottery. *Grès* comes in a wide range of original forms and is decorated with a rainbow of polychrome glazes that range from gentle variegated green-pink to earthy brown-speckled blue. The artists who use this medium draw inspiration from the pottery of the Orient as well as Provence and strive to reinterpret the classic beauty of traditional craftsmanship with originality.

Two leading exemplars are P. Voelkel, who works in St-Zacharie and displays his work there and in Cassis, and Roger Collet of Vallauris. Although long a pottery centre, Vallauris

became internationally famous after Picasso joined the local "Madoura" workshop in the 1940s; unfortunately, it is now crammed with cheap tourist ware. Collet, a master of *grès* and porcelain, was a colleague and friend of Picasso and is one of only a handful of reputable potters left in the town. You can still, however, visit the Musée Nationale de Céramique *(see page 256)*, next to the church, to see the products of Vallauris's illustrious past.

Biot glass

The nearby town of Biot offers a refreshing contrast to the shoddy tourism that has overwhelmed Vallauris in recent years. In Biot, a unique system is used to create swirls of bubbles in clear or iridescently coloured blown glass. Founded in 1956 by Eloi Monod, a potter and engineer who wanted to revive the craft of glass-blowing in Provence, the original Biot glass factory has grown from one blower, Raymond Winnowski, and one glassmaker, Fidel Lopez, to 70 workers. The workshop where all the glass is blown is open to visitors, with the bare-chested Winnowski presiding amidst the glowing coals. The adjoining store offers an array of beautiful yet surprisingly sturdy glassware in more than 100 different forms including glasses, goblets, jugs, vases and bowls, as well as numerous miscellaneous items from decanters and oil lamps to knife stands.

New traditions

Today, most handicraft artisans working in Provence are not natives of the region. In the 1950s artists as well as movie stars were drawn to the Alpes-Maritimes. The 1960s, a period of social upheaval in France when many sought a "return to nature", brought an even greater wave of artists – known as the "Romantics of '68" – to the entire region. Trained in art schools, the new artisans freely experiment, creating new decorative forms and introducing innovations to the traditional utilitarian ones.

Visiting art galleries in towns such as Aix-en-Provence, Avignon, Marseille and along the Côte d'Azur, walking through the many craft fairs such as the *Foire aux Croutes* on the cours Mirabeau in Aix, or stopping by communal workshops scattered around the countryside, you can find an eclectic variety of forms and styles. Much of the work, notably painted silk, woven murals, mobiles, olivewood sculptures, jewellery, watercolours, pastels, leather goods and wooden toys, has no specific link to traditional Provençal folk arts, although some of the more traditional Provençal handicrafts such as pottery and puppetry are also still going strong.

Despite the great changes brought on by the industrial age and the advent of the new artists, the traditional handicrafts of Provence have not been lost to the present, and the richness of the craft tradition continues to be both a foundation and rich source of inspiration for the Provençal artisan. ❑

Left: Moustierware motif.
Right: a master *santonnier* at work.

THE CANNES FILM FESTIVAL

Glamorous or tawdry? Unmissable or irrelevant? It's the annual event that movie makers love to hate – and hate to miss

Cannes's "Festival International du Film" was the brainchild of Edouard Daladier's government, devised to provide an alternative to the Venice Film Festival, where only those films meeting the approval of Mussolini's censors were shown. Cannes, one of the glittering holiday resorts on the Cote d'Azur, was elected for its "sunny and enchanting location", and the first festival was scheduled for 1939. Plans were scuppered, however, by the onset of World War II and it was not until 20 September 1946 that reels were rolled and glasses raised at the belated inaugural festival.

The 10-day event, which since 1951 has occupied its current slot in the spring calendar, is held in the Palais des Festivals et des Congrès, a massive and rather tasteless architectural eyesore that dominates the landscape of this little coastal town and is nicknamed "the bunker" by the locals. The Palais was enlarged in 1970, to honour 75 years of French film; a second extension was completed in May 2000.

The judging

In the festival's early years, productions due to feature were selected by their country of origin, but since 1972 that honour has been reserved for the festival's general delegate, aided by two selection committees, one for French films and the other for foreign productions. Each year the festival's board of directors chooses a 10-member international jury: nine artists and a president, who is almost exclusively — give or take a few authors such as the Belgian crime writer Georges Simenon and the US playwright Tennessee Williams, in 1960 and 1976 respectively – a leading figure in the film world. Past presidents range from Jean Cocteau (1953 and 1954) to the first woman president of the board, Olivia de Havilland (1965) and, in more recent years, Martin Scorsese (1998), David Cronenberg (1999), Luc Besson (2000) and Liv Ullmann (2001).

The jury's job is to award the prestigious "Palme d'Or" (literally, golden ear of corn; called the Grand Prix from 1949–55 and 1964–74) for Best Film as well as prizes including Best Actor, Best Actress, Best Director and

PRECEDING PAGES: 1953 Cannes Film Festival: Dany Robin, Kirk Douglas, Olivia de Havilland, Edward G. Robinson and members of the festival's jury.
LEFT: Cathérine Deneuve.
RIGHT: Sophia Loren's handprint, Cannes.

"BB"

It was the film *And God Created Woman*, made in 1956 by Brigitte Bardot's then-husband Roger Vadim, that rocketed the overtly sexy star to fame. The daughter of bourgeois Parisians, Bardot was a mere 15 years old when she met Vadim. She soon became an international star, with her love life as famous as her films. She was a regular at the Cannes Film Festival and the darling of the photographers. Animals, however, were her passion, and she has famously declared that she prefers them to men. Further scandal was caused by her marriage in 1992 to Bernard d'Ormale, a leading member of the Front Nationale and her controversial autobiography of 1996.

Best Screenplay for feature films that have been made in the year leading up to the Festival. (To qualify, entries must not have been shown outside their country of origin nor entered for any other competition.) A second jury gives awards for short films (that is, those that last for a maximum of 15 minutes) and for the best three films presented by the Cinéfondation, Cannes' champion for productions from film schools or by new talent. A special award is also given for the best first feature film.

WANT TO KNOW MORE?

For further details, contact the Bureau du Festival International du Film, 99 boulevard Malesherbes, 75008 Paris (tel: 01 45 61 66 00) or visit www.festival-cannes.fr.

Money talks

Critical cinematic appreciation and highbrow prize-giving are not the sole concerns of the Cannes festival, however. It's also a major venue for the hard-nosed buying and selling of film rights, for industry schmoozing and boozing. Much of this wheeler-dealing goes on in the basement of the Palais, at the Marché du Film.

However, this aspect of the festival is often criticised, accused of being a marathon homage to bad taste and conspicuous consumption, a big excuse to take advantage of swollen expense accounts at Cannes's luxury *Belle Époque* hotels such as the Carlton, Martinez or Majestic. It could be argued that the invisible hand of capitalism – the driving force behind the Marché du Film – is why over 12,500 film producers, directors, distributors and actors from around 80 countries, more than 3,000 journalists and no less than 2,500 hangers-on come to Cannes for two weeks every year.

Glamour and glitz

Officialdom and cynicism aside, however, much of the hullabaloo surrounding Cannes is without doubt due to the pull of the stars. Ever since the festival's glitzy heyday during the 1950s and 1960s the paparazzi have travelled to the southern French shores in May to snap gorgeous stars in glamorous evening attire and – more popularly – scantily-clad, wannabe cinema-lovelies on the beach at Cannes.

Bathing wear is certainly not, however, reserved for the female guests – 1947 goes down as the year when Jean-Paul Sartre strolled down Cannes's palm-lined main street in a bathing suit. Brigitte Bardot made the biggest splash of them all, however, in 1953, when she attended her first Cannes festival – then unknown, Bardot went on to be a screen sensation in films, most notably in films by her then-husband, Roger Vadim.

Other eternal Riviera beauties include the American actress Grace Kelly, for whom romance was in the air in 1955, when she visited the Monagasque royals during her fortnight at Cannes. The filmstar married her prince, and the Grimaldis have been a source of celebrity gossip ever since.

Recent star-spotting involves sighting the eccentric Icelandic songstress Bjork, who won Best Actress in 2000 for her role in Lars Van Trier's *Dancer in the Dark* – her debut acting role. In 2001 the Palme d'Or went to Italian director Nanni Moretti for *The Son's Room* but much of the attention went to *Moulin Rouge* show-stopper Nicole Kidman.

A MAN'S WORLD

Female directors have fared less well at Cannes than male ones. In 1993 Jane Campion became the first female director to win the Palme d'Or for her film *The Piano*.

Success stories

Although winning the Palme d'Or at Cannes does not guarantee box-office success – some past winners have received little or no attention outside the festival – this is not the absolute rule. Enduring past winners include Carol Reed's *The Third Man* (1949), Federico Fellini's *La Dolce Vita* (1960), Martin Scorsese's *Taxi Driver* (1976), Steven Sonderbergh's *Sex, Lies and Videotape* (1989), David Lynch's cult classic *Wild at Heart* (1990) and Quentin Tarentino's 1994 trigger-happy *Pulp Fiction*.

Invitations

The festival is supposed to be for industry insiders only, with tickets to screening and other evening events notoriously difficult to come by. However, if you're determined to get in to see the stars, you have a talent at charming bodyguards and local *gendarmes*, and your holiday budget stretches to the extortionate prices charged at the luxury hotels on the Cannes waterfront (around €16 a pop for an alcoholic drink), you may yet get to take part in the action.

Not to be recommended, however, is taking a leaf out of the book of the previously unknown Simone Sylva, who in 1954 parted company with her bikini top in close proximity to the American actor Robert Mitchum. To the delight of the paparazzi – and the dismay of Mitchum's wife – the latter gallantly tried to protect the young lady's modesty with his hands, creating the perfect photo opportunity and sparking acres of press coverage. Tragically, however, Sylva committed suicide six months later. ❑

LEFT: entrance to the "Bunker".
ABOVE: George Clooney and Holly Hunter.

A Short History of the Bikini

When the first two-piece bathing suit was unveiled in Paris on 5 July 1946, it had such an impact that its designer, Louis Réard, named the garment "bikini" after a then-recent atomic explosion in the Pacific Ocean. The *Paris Herald Tribune* reported: "For the first time in history, the entire staff of the European edition and the foreign service of the *New York Herald Tribune* now in Paris insisted yesterday on covering

the same assignment. Each was so determined to do that job that, for the sake of organisational morale, they were all assigned to the story. It turned out to be an exhibition of the world's smallest bathing suit, modeled at the Piscine Molitor."

The bikini's arrival launched the beginning of a whole new era in bathing attire as well as a fresh attitude towards women's bodies. Nowadays, it seems quite unbelievable that such a small amount of fabric could be interpreted in so many different ways and find itself at the centre of so much controversy.

During the late 19th century, bathing suits came in two pieces, but they were very different from today's typical bikini. Composed of a long tunic and knickers – generally of wool or serge – their integral purpose was to cover up the body. In fact, for a long time, bathing suits were designed for beachwear rather than for swimming.

It was only at the beginning of the 20th century that one-piece garments were produced. The first rib-knit, elasticised, one-piece bathing suit was made in the United States in 1920 by the Jantzen Company. This change of attitude from prudishness to practicality can be attributed largely to swimmer Annette Kellerman, who joined many competitions against men in swimming events held in the River Thames in London, the Seine in Paris and in the English Channel.

In 1924, the designer Jean Patou added a fashionable touch by introducing bathing suits bearing Cubist-inspired designs. And, of course, the ubiquitous Coco Chanel was also instrumental in the bathing suit revolution. During her much-publicised affair with the Duke of Westminster, Chanel was one of the first women to sport a tan, acquired during long vacations in Spain and on the French Riviera, where she wore the most up-to-date swimsuits and beachwear.

However, of the many designers who contributed to promoting the bikini over the years, Jacques Heim was probably the most innovative. Having opened a chain of boutiques selling sportswear as early as 1946, he popularised the use of cotton for beachwear when he used the fabric in his couture collections.

With the end of World War II, beaches on both sides of the Atlantic reopened and seaside holiday became possible once again. But, although dressier swimsuits in brighter colours were emerging, as well as backless models in the new lightweight fabrics, the attitude towards baring one's skin was still prudish. Peggy Guggenheim told of being fined on a Spanish beach where she was holidaying with the painter Max Ernst during the early 1940s. The local *carabinieri*, having gone to the trouble of measuring her back *decolleté*, deemed it indecent.

The American magazine *Vogue* began giving advice on how to choose a good swimsuit: "Don't spoil the looks of your perfect dive with a fluggy-ruffles, cutie-pie suit... don't go in for violent water sports in a suit with trick fastening... take off your girdle before you try it on for it's likely to give you delusions of grandeur about your figure... don't overdo the little girl angle when you are chronologically or anatomically unsuited... don't stop at one bathing suit..."

But it was really only in the 1950s that the attitude towards the bathing suit started to ease. Even though swimming siren Esther Williams and her nautical extravaganzas did a great deal for the glamour of sophisticated swimming attire, it was not until Brigitte Bardot came on the scene that bikinis found their role model.

Right from the start, the French Riviera was the focal point of the bikini's development, particularly in St-Tropez. In 1956, Bardot was photographed there wearing a gingham bikini decorated with frills. Instantly, gingham became the rage.

During the 1960s, swimwear was designed to emphasise the body with underwiring added to emphasize the bosom. "The new way for a bikini," said British *Vogue* in 1963, "is little-boy shorts and a built-up bra." But, by the end of the decade, when smaller busts became the look, the costumes were more severely cut.

And bikinis were designed at their scantiest: "the minimum two-piece for a perfect tan, leaving the least possible marks from sunbathing", reported French *Vogue* in 1969. The arrival of nylon was also important: "The quick-change *maillot* – when it's dried in the sun it's a sinuous velvety black, and when it's soaked with water it glistens like a seal on the rocks. In the miracle fibre Vyrene." (British *Vogue*, 1965).

In keeping with the hit song "She wore an itsy-bitsy, teeny-weeny, yellow, polka-dotted bikini," two-piece suits inched their way to nothingness. By the mid-1970s the more daring sunbathers had even begun to remove their tops. The arrival of the monokini (just a bottom) was inevitable.

While going topless is still taboo in many countries, it is accepted easily in the majority of Western Europe, especially on the French Riviera. However, the one-piece is finding new interest. Take it from Felix Palmari, the knowledgeable owner of the Tahiti beach club, one of the oldest "private" beaches on the "Route des Plages." When Felix opened his concession on the 10-km (6-mile) stretch of pure white sand, he was alone. Nowadays, the beach is staked out with sprawled bodies in every stage of undress and dozens of exotically named concessions renting parasols, mattresses and other sunbathing paraphernalia.

"We've seen it all," says Felix, who remembers how wonderfully deserted the beach was when he first arrived here some 40 years ago. "Fashions move, but I think that women today are less into showing off their nudity. They take off their tops in order to tan, but there is a definite comeback of the one-piece bathing suit." ❑

LEFT: an early advertisement for Jantzen one-piece bathing suits.
ABOVE: Brigitte Bardot, the ultimate bikini siren.

MARINE

PLACES

A detailed guide to the entire region, with principal sites clearly cross-referenced by number to the maps

Provence consists of six *départements* with two sub-regions. Of them, the Vaucluse is known for lush landscapes, fruits and the sophisticated papal city of Avignon. The ancient Bouches-du-Rhône combines dry wide plains of olive trees and cypress with a Mediterranean coastline and includes the distinctly Roman city of Arles, the fountain-bedecked university town of Aix-en-Provence and the seaside metropolis of Marseille. Within the Bouches-du-Rhône, the Camargue is an ecologically fascinating mixture of marshland, salt plains and beaches, populated by flamingoes, wild horses, bulls and French cowboys *(gardians)*.

Crowned by the naval capital of Toulon, the southern reaches of the Var also lie along the Mediterranean, while huge inland forests make this France's most heavily wooded *département*. To the north, the Alpes-de-Haute-Provence rises to alpine heights, with fortified villages clinging precariously to mountainsides. Its neighbour, the Alpes-Maritimes, is equally renowned for its hill-towns, becoming increasingly Italian in character towards its eastern border. Nearer the sea are beaches and harbours, yachts and villas – the Côte d'Azur, often referred to as the French Riviera.

Along with disparities, certain Provençal characteristics can be found regionwide. The region is famed for its culinary tradition – fresh local produce and excellent wine contribute to a hearty but delicious cuisine. Across this part of France, the people are warm and down-to-earth, and a love for folklore is reflected in much of their daily lives.

All is not rustic in Provence, however – the region also has a sophisticated side, with considerable cultural riches to offer. The artists who have lived here – inspired by the region's legendary light, which dazzles mountains, plains and seaside – include Van Gogh, Cézanne, Picasso and Matisse. These great masters have left a legacy of art, and there are many important art museums in the region – in Nice, St-Paul-de-Vence, Marseille, Nîmes, Arles, Aix-en-Provence, St-Tropez, Antibes and Avignon – in which numerous works inspired by Provence and its Côte are on display. There are also many smaller museums and galleries exhibiting a huge variety of art and crafts.

Summer festivals abound, where everything from flowers to lemons and garlic is celebrated. Avignon is famous for its theatre festival, as is Cannes for film, and there is also the opera festival of Orange and the jazz festivals of Nice and Juans-les-Pins. Welcome to the many delights of France's sunny, southeasternmost region. ❑

PRECEDING PAGES: lavender fields on the plateau de Valensole; evening on the Cassis waterfront; hill town in the Var.
LEFT: the village of Saignon.

Provence
0
20 km
0
20 miles
N
MEDITERRANEAN SEA
Valence
Crest
Die
Lalley
Saillans
Privas
la Cluse
Drôme
Luc-en-Diois
Rhône
A7
Bourdeux
Aubenas
Aspres-sur-Buëch
Veynes
Montélimar
Ardéche
Serres
Grignan
N94
D994
Rocher de Beaumont
1545
N86
E15
N75
Pierrelatte
St-Paul
Valréas
Nyons
Baronnies
N7
Ardèche
Laragne-Montéglin
Barjac
Tulette
Buis-les-Baronnies
Bollène
D938
A7
Vaison-la-Romaine
Séderon
N86
Mont Ventoux
1909
Bagnols-sur-Cèze
Violès
Signal de Lure
1826
Orange
Lussan
Beaumes-de-Venise
Montagne de Lure
Sault
N580
A9
Villes-sur-Auzon
A7
Carpentras
Banon
St-Etienne
Sorgues
Uzés
N86
Vaucluse
Plateau de Vaucluse
Gard
Villeneuve-lès-Avignon
Forcalquier
Remoulins
Pont du Gard
Avignon
l'Isle-sur-la-Sorgue
E15
Aramon
N100
N96
Châteaurenard
Apt
N100
Nîmes
Marguerittes
E714
Cavaillon
Manosque
N999
Bonnieux
Montagne du Lubéron
Beaucaire
Tarascon
Parc Régional du Lubéron
Montpellier
A9
St-Rémy-de-Provence
Durance
A51
A54
Cadenet
Mirabeau
E80
Eyguières
A7
Pertuis
St-Gilles
N572
Arles
Mouriès
Salon-de-Provence
N96
N113
Rians
Parc Naturel Régional de Camargue
Grand Rhône
N7
Mont Ste-Victoire
Miramas
Bouches-du-Rhône
St-Chamas
A8
Aix-en-Provence
Etang de Vaccarès
N568
Istres
A7
Etang de Berre
N7
N569
E80
St-Maximin la-Ste-Baume
A51
Gardanne
Saintes-Maries-de-la-Mer
Salin-de-Giraud
Port-St-Louis-du-Rhône
Martigues
Port-de-Bouc
Marignane
N8
N560
Golfe des Stes-Maries ou de Beauduc
N568
Golfe de Fos
Carro
Carry-le-Rouet
Allauch
A52
Marseille
A50
Aubagne
Île Pomègues
N8
Cap Croisette
Cassis
N8
la Ciotat
A50
Île de Riou
Cap Canaille
Six-Fours les-Plages

UNITED KINGDOM
BELGIUM
GERMANY
LUX.
Nord-Pas-de-Calais
Picardie
Haute-Normandie
Basse-Normandie
Lorraine
Alsace
Bretagne
Île-de-France
Champagne-Ardenne
Pays de la Loire
Centre
Bourgogne
Franche-Comté
SWITZ.
Poitou-Charentes
Limousin
Rhône-Alpes
Corse
Auvergne
ITALY
Aquitaine
Midi-Pyrénées
Provence-Alpes-Cote-d'Azur
Languedoc-Roussillon
SPAIN
ANDORRA
Hautes-Alpes
Guillestre
Pic de la Font Sancte
3387
Monviso
3481
Dents de Maniglia
3171
N94
Embrun
Chorges
Gap
Lac de Serre-Ponçon
Grand Parpaillon
2899
ITALY
D900
Dormillouse
2505
Barcelonnette
Seyne
Grande Séolane
2909
l' Oratoire
2071
D900
Mont Pelat
3051
Parc National du Mercantour
Tête del l'Autaret
2661
Cima d'Argentera
3297
Sommet du Caduc
2654
Colmars
Mont Mounier
2817
Laupon
2434
la Javi
Thorame-Haute
Mont Bégo
2873
Guillaumes
St-Sauveur-sur-Tinée
St-Martin-Vésubie
Digne-les-Bains
Dome de Barrot
2137
Parc National du Mercantour
N85
N204
Alpes-de-Haute-Provence
Alpes-Maritimes
St-André-les-Alpes
N202
Entrevaux
Puget-Théniers
Breil-sur-Roya
ITALY
San Remo
N85
la Bégude-Blanche
Senez
Lac de Castillon
Sospel
Levens
Chiran
1905
Castellane
Var
Montagne du Cheiron
N202
Ventimiglia
Coursegoules
A8
Menton
Lac de Ste-Croix
N85
Monte-Carlo
MONACO
Monaco
Vence
E80
N7
Nice
Grand Plan de Canjuers
Comps-sur-Artuby
N85
Cap Ferrat
Grasse
Cagnes-sur-Mer
Montmeyan
Aups
Fayence
N7
Vallauris
Antibes
Salernes
Draguignan
Cap d'Antibes
Cannes
Cotignac
N555
A8
Îles de Lérins
N7
Carces
Lorgues
E80
le Muy
Argens
N98
Var
A8
Fréjus
St-Raphaël
Corse
N7
Brignoles
E80
le Luc
Côte d'Azur
N97
Massif des Maures
Ste-Maxime
Cap St-Pierre
A57
St-Tropez
Cogolin
la Croix-Valmer
N98
Cavalaire-sur-Mer
Bormes-les-Mimosas
MEDITERRANEAN SEA
Hyères
le Lavandou
A570
Cap Bénat
Rade d'Hyères
Îles d'Hyères
Parc National de Port-Cros
Corse
Corse

EST
ature et effort
NOUVELLE VIE
FLASHES
« March ou rouille ! »

Découverte du cadavre d'une femme à Bollène
Les colis étaient bourrés de bijoux
Vaucluse Matin
le dauphiné
FESTIVAL INTERNATIONAL DE FOLKLORE
La rupture

Map
n pages
12–113

THE VAUCLUSE

Provence's most northwesterly corner is home to Avignon, often lauded as the jewel in the Provençal crown, and such Roman sites as Orange and Vaison-la-Romaine. Nearby are Nîmes and the Pont du Gard aqueduct

In a survey conducted by *Le Point* magazine, the Vaucluse came second only to Paris in a list of France's best areas for cultural activities. However, anyone journeying through this region's beautiful countryside will quickly become aware of a richness far beyond staged events.

Each town and village within the Vaucluse guards its own character, overtly expressed through unique and traditional *fêtes* and customs. Differences exist between mountain and valley people, town and rural life, and even the Provençal and French mannerisms, and these all add to the joy of discovering the region.

A similar diversity in terrain provides the visitor to the Vaucluse with a wonderful choice of things to do. You can go mountain-climbing, bird-watching, pony-trekking or canoeing, taste some of France's finest wines in such vineyards as Châteauneuf-du-Pape or indulge in a cuisine that draws on an abundance of locally produced herbs, fruits and vegetables. Or you can simply let the fragrance of lavender, the freshness of rosemary and the softness of pine waft through your open car windows as you drive.

Unless you are visiting for one of the many summer festivals, there are good reasons to visit the Vaucluse in early spring or late autumn, when the region is less hot and crowded than in summer. Whenever you go, however, the colour and texture of a land that embraces the snow-capped peak of Mont Ventoux, the cherry blossoms of Malaucène, the ochre cliffs of Roussillon and the light that has inspired numerous painters should be incentive enough to lead you away from the main cities and motorways into the countryside. As a general rule, the adventurous spirit is rightly rewarded in the Vaucluse, as some of the best finds are tucked away along mountain tracks or forest-lined backroads.

ECEDING GES: tching up on e local news. **FT:** vineyards front of the ntelles de ontmirail. **GHT:** ignon's lais des pes.

From the north in Valréas to the west along the banks of the Rhône, south to the River Durance and east through the Lubéron, the Vaucluse has virtually natural borders. Historically, the region has always been a sort of crossroads. For centuries a trampling ground of marching armies, it has seen conflict between Romans and Gauls, Arabs and Christians, Catholics and Protestants and between French Resistance groups and Germans. These many different conflicts have come together to shape the rich architectural heritage of the region.

Popes, bridges and festivals

Nowhere in the Vaucluse is this rich heritage more apparent than in the papal city

Lyon
Donzère
St-Montant
St-André-de-Mitroys
Roche Colombe
Les Granges-Gontardes
La Garde-Adhémar
Chapelle du Val-des-Nymphes
Roussas
Valaurie
Réauville
Taulignan
Grignan
Grotte de Rochecourbière
La Clarte Notre-Dame
Montbrison
le Pègue
N.D. de Beauvoir
St-Pantaléon-les-Vignes
St-Ferréol-Trente-Pas
Condorcet
Venterol
Curnier
Arpavon
Aubres
Nyons
Montaulieu
Ste-Jalle
Drôme
Grillon
Chamaret
Valréas
Richerenches
Vaucluse
Montségur-sur-Lauzon
Solérieux
la-Baume-de-Transit
Pierrelatte
Ardèche
Bourg-St-Andéol
Vinsas
Faveyrolles
St-Paul
St-Marcel-d'Ardèche
le Bosquet
St-Just
Lapalud
Rhône
St-Ferréol
Gourdon
St-Turquoit
Bouchet
Tulette
Visan
St-Maurice-sur-Eygues
Vinsobres
Verone
Mirabel-aux-Baronnies
Beauvoisin
Gorges d'Ubrieux
Propiac
Buis-les-Baronnies
Villedieu
la Baude
Buisson
Puymeras
Faucon
Pierrelongue
Mollans-sur-Ouvèze
Suze-la-Rousse
Lez
Bollène
Pont Antique
Pont-St-Esprit
St-Paulet-de-Caisson
Carsan
St-Alexandre
Mondragon
Rochegude
Ste-Cécile-les-Vignes
Cairanne
Rasteau
Roaix
St-Roman-de-Malegarde
Vaison-la-Romaine
Notre-Dame d'Aubusson
Crestet
Séguret
Sablet
Entrechaux
St-Léger-du-Ventoux
Lagarde-Paréol
St-Estève
la Galle
Sérignan-du-Comtat
Aygues
Travaillan
St-André
Cirque de St-Amand
Beaumont-du-Ventoux
Malaucène
Suzette
Notre-Dame-du-Groseau
Ste-Croix
Mont Ventoux
St-Laurent-de-Carnois
St-Nazaire
Vénéjan
St-Étienne-des-Sorts
Piolenc
Aigueville
Camaret-sur-Aigues
Violès
Gigondas
Dentelles de Montmirail
la Madeleine
Lafare
le Barroux
Bédoin
Crillon-le-Brave
Flassan
Donnat
Cèze
Bagnols-sur-Cèze
Chusclan
Orange
Martignan
Causans
Vacqueyras
Beaumes-de-Venise
Aubignan
Modène
Caromb
Mégier
Tresques
Orsan
Codolet
Caderousse
Jonquières
Laudun
Courthezon
Sarrians
Loriol-du-Comtat
St-Pierre-de-Vassols
Mormoiron
Villes-sur-Auzon
Connaux
Gaujac
St-Paul-les-Fonts
Montfaucon
Tourreau
Ouvèze
le Martinet
St-Laurent-des-Arbres
Corrénson
Châteauneuf-du-Pape
la Fortia
Carpentras
Mazan
Masmolène
St-Victor-la-Coste
Roquemaure
Bédarrides
Monteux
Malemort-du-Comtat
Blauvac
Pouzilhac
Lirac
Tavel
Sauveterre
Sorgues
Entraigues-sur-la-Sorgue
Althen-des-Paluds
St-Didier
Notre-Dame-de-Vie
Méthamis
Nesque
Valliguières
Gard
Pujaut
Tringuevédel
Pernes-les-Fontaines
Venasque
Castillon-du-Gard
St-Hilaire-d'Ozilhan
Rochefort-du-Gard
Villeneuve-lès-Avignon
Barthelasse
Vedène
les Valayans
Sorgue
Velleron
Vaucluse
Plateau
Vers
Cassagner
Morières
Jonquerettes
Saumane-de-Vaucluse
Abbaye de Sénanque
Remoulins
Pont du Gard
Estézargues
Domazan
Avignon
Grotte de Thouzon
Châteauneuf-de-Gadagne
Fontaine-de-Vaucluse
Fontaine
Gordes
Fournès
St-Bonnet-du-Gard
Théziers
Durance
Caumont-s-Durance
l'Isle-sur-la-Sorgue
Cabrières-d'Avignon
Nîmes
Meynes
Aramon
Barbentane
Rognonas
Châteaurenard
les Vignères
Lagnes
St-Pantaléon
Musée les Boullons
Montfrin
Abbaye St-Michel-de Frigolet
Noves
les Baumianes
Coulon
Beaumettes
Lumière
Campredon
Boulbon
Graveson
Cabannes
Cavaillon
Maubec
Robion
les Poulivets
Taillades
Ménerbes
Lacoste
Oppède-le-Vieux
Comps
Vallabrègues
Bournissac
St-Saveur
St-Andiol
Jonquières-St-Vincent
Abbaye de St-Roman
Maillane
Eyragues
Paluds-de-Noves
Lagoy
Gres-Hauts
Mollégès
Plan-d'Orgon
Cheval-Blanc
Beaucaire
Tarascon
St-Rémy-de-Provence
Roussan
les Antiques
Orgon
Valdition
Mont
Bellegarde
St-Etienne-du-Grès
Cathédrale d'Images
Chaîne des Apilles
les Baux-de-Provence
Eygalières
St-Sixte
Sénas
Mérindol
Viguier
Estoublon
Pierredon
Roquemartine
Fontvieille
Escanin
Maussane-les-Alpilles
Castelas de Roquemartine
Mallemort
Durance
Moulin de Daudet
Paradou
Servanne
Aureille
Grottes de Calès
Charleval
Pont-Royal
Abbaye de Montmajour
Fourques
le Grand Barbegal
Eyguières
Lamanon
Allens
St-Martin
Cazan
Mouriès
Richebois
Arles
Bouches-du-Rhône
Bas
Parc Naturel Régional de Camargue
Villepail
Raphèle-les Arles
Salon-de-Provence
Marseille
Marseille

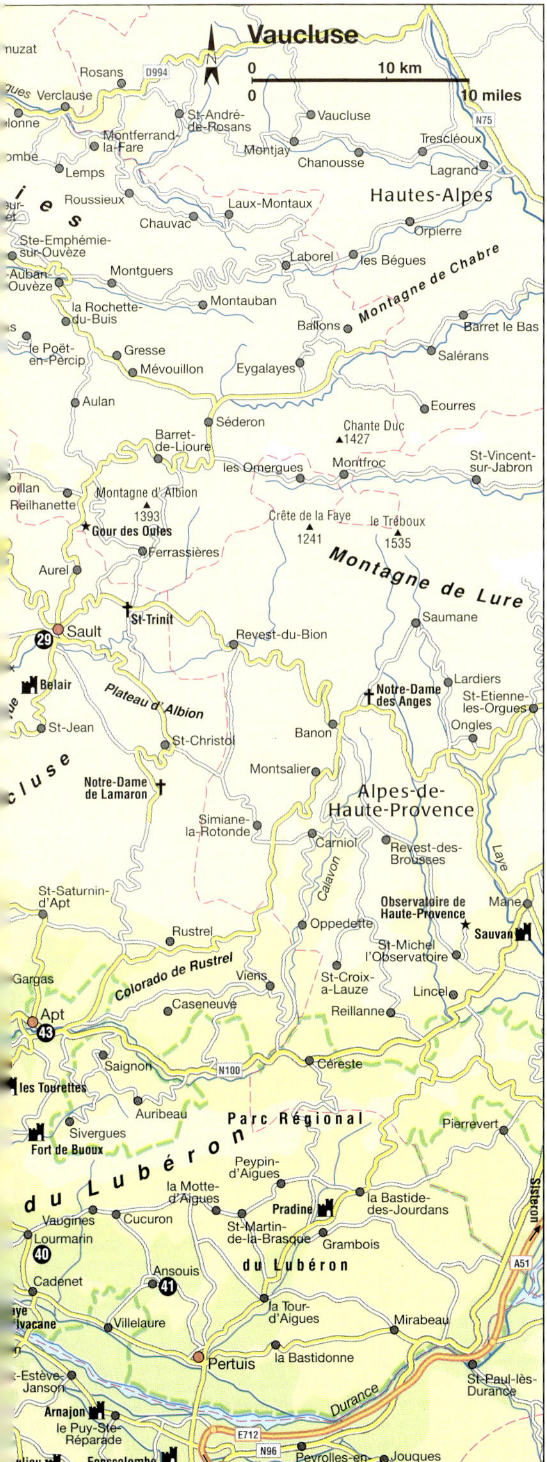

of **Avignon ❶**, *préfecture* of the *département* and gateway to Provence. Strategically situated near the junction of the Rhône and Durance rivers, Avignon was first established by the early Gauls as a tribal capital, and it was known to the Greek traders of Marseille. During the Roman period, however, it was overshadowed by Orange and although some Roman artefacts can be found in the Musée Lapidaire *(see page 117)*, most buildings that you can see today belong to its medieval past.

Avignon is a walled city, with 5-km (3-mile) fortifications enclosing its inner core. A walk around these ramparts, broken up by 39 towers and seven gates, reveals a cornucopia of historic buildings, churches and palaces. The French writer Rabelais called Avignon "*la villa sonnate*" because of the number of steeples that adorned its skyline; nowadays, buildings of a religious character still outnumber the secular ones. On a less lyrical level, the battlements now also bear witness to the modern growth of the city. Factories and modern suburbs extend outwards from under the shadow of the wall to accommodate the city's 180,000 inhabitants.

The **tourist office** (41 cours Jean Jaurès, tel: 04 32 74 32 74) provides information on the best methods of getting to know the **vieille ville** (old town) They offer an excellent guide service that takes you on either a half-day or full-day walking tour of the town, with commentary available in most major European languages. For the tour, it is best to book in advance as space is restricted. If you are travelling as a family or small group you can arrange to have your own guide. If you're not keen on walking, you can tour the old town on a miniature train, which covers all the key points and the shopping zone.

Sur le pont d'Avignon

Whether you go by bus or on foot, you should not miss the famous bridge, **Pont St-Bénézet Ⓐ** (rue Ferruce; open daily; entrance fee; tel: 04 90 27 50 83) immortalised in the popular children's song ("*Sur le pont d'Avignon...*"), although only four of its original 22 arches remain today. Inspired by heaven, a young shepherd from the Ardèche (the future St Bénézet) built the bridge at the end of the 12th century; it was destroyed during the Albigensian War of 1209–28 and reconstructed in 1234. The Chapelle St-Nicholas, which stands halfway along the remaining structure, was also altered during this period and a Gothic apse was added to it in 1513.

Home of the Papacy

The **Palais des Papes** Ⓑ (Papal Palace; place du Palais; open daily; entrance fee; guided tours and individual audio-guides available; tel: 04 90 27 50 74), symbol of the papal residency in Avignon (1309–77), is easy to find, as – according to a traditional French saying – all roads, or at least those in Avignon, lead there. The "route rapide", rue Vieille Porte and rue de la Monnaie do indeed all lead to the vast square in front of the monumental yellowstone edifice, which from this spot and set against a dazzling clear-blue sky makes an imposing sight.

When you face the façade, with its two flanking towers, it is immediately apparent that the palace was built for defensive purposes as well as for residency. The former aspect of the structure was necessary because the original city walls, which were built by popes Innocent VI and Urban V, were not strong enough to ward off attack by the bands of wandering knights that plagued the countryside.

You enter the palace through the **Porte des Champeaux**. Once you step into the **Grande Cour** (Great Courtyard), this fortress palace quickly takes on the sense of being a city within a city. It takes between an hour and two hours to walk through the palace, which is divided into two sections: the "old" part, built by Pope Benedict XII between 1334 and 1342, and the "new" palace, begun under Benedict's successor, Pope Clement VI, and completed in 1348. The old palace has a monastic simplicity and austerity that

BELOW: making mus in Avignon's place de l'Horloge.

Maps:
Area 112
City 116

reflect the sombre character of Benedict XII. The new palace, on the other hand, is brightly decorated with elaborate fresco work and flamboyant ceilings, which reflect Clement VI's status as a patron of the arts and lover of the high life. Both parts of the palace, however, are far from modest, and their grandeur was received with some controversy. Petrarch, who spent time in Provence but was no fan of the court of Clement, called the palace "the habitation of demons".

As you make your way around, be sure to look in on the row of portraits of the popes who resided in Avignon that hang in the **Aile du Consistoire** (Hall of the Consistory). You should also look for the **Chambre du Cerf** (Deer Room), in the new palace, where you can feast your eyes on the elaborate frescoes painted by Matteo Giovanetti in 1343. These lively scenes of hunting, fishing, falconry and youths picking fruit and bathing give valuable insight into life at the papal court during the 14th century.

If you were in any doubt about the sumptuous tastes of Clement VI , the star-studded ceiling of the **Aile de Grande Audience** (Audience Hall), in shades of blue and gold, should dispel any last reservations. If it doesn't, the grand walls and windows of the **Chapelle St-Martial** certainly will.

Eventually, you will find the guardroom that leads back to the entrance. Before leaving, it is worth taking one last glimpse across the great courtyard.

City of churches

By way of contrast to the grand Palais des Papes, Avignon's cathedral, **Notre-Dame-des-Doms** **C**, where John XXII is buried, is a strictly serious affair. Although this Romanesque, 12th-century building has undergone many architectural changes over the years, it retains its original spiritual simplicity. Unfortunately, the addition in 1859 of a gilded cast-iron statue of the Virgin means that it rather resembles a wedding cake.

.OW: Palais des ...es, Avignon.

A church that has changed little since its consecration in 1359 is the **Eglise St-Didier** Ⓓ. This was the largest church to be built in the town during the Avignon papacy and owes much of its clean-lined appeal to the influence of "old palace" Pope Benedict XII. The elegant restriction of internal decoration is a reflection of the "purity" that Benedict supported.

When you enter St-Didier's first chapel, you'll come upon one of the church's vantage points: an early Renaissance work by Francesco Laurana called *The Way of the Cross*. In 1953 other 14th-century wall paintings of the Crucifixion were uncovered, which are now gradually being restored. Another notable feature is the hexagonal Gothic pulpit that stands in the centre of the church – a certain indication of the important role sermons played during the 14th century.

Shopping facilities are good in this area, and there are several spacious pedestrian zones that are lined with boutiques as well as open-air bars and cafés. As a general rule, prices become more reasonable the further away you go from the Palais des Papes. However, in July and August, all the streets of the old town (as in most of Provence) become hot and crowded, and even the smarter restaurants hereabouts do not offer the quality of menu or service that their exteriors promise.

Galleries and museums

Avignon has several good museums, with diverse collections, making it a great spot for culture lovers. At the northern end of the place du Palais is the **Musée du Petit Palais** Ⓔ (closed Tues; entrance fee; tel: 04 90 86 44 58), which has a superb collection of medieval painting and sculpture, Romanesque sculptures, frescoes and a fine collection of work in the International Gothic style. Most stunning of all is Botticelli's late 15th-century *Madonna and Child*.

Housed in an elegant former *hôtel particulier* to the southwest of the Palais des Papes is the **Musée Calvet** Ⓕ (65 rue

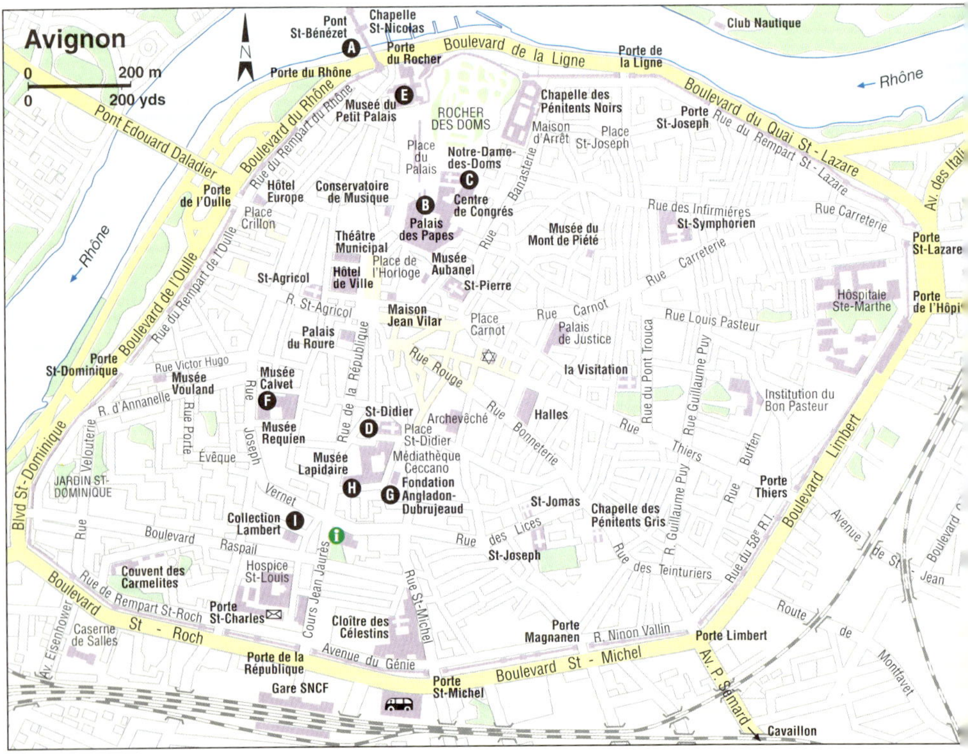

Maps:
rea 112
ity 116

Joseph Vernet; closed Tues; entrance fee; tel: 04 90 86 33 84). This airy museum was named after a doctor-cum-archaeologist-cum-bibliophile, who bequeathed to the city his library, art collection and funds to start the museum.

On show is an extensive collection of the French and Avignon schools of painting and sculpture from the 14th to the 20th century. Jacques-Louis David, Théodore Géricault, Eugène Delacroix, Camille Corot and Edouard Manet are just a few of the important painters whose works hang here. There is also a good modern section, showing work by Chaïm Soutine, Alfred Sisley, Albert Gleizes, Maurice Utrillo, Raoul Dufy and Camille Claudel.

Musée Calvet's archaeological collection is a treasure trove of objects from the neo-Gothic period. Its holdings include finds discovered in the 1960s that have changed theories about the origins of Avignon and have suggested that its culture has much earlier roots than was previously believed.

Other museums in Avignon worth visiting include the **Fondation Angladon-Dubrujeaud** **G** (5 rue Laboureur; closed Tues; entrance fee; tel: 04 90 82 29 03), housed in an 18th-century mansion, with a fine collection of Dutch oils and modern French art, most notably the only painting by Van Gogh in Provence, *Les Wagons du Chemin de Fer*.

The **Musée Lapidaire** **H** (27 rue de la République; closed Tues; entrance fee; tel: 04 90 86 33 84), housed in the former chapel of a 17th-century Jesuit college, is worth a visit if you are interested in archaeology. The collection, which includes Greek, Gallo-Roman and Etruscan ceramics, sculpture and glassware, is wonderfully displayed.

Contemporary art fans will delight at the excellent **Collection Lambert** **I**, (Hotel de Caumont, 5 rue Violette; open daily; entrance fee; tel: 04 90 16 56 20), which includes works by Carl André, Anselm Keifer, Julian Schnabel and Cy Twombly. Exhibitions change regularly.

CULTURAL AVIGNON

Don't be surprised if, while sitting in a café in Avignon any time between the first week of July and the eginning of August, you find yourself surrounded by a oupe of strolling players in medieval costumes, carrying rums, pipes and lyres and acting out a full-blown drama. his may all be part of Avignon's internationally renowned ummer festival, which was established in 1947 by the ctor Jean Vilar and his Théâtre Nationale Populaire to ıake the performing arts accessible to all. Performances clude theatre from Shakespeare and Racine to Ionesco, ıus "fringe" productions, street theatre, puppetry, dance, ime, orchestral concerts and café cabarets. You'll robably also see fire-eaters, stilt-walkers and similar aring street performers in the area around the Palais des apes, not to mention innumerable human statues.

Given their own dramatic flare, the Avignon popes would ndoubtedly have approved of the festival. At any rate, ıany of the shows are given in the court of their one-time esidence. Other performances make imaginative use of cal churches and cardinals' houses. For bookings and formation on the festival, contact: Bureau du Festival Avignon, 8 bis rue de Mons; tel: 04 90 27 66 50; fo@festival-avignon.com; www.festival-avignon.com.

HT: street formers he Avignon tival.

A good way to find out what is going on in Avignon is to the visit the second-hand bookshop, Shakespeare (155 rue Carnot; closed Sun; tel: 04 90 27 38 50), which stocks a wide range of foreign-language titles, English magazines and local-listings papers. Homesick Brits will be happy to hear that tea and scones are served here.

Avignon's calendar

Avignon is world famous for its festival , which takes place in July and early August *(see page 117)*, but there is actually plenty going on here all year round. January welcomes an equestrian fair, in February there is an antiques fair here and mid-November heralds the Baptème des Côtes du Rhône, the festival celebrating the yearly first tasting of the regional wine. There are also regular open-air flea markets in the city.

Avignon has lots of late-night bars, cafés and discos. There are also several cinemas, some of which show original-language *(version originale)* films, most notably **Cyberdrome**, on rue Guillaume Puy, and **Utopia**, which is tucked away behind the Palais on rue des Escaliers Ste-Anne. Utopia is also home to a lovely laid-back café.

Villeneuve-lès-Avignon

If you want to escape the hustle and bustle of Avignon, you may prefer to stay across the river at **Villeneuve-lès-Avignon** ❷. Much smaller than Avignon, Villeneuve nevertheless has a rich and celebrated history of its own, albeit without the hectic frenzy of its neighbour.

Towering over the attractive little town is the **Fort St-André** (west tower open daily; entrance fee), which guarded the frontier of France when Avignon was allied to the Holy Roman Empire. Built in the second half of the 14th century by John the Good, the fort still retains a military prowess so palpable that you feel it the moment you pass through its magnificent defensive entrance, which features mighty twin towers. The massive crenellated walls number among the finest examples of medieval fortification extant. Inside the fort's ramparts are the gardens of the **Abbaye St-André**, a restored Romanesque chapel, and the ruins of the 13th-century church (closed Jan and Mon; entrance fee; tel: 04 90 25 55 95).

The other militaristic building in Villeneuve is the isolated **Tour Philippe le Bel** (Philip the Fair Tower), which was once the starting point of the Pont St-Bénézet *(see pages 113–4)*. Both the Fort St-André and this tower give excellent views over the papal city. On a clear evening you can witness some gorgeous twilight colours, as the sun sets on Avignon's golden stone, with the bulk of Mont Ventoux silhouetted in the distance.

Villeneuve rose to splendour during the Avignon papacy. As the papal court increased in importance, the number of adjunct cardinals rose. Finding that Avignon had no more suitable space available, many of these cardinals chose to build their magnificent estates in Villeneuve instead, and at one point, there were as many as 15 of these.

LEFT: *herbe de Provenc* at market.

Map
1 pages
12–113

Ironically, the one structure to survive from that period is the simple and austere **Chartreuse de Val de Bénédiction** (allée des Mûriers; open daily; entrance fee; tel: 04 90 15 24 24). This Carthusian monastery was founded in the mid-14th century by Pope Innocent VI (whose tomb lies in the adjacent church) to commemorate the general of the Carthusian Order, who had himself been elected pope in 1352 but had refused the position out of a sense of humility. A small vaulted chapel off the Cloître du Cimitière features beautiful frescoes by Matteo Giovanetti, whose work also features in Avignon's Palais des Papes. The Chartreuse now functions as a state-funded centre for playwrights.

The **Musée Pierre de Luxembourg** (rue de la Republique; closed Feb and Mon; entrance fee; tel: 04 90 27 49 66) contains some wonderful works of art, including a carved-ivory *Virgin and Child* from the 14th century, and 16th- and 17th-century religious paintings by Pierre Mignard and Philippe de Champaigne; the cream of the crop is undoubtedly the *Coronation of the Virgin* (1453–4) by Enguerrand Quarton, which is set in a room of its own and shows an exquisitely detailed medieval view of the world.

Just to the south of the museum is the 14th-century church of Notre-Dame, home to paintings by Mignard and Levieux, a notable 18th-century altarpiece and a 14th-century cloister.

Villeneuve is a good alternative to Avignon for accommodation, with some very decent small hotels and an excellent campsite on the outskirts of town.

Châteauneuf-du-Pape

There are three basic journeys that can be easily made from Avignon or Villeneuve-lès-Avignon. The first trip is towards **Châteauneuf-du-Pape** ❸. From Villeneuve you'll need to cross the busy bridge towards Avignon, but you can avoid the main-town traffic by joining the N7 immediately and heading off in the direction of Sorgues. At Sorgues, join the D17

LOW:
medieval
t St-André,
eneuve-
-Avignon.

going northwest. On both sides of the road, rows of green vines rise out of what looks like a pebbled beach. In fact, this land was once washed by the waters of the Rhône. Today, the curious landscape marks the beginning of the villages with vineyards that are classed under the Châteauneuf-du-Pape *appellation*.

The legal history of the area is interesting, since it marked a major change in the history of French wine. In 1923, the local wine-growers applied to the courts for exclusive use of the Châteauneuf-du-Pape designation. Until that time, there were no such restrictions on the labelling of wines. Six years later, after a slow legal process, judgement was passed in their favour by an Orange court. The action gave rise in 1935 to the *appellation contrôlée* label that now appears on French wine bottles.

The vineyards of Châteauneuf-du-Pape are planted with 13 different grape varieties. The best wines achieve their complexity and character from blends of these grapes. Most red wines are the result of a blend of at least four grape types. Grenache is the dominant red-wine grape, followed by Mourvèdre, Syrah and Cinsault.

The end-product is what the writer Alphonse Daudet (1840–97) nicknamed "the king of wines and the wine of kings". Châteauneuf-du-Pape is a supple, warm and full-bodied wine that goes well with strongly flavoured dishes such as game and red meat and pungent cheese. This noble wine, perfumed with the scent of the Garrigues, can be sampled at any of the local vineyards. Reds and whites are produced but there are no Châteauneuf rosés.

Châteauneuf has its own wine museum: the **Musée des Outils de Vignerons** (place du Portail; open daily; free; tel: 04 90 83 70 07), which is devoted to the wine-making traditions of the region. Here, you can see baskets, pruners and wine-making equipment galore, followed by a tasting opportunity and the chance to buy a good selection of the local wine.

Above the village of Châteauneuf-du-Pape are the ruins and tower of the 14th-

BELOW: vineyard owner.

Map
n pages
112–113

century **château**, which was built by Pope John XXII as a summer residence. From here, you can look down the Val du Rhône, over the tiled roofs of Châteauneuf, right across to Avignon. Sadly, the château's strategic importance led to its almost total destruction in 1944, when German troops fought a scathing battle against Resistance forces.

Courthézon and Beaumes

Further opportunities to visit *caveaux de dégustation* (wine cellars, where tasting is available) lie along D92, towards the market town of **Courthézon** ❹. One valuable tip to remember when visiting the wine cellars is that it's always a good idea to offer to buy at least one bottle.

Real wine lovers should head a little further along the route to **Beaumes-de-Venise** ❺, where the wines are excellent. This spot was made famous by the troubadour Raimband d'Orange, who wrote and sang about medieval life in its castle. The attractive drive to Beaumes takes you along a road lined with vineyards and neat rows of cypress trees.

LOW: the
ed roofs
Beaumes-
-Venise.

Carpentras

Back in Courthézon, it's around 8 km (5 miles) to **Sarrians** ❻, where there is a fine example of late 18th-century architecture in the eccentric **Château de Tourreau**. From here it's a straight run along D950 to **Carpentras** ❼. En route, any of the side roads that lead in the direction of the River Auzon will take you to beautiful shady groves that are perfect for escaping the heat of the midday sun and enjoying a laid-back picnic.

Carpentras's peculiar mix of architectural styles – from Roman to rococo – reflect its history. The town's name is said to have been derived from the Latin word *karpenton*, meaning a two-wheeled cart drawn by horses. (For centuries the town was famous for its wagoners.) Even before it was conquered by the Romans, however, it was called Carpentoracte and was the tribal capital of the Celto-Ligurian Memini. The conquest itself is recorded in the carvings on the monumental gate in the courtyard of the **Palais de Justice**.

By the 4th century, Carpentras had become a bishopric. From 1274 until 1797 it was elevated to the position of capital of the Comtat-Venaisson and, as such, was part of the Holy See. During the first couple of centuries of this period, a thriving Jewish population enjoyed a liberal freedom of worship and were known as the *juifs du pape* ("papal Jews"). In testament to this singular period of religious tolerance, France's oldest **synagogue** stands behind the town's **Hôtel de Ville**. The synagogue dates from the 14th century and parts of it can be visited. Sadly, the Jewish cemetery outside town was desecrated some years ago, and the rise of the Front National in the locality has tarnished any reputation for racial tolerance.

Dating from the 15th century, the Romanesque **Cathédrale St-Siffrein** is further evidence of the church's good relationship with the Jewish community at that time, for the south portal is known as the **Porte des Juifs**. Note the marble sphere, depicted as being gnawed by rats, that stands above the gate. Historically, the sculpture is interpreted as connoting God's anger, as the rat was considered the spreader of plagues. (Over the centuries, the Vaucluse was no stranger to the dreaded arm of the plague.)

One man who was less than kind to the Jewish population, however, was the Bishop d'Inguimbert. In the 18th century, he decreed that the Jews had to remain within their own ghetto and couldn't traffic with the better houses. Nonetheless, he played a major role in the cultural and architectural development of Carpentras. He ordered the building of the rococo **Chapelle Notre-Dame-de-Sainte** and founded the **Hôtel-Dieu** hospital in 1750.

Carpentras has several museums, most notably the **Musée Comtadin** and **Musée Duplessis**, which are housed in the same building (234 boulevard A. Durand; closed Tues; entrance fee; tel: 04 90 63 04 92). The two museums cover the customs and history of the region and feature works by Hyacinthe Rigaud, Joseph Vernet and local painters. The building has a magnificent library, bequeathed by Bishop d'Inguimbert, which contains more than 150,000 volumes including some rare editions of work by Petrarch. The **Musée Sobirats** (rue du College; closed Tues; entrance fee; tel: 04 90 63 04 92) preserves the atmosphere and contents of an 18th-century mansion. The **Musée Lapidaire** (rue des Stes-Maries) is an 18th-century chapel with columns from the cloisters of the city's original Romanesque cathedral (currently closed for restoration).

Carpentras hosts arts and music festivals during the summer months and it has an excellent market every Friday. Look out for the town's sweet specialities: its strawberries and a kind of caramel candy called *berlingots*. Above all, however, the town is famous for its truffles, which some call "*les perles noires du comtat*" ("the black pearls of the county").

On the return journey along the D942 towards Villeneuve and Avignon, make a short detour at **Monteux** ❽, southwest

BELOW: picnickers in the Vaucluse.

Map
›n pages
112–113

along the D31, to the **Saule Pleureur**. Set in the Quartier Beauregard, this restaurant has established a well-deserved reputation for gastronomic delights, using mostly local produce.

Back on the main road, the D942, you will go through **Entraigues-sur-la-Sorgue** ❾. This village was a stronghold of the Templars during the 12th century, and one tower still stands of the fortress that this powerful group once commanded. From here, the road leads directly back to Avignon.

Nîmes and the Pont du Gard

The second journey you might like to take from the Avignon area is to **Nîmes** ❿. Although technically this will take you outside the borders of the Vaucluse and Provence, it's a great introduction to Roman Gaul and is generally included in tours of the area.

To reach Nîmes you pass the **Pont du Gard** ⓫. This bridge and aqueduct are a testament to the Romans' superlative technology. The aqueduct spans the Val du Gardon (Gardon Valley) and remains in excellent condition 2,000 years after its construction. At 48 metres (157 ft) it was the highest bridge that the Romans ever built and it originally carried water from the springs at Uzès to Nîmes, along a 50-km (31-mile) channel, much of which was underground, dug out of solid rock. Three great storeys of golden limestone arches have resisted the erosion of time and the tampering of more ignorant generations. In the floods that devastated Nîmes in 1988 the Pont du Gard stood firm when several other bridges collapsed – a tribute to Roman engineering.

The aqueduct is most stunning seen early in the morning or at dusk, and is best viewed from the 18th-century road bridge that runs alongside. Recent renovation work on the site included the building of a visitors' centre: **le Portal** (open June–Aug: daily; entrance fee; tel: 04 66 37 50 99), an auditorium in a former quarry, a pedestrian promenade and restaurants.

ELOW: the
nt du Gard.

Vineyards slope away on either side of the route to Nîmes, and it is here that the increasingly successful Costières de Nîmes wines are grown. However, modernity is the prevalent force in the area. Even as you approach the outskirts of the city, you will become aware of the emergence of modern architecture.

Urbanisation had already taken a firm hold of Nîmes 100 years ago. When the novelist Henry James sojourned here in 1884, he described the square where he stayed as having "the air of Brooklyn and Cleveland". When you gaze at the all-too-visible skyscrapers to the southwest, it is easy to agree with him that the city's "only treasures are its Roman remains, which are of the first order".

Nîmes was the first French city to be colonised by the Romans and for many years it was their link with Spain. As a result, a number of impressive Roman structures were built here, several of which still stand. The most outstanding monument is the amphitheatre, the **Arènes** (boulevard des Arènes; open daily; entrance fee; tel: 04 66 76 72 77), built in AD 50. Slightly smaller than its counterpart in Arles, the arena could originally seat 21,000 spectators and was designed so that it could be flooded for aquatic events; it also housed a gallery where slaves could sit.

Over the centuries, the amphitheatre experienced a variety of indignities. Visigoths substantially altered its form for use as a fortress. It suffered further changes to accommodate a village for 2,000 poor people, including the addition of many houses and a chapel. Finally, in the 19th century, attempts were begun to unearth the original structure, which was by then hidden under 8 metres (25 ft) of rubble.

Today the amphitheatre has been restored to something approaching its early glory. It now welcomes Spanish, Mexican and Provençal matadors *(raseteurs)* in both traditional bullfighting (in which they do kill the bull) and Provençal-style (in which they don't).

FAR LEFT: schedule of th *corridas*, Nîme **BELOW:** youn matador.

Map on pages 112–113

Other Roman sights in Nîmes include the recently discovered **Castellum**, a water tower on rue de Lalpèze, which was the original distribution point for the water from the Pont du Gard. **Porte Augustus**, on boulevard Gambetta, was one of the original Roman gates of the city; it has two large arches that provided a dual carriageway for carts and chariots and two smaller arches for pedestrian traffic.

Like the amphitheatre, the **Maison Carrée** went through several incarnations before reaching its present state. This 1st-century BC temple was even used as a stable for a while, as well as a town hall and a monastery church. Although its original dedication is a matter of discussion – some say it was dedicated to Juno, while others claim it was to Jupiter or Minerva – the Maison Carrée is generally considered to be the best-preserved Roman temple still standing. For centuries the building has been known as the "Square House", despite the fact that it is twice as long as it is wide. It now houses drawings and photographs of current archaeological work, one splendid result of which is a fresco that was only discovered in 1992 when the Carrée d'Art *(see below)* was built.

Opposite the temple is the **Carrée d'Art** (place de la Maison Carrée; open 11am–6pm; closed Mon; entrance fee; tel: 04 66 76 35 80), a vast art gallery in a glass-and-steel building that was designed by the British architect Lord Norman Foster and is a tribute to the ancient temple opposite. The collection focusses on European art since 1960, with particular emphasis on avant-garde movements such as Arte Povera and New Realism and work by Mediterranean artists. Artists well represented include Martial Raysse, Christian Boltanski, Claude Viallet, Arman and Bertrand Lavier.

This mix of ancient history and modern development is typical of Nîmes. There are commissioned art works all over the city, notably a Philippe Starck bus-stop and a fountain – a modern version of a crocodile tied to a palm tree – that was

ELOW: ıllfight in the ımes arena.

designed by Martial Raysse and stands in the place du Marché, where the corn market used to be held.

On a hot summer day in Nîmes, you might want to quench your thirst with a bottle of Perrier. This natural mineral water comes from a spring a short distance southwest of Nîmes, towards Vauvert. To find out more about the history of Perrier, visit the plant at **Vergèze**.

It was Hannibal and his 30 elephants who supposedly first discovered the spring here, in 218 BC. Some 300 years later, the Romans also were enchanted by the cool, naturally sparkling water. In 1863, Napoleon III took up its case and decided that the water should be bottled "for the good of France". However, it was an Englishman, St-John Harmsworth, who in 1903 first put the water in a bottle and marketed it, spurred on by a meeting with a Dr Perrier in Vergèze. They collected the abundant natural gas, found in the underground lake formed by the spring, and reinserted it into the water under pressure.

For a striking contrast to the modernity of the Perrier plant, take a look at the adjacent château with its Louis XIV architecture and attractive gardens.

Orange

The last excursion from Avignon is a full-day's outing and brings together two of the main Roman towns in France: Orange and Vaison-la-Romaine. From Avignon, take the N7 direct for 24 km (15 miles) to **Orange** ⓬, a city that in the 2nd century was of much greater importance than Avignon. The main reason for Orange's fame nowadays is the opera festival, the Chorégies d'Orange, which is held here in the summer and attracts some of the biggest stars in opera. The town is fairly busy all year round, however, partly because of its location near to the autoroute, making it a popular stopping-off point, and partly because of the large daily market that is held between mid-April and mid-October.

The city's name has nothing to do with the fruit but, rather, is connected with the

BELOW: Provençal produce.

Map on pages 112–113

Royal Dutch House of Orange, who inherited the city in 1559 from the Chalon family. Orange's two most outstanding monuments – the Théâtre Antique and the Arc de Triomphe – both date back to the earlier days of the Romans, and each, in its own way, represents the force of Roman colonisation.

The well-preserved **Théâtre Antique** (open daily; entrance fee; tel: 04 90 51 17 60), which at one time could hold up to 10,000 spectators, is still in use today. This is where the Chorégies d'Orange, the town's summer theatre festival and other cultural events are held. The acoustics are excellent in the auditorium, but don't forget to bring a cushion to a performance here, as the stone seats are hard and cold.

Next to the Théâtre Antique is the **Roman forum**, which is one of only three Roman gymnasia still extant. Unfortunately, the forum suffered some drastic changes in the period of William of Orange, but you can still get a fairly good idea of its original size and shape.

The **Arc de Triomphe** comprises three archways. The decorative friezes and carvings tell a proud tale of Roman success on land and on the sea, but their message is subtle. The weaponry, shields and helmets depicted on the lower part of the side arches are Celtic, and their positioning suggests Rome's triumph over Gaul.

For a clear explanation of how Roman colonial policy worked in Gaul, visit the **Musée Municipal** (open daily; entrance fee; tel: 04 90 51 18 24), just opposite the forum on rue de Pouillac. Inside is a marble tablet, discovered on an archaeological dig in 1963, on which land holdings were recorded. This example of land registry from AD 77 has markings that extend some 850 sq. km (510 sq. miles) from Bollène to Auzon. It not only reveals what areas were settled but also to whom the better plots belonged. This finding has given archaeologists a superb avenue for investigating the nature of early property ownership, on both a geographical and sociological scale.

ELOW: range's nphitheatre.

The museum also has two other sections, one on the history of Orange and the other on paintings. Of special note are the gallery's portraits of members of the Royal House of Orange and the paintings by British artist Sir Frank Brangwyn.

At the Treaty of Utrecht in 1713, Orange was yielded to France. When Louis XIV said that the city's theatre possessed "the most beautiful wall of the kingdom", it is quite likely that he was expressing his joy in having finally won over this valiant town as much as his wonder at the survival abilities of Roman architecture.

There is a great deal more to Orange, however, than its Roman heritage. If you take the time to stroll through its streets, you should stumble upon some delightful old houses on attractive tree-lined squares and avenues. A particularly pleasant walk leads you up the hill behind the theatre, where the ruins of the **château** constructed by the Orange family can be seen; note that there are some fine views to be had from here.

Vaison-la-Romaine

The drive on the D975 to Vaison-la-Romaine passes one large vineyard after another and encompasses some of the most picturesque countryside in the Vaucluse. The D8 brings you down to the hamlet of **Vacqueyras** ⓭, located near to Beaumes-de-Venise *(see page 121)*.

Before reaching Beaumes, however, you might prefer to switch onto the D7 towards the beautiful medieval village of **Gigondas** ⓮. The excellent wines produced here are established enough to be expensive, but there are still several lesser-known *caves de dégustation* where you can pick up a bottle or two without feeling you've spent a fortune.

Continuing along the D7 will take you towards the prototypically Provençal village of **Sablet** ⓯, which in turn leads into **Séguret** ⓰. The latter is a charming village, with steep streets, an old gate, a fountain, belltower, church and castle.

The sharp limestone peaks that frame the area are **les Dentelles de Montmirail**.

BELOW: wine château in Gigondas.

Map
n pages
12–113

Dentelle means "lace" in French, which gives a good indication as to the appearance of this rock formation. The jagged edges that jut into the clear blue sky present an attractive challenge to climbers, many of whom make special trips here just to tackle the slopes. Less-energetic visitors will also find the area excellent for rambles through the surrounding pine and oak woods and over the wild but beautiful countryside.

From Séguret take the D88 back to the D977 and you will soon reach **Vaison-la-Romaine** ⓱. By a direct route Vaison is only 28 km (17 miles) from Orange but, unlike Orange, Vaison's Roman past is very much a 20th-century discovery – excavations only began in 1907.

Vaison is divided into two distinct parts. The Roman town was built on a flat area of land on the east bank of the Ouvèze River and this is where the bulk of Vaison is located today. Walk down through the town and cross the **Pont Romain** (Roman bridge), which has been restored since it was severely damaged by floods in 1992, and you will see the medieval village perched on a rocky outcrop. With the fall of the Roman Empire the villagers no long found it safe to live on the exposed river bank and retreated to the hill across the river.

The digs in the ancient part of the city have been done in such a way that you can begin to visualise life in Roman Gaul. There are two open sites: the Quartier de Puymin and the Quartier de la Villasse (open June–Sept: daily; Oct–May: closed Tues; entrance fee; tel: 04 90 36 02 11).

Within the Quartier Puymin there is a park dotted with attractive cypress trees and a handful of buildings. The **Maison des Messii** (Messii House), the **Portique de Pompée** (Pompey's Portico), a type of pillared hall, and a nymphaeum, the source of the town's water, have all been uncovered here.

Reproductions of the statues that are housed in the adjacent museum decorate the park's promenade. Within the museum are the originals, plus a helpful historical map of the province of Gallia Narbonensis and a variety of antiquarian exhibits such as jewellery, weapons, coins and ceramics. The imposing statue of Tiberius and two larger-than-life marbles of the Emperor Hadrian and Empress Sabina say much about the one-time arrogance of Rome.

The second excavated spot lies to the southwest of the Puymin site. Here, the ruins of a Roman villa and a well-restored Roman street with a mosaic floor that leads to the arch of a former basilica, give the visitor an impression of the size and layout of the commercial part of the town in Roman times.

The last major ruin in Vaison is the **Théâtre Antique**. Like the amphitheatre in Orange, this Roman theatre provides the stage for much of the town's summer festival, although Vaison's example is much smaller. Cut out of rock from the north side of the Puymin Hill, it has been appreciated by theatre lovers for over 25 years for its drama, opera and ballet productions. The festival begins in the first

HT:
ned château
Vaison-
Romaine.

week of July, usually with a colourful and expensive folkloric and international gala, and runs through August.

Vaison's **Cathédrale Notre-Dame-de-Nazareth** is a well-preserved, 12th-century church with arcade pillars featuring beautifully decorated capitals. Other attractions include a walk through the maze of old streets to the **haute ville** (upper town), where you will find an interesting if dilapidated church and a ruined château that was once the country seat of the counts of Toulouse. Looking east from the top of the upper town will give you one of the best views over the valleys and foothills that lead to Mont Ventoux. This spot is slowly becoming an artists' colony and might be a good place to purchase local pottery and paintings.

A day-trip from Vaison will take you across the Aigues River northwards to **Valréas** ⓲. Valréas marks the northernmost frontier of the Vaucluse and it is included in this *département* for historical reasons, despite the fact that the town is surrounded by the Drôme River. The witty, literary Madame de Sevigné spent considerable time in this old Roman town and eventually built a château in nearby **Grignan** ⓳. There is more than a slight ring of truth to her criticism of the climate, since the mistral wind is particularly virulent here. However, she did have much praise for the local food and the immediate countryside, which is enlivened with fields of bright yellow sunflowers.

Heading west from Vaison-la-Romaine will take you to a number of new communities such as **Pierrelatte** and **Bagnols-sur-Cèze**. These settlements have sprung up as a result of the construction of nuclear and military centres, which you won't be able to see from the road and probably won't want to see anyway. The old town of Bagnols-sur-Cèze has some lovely houses and a good museum, the **Musée Albert André** (closed Feb and Mon; entrance fee; tel: 04 66 50 50 56). After a fire at the museum in 1923, an appeal was made to the artists of France,

BELOW: girls from Vaison-la-Romaine i local costum

Map n pages 12–113

who responded magnificently and there are works by Auguste Renoir, Paul Signac, Pierre Bonnard, Henri Matisse, Paul Gauguin and others.

Hill-top villages

It's certainly worth devoting a decent amount of time to visiting the mountains and hill-top villages of the Vaucluse, since there is much to see in a relatively concentrated area. Among other things, the area around Mont Ventoux gives you the chance to go horse-riding, climbing or hiking. Travel by car around here takes a little longer than elsewhere, because many of the attractions involve fortified hill-top villages that can often only be reached by winding roads, followed by a walk on foot to a lofty castle or church.

Crestet ⓴, south of Vaison-la-Romaine, is just such a hill-top village. It is set above olive groves and has both charm and a ghostly quality. At times it almost seems as if this 12th-century village has no inhabitants at all, it's so tranquil. To visit the town, you have to leave your car at the outlying park and set out on foot. A climb up the cobbled alleyways brings you to the church and, after a further ascent, to the village castle. From the lookout point on top of the castle, there are some stunning views across the valleys and the peak of Mont Ventoux. There are also some good picnic spots here.

If you return to the D938 and head south, you will reach **Malaucène** ㉑. The lively main street bustles with cafés and restaurants where, when in season, you can sample some of the cherries for which this town is a capital. Malaucène also produces some delicious local honey.

The town's church offers a good example of how closely connected war and religion have been in this part of France. Built by Clement V in the 14th century, it is both fortified and castle-like in appearance from the exterior. As the iron-plated front door suggests, the church was the place of refuge for the townspeople during times of war. Today, it functions on a more

LOW: an ening scene Sérignan.

traditional level, and you will have to attend a service to hear the tone of the impressive 18th-century organ.

If you head west from here in the direction of Mont Ventoux, you will be following the route that Petrarch took in 1336 when he undertook to climb the legendary mount – the Italian poet was the first person to climb the mountain for reasons of pleasure alone. First, however, you might want to make a quick dip south to Caromb. This route, the D938 to the D13, will take you over a lovely scenic backroad. Even if you don't stop along the way, you will be able to see a series of small fortified villages on both sides of you, which have hardly changed since they were first constructed.

Caromb ㉒ is another medieval hill-top village. Long famed for its vines, its well-preserved exterior walls enclose another typical feature of the area: a bell-towered church with an 18th-century wrought-iron cage for the bell, designed to protect it from the fierce mistral. The interior of the church is decorated with frescoes and woodcarvings. Be aware, however, if you elect to stay in the town's hostel, that the church's bell chimes all night long.

Another fortified town in the Mont Ventoux area is **le Barroux** ㉓, with a château and fine Romanesque church that illustrate the locale's transition from royal to country seat.

The base of Mont Ventoux is surrounded by many other pretty villages. **Mazan** ㉔, **Crillon-le-Brave**, **St-Pierre-de-Vassols** and **Bédoin** ㉕, to name a few, are all lovely in their own individual way, and many are wine-tasting centres for the produce of the vineyards in the Mont Ventoux area. Bédoin, in particular, is a popular starting point for hikes up Mont Ventoux. A good number of these *villages perchés* (literally, "perched villages") are best investigated on foot. Because of their defensive physical characteristics and dramatic locations, they fire the imagination with colourful images of knights, sieges and other such scenes from the

BELOW: vineyard nea Ménerbes.

Map
n pages
12–113

Vaucluse's turbulent past. A visit here will bring to life the songs of the troubadours.

Mont Ventoux

After you've had your fill of picturesque hill-top villages, rejoin the D974 for the best route to **Mont Ventoux** ㉖. Placed along the immediate ascent, the small, Romanesque, 11th-century **Chapelle de Notre-Dame-du-Groseau** is worth a look. If it's a hot day, cool down by sampling the fresh water from the nearby Source du Groseau.

Mont Ventoux divides into two very distinctive sections: the lower area, which lies below the ski resort and is ferny and forested, with many beautiful spots where you can stop to enjoy a packed lunch, and the upper, harsh limestone area that approaches the summit.

When the sun reflects off the white of this higher part, the glare is so great that it can leave you momentarily blinded. The peak is snow-capped for approximately three-quarters of the year.

There are two interpretations of the origin of the mountain's name. One suggests that it is a derivation of the Celtic phrase *ven top*, which means "white mountain". The other interpretation associates the name Mont Ventoux with the French word *venteux* (meaning "windy"), which seems logical, as there are always winds blowing around this area. Watch out for these gusts, as they do become quite powerful as you climb and are certainly strong enough to blow some of the lighter cars off the road.

The mountain peak is always white, whether from snow or limestone, and it has a certain science-fictional quality about it. This impression is emphasised by the placement of a radar station, from which numerous aerials protrude, and the adjacent observatory.

A stop in the peaceful **Chapelle de la Ste-Croix** ㉗, which stands nearby, should give you the chance to spend a moment meditating on the glories of nature rather than the intrusions of man.

LOW:
e unlucky
ovençal
ose – *foie*
as is a
eciality here.

From this elevated point, at 1,909 metres (6,263 ft), it is easy to appreciate why the Vaucluse has always been such an important crossroads. On a clear day – although mist and haze are more typical – you can see the Rhône, the Alps and the Mediterranean from here. Some people even claim to have caught sight of the Pyrenées from this spot.

The drive downhill in the direction of **Sault** takes you through a nature reserve of particular interest to botanists. The 19th-century Provençal entomologist Jean-Henri Fabre (1823–1915), who is best known for his observations on the behaviour of insects, discovered a rare species of yellow poppy growing here as well as a collection of other plants to which he attributed unusual medicinal qualities. Now, almost a century after his death, practitioners of various forms of alternative medicine – generally of the homeopathic variety – are finally proving his theories to be correct.

Fabre was also influential in reforesting this area, and nowadays pine trees give way to oak, followed by fields of wild thyme and, eventually, in the lower valleys, the resilient mauve of lavender. As he observed at the turn of the 20th century, "half a day's journey, in a downward direction, brings before our eyes a succession of the chief vegetable types, as we should find in the course of a long voyage from north to south along the same meridian."

A benign statue of Fabre overlooks the main thoroughfare of **Sérignan-du-Comtat**, which is well to the west of the *département*, near to Orange. The unassuming home and rocky outdoor "laboratory" where this celebrated scientist, affectionately dubbed by the public *l'homme des insectes* ("the insect man"), conducted his research are also here and are open to visitors.

Not surprisingly, the Ventoux area is equally popular with ornithologists. They come in early summer with an eye to spotting sub-alpine warblers, sea crossbills and mountain thrushes. However, the

BELOW: the misty heights of Mont Ventoux

Map
on pages
112–113

decline in species of all sorts of wildlife, due to the rash of forest fires in Provence, is unmistakable. Campers, climbers and picnickers should take particular care not to leave any campfires, matches or cigarettes smouldering.

The climate of **Buis-les-Baronnies** ㉘, which is actually located in the *département* of the Drôme, nestled between Mont Ventoux and the Baronnies ridge to the north, is especially suitable for growing apricots, olives, almonds and limeflowers, which are used for making *tisane* (herbal tea); in early July, the delightful fragrance of lime blossom fills the town. Not surprisingly, in the old quarter of town, many of the shops sell excellent samples of Provence's most genuine – and popular – souvenirs: lavender soap, lime-blossom *eau de toilette* and olive oil.

The Gorges de la Nesque

If you don't want to go north from Mont Ventoux, you should probably head southeast towards **Sault** ㉙. Although this town was a baronial seat in the 15th century, nowadays the only remnants of glory are the towers of the 16th-century castle. The Romanesque Eglise de St-Saveur stands guard over the town, which acts as a lively marketplace for the surrounding lavender mills.

The drive along the D942 towards the lively village of **Monieux** ㉚ is lush, green and lined with fields of lavender. The Monieux road takes you through the **Gorges de la Nesque** ㉛, which offers breathtaking views and a sensational cascade of colours all year round. In some spots, the gorge plunges to depths of over 300 metres (984 ft), and scrub and rocks camouflage deep caves. Despite the fascination of the mountain views, the driver should be sure to watch out for tunnels and hairpin bends.

The Nesque gorges have their own share of attractive Provençal villages. **Villes-sur-Auzon** ㉜ has had, like Mazan *(see page 132)*, its fair share of disasters in the form of invaders, sieges and outbreaks

...LOW: ... afternoon ...noke in Buis-...s-Baronnies.

of the plague. On top of that it was the battleground of Baron des Adrets. Nonetheless, the village managed to survive and nowadays it has a steady – if small – population of a little less than 1,000.

The close-knit community lives off the cultivation of the vineyards that surround the town. You may want to stop at one of the town's *caves de dégustation* to sample the local Côtes du Ventoux, a light-coloured so-called "café" wine, which is best drunk when it is young and which, since 1974, has qualifed to bear an *appellation contrôlée*. Like many mountainous areas in Provence, the Gorges de la Nesque make this into wonderful climbing and hiking country.

Southern Vaucluse

As is evident from the descent from Mont Ventoux, the countryside of the Vaucluse can change rapidly. Further proof of this will come along the journey south and slightly west to **Venasque** ㉝ through the **Plateau de Vaucluse**.

Venasque is tucked away between two small but steep hills, cupped to the east by a deep and dense forest, in which it is easy to get lost. The village has an unaltered charm and is a good example of the benefits of careful restoration. Once the capital of the Comtat-Venaisson, to which it gave its name, Venasque still retains an identity of its own, although rather drastically subdued. In the early summer, it comes alive as a market centre for cherries and during the rest of the year has a couple of buildings worth viewing.

The baptistry within the **Eglise de Notre-Dame** is one of France's oldest religious buildings. Built in the 6th century and remodelled during the 11th, it still causes dispute among historians as to its specific function.

Also worth visiting in Venasque is the **Chapelle de Notre-Dame-de-Vie**. Constructed during the 17th century, on top of a 6th-century site, the chapel still houses the tomb of Boetius, one-time bishop of Carpentras and Venasque. The

BELOW: lavender field near Sault.

Map
n pages
12–113

tombstone is a particularly fine example of Merovingian sculpture.

From Venasque, follow the D4 to the D177 south through the plateau. Looking down over the **Vallée de la Sénancole** will reveal the path to the **Abbaye de Sénanque** ㉞ (open Mar–Oct: Mon–Sat 10am–noon and 2–6pm, Sun 2–6pm; Nov–Feb: Mon–Fri 2–5pm, Sat–Sun 2–6pm; entrance fee; tel: 04 90 72 05 72). The curved road at its side leads to an area for parking your car, approximately 2 km (1¼ miles) away from the abbey itself.

The 12th-century Cistercian abbey stands at the edge of a grey mountainside and is surrounded by oak trees and lavender. Its one curiosity is the manner in which the limestone from which it is constructed changes colour as the day heats up. The buildings seem to change from grey to a deep yellow.

Sénanque possesses a natural serenity. Since 1989 the abbey has been restored and there are monks living there again. Some of their home produce is for sale. There is a remarkable quietness reflected in the pastoral setting, the simplicity of the building and the austerity of its interior. If you find the mood persuasive, you can retire to a room that has been set aside for meditation. This room also happens to be the coolest spot in the monastery, so you can emerge from it with both the spirit elevated and the body refreshed.

The nearby town of **Gordes** ㉟ is linked to Sénanque by a narrow, winding and bleak road. Don't expect to find it deserted, however. During the summer, this town is one of the most popular tourist spots in the Vaucluse. At first glance, Gordes looks as though it is about to slip off the small mountaintop over which it is spread. Through the centuries, however, this peculiar location has contributed to the village's natural defence. Gordes has had a turbulent history, especially during the 16th-century Wars of Religion and then again in World War II when the town was a stronghold for the Resistance movement.

THE FONTAINE DE VAUCLUSE

While in this area, you may want to visit the town of **Fontaine de Vaucluse** and the fountain after which he town is named. Although it's a delightful spot, it's also ery busy – over a million tourists visit each year. The own's most important architectural sights – several nuseums, a ruined castle and an 11th-century church – on't add up to anything much, although the Romanesque glise de St-Véran possesses the tomb of the 6th-century ishop of Cavaillon, who is said to have freed the area of ne Coloubie monster *(see page 142)*.

The real attraction, however, is the fountain, which is fed y rainwater that drains through the Vaucluse Plateau and is elieved to be the source of the Sorgue. The water emerges om within a cave, and in winter and spring the flow can se to 150 cubic metres (32,985 gallons) a second.

By far the fountain's most celebrated observer was etrarch. The Italian poet lived here from 1337 to 1353, etween stays in Avignon, and it was here that he comosed his sonnets to Laura *(see page 39)*. As with so nany places in the Vaucluse, poetry and legend play large arts in the village's popularity. There is a museum devotd to the great Italian: **Musée Petrarque** (quai du Château ieux; closed Tues and Nov–Mar; tel: 04 90 20 37 20).

ɜHT: the
ntaine de
ucluse.

The majority of tourists to Gordes come to see the "ancient" village of 20 restored *bories* (drystone huts) that lies just beneath the central town. This group of curious, wind-resistant dwellings in round or rectangular shapes are believed to date from the 17th century, but don't be surprised to find 19th-century tools and furniture in some. Others are privately owned and have been modernised for use as holiday homes.

As a bridge to the contemporary world, stop in at the **château**. The castle itself is Renaissance and old but, in more recent times, five rooms were set aside for the contemporary artist Victor Vasarely. Within them, he established a study centre for the "interaction of the arts and sciences." Now there is a semi-permanent exhibition of works by Belgian artist, Pol Mara.

Overall, the château has a sobering effect. Initially constructed during the 12th century, it was radically altered during the 16th century to emphasise the strength of its fortifications.

The Lubéron

From here, the drive south along D104 will take you into the foothills of the **Lubéron**. This third, and last, mountain range in the Vaucluse is also a general favourite. It is an increasingly popular spot for well-heeled Britons and Parisians to have summer homes. Appreciation for its natural beauty spurred the creation of a 100,000-hectare (247,000-acre) regional park in 1977.

Outside the park, the foothills make for great walking. Remember, however, that come autumn the hunters here take their sport very seriously. Once a so-called "boar drive" is under way, it's like driving in Paris – pedestrians are considered fair game. After the hunting season has opened, be sure to walk with your eyes and ears open.

On a lighter note, *pastis*, the legendary drink of the Provençal, had its origin in this part of the Vaucluse. First blended within the small villages of the Lubéron, this potent herbal brew is supposed to be

BELOW: playi *boules* benea the plane tre

Map
n pages
12–113

the secret of the Provençal people's reputation for good health. Nowadays *pastis* is usually associated with old men and Ricard, an aniseed-flavoured drink that is commonly referred to as the "good-natured thirst quencher".

The force of tradition is very strong in the Lubéron. The mountain village of **Lacoste** ㊱, where stone quarries are still worked, is a good example of how slowly change comes to some parts of the Vaucluse. Rural life here resembles that depicted in the Pagnol films, and Lacoste's major acknowledgement of the 20th-century comes in the form of the floodlit *boules* court located behind the local church.

Elsewhere in the village, traditional life continues much as it has for the last few decades: hanging out in the cafés, sipping *pastis*, playing the popular card game of *belote*. Perhaps all that is missing is the Marquis de Sade, who lived here from 1774 until his arrest in 1778. The ruins of his huge **château** look down on the village and, as the guide is wont to say, "If walls could talk…"

From the heights of **Bonnieux** ㊲, southeast along D109 to D3, you can see the junction of the Plateau de Vaucluse and Mont Ventoux. On one side of you, through an attractive mist, you'll look out over a forest of cedars and, to the other, south towards the Plateau de la Crau, you can catch the glimmer of the Lac de Beise and, beyond it, the Mediterranean.

The easternmost section of the Vaucluse, running from Bonnieux to **Oppède-le-Vieux** ㊳ has the distinct touristic advantage of being less crowded during July and August than many other parts of the *département*, even though the area is as rich in both natural beauty and historical interest as many of the more accessible parts of the Vaucluse.

Many of the stories written by the Provençal novelist Jean Giono (1885–1970) dwelt upon the dying out of local villages in the 1920s and 1930s, and the "Petite Lubéron" could easily have gone

LOW: church
Lacoste.

that way. In recent years, however, a new brand of year-round resident has brought a fresh spirit to these small villages.

Writers and artists from all over the world, attracted by the tranquillity and the climate, have undertaken the careful restoration of many of the houses. Their tasteful work shows a great understanding and respect for the Lubéron's past, and their appearance has done much to improve the region's economic future. Not least, of course, Peter Mayle, whose best-selling autobiographical novel *A Year in Provence* confirmed the region's mythical quality. The village of **Ménerbes**, which featured in the book, remains as sleepy as ever. All over, the soft yellow and red shades of the houses are both startling and attractive. Magic descends with the setting of the sun, as the colours become illuminated with unearthly light.

Particularly beautiful is the southerly village of **Roussillon** 39. This hill-top village, located just east of Gordes, is constructed of a brilliant red stone, set off by the grey-green landscape that surrounds it. First made known as the subject of sociologist Laurence Wylie's *Village in the Vaucluse*, under the pseudonym of "Peyrane," Roussillon became the site of a property boom in the 1960s. Although it is still quite delightful, contemporary visitors will have to read the book to find its impoverished heritage.

The capital of the Lubéron is **Lourmarin** 40. The countryside that surrounds this small "city" is colourful all-year-round, because the large variety of trees, wild flowers and vegetables that thrive in the region benefit from having the longest growing season in France. Lourmarin is rich in culture, and on the west side of town is the house (open to visitors), where the French author, philosopher and existentialist Albert Camus (1913–60) once lived. Camus chose to be buried here, and his grave lies amidst a tangle of wild rosemary. The Provençal writer Henri Bosco (1888–1976) is also buried here. Reading his novels is a good way of understand-

BELOW: herb-flavour vinegar.

Map
n pages
12–113

ing the area, for they often draw nostalgically on his memories of the childhood he spent here.

Works of art are still produced at the 16th-century **château**, located just outside Lourmarin. The building was restored in 1920 by Laurent Vibert and today it acts as a study centre for artists, musicians and writers. Concerts and exhibitions are held here on a regular basis, and organised tours of the château are also available.

If you take the tour, be sure to ask for an explanation of the graffiti, scrawled on one of the walls, that depicts a small sailing boat surrounded by mysterious birds with human faces. Before the château was taken over by Vibert, it had acted for many years as a stopping place for gypsies on route to Stes-Maries-de-la-Mer *(see page 192)*. Many people say that the graffiti is a curse put on the place by them after their expulsion.

A short detour 10 km (6½ miles) east will bring you to the delightful 10th-century village of **Ansouis** ㊶. As in many of the tiny Provençal towns, Ansouis's narrow, twisting and climbing streets were certainly not designed for motorised traffic. Unless your car is tiny, you may prefer to park in the central square and do your exploring on foot.

Ansouis's **château** is an interesting combination of styles, as it has been in the same family for centuries, and each member to live there has left his or her own mark. It commands the top of the hill where the town stands. Also a novelty is the **Musée Extraordinaire de Georges Mazoyer** (rue du Vieux Moulin; open afternoons only; closed Tues; entrance fee; tel: 04 90 09 82 64), dedicated to marine life and, in particular, to the underwater creatures that once occupied the Vaucluse, and includes a recreated underwater cave in the cellars. (Mazoyer was a painter with a passion for marine life.)

Cavaillon

From Ansouis, follow the bank of the Durance River west along the D973 to

LOW: picking
eul, which is
d for tea.

Cavaillon ㊷, the melon capital of the Vaucluse. (You may be tempted to buy fresh melons from a roadside vendor en route.) The fertile fields that surround this town contrast with the rocky terrain of much of the land that you have been passing through and make for a fine crop of fruits and vegetables. A typical morning sight is that of the farmer on his Velosolex motorcycle with a sidecar carrying huge baskets of some type of produce, as he heads for Cavaillon's marketplace.

Outdoor markets are a year-round feature of life in this *département,* where so many of the fruits and vegetables are grown that feed the rest of France. Far from a side attraction, the markets remain the centre of business as well as social activities for a large number of the area's towns and villages.

Whether you speak French or not, you can gain real insight into the Provençals and their way of life by visiting their markets. These people take their food seriously, and the beginning of any good Provençal dish invariably involves fresh tomatoes, peppers, herbs and garlic. Colourful fruits decorate the stalls, and you can generally find specialised stands selling local sausage and goat's cheese. People travel from all over to shop here at the market in Cavaillon.

The melon is not the only thing that is legendary in this town. Popular mythology suggests the area around Cavaillon was once flattened by a monster called the "Coulobie". Basically an oversized lizard, he later either flew away to the Alps or was chased away by St Véran, the patron saint of shepherds *(see panel, page 137).*

The Coulobie is the subject of a painting by Pierre Mignard that can be seen in the **Cathédrale Notre-Dame et St-Véran** on place Joseph d'Arrard. The building itself is a rather uncomfortable mix of styles with a 16th-century façade and some unfortunate 19th-century additions. However, its little 14th-century side chapel was nicely restored after the Wars of Religion during the 17th century and

BELOW: typical busy market sce

Map
n pages
12–113

has a very attractive interior. Located to the left of the church is the **Musée de l'Hôtel-Dieu** (Grand Rue; closed Tues; Oct–Apr also closed weekends; entrance fee; tel: 04 90 76 00 34), a former hospital, which now houses a collection of local archaeological finds.

Like Carpentras *(see page 121)*, Cavaillon "tolerated" a significant Jewish community during the time of the Papal residency in Avignon, although the number of its members never exceeded 300. A first **synagogue** was built in the 16th century, but it later fell to pieces; the elegant building that now stands was erected in its place in 1772.

The small **Musée Juif-Comtadin** (rue Hebraique; closed Tues; Oct–Apr also closed weekends; tel: 04 90 76 00 34) occupies part of the ground floor of a synagogue in what was once a bakery in which the Jews made their unleavened bread. The museum contains Jewish prayer books and Torahic relics, as well as the original oven.

Cavaillon's **cultural centre**, which was built in the late 1990s, has its feet firmly planted in the 20th century. Apart from staging jazz concerts during the town's annual summer festival, the staff at the centre also organise a lively year-long programme of performing and visual arts.

Also striving to keep up with modern times is bustling **Apt** ㊸. This city's particular contributions to the economy of the region are crystallised fruits and preserves, the making of truffles and the bottling of lavender essence. In addition, it is one of the few places in the region still to mine and refine ochre.

On a more spiritual level, Apt is the seat of the **Ancienne Cathédrale Ste-Anne**. The main structure dates from the 12th century, but the Royal Chapel, which is also the major point of interest, was erected in 1660, the year that Anne of Austria arrived in pilgrimage. It is now the destination of an annual pilgrimage by Catholic devotees that takes place on the last Sunday in July. ❑

LOW:
althy local
sident.
GHT:
ity regional
oduce.

laps:
ea 148
ty 151

THE BOUCHES-DU-RHÔNE

This area, immortalised in the paintings of Cézanne and Van Gogh, contains Provence's largest city, Marseille, the university town of Aix-en-Provence, and Arles, once a Roman stronghold

The Bouches-du-Rhône ("mouths of the Rhône") is located in a prime position between the Mediterranean and one of France's greatest rivers. The region is characterised by acres of arid land dotted by crooked olive trees and dark vineyards, alternately scorched by a merciless sun and threatened by the violent gales of the mistral wind. Yet the area is also home to Marseille, France's second-largest city, and two especially renowned cities of cultural excellence: Aix-en-Provence and Arles.

It takes an informed eye to appreciate the historical bounty of the Bouches-du-Rhône. Many of the region's monuments are either in ruins or hidden amidst the desolate countryside. Other sites become interesting only after learning the myths and traditions that surround them.

Although a fairly small *département* in size, the Bouches-du-Rhône can be divided into at least three distinct areas. The divisions centre around the major cities: Marseille and its industrialised coastal territory; Aix-en-Provence, an elegant and bourgeois university town, and its slightly mountainous and fertile surroundings; Arles, ancient and distinctly Roman, set in the midst of dry, flat and poor plains with menacing ridges of the Alpilles to the north. A fourth area, the marshy Camargue, is so individual that, although administratively a part of the Bouches-du-Rhône, it deserves (and has been given) a chapter of its own.

Provence's oldest city

It was 2,600 years ago that Greek sailors from the Ionian city of Phocaea first sailed into the harbour at **Marseille ❶**. According to legend, they arrived just as Gyptis, the local Ligurian princess, was selecting a husband. Suitors stood in a circle awaiting her decision when, eschewing local blood, she handed the chalice that marked her choice to Protis, captain of the Greek entourage. From their union flowered a prosperous Greek trading post, called Massilia. Over the centuries, the Massilians knew numerous high and low points of fortune, all the while developing a strong and independent character still apparent in their modern descendants.

Today, the city is still a major sea port and harbour, with a somewhat salty reputation. The latter is due to the fact that, as a centre for trade and commerce, a certain amount of drug traffic and black marketeering inevitably passes through its ancient waters. Also, the city is one of the major French entry points for North African immigrants, and their emergence as an integral part of the French work

:EDING
:S: splash
nflowers.
: view of
seille from
-Dame-
-Garde.
T: Mt Ste-
ire and
Barrage
imont.

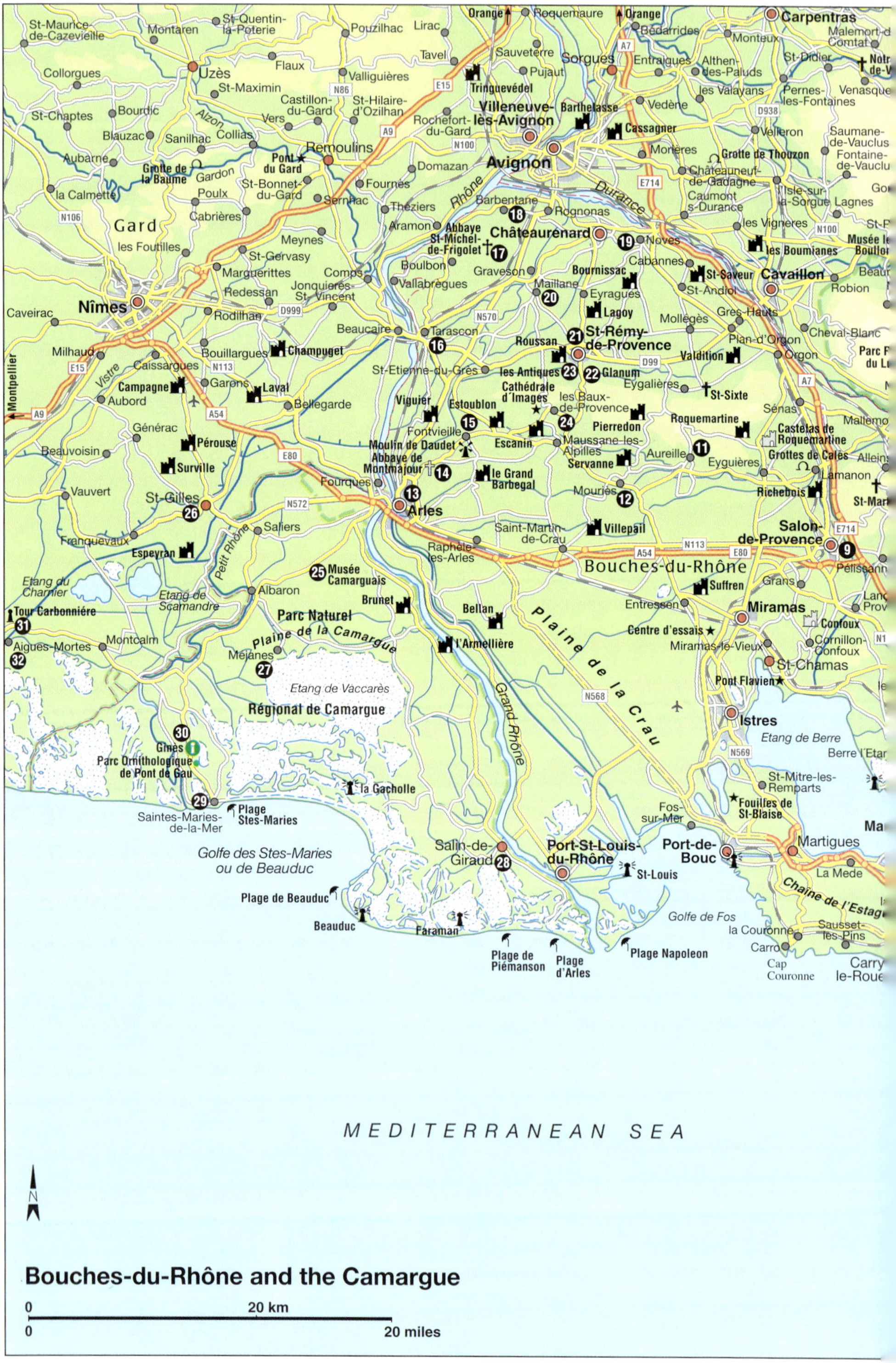

Bouches-du-Rhône and the Camargue

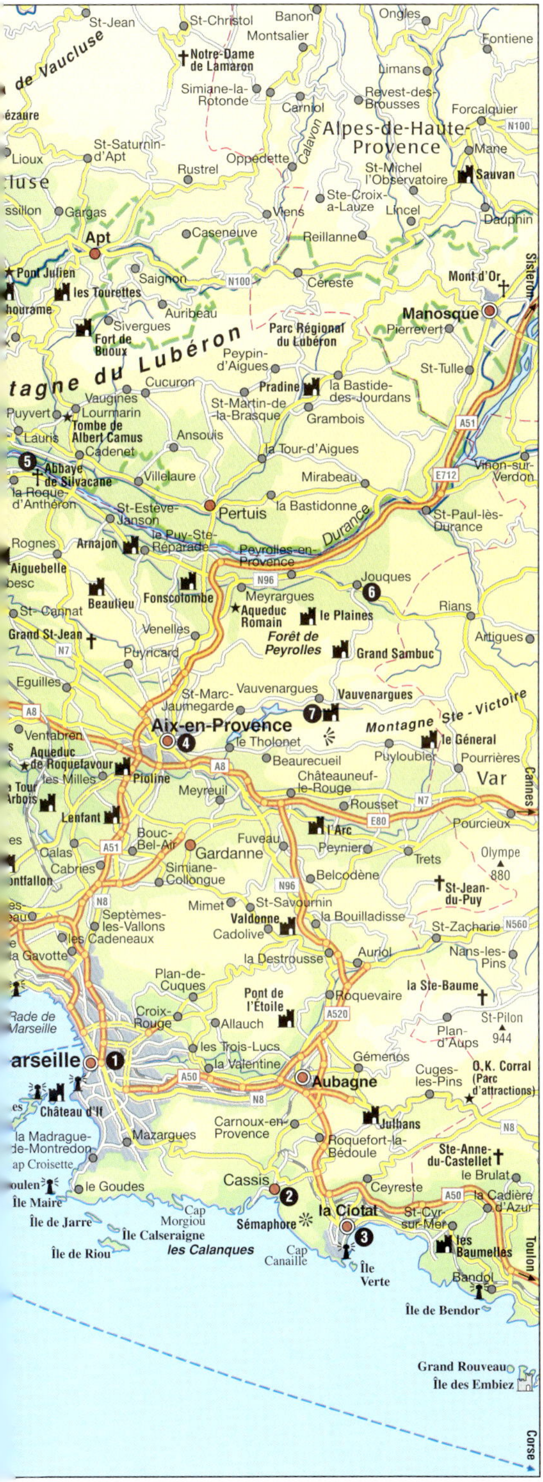

force has engendered a strong local following of the reactionary Front National party headed by Jean-Marie Le Pen.

Until recently most visitors to Provence considered Marseille a spot either to avoid or to pass through as quickly as possible, looking over their shoulders and clasping their wallets all the while. Now, however, massive investment in urban regeneration, particularly the renovation of the old docklands, new museums and cultural programmes that have attracted artists to the city, is all helping to change the city's image. The advent of the new TGV connection to Paris, cutting the journey to just three hours, is also a key development.

The old port

Any visit to Marseille should begin at the **Vieux-Port** Ⓐ (old port). Here, fancy yachts share the waters with fishing rigs, and a lively fish market, complete with very live fish, heralds each morning along the wharfs. Although the city's other harbours now handle incoming commerce, the Vieux-Port is Marseille's oldest and most picturesque harbour.

At the very base of the Vieux-Port a ferry that taxis visitors out to a tiny rock island just off the coast docks. The island is the site of the **Château d'If** Ⓑ, from where the legendary Count of Monte Cristo was fabled to have made his escape. There's not really much to see on the island itself but you can enjoy a great view of the city, and even take a swim off the rocky shores.

On the northern side of the port is the **Quartier Panier**, Marseille's oldest quarter, characterised by narrow climbing streets and colourful streetlife. The quarter is safest explored during the day, when the new galleries and cafés there are open.

Within the Quartier Panier are several of the city's museums. The **Musée du Vieux-Marseille** Ⓒ (rue de la Prison; guided visits possible Wed and Sat; tel 04 91 55 28 68) is due to reopen in summer 2001 after restoration. It gives the newcomer a fine introduction to the folk life of Provence. Housed within the remarkable Maison Diamantée (1570–76), this museum is dedicated to Provençal culture, with entire rooms of traditional costumes, tarot cards, *crèches* etc. Also on display are a variety of engravings and models of Marseille over the centuries.

While you are in the area, you might as well look in on the **Musée des Docks Romains** ❶ (place du Vivaux; closed Mon; entrance fee; tel: 04 91 91 24 62), which shelters a series of uncovered Roman docks on the site of their excavation. The open amphores once stored grain, olives and wine for the Romans. To the north of this museum is the neo-Byzantine **Cathédrale de la Major** Ⓔ, which is the largest cathedral constructed in France since medieval times. Adjacent to la Major is the 11th-century **Ancienne-Major** Ⓕ, home to a particulary notable Renaissance altarpiece by Thomas de Como and Francesco Laurana.

Also in the neighbourhood are the **Galeries de la Charité**, which were erected as a hospital in the 17th century with decoration by the sculptor Pierre Puget. The restored buildings are now the site of the **Musée d'Archéologie Mediterranéenne** Ⓖ (closed Mon; entrance fee; tel: 04 91 14 58 80).

Ancient walls

Much of Marseille's ancient ramparts were destroyed in the continual battles of the centuries and most of what was left was decimated in World War II. However, among the modern buildings and bobbing shipmasts, a few ancient walls still stand.

Numerous excavations at the **Centre Bourse** (1 square Belsunce; closed Sun; entrance fee; tel: 04 91 90 42 22) have unearthed fortifications, wharfs and a road, dating from somewhere between the 3rd century BC and the 4th century AD. Called the **Jardins des Vestiges**, the remains now form a public garden beside the Centre Bourse shopping mall and the **Musée d'Histoire de Marseille** Ⓗ.

The museum is itself a fascinating place, filled with an excellent selection of Ligurian, Greek and Roman artefacts found over the ages in Marseille. Every-

BELOW: Cathédrale de la Major, Marseille.

Maps:
ea 148
ity 151

thing is extremely well documented. Be sure to note, directly on the left when you first enter the museum, the terrifying "Gros Repasse". Once the doorway to a Ligurian sanctuary, frontal ledges are filled with the skulls of unlucky enemies.

Nearby, in the Palais de la Bourse is the **Musée de la Marine et de l'Economie de Marseille** ❶ (9 la Canebière; open daily; entrance fee; tel: 04 91 39 33 33), which documents Marseille's maritime history from the 17th century to the present day. The Palais de la Bourse is set on Marseille's throughway, **la Canebière** ❸, which runs up from the centre of the harbour. Despite its fame, this is a pretty unattractive street, lined with bland department stores and busy with traffic.

Situated at the port end of la Canebière, just a few doors east of the Musée de la Marine, is the **Musée de la Mode** Ⓚ (11 la Canebière; closed Mon; entrance fee; tel: 04 91 56 59 57), a fashion museum concentrating on 20th-century style. South of la Canebière is the **Musée Cantini** Ⓛ (19 rue Grignan; closed Mon; tel: 04 91 54 77 75), Marseille's modern-art museum, which holds a notable collection of Surrealist paintings.

The northern end of la Canebière is dominated by the neoclassical **Palais Longchamp** Ⓜ, which houses the **Musée des Beaux-Arts** and **Musée d'Histoire Naturelle** (boulevard Longchamp; closed Mon; entrance fee; tel: 04 91 14 59 30). The art collection includes works by Marseillais sculptor Pierre Puget, as well as 16th- and 17th-century French, Provençal, Italian and Flemish works. The Musée d'Histoire Naturelle features a variety of zoological exhibitions.

On the south side of the harbour off the quai de Rive Neuve, is the pedestrian area around **place Thiars**, its streets lined with galleries, shops and outdoor cafés. Parks and fountains laid out during the late 20th century make it a pleasant spot to lunch or take an afternoon stroll. Also on this side of the harbour, at 47 rue Neuve St-Catherine, is a small shop of special interest

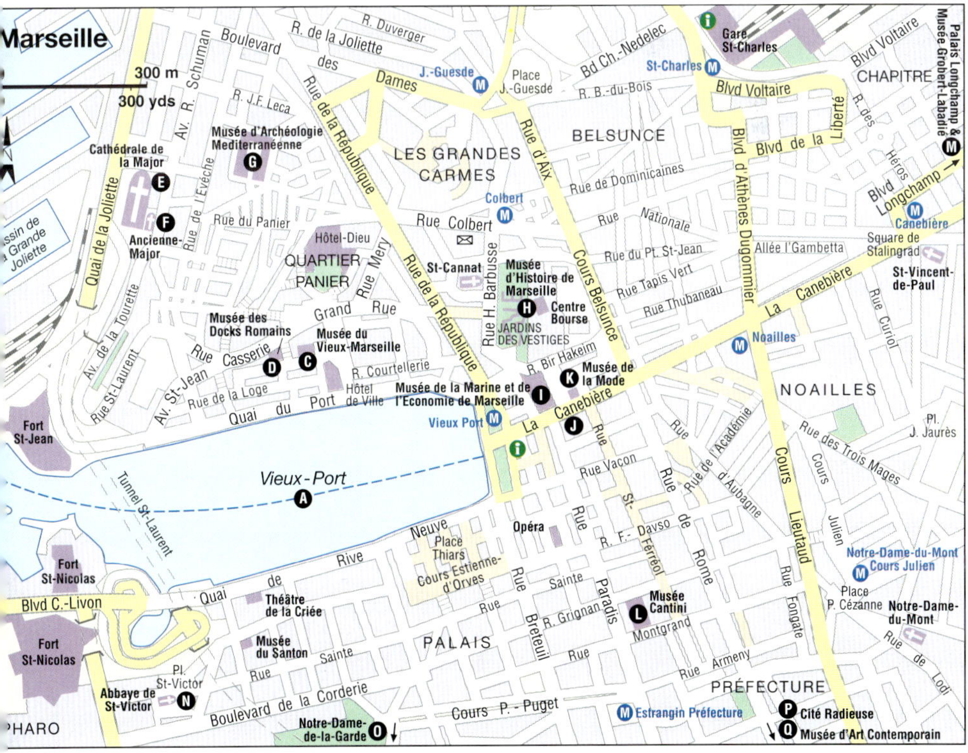

to the *santon* (small clay traditional Provençal figures, *see page 85*) enthusiast. At the **Atelier Marcel Carbonel**, visitors are welcome to watch some of the best-regarded *crèche* figures being made and view M. Carbonel's personal collection of Christmas cribs from around the world.

Just down the street, at 136 rue Sainte, is another enclave of Marseillaise tradition, **le Four des Navettes**. First created in 1781 in this very shop, *navettes* are biscuits cooked in the shape of the boat that is said to have brought Mary Magdalene and a host of other saintly Marys to the shores of Provence 2,000 years ago. Made according to a secret method, these biscuits are the special mark of the annual Fête de la Chandeleur, which takes place on 2 February.

The rue Sainte ends at the **Abbaye de St-Victor** **N**. In the 3rd century BC the site was a Greek burial ground and, in the 1st century, it became a Roman monument. Then, during the 3rd century AD, a Christian cemetery began to grow around the tombs of two martyrs who were slain during the persecution of Dece in AD 250.

The basilica itself was built in the 5th century by St-John Cassian, an Egyptian monk who named it after a third local martyr, St Victor, the patron saint of sailors, millers (Victor was ground to death between two millstones) and Marseille. The primary structure now standing is an 11th-century reconstruction, with high Gothic arches that resound with distant taped music. Deep below, in the crypt, is the original church. Ancient sarcophagi, some hidden in candle-lit alcoves, line the walls; in the centre stands the sombre tomb of the two slain martyrs. Even more eerie, in a rocky alcove to one side, is the 3rd-century tomb of St Victor. His grave image, carved into the wall on the right as you enter, watches over the shadowy corner.

Once back on the port, if you still have an appetite, you might want to try the *bouillabaisse* dining experience. Anyone

BELOW: mansion on Corniche J.F

Maps: Area 148 City 151

seeking to understand Marseille should attempt this traditional fish stew, but be warned: only a few restaurants still offer an authentic *bouillabaisse*, it won't come cheap and don't expect a refined meal. *Bouillabaisse* was created by fishmonger's wives trying to use up the catch their husbands hadn't sold, and in basic ingredients and recipe it hasn't changed much. Fish-lovers should find it delicious.

If you can still stand after three bowls of fish soup and are in the mood for some night-time panorama, climb to the site of **Notre-Dame-de-la-Garde** ⓞ. No matter where you go in Marseille, you can't miss noticing the airy 19th-century basilica. Erected on a bluff of 162 metres (530 ft), it offers, without question, the best view over the city.

However, the most beautiful view in Marseille is to be found along the **Corniche Président-John-F.-Kennedy**. Following the coastline, this 5-km (3-mile) road looks out over the sea, the offshore islands, the surrounding *massif* and the winding shore ahead. In the late 1990s it benefitted from the addition of new bars and restaurants and it is also adorned by some of the most beautiful war memorials to be found anywhere. Of special note is the one that commemorates the Far Eastern troupes of World War II. Even the staunchest of hearts will heave a little beneath its outstretched arms.

The road eventually leads to the **Plage de Marseille**. The beach here has been split into two parts, the first half being pebble and the second sand, and the water is quite clean. Bearing a striking resemblance to Southern California, this area is a lively and chic place to dine at night.

South of the city centre for modern architecture enthusiasts, is the acclaimed **Cité Radieuse** ⓟ by the French architect Le Corbusier (guided tours only; tel: tourist office, 04 91 13 89 00 for details). Also to the south is the **Musée d'Art Contemporain (MAC)** ⓠ (69 avenue d'Haïfa; closed Mon; entrance fee; tel: 04 91 72 17 27), Marseille's hangar-like contemporary art museum, which has an impressive international collection including artworks by Robert Rauschenberg, Marseille-born César, Andy Warhol, Dieter Roth, Martial Raysse, Ben, Niki de Saint Phalle and Absalon.

Cassis

Hard-core beachgoers may want to continue down the coast for a further 23 km (15 miles) to **Cassis** ❷. First of the Riviera resorts, Cassis possesses none of the glamour or urbanity of St-Tropez or Cannes and therein lies its special charm. It is blessed with the coolest water along the French Mediterranean, thanks to a series of mainland streams. Numerous modern painters spent many summers in this delicate port, and it is easy to see why.

The town has three beaches, the best being the **Plage de la Grande Mer**. To the west is the Plage du Bestouan, sheltered behind a breakwater. Cassis has a casino and a couple of little nightclubs, but don't expect to find a wild nightlife here. This is a resort mostly for families or young couples, and after-dark activities centre around the harbourfront and its row

GHT: traditional kery.

The Underworld and Marseille

As a thriving port, Marseille has long born the unsavoury associations that come with trade and passing sailors. By the 1930s the city's reputation was such that every employee in the town hall was said to have a criminal record. Although the statistics were far from conclusive, the city cemented its reputation as France's capital of organised crime and corruption.

If this sounds rather like New York during the 1920s, it comes as no surprise to find that Marseille was a transit port for Sicilian emigrants on their way to New York. Many never reached Ellis Island, finding hope in France's second largest city instead. Some brought the code of the mafia, which then mixed with the traditions of the native Marseillaises and the Corsican clans who had come to the mainland in search of jobs. Over generations, this heady brew took to an extreme the Phocaean city founders' vision of Marseille as a trading post.

In 1971 the "French Connection" was broken up, exposing a web of drug smuggling, with Marseille as the linchpin. Illicit raw materials had been hidden in cargo ships from Pakistan and the Middle East, refined in the south of France and shipped to New York. Much of the money was laundered, finding its way to bars, clubs and casinos all along the southern French coast.

However, busting the French Connection did not put an end to Marseille's criminal activity, and the *milieu* (underworld) is still going strong. Several years ago, the police seized 40 fruit machines in a clampdown on illegal gambling. Their faith in the security of local warehouses was minimal, so the evidence was stored overnight in the main police station. By the next morning 36 of the machines had been meticulously stripped down and their mechanisms removed for further use elsewhere. The great risk is when the dashing brigands of one day turn into killers the next, in order to "settle accounts".

Attempts are often made to strip the core from the *milieu*. The imprisonment in 1983 of one of the gangland bosses, Gaetan Zampa, was thought to have ended the *guerre des clans*, a war of underworld families. However, the *milieu* simply restructured. The *parrains* (godfathers) have virtually disappeared, and five groups are said to share Marseille, occasionally cooperating on joint ventures.

When the "new" underground does come out of its shell, it is ruthless. An examining magistrate, Judge Michel, was shot dead in 1983 as he rode home on his motorcycle. It was the first time anyone had dared to touch a senior judicial figure in the city. Two people were sentenced for the murder five years later, but the identity of whoever ordered the killing remains unknown. However, Michel's investigations into drug smuggling, and the massive surge in local drug addiction, leave the police in little doubt that the drug trade has come back to roost in Marseille.

An ironic turn of events in the late 1990s was the conviction of local politician, Bernard Tapié, who was also president of Marseille's football team. In 1998 he was convicted of match-fixing and embezzling team funds and was sent to prison. ❑

LEFT: heroin is not chic.

Map
on pages
148–9

of excellent restaurants. While enjoying a meal along here, be sure to sample the delicious local white wine. And most visitors make at least one trip to the town's spectacular *calanques*.

The *calanques*

The *calanques* (literally "rocky inlets") are like fjords carved out by the sea from the limestone cliffs, superb for swimming, and still unspoiled, mainly because they are so difficult to get to by car. You can reach them by ferry from Cassis, or by walking along the GR98 footpath between Marseille and Cassis.

The first inlet, the only one reachable by car, is Port-Miou; this is dedicated to harbouring yachts. The second is Port-Pin, so named for the shrubby pines that decorate its rocky walls. Port-Pin must be approached either by boat or on foot, as must En-Vau, the last and most incredible of the *calanques*.

En-Vau is breathtaking. Similar in appearance to a Norwegian fjord, sky-high white cliffs cut directly down into water of the deepest blue-green imaginable. A sandy white beach adorns one end. The view from the top is something never to be forgotten, but be warned – getting there isn't easy and neither is getting down. The paths that lead to both of the last two *calanques* are more or less unmarked, and inexperienced walkers may find themselves lost on arid clifftops.

In the long run, all but the most adventurous would be better off taking a native guide or a boat to En-Vau. And remember, if you're there during the high season, none of these places are going to resemble a deserted paradise. (Ferries from Cassis: Visite des calanques, 13 rue Lamartine; tel: 04 42 01 03 31.)

Cap Canaille and la Ciotat

Dominating the little village is **Cap Canaille**, which at 416 metres (1,400 ft) is the highest cliff in all of continental Europe. For a panoramic thrill, take a drive along the **Route des Crêtes**, which

LOW:
e calanque
rt-Miou.

climbs up, over and down to the neighbouring city of **la Ciotat** ❸. From summer homes to clinging vineyards to rubble, the road seems to disappear up into the sky. The view is fabulous, as is the lightheadedness it gives the viewer.

Down on the other side of the cliff, la Ciotat has a very different character. First called Citharista and an outpost to Marseille, its harbour now rather resembles a resort in Florida. The people are friendly and unpretentious, and the long flat beachfront is lined with souvenir shops.

Some of the town is quite pretty, particularly around the old port and the 17th-century **Notre-Dame-de-l'Assomption**. Unfortunately, the huge shipyards at one end of the waterfront, where oil and methane tankers are built, keep la Ciotat from being wholly picturesque.

Like Cassis, la Ciotat possesses a set of *calanques*, but **Muguel** is not good for swimming and **Figuerolles** is polluted and ugly. A more enjoyable tourist attraction is the beachfront monument to the Lumière brothers. These two illustrious sons of the city were the inventors of the moving picture. **L'Espace Lumière** (20 rue Foch; Sept–June: closed Mon, Tues and Sun; July–Aug: closed Mon, Tues and Sun pm; tel: 04 42 71 61 70) has photographs, posters and a film archive in their honour.

Travelling inland along the A50, north of la Ciotat and east of Marseille, will bring you to **Aubagne**, hometown of another inestimable Provençal native: Marcel Pagnol *(see box below left)*. The other main attraction in this town are the producers of *santons* (clay figures), who have many workshops here.

Aix-en-Provence

Although physically but a stone's throw north of the coast, in character **Aix-en-Provence** ❹ is a million miles away from the glitzy Riviera hotspots. Bastion of culture and bourgeois niceties, seat of one of France's finest universities since 1409, Aix embodies grace and gentility.

The Romans first founded Aquae Sex-

MARCEL PAGNOL

The writer and film director Marcel Pagnol, one of the figures most responsible for perpetrating the myth of idyllic rural Provence, was born in **Aubagne** in 1895. Pagnol captured the spirit of the region in works such as *Manon des Sources, Jean de Florette, La Femme du Boulanger, Le Gloire de mon Père, Le Château de ma Mère* and *Souvenirs d'Enfance*. Movie fans are best advised to avoid the rather unattractive Aubagne and drive instead through Cuges-les-Pins and up to **Riboux**, where the pastoral scenes of the films *Jean de Florette* and *Manon* were shot. Here, you can imagine Manon tripping through the rugged mountainside with her goats, and enjoy the great view afforded by the hair-raising drive. The tourist office in Aubagne can give full details of the Circuit Pagnol, which covers many of the sites mentioned in his works. One stop is **la Treille**, where Pagnol is buried.

Maps:
Area 148
City 156

tiae – so named for its hot springs – in 122 BC, after conquering the nearby Ligurian settlement of **Entremont**. It was overshadowed, however, by Massilia and Arles until the 12th century when the beloved "Good" King René, count of Provence, made it his city of preference. René's death brought Provence under the rule of the French crown, and Aix was made the seat of a parliament designed to keep the region under Gallic control. By the 17th and 18th centuries, it had become the leading city in the Bouches-du-Rhône.

Much of Aix's renowned architecture dates from this period of prosperity. Buildings erected during the 17th century can be distinguished by the single iron balcony placed over their central front door, frequently embellished by a cornice underscored with little teeth. The 18th-century structures, on the other hand, typically have iron balconies on all the windows and the door on the right.

The architecture also bears witness to the eventual decline of the city's power. Across the city you find homes with closed-in windows, because taxes were assessed according to the number of windows a house possessed, and owners were gradually unable to pay them. Eventually, most of the grand homes were repossessed by the banks.

During the Industrial Revolution, Aix fell back under Marseille's shadow. In the 20th century, however, new industries managed to find a niche here and the city remains the European capital for prepared almonds (some of which can be sampled in the local specialty: white iced diamonds of almond paste, called *calissons*). Nowadays, however, Aix is most renowned as a university town, and of its 150,000 inhabitants around 40,000 are students.

Around the cours Mirabeau

The best place to begin your investigation of the city is the **cours Mirabeau** Ⓐ, a long, wide avenue, lined with cafés on one side and venerable old houses on the other. Four rows of benevolent and stately

ELOW: the ntaine de la tonde, Aix- -Provence.

plane trees run down the centre of the avenue, punctuated by three 19th-century fountains. The most celebrated of these is the **Fontaine de la Rotonde** B, on place du Général de Gaulle, which dominates the western entrance to the avenue.

The avenue's original purpose was to separate the southerly **Quartier Mazarin** from the northerly Quartier Ancien. Only parliamentarians and nobles were allowed to grace the cours Mirabeau's elegant thoroughfare, and the Quartier Mazarin was designed specifically to accommodate them. Many lovely parliamentarian homes can be found within this quarter.

Of these homes, the **Hôtel Arbaud** is generally considered the most beautiful. It was built in 1730 directly on the cours by the first president of the parliament. A good runner-up, however, is located within the quarter, at the corner of rue Joseph Cabassol and rue Mazarine. The only house in Aix aside from the Hotel Arbaud to have been designed by a non-local, the **Hôtel de Caumont** was constructed in 1720 by Louis le Vau, one of the illustrious architects of Versailles. It is now the Ecole Superior d'Art et de Danse de Milhaud. Go inside to see the foyer fountain and the Atlanteans that hold up the ceiling. Many of the older houses in Aix possess similar interior fountains, remembrances of the city's aquatic origins; the Atlantean is a popular local motif, borrowed from the Genoans.

East down the rue Cardinale lies the **Fontaine des Quatres Dauphins** C (Fountain of the Four Dolphins). Built in 1667, it was the first fountain in Aix to be placed in the middle of a street rather than against a wall, giving it an unprecedented decorative purpose. Alain Delon fans will be interested to know that the beloved French celebrity owned the home on the northeast corner until the mid-1980s.

The **Musée Paul Arbaud** D (2 rue du Quatre-Septembre; open Mon–Sat, 2–5pm; entrance fee; tel: 04 42 38 38 95) stands very near to the Fontaine des Quatres Dauphins. Immediately as you enter its

BELOW: cours Mirabeau, Aix

Maps:
rea 148
City 156

large foyer, you will see a plethora of reliefs and capitals from different ages. Be sure to check out *Les sept péchées capitaux (The Seven Deadly Sins)*, hanging directly on your right.

The first room in the museum has one of the most important collections of Moustiers-Ste-Marie-style faïence to be found in Provence. Among the numerous examples of traditional work are such whimsical pieces as one marking the hot-air balloon ascent of 1783.

Going up the stairs, note the 18th-century, hand-painted, ornamental trimming. This decoration is lavish and the detail upstairs is incredible, with acorns and leaves carved directly out of the wood portals and exquisitely handcrafted fireplaces.

Another museum within the Quartier Mazarin is the **Musée Granet** Ⓔ (place St-Jean-de-Malte; closed Tues; entrance fee; tel: 04 42 38 14 70). The ground and first floors are devoted to numerous fairly unremarkable paintings, though there are the eight Cézanne canvasses, of which the museum is extremely proud. Granet's true interest lies in the basement where an excellent collection of lengthily documented Celto-Ligurian artefacts have been assembled, with maps and text describing early geological and prehistoric activity.

Next door is the 13th-century **St-Jean-de-Malte**, former priory of the Knights of Malta and Aix's oldest Gothic building.

The Quartier Ancien

When you cross over the cours Mirabeau to the **Quartier Ancien** ("Old Quarter"), you will notice a distinct change in atmosphere. Whereas the Quartier Mazarin oozes a sense of serenity, the narrow streets of the Quartier Ancien are filled with the lifebeat of the city.

This part of town also possesses the lion's share of interesting museums and splendid architecture. The **Hôtel Boyer d'Eguilles**, around two blocks in from the Cours, at 20 rue Espariat, combines both. Dating from 1675, the architectural plan is Parisian while the exterior décor is Italian

ELOW: city-
ntre flower
arket, Aix.
GHT: Place
l'Hôtel de
lle, Aix.

in style. The **Musée d'Histoire Naturelle** (6 rue Espariat; open daily; entrance fee; tel: 04 42 26 23 67) is located inside the Hôtel, with a number of large dinosaur eggs as its star attraction.

Down the street is the delightful **place d'Albertas** Ⓕ. When the parliamentarian Albertas built his home in the 1720s, he also bought all the land in front of it – to "protect his view". The four contiguous buildings that now enclose the square were not constructed until 1740. The fountain was added in 1912.

The place d'Albertas lies at the base of **rue Aude**, home to many of Aix's most fashionable stores and best-loved tourist sites. However, the first square that you come upon when heading up it, **place Richelme** Ⓖ, may seem slightly incongruous. Young rockers, often found holding impromptu concerts, have claimed this square for their own; it is now the main centre for illegal substances in the city.

Gentility is restored at the **place de l'Hôtel de Ville** Ⓗ, just up rue Aude and an excellent place to stop and have a drink or a bite to eat. On the western side of this square is Aix's **Hôtel de Ville** (town hall). If you go into the town hall, glance up at the beautiful wrought-iron work above the entrance, which fans out in a representation of the sun. Crossing the pretty paved courtyard will lead you into the foyer, with an elegant staircase that was the first in France to be built in the double style.

To the south side of the square is **la Poste** (post office). This building was first begun in 1718 as a granary, but work was halted two years later because of the plague. Another 40 years passed before work was resumed, and by then the building had been designated as a public structure – hence its windows and decorations are far more elaborate than those one would usually find on a granary. Particularly engrossing are the cavorting figures, intended to represent the Rhône and Durance rivers, that drape themselves into the stone beneath the central eave.

On the north side of the square is the whimsical **Tour de l'Horloge**, dating from 1510. This tall clock tower houses four different statues, each of which marks a season and appears alone for an appropriate three-month stretch. In the summer, you will see a woman holding wheat; autumn shows the wine harvest; winter has a wood bearer, and spring appears as a woman carrying fruit and a young salmon.

Every Tuesday, Thursday and Saturday morning the place de l'Hôtel de Ville welcomes the *marché d'Aix*, undoubtedly one of the largest and most colourful markets to be found in all of Provence. In front of the Hôtel de Ville are the flower stands. Over by the Palais de Justice are produce on one side and second-hand goods on the other. In between, the narrow stone streets spill over with additional merchants selling everything from kitchen utensils to underwear.

Passing under the arch of the Tour d'Horloge and up the rue Gaston-de-Saporta will bring you to the **Musée du Vieil Aix** Ⓘ (17 rue Gaston-de-Saporta; closed Mon; entrance fee; tel: 04 42 21 43 55). This funny little museum is badly

LEFT: Aix's Tc de l'Horloge.

Maps:
rea 148
ity 156

lit but it is home to an entertaining hall of mechanised *crèche* marionettes and also contains a fascinating room documenting the *Jeux de la Fête-Dieu*.

The Fête-Dieu, half-religious and half-profane, takes place during June and is a long procession in honour of the battle of Christianity against paganism. Its origins lie in the 13th century, but it wasn't until 1836 that the marionettes of Bontoux, displayed within the Musée du Vieil Aix, were created. Also shown are some of the participants' masks and a large painted screen. Don't miss the emphatic devil masks hanging up on high or the demonic puppets with red faces and pitchforks.

The **Cathédrale St-Sauveur** J (place de l'Université; open daily but closed to tourists during services; cloister closed Sun; tel: 04 42 21 10 51). At first there was just a small Roman church on this site. Then, in 1170, after the Crusades caused the population of Aix to swell, the little church was deemed no longer large enough, which then led to the planning of the cathedral.

Soon after work had begun, however, the plague struck, and it was closely followed by the Hundred Years' War (1137–1453). Around 140 years went by before construction could be continued, and, as a result, the cathedral is an eclectic structure. Its façade combines the 12th century with the 16th, the belfry belongs to the 15th and the Gothic nave to the 16th.

Slightly more coherent is the cathedral's 5th-century **baptistry**. This encompasses all that is left of the initial Roman settlement in Aix and is one of only three original baptistries in France (the others are in Fréjus and Riez).

The baptistry is a particularly fine example of symbolic architecture. The exterior plan and cupola are cubic to represent the four apostles. The interior pool is octagonal with eight marble columns. Water flowed in from the west and out to the east, in keeping with the direction of the sun and its light. The two westernmost columns were formed of black granite (for the darkness of unenlightenment), and it

LOW:
ditional
y *santons*.

was between these that the soon-to-be-baptised would enter the pool. The other six columns, through which the newly baptised left the pool, were made of green marble, signifying the light of redemption.

Also notable are the cloisters and Nicolas Froment's 15th-century triptych, *Buisson Ardent (Mary in the Burning Bush).* Next door, the baroque Palais de l'Archevêché contains a **Musée des Tapisseries** Ⓚ (Tapestry Museum; closed Tues; entrance fee; tel: 04 42 23 09 91) and hosts productions in the courtyard in the Festival d'Art Lyrique.

Pavillon Vendôme

One last, although definitely not least, local architectural feat is the **Pavillon Vendôme**. To reach it, you must leave the central city and head down rue Célony – the Pavillon's original owner, Louis de Mercoeur, Duke of Vendome and governor of Provence, built this home in 1665 outside the central confines of Aix for very specific reasons.

Louis was the grandson of Henry IV and the nephew-in-law of Cardinal Mazarin. After his wife died, however, he had the misfortune to fall madly in love with Lucrèce de Forbin-Soliers, "La Belle du Canet". Although Lucrèce was available, being a widow, she was not of a high-enough social stature to become the official consort of the duke. Desperate, Louis had this second home built outside the town, so that they might continue to rendezvous in secret. Eventually he decided to marry her anyway, at which point an outraged Mazarin made him a cardinal and thereby elevated his status to a level where any legitimate union was forever impossible.

Outside, the Pavillon looks much like an English country home, enhanced with *quatrepartite* formal gardens. The only disturbance to the symmetry of the grounds and building is the unfortunate third floor, an 18th-century addition.

Close to the Pavillon are the **Thermes Sextius** Ⓛ, now a luxury glass-and-marble spa but originally a series of 1st-century BC Roman baths (these can be seen to the right of the present entrance), fed by the water from the *Source Imperiatrice*. The baths were expanded in the 18th century and a fountain from this period is still on view to visitors.

Artists in Aix

The **Atelier Paul Cézanne** Ⓜ (9 avenue Paul-Cézanne; open daily; entrance fee; tel: 04 42 21 06 53) lies behind a little wooden gate, situated just north of the Quartier Ancien. The renowned modern artist was born in Aix in 1839 but left during the 1860s to join the Impressionists in Paris. He soon became disenchanted, however, and in 1870 he returned to his home town, where he remained until his death in 1906.

This studio was built in 1900, and it was here that Cézanne painted his last works. The large windows are testimonials to the fact that the artist designed the building himself. Inside there are a couple of reproductions of his works, his easel, rucksack, cape, books and many of the objects that he used in his still life paintings.

LEFT: statue, Pavillon Vêndome.

Maps:
Area 148
City 156

To see one of Cézanne's greatest inspirations, drive out of the city along the D17, or route de Tholonet. This will bring you to the foot of the huge, silvery **Mont Ste-Victoire**.

Another artist who left his mark on Aix was Hungarian-born Victor Vasarely. A museum to his work, which Vasarely himself constructed, named the **Fondation Vasarely** N (1 avenue Marcel-Pagnol, Jas de Bouffan; open daily; entrance fee; tel: 04 42 20 01 09; take bus No 8 from la Rotonde) stands just to the southwest of Aix on the Jas de Bouffan. The building is unmistakable, with its bold black-and-white Op Art design.

All of the 42 works, which the artist described as "mural integrations", were painted directly onto the high walls in 1975. Also on view are 800 "experiments" and a gallery of contemporary work.

Painting is not the only art form that can be enjoyed in Aix. During the July summer festival, original productions of opera and chamber music can be seen almost every night. (Festival International d'Art Lyrique; box office, 11 rue Gaston de Saporta; tel: 04 42 17 34 34). There are also jazz and dance festivals in July and August. The Aix festival is just one source of nocturnal distraction. Jazz clubs, encouraged by the large student population, swing all year round, as do numerous other clubs.

North of Aix

On days when you feel like escaping from the hustle and bustle of the city, you may want to head north towards the Durance River and the solemn **Abbaye de Silvacane** 5 (Apr–Sept: open daily; Oct–Mar: closed Tues; entrance fee; tel: 04 42 50 41 69). Constructed by the Cistercians in 1144, Silvacane's name is derived from the Latin for wood *(silva)* and reed *(cane)*, after its marshy surroundings.

True to the Cistercian spirit, the appearance of this abbey is anything but frivolous. Here, there is no stained glass, no statuary and no extraneous decoration.

LOW:
e striking
) Art
ndation
sarely,
ar Aix.

Add to the original austerity an empty interior and a poorly reconstructed exterior and Silvacane makes for a rather bleak destination.

The area along the Durance, however, does provide a nice break from the dry plains of Aix. As you head north, the land begins to rise, coniferous trees appear and green surrounds you. Occasional meadows, deep reservoirs and distant mountains are a welcome sight. You are now heading into wine country.

Those with a yen to visit a working wine château from the *Côteaux d'Aix* should follow the river east to the pretty little town of **Jouques** ❻, with its attractive central fountain. The owners of the **Château Revelette**, who speak French, German and English, are happy to offer a tour of their *cave* and a *dégustation*.

Afterwards, head south on D11 through the **Forêt de Peyrolles**, past numerous fields, vineyards and sheep-crossing signs, and you will find a number of shaded groves suitable for picnicking. You'll need some fortification before embarking on the climb up over the mountains and back down towards Aix. The curvy, shoulderless road resembles nothing more than a goat path that has been mildly picked over to accommodate modern civilisation. Even its surface undulates.

Once you've hit the crest of the **Col de St-Buc**, the road begins to wind down through cliffs of sheer rock, cut into natural tiers. At the bottom, head just west and you reach the **Château de Vauvenargues** ❼. Perched on a little hill, but within a deep valley and surrounded by green mountains, the château is incredibly picturesque. Apparently, Picasso thought so too, for it was here that he elected to be buried, following his death in 1973, aged 91. His tomb lies within the park, but the grounds are not as yet open to the public.

Continue west, in the direction of Aix, and you will pass the **Barrage de Bimont**. This dam makes for a pleasant afternoon trip, with its tremendous James Bond-style waterworks and large nature reserve. Hikers will find numerous trails to choose from, several of which lead to the **Barrage Zola**, designed by Emile Zola's father in 1854.

Heading West from Aix

Another day trip from Aix lies to the west of the city on the road to Arles. However, a visit to the impressive **Château de la Barben** ❽ (11 km/7 miles east of Salon-de-Provence on the D572/D22; open daily; entrance fee; tel: 04 90 55 25 41) and its **zoo** best serves to show the public the perils of tourism in Provence.

Architecturally the château is a lovely place. Originally built in the Middle Ages, it was enlarged in the 14th and then the 17th centuries. The formal gardens were laid out by the garden designer of Versailles's, Le Nôtre, and in their centre is a sweet fountain, in which Napoleon's little sister, Pauline, liked to bathe *au naturel*. To protect her modesty as she frolicked, servants would hold up sheets of black cloth. Inside are a number of rooms worth seeing, such as Pauline's delicate boudoir, with its hand-painted wallpaper.

LEFT: Mont Ste-Victoire.

Map
n pages
148–9

Salon-de-Provence

Situated on the edge of the arid Crau Plain, **Salon-de-Provence** ❾ has been dubbed the "crossroads of Provence." And, indeed, it lies within 50 km (30 miles) of Arles to the west, Avignon to the north, Aix to the east and Marseille to the south. The town is also at the heart of olive-growing country, making it France's number-one marketplace for that silky oil.

Salon is certainly a very laid-back city with a warm, small-town feel. Brightly coloured standards hang from the 17th-century **Hôtel de Ville**, and more flags decorate the heavy arches that give passage into the cobbled streets of the central **Vieille Ville** (Old Town). Above the arches, imposing towers mark what remains of ancient ramparts.

The old town is dominated by the grim **Château de l'Emperi**, built between the 10th and 16th centuries and around which Salon originally sprang up. Inside, the **Musée de l'Emperi** (place des Centuries; closed Tues; entrance fee; tel: 04 90 56 22 36) showcases France's largest collection of military art and history. Under the vaulted Gothic ceilings there are copious exhibits of saddles and sabres, guns and medals, toy soldiers and life-size figures. The tour culminates with several rooms dedicated to the Napoleonic era, including the diminutive general's short blue bed among its treasures.

The museum has been marvellously arranged, with great attention to presentation and documentation. And, while only a quarter of the collection is on view at any given time (all objects date between 1700 and 1918 and pertain to French – not just Provençal – history), the tour still seems gargantuan. Serious military history buffs should make the trip to Salon just to visit this museum.

Spiritualists, on the other hand, should come to see the **Maison de Nostradamus** (Nostradamus's House; 13 rue Nostradamus; open daily; entrance fee; tel: 04 90 56 64 31). The renowned physician-turned-astrologer settled in the town,

LOW: inside
e Château
velette.

birthplace of his wife, in 1546, and it was here that he both wrote his famous book of predictions, *Centuries*, and spent the last 20 years of his life.

Salon has made much of this famous inhabitant but, if truth be told, he was not as warmly welcomed during his lifetime. The townspeople regarded him with suspicion, partly because of his star-gazing and partly owing to of his conversion to Judaism. Indeed, he was only saved from condemnation as a sorcerer by his ties to King Charles IX.

Nostradamus's house is a modest affair. All his original manuscripts are under lock and key in the mayor's office, and most of his household objects were lost in a fire. Restoration, however, is at long last under way, and the authorities intend eventually to move the priceless manuscripts back to their rightful home.

Also within the ancient ramparts of the old town is the beautiful **Eglise St-Michel**, dating from 1220 to 1239 and built in the Roman Gothic style. The church possesses two belltowers, one is contemporary to the construction of the building, while the other is a delicate 15th-century addition. Inside, cobwebs hang from the skylights above a tiny cool chapel. Be sure to note the stone tympanum that decorates the wooden front door, which shows the Archangel Michael killing a snake above the paschal lamb. This pre-dates the church, having been carved in the 12th century.

A second church lies just outside the ancient walls of the original citadel. **St-Laurent** was built between 1344 and 1480 and presents a much grander spectacle than its forerunner. Executed in true Provençal Gothic, its exterior presents a simplicity that is reiterated by the church's sombre and majestic interior.

Only the largest of the chapels, placed directly across from the entrance, is lit. Dedicated to the Virgin, this chapel features a 16th-century alabaster statue commemorating her maternal piety.

Nostradamus's **tomb** stands beside the statue of the Virgin. On the wall behind it

BELOW: giraf
Barben zoo.

Map on pages 148–9

is an inscription that reads: "Here lie the bones of Michel de Nostradame, alone at the judgement of humans worthy of knowing the stars of the future. He lived 62 years, 6 months and 17 days. He died in Salon in 1566. May future times not trouble his repose. Anne Ponsard, his wife, wishes him true happiness."

A second famed inhabitant of Salon, Adam de Craponne, has been remembered with a statue on a small square across from the Hôtel de Ville. De Craponne was the 16th-century engineer who brought fertility to the region by building an irrigation canal from the Durance River down through the dry plains of the Crau and out into the sea.

Olive country

Although Salon has served as a centre for the olive trade since the 15th century, insiders flock to three neighbouring towns to buy their oil. Before going off in search of that perfect bottle of olive oil, it is important to know what to look for. First, check whether the bottle is marked *premier pression à froid vièrge extra*. If it isn't, don't buy it. If it is, then hold the bottle up to the light. The best oil will be a delicate green in colour.

South of Salon is the first town, **la Fare-les-Oliviers** ⑩, which many say offers the best oil in all of France. The local oil mill and wine cooperative are open to the public, and products can be bought on site. It's best to go during the harvest season, if possible.

Other locals swear by the olives of **Aureille** ⑪, a half-forgotten town on the road westward to Arles in the midst of grassy plains and vast expanses of olive trees. Aureille is a poor town but it is a pleasant enough place with a friendly central bar and a ruined 11th-century castle rising up on a hill above it that is only accessible on foot. For those in search of the "real" Provence, this can be both a relief and a point of interest. Aureille's olive mill, just off the D17, can also be visited by the public.

LOW: ural of ostradamus, lon-de-ovence.
GHT: statue Adam de aponne.

A third town with a claim on the olive market lies more within the jurisdiction of Arles than Salon. Like Aureille, **Mouriès** ⓬ gives the outsider an opportunity to generalise about the Provençal character. Although hardly more than a village, with just one main street, Mouriès boasts several cafés, a handful of markets and two hotels. It also has two olive oil mills, one of which is a local cooperative. The other, on the cours Paul Revoi, is open to the public, with on-premises sales.

Since Mouriès is just outside Arles, it's a good place to stay if you have a car and can't find a room in the city during one of its festivals.

Arles

For many, **Arles** ⓭ *is* Provence. No other city in the region offers a more colourful atmosphere or possesses a greater awareness of its Provençal heritage. The proud inhabitants of this old city are the first to tout themselves not only as "*vrai* (true) Provençals" but as "*Arlesiens*". Societies dedicated to upholding local customs flourish, and a "queen of Arles" is selected every three years on the basis not of her beauty but of her knowledge of Provençal traditions and her ability to speak the regional dialect and dress in its costume.

Arles bears none of the shrewd urbanity of Marseille nor the cultured sophistication of Aix. Instead, it seems to live in its past, haunted by the spectre of the Romans, populated by fierce upholders of tradition and deeply affected by its proximity to the wild marshes of the Camargue.

Founded by the Massilians as a trading post in the 6th century BC, Arles's position at the crossroads of the Rhône and the Roman Aurelian Way made it a natural choice for development by the Romans. The town grew slowly for several hundred years, with some special help from Marius in the 2nd century BC. Then, during the struggle for power between Caesar and Pompey, Arles got its lucky break. Marseille made the fatal error of showing friendship towards the latter, and

BELOW: olive country.

Maps:
rea 148
ity 173

Caesar turned to Arles, which was already known for its skilled boat-builders, with the request that 12 war vessels be built for him within 30 days. The city complied, and Arles's good fortune was sealed. After squelching the claims of Pompey in 49 BC, Caesar squelched Marseille and designated Arles as the first city of Provence.

The city continued to prosper and in 418, under Honorius, it was made the administrative capital of the territory for Gaul. Although its predominance would waver over the following centuries, Arles remained a central maritime and river port right until the advent of the steam engine, when transportation by train overtook the tugboat method.

Train travel spelled disaster for the Arlesian economy, which had from the very beginning depended on its port activity for importance. As gateway to the Camargue (the top producer of rice in France), Arles has managed to recoup some of its value as a trading centre, but its days of eminence are long gone.

Lacking any major industry or university, the Arles of today relies heavily on the glorious Arles of yesteryear for its livelihood. At the heart of Arles is the **Vieille Ville** (old town), an attractive maze of narrow stone streets, where crumbling Roman edifices mingle with sturdy medieval stonework.

The old town is bordered to the south by the wide boulevard des Lices, to the east by the remnants of ancient ramparts and to the north and west by the grand sweep of the River Rhône. Surrounding all of this is the somewhat innocuous spread of the more modern city, including the large Trinquetaille section of Arles.

Most visitors will first arrive in Arles via the boulevard des Lices. If you have a car, it might be a good idea to leave it in the municipal parking garage to be found on this street's south side. Almost all of the city's tourist sites are within easy walking distance of each other, and the narrow lanes of the old town are not hospitable to automobiles.

LOW:
downer and
daughter
side Arles.

The boulevard des Lices is a busy spot with many cafés and the local tourist office, but it lacks the charm of Aix's cours Mirabeau and the commerciality of Marseille's la Canebière. Its highest points come on Saturday morning during the extensive produce market and every first Wednesday of the month, when a fabulous flea market spills over its streets. At other times, the boulevard serves mainly as a thoroughfare past the Vieille Ville.

Before heading into the old city, take a quick detour south along the avenue des Alyscamps, named after the site of the same name: **les Alyscamps** Ⓐ (open daily; entrance fee; tel: 04 90 49 36 87). Not much is left of this ancient necropolis, but no first-time visit to Arles is complete without a stroll down the leafy **allée des Sarcophages**, which was painted vibrantly by former Arles resident, Vincent van Gogh. As you walk down the tomb-lined lane, notice the plaque that reads: "Van Gogh. Here, struck by the beauty of the site, he came to set up his easel."

The Alyscamps cemetery was begun by the Romans but by the 4th century it had been taken over by Gallic Christians. Its fame spread during the Middle Ages, but the necropolis gradually fell into decline as its stone began to disappear; some of it went towards the building of other religious structures, some to antiques dealers and some as presents to illustrious guests of the city.

All the tombs are now empty, and the stone shells that are left bear an uncanny resemblance to a long line of molars. Nonetheless, there is a peacefulness under the poplars that guards the solemnity of the spot and makes it a favourite for meditative afternoon walks.

At the very end of the lane stands what remains of **St-Honorat des Alyscamps**. Once upon a time a large Romanesque church, St-Honorat now functions mainly as a backdrop for some of the city's theatrical activities.

To enter the old city, return to the boulevard des Lices and walk a block towards

BELOW: the Roman town of Arles along the Rhône.

Maps:
rea 148
ity 173

the centre, up the cobbled rue Jean Jaurès. This will bring you to the spacious **place de la République** Ⓑ, with the **Hôtel de Ville** (town hall) at one end. The most impressive building on the square, however, is the **Eglise St-Trophime** Ⓒ, with a stunning front portal that dominates the eastern side of the square.

The doorway of St-Trophime (the saint who is credited with having brought Christianity to France) is a glorious example of Provençal Romanesque style. Constructed between 1152 and 1180, its intricate tympanum shows the Last Judgement being overseen by a barefoot and crowned Jesus. He is flanked by the four apostles (Matthew with wings, Mark as a lion, Luke as an ox and John as an eagle). To the left of this group, the elect are presented to Abraham, Isaac and Jacob by an angel. To the right, the damned are refused admission to Heaven by an angel brandishing a sword of fire.

Inside, the lofty tone continues. The church's broken-barrel-vaulted nave is, at over 20 metres (60 ft), the highest in Provence. By the left of the entrance, a 4th-century sarcophagus serves as a baptismal font. Further in, the life of the Virgin is depicted on a huge 17th-century Aubusson tapestry.

St-Trophime's **cloisters** (open daily; entrance fee; tel 04 90 96 07 38), which stand to the right of the church, are more cheerful. The sound of birds fills the air as you enter, and in warm weather pink flowers dot the bright courtyard, which is enclosed by solemn 14th-century figures posted as columns.

Although work began on the cloisters during the second half of the 12th century, it was interrupted for around 100 years, and they were not completed until the 14th. The northern and eastern galleries belong to the earlier period, while the western and southern ones were built later.

Be sure to climb up to the top of the church before leaving. As you step out onto the "roof", you will be struck by the brilliant sun, reflected off the white stone. Look down into the courtyard, then to the lofty belltower circled by birds. Delicate columns and the stone tiles that were used for eaves complete the exquisiteness of this lofty perch.

The **Museon Arlaten** Ⓓ (July–Aug: open daily; Sept–Jun: closed Mon; entrance fee; tel: 04 90 93 58 11) waits a couple of blocks away down the rue de la République. Native-born poet Frédéric Mistral founded this ethnographic museum with the money he received for winning the Nobel Prize for literature in 1904, with the stipulation that it be dedicated to all that is Provençal. Accordingly, the name is Provençal (for "Musée d'Arles"), all the documentation within is in dialect (as well as in French) and the *gardiennes* are dressed in traditional costume.

Room after room leads you through the world of the Provençal. One hall is filled with costumes and explanations of how they should be worn, others feature amulets and magic charms, *tambours* and other instruments, nautical and agricultural equipment, wallhangings and paintings. There are even several re-creations of Provençal domestic scenes.

HT:
ormer
ueen
Arles".

The *museon* is not the only mark left on the city by the poet. A formidable **bust of Mistral** looks down over the place du Forum, just a stone's throw away. Most of the nightlife that doesn't involve a festival or cinema takes place in this lively square. There is a variety of cafés here, making it a great place to enjoy a laid-back meal. Bullfighting aficionados may prefer to head into the Tambourin, patronised by the local champions; the walls are lined with their autographed photos.

If you continue towards the river, you will come to the **Thermes de Constantin** E. These 4th-century baths were once the largest in Provence, but little of them still exists. The **Musée Réattu** F (10 rue du Grand Prieuré; open daily; entrance fee; tel: 04 9049 3674), across the street, is far more interesting. It isn't worth paying the entrance fee to see most of the paintings, many of which are badly in need of restoration and some of which have not even been attributed. However, the collection does include some intriguing modern sculpture from the region, including one fascinating metallic piece with "living beads", and a collection of 57 Picasso sketches dating from 1971, donated by the artist himself.

If the inevitable press of tourists has begun to get to you, steal a quiet moment walking down the ramparts that line the Rhône. Here, with the wide river on one side of you and crumbling stone façades on the other, you may recapture a sense of the Roman spirit that once dominated this city. (Try not to look at the late 20th-century five-storey tenements on the facing bank.)

On the other side of town is the **Musée de l'Arles Antique** G (avenue de la Première Division Française Libre; open daily; entrance fee; tel: 04 90 18 88 88), which should not to be missed, as it offers a key to understanding the history of Arles. It is housed in a splendid new building containing many antiquities that were previously scattered round various Arles museums, including statues, capi-

BELOW: festivities at the Arènes in Arles.

Maps:
rea 148
ity 173

tals, carved friezes, pottery, glass, jewellery, mosaics and a large collection of marble sarcophagi.

The **Arènes** **H** (amphitheatre; Rond-point des Arènes; open daily; entrance fee; tel: 04 90 49 36 86) is another place to chase Roman ghosts. Enormous in size – it measures an impressive 136 by 107 metres (440 by 345 ft) and is capable of accommodating more than 20,000 spectators – this Roman arena is both larger and older than its cousin in Nîmes, having been built in the 1st century AD. A visit to its tower offers a view out over the expanse of the red-roofed old city, its modern environs, the Rhône and the Alpilles Ridges to the north.

Bullfights of various types are still held in the Arènes. Saturday afternoons find locals munching peanuts and drinking sodas as they watch their favourite *cocarde* champions cavort in front of snorting bulls. The first of May welcomes the Fête des Gardians, when cowboys from the Camargue gather for a yearly spectacle.

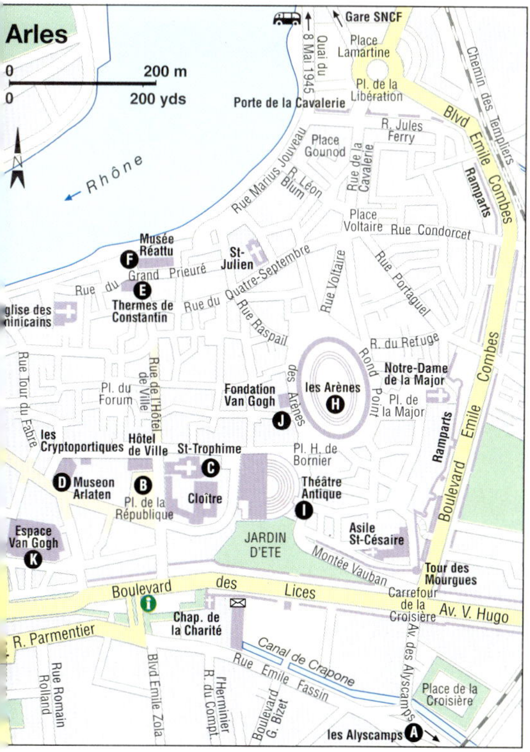

More annual bullfights take place during the Feria Pascale of Easter and the Prémices du Riz in mid-September.

It's probable that if you enter the old city on a warm summer night, you will be greeted by the sound of flamenco, opera or jazz wafting out from within the walls of the neighbouring **Théâtre Antique** **I** (rue de la Calade; open daily; entrance fee; tel: 04 90 49 36 25). During summer days, this 1st-century BC theatre equates to little more than a few piles of rubble, a siding of worn stone seating and two half-standing columns. At night, however, the Théâtre is transformed into a magical backdrop for the Festival d'Arles.

Like all the other cities of Provence, Arles puts on a special cultural festival during the summer. The Festival d'Arles is particularly successful, wisely taking advantage of Arles's many antiquities as wonderfully atmospheric stages for everything from folkloric dance to classical music to high-fashion shows.

The festival is accompanied in July by another widely applauded annual event: the Rencontres Internationales de la Photographie. This festival brings together photographers from around the world to compare techniques, peruse exhibits and enjoy nightly spectacles. Workshops with respected masters are also available. Like the festival, the Rencontres use many of the Arlesian monuments and museums to enrich their productions.

Artists who come to Arles with the intention of making a pilgrimage to the haunts of Van Gogh may be disappointed, however. The house where he and Gauguin once lived, worked and argued no longer stands, and the Café de la Nuit on Place du Forum is a reconstruction. However you can visit the **Fondation Van Gogh** **J** (Palais de Luppé, 24 bis rond-point des Arènes; closed Mon; entrance fee; tel: 04 90 49 55 49), which has a collection of work from contemporary artists in tribute to Van Gogh. Otherwise devotees must content themselves by seeing some of the sites the master once painted, the fabulous light he once saw and the copious fields of sunflowers from where he once gathered bouquets for still lifes.

The **Espace Van Gogh** Ⓚ (place Docteur Félix Rey; open daily; admission free; tel: 04 90 49 37 53) is on the site of the hospital where Van Gogh was treated and which has now been restored to look as it did when the artist was there. The building, which is set around a garden courtyard, incorporates a bookshop, library and exhibition space, where temporary shows are held.

The Alpilles

The dry flat land that surrounds Arles, circled by jagged, white stone peaks called the **Alpilles**, is filled with sunflowers, not to mention cypress and olive groves. Arles holds reign over this region, generally referred to as the Pays d'Arles.

If you don't have a car and are energetic, you can try cycling to get around, but be wary of the hot midday sun in summer and the steep inclines of the Alpilles. Local buses will get you where you want to go, but they will take both time and money. As a final choice, try hitchhiking. It's never the best idea but probably safer and easier here than in most places.

Just 7 km (4 miles) northeast of Arles, past a long field of peppers, lies the **Abbaye de Montmajour** ⓮ (route de Fontvieille; closed Tues pm; entrance fee; tel: 04 90 54 64 17). Founded in the 10th century by Benedictine monks on an island amidst a swamp that was passable only by raft, the monastery fell into decline by the 1600s. Total collapse came during the next century, when the head abbot, Cardinal de Rohan, became entangled in a scandal concerning Marie Antoinette. In the 1790s, the property was bought and then stripped by antique dealers. Restoration was begun in 1872, but there is still something akin to a movie façade about the abbey: grand from the front, empty at the back. To add to its problems, it was occupied by foreign forces in 1943 and burned a year later.

Nonetheless, the plan of the abbey is fabulous and it is touted as being the most elaborate of any Romanesque church in

BELOW: local painter

Maps:
rea 148
ity 173

Provence, along with the Abbé St-Gilles. The central crypt, which is found above ground and marked with cryptic inscriptions, forms a perfect circle with five evenly radiating chapels. The enormous 12th-century **Eglise de Notre-Dame** possesses a never-completed nave that is considered one of the masterpieces of Romanesque art.

Stepping out of the cloister and onto the ruins offers a wonderful view of the outlying countryside, with the city of Arles in the distance. For an even grander panorama, climb to the top of the imposing tower erected by the Abbot Pons. From there, you can see the nearby town of **Fontvieille** ⓯. Following the road just northeast will take you right into this pleasant little town. As you enter, note the modest oratory, erected in 1721 in thanks for the end of the plague. Similar oratories mark each corner of the town.

Fontvieille is a charming spot, but one that has clearly been marked for tourism, with prices to match. The town's primary attraction is the **Moulin de Lettres**, as they call the mill where Alphonse Daudet (1840–97) presumably wrote *Letters from My Windmill*. The fact that the windmill actually belonged to friends (not the author) and probably witnessed little penmanship (although Daudet did visit it) has done little to deter the hordes of tourists that crowd its tiny interior.

Set in a picturesque spot, the mill does contain some interesting features, such as a round ceiling marked in compass fashion with the names of the winds that sweep the hill. Unfortunately, you can't hear these winds above the din of tourists. The narrow subterranean museum is equally disappointing.

Daudet also left his mark on the neighbouring town of **Tarascon** ⓰. This small city was founded by the Massillians in the 3rd century BC and became a Provençal legend in AD 48 when its horrible resident monster, the amphibious Tarasque, was tamed by the sweet St Martha. Widespread fame came in the personage of

LOW: fields sunflowers round Arles.

Christian Lacroix

It is no secret that the internationally acclaimed haute-couture designer Christian Lacroix (*b.*1951) is strongly inspired by his native region of Provence. His madcap designs reflect his love for the sunniest area in France and his palette is reminiscent of the colours one finds in Van Gogh's paintings: sunflower yellows, poppy reds, purples and blues, and swirling prints.

Despite his fame, Lacroix admits that he often feels the need to go back to his childhood Provençal roots. "I've always been crazy about terracotta floors, primitive people, sun and rough times," he says . "This is my real side – goat's cheese and bread, elementary things. I am fascinated with Paris, its elegance, its women, even its artificiality. But with my heart and skin I love the south – bullfighting, pleasure, music, nature, the sea."

Lacroix grew up in Arles, which he still speaks of with a feverish nostalgia for his golden youth: the now-deserted rue de la Roquette, then alive with gipsies; the rue des Porcelets, where he bought the *fougasse aux gratillons*, a delicious bread that Marcel Pagnol often talks about in his novels; the rue de la République, where he used to be fascinated by the shop of *santons*. Some of Lacroix's favourite landmarks around Arles include the entrance hall of the Hôtel de Ville, the Cathédral St-Trophime and the Eglise Notre-Dame-de-la-Majeur, near the Arènes.

Following the sinuous rue Parade leads to the Musée Réattu, in the former palace of the Maltese knights. When the young Lacroix played truant from school, it was often to go and look at *L'Arlésienne* and *L'Atelier de couture en Arles*, painted by Antoine Raspal in the 18th century.

"Our local hangout was le Mallarte," remembers Lacroix. "It was the bourgeois café in town, where we liked to spend long hours practising the art of conversation, seated at smoky tables in our navy pea coats and long hair."

When he can escape from his obligations as a master of haute couture, Lacroix can generally be found somewhere in the golden triangle of Provence: in the Alpilles, from Maussane to Mouriès, from les Baux to St-Rémy-de-Provence, and eventually down into the Camargue region.

"Arles is really a passage between my two worlds: Provence and the Camargue," the designer says. "On the one side, the laughing universe of the Alpilles commemorated by Alphonse Daudet; on the other, as soon as one crosses the Rhône and enters the Trinquetaille, where my grandparents lived, it is already the door to the Camargue and its flat countryside. Since I am both Cévenol and Provençal, I am very sensitive to this double aspect."

It's just a short drive south to the region of the Camargue and the town of Stes-Maries-de-la-Mer, where Lacroix remembers with great fondness spending long lazy summers. "I have always loved the swampy landscapes of the Camargue," he says. Proof of this is the lovely *mas* (the local name for a traditional Provençal farmhouse) that he bought once he had established himself in Paris. "I come here as often as possible with my wife Françoise and renew my relationship with my friends, to whom I am just Lacroix, the old pal from years ago." ❑

LEFT: desigr for Lacroix haute coutu

Map pages 148–9

Tartarin, fictional "hero" of the book of the same name by Daudet.

Tartarin was Daudet's revenge against what he saw as the smallness of the provincial spirit. Despite a superficially sympathetic aspect, the character was a liar, braggart and all-in-all ridiculous figure. The people of Tarasque, from where Tartarin was supposed to have come, have never been able to live this reputation down. Without too much prodding, they'll probably tell you just how little they appreciate being known as the compatriots of Tartarin.

However, this has not prevented them from creating a tiny museum to the character, the **Maison de Tartarin** (Tartarin House). Opened in 1985, the house features wax figures in re-creations of scenes from the book. It's only really worth a visit if you're very familiar with the story.

All visitors to Tarascon will want to stop by the **Collegial Ste-Marthe**. Like many other churches in the region, this imposing edifice presents an interesting eclecticism of architecture, since one half of it was built during the Romanesque 12th century and the other half was erected during the Gothic 14th century. Unfortunately, most of the bas-reliefs that once decorated its doorway were destroyed in the Revolution.

Nothing, however, has touched its remarkable crypt. Descending into its tiny alcove, you are immediately overwhelmed by the cool hush. A button on one side illuminates the oratory just long enough to expose the relics of the saint, hostess to Christ at Bethany, passenger on the *navette* from Jerusalem and tamer of the menacing Tarasque. Her crypt is one of those unique places where the unseen overtakes the everyday. From the moment you enter its dark and damp confines, you feel a shroud of sanctity fall over you. It's not grandiose – but it is convincing.

Grandiose would more accurately describe the feudal **Château de Tarascon** (boulevard du roi Renée; Easter–Sep: open daily; Oct–Easter: closed Tues; entrance fee; tel: 04 90 91 01 93). Con-

ow: the ne near ascon.

structed directly on the banks of the Rhône during the first 50 years of the 15th century, this building proudly rivals the Château de Beaucaire, which stands across the river on the opposite bank.

The interior of the Château de Tarascon is mostly empty. In the first gaping hall, a changing exhibition of modern abstracts creates a striking effect against the severe medieval walls. Aside from this exhibition and six magnificent 17th-century tapestries that recall the glory of Scipion, the castle has no furnishings.

Tarascon puts on several *fêtes* each year but none is more celebrated than that of the *Tarasque*. Among the activities that accompany this festival, which takes place during the last weekend in June, is a colourful parade led by a *papier-mâché* facsimile of the monster.

From Tarascon, travel north along the D35 towards Avignon to reach the 10th-century **Abbaye St-Michel-de-Frigolet** ⓱ (open for group visits only Mon–Sat at 2.30pm and Sun 4pm; tel: 04 32 74 32 74), where a handful of monks still dwell. The land seems slightly less forbidding here than around Tarascon, as the Alpilles meld into the gentler **Montagnettes**. These hills cover the area between the curve of the Rhône and the east–west stretch of the Alpilles and harbour numerous alcoves of cypress and poplars, olive and almond trees, straggly pines and fragrant herbs.

Barbentane ⓲ is a friendly little town just north of the abbey and it has a warm, laid-back atmosphere. Despite the town's modesty, a wonderful **château** (open: Apr, May and Sept–Nov: Thur–Tues; June–Aug: daily; Dec–Mar: Sun only; entrance fee; tel: 04 90 95 51 07), constructed in 1674 and still occupied by the Marquis of Barbentane, stands right off its main street. Step through the gates and you'll wonder whether you have suddenly been transported to the Ile-de-France.

The interior is filled with an impressive collection of antiques and *objets d'art*. The grandson of the first owner spent 20

BELOW: plar
trees in the
Pays d'Arles

Map pages 48–9

years as ambassador in Florence and brought home from his Italian voyages masses of marble and 18th-century furniture. Everything within is original, and many items, such as the wrought-iron bannister, are handmade.

Among the most amazing articles are: the marble floor and circular mosaic ceiling of the "statue" salon; the hand-painted 18th-century wallpaper of the "Chinese" sitting room; the Italian-style wall fountain in the parlour (it was once the dining room, but lack of servants and distance from the kitchen forced the marquis to switch their uses); and the Provençal-style library and upstairs bedroom, also with original hand-painted wallpaper. Note that the beds were short because people never lay on their backs – considered the position of death.

Above the stairwell is a stone-carving of the blustery mistral. From the front door you can see the ominous **dungeon**, but it is not open to the public. Also within sight is the crumbling church of **Notre-Dame-des-Graces**.

A more contemporary attraction on the outskirts of town is the **Orchidées de Provence** greenhouse, where you will find a vast offering of prize-winning orchids on view and for sale. The best time to visit is between October and May, when the flowers are in full bloom.

Before heading back south, you may want to make a quick sweep east through **Noves** 19. The town today boasts little to attract tourists (all that remains of its château are segments of the 14th-century ramparts), but it does have an almost mythical past. Founded in the 5th century BC, it was here that Petrarch first laid eyes on his beloved Laura, about whom he would later write some of the world's most famous love poems *(see page 39)*. The wine grown on the neighbouring hillsides is called, most appropriately, the *Cuvée des Amours* (Love Vintage).

Another town of literary significance lies on the D5 between Graveson and St-Rémy-de-Provence. **Maillane** 20 was both the birth and burial place of Frédéric

ow:
ato picker.

Frédéric Mistral and the Félibrige

Greetings, empire of the sun, bordered
Like a silver edge by the glistening Rhône!
Empire of pleasure and of joy,
Wondrous empire of Provence, who
Enchants the world with your name alone.
Frédéric Mistral (1830–1914)

Mistral, the man not the wind, is a hallowed figure in Provence, a poet who dedicated his life to the revival and preservation of the Provençal language and culture. Provençal is not a dialect of French but a Latin-based language spoken throughout most of Southern France until quite recently. The imposition of standard French throughout the country in the 19th century, and the banning of regional languages in schools, press and government meant the decline of Provençal, along with other regional languages, such as Basque and Breton.

Mistral was a Provencal patriot, who resented the standardisation of French imposed by Paris, refusing even to be considered for the Académie Française. He was a founding father of the group of like-minded poets known as the Félibrige, who wished to encourage a revival of the language through the promotion of literary works celebrating the Provençal tongue.

Other members of this group of latter-day troubadours included the well-respected Avignonnais printer Théodore Aubanel, and Joseph Roumanille, Mistral's teacher and inspiration. It is said that Roumanille first had the idea for the Félibrige after discovering his Provençal speaking mother in tears because she could not understand the French poems her son had written.

With his flowing white beard and broad-brimmed hats Mistral looked like Buffalo Bill, who once came to see him he was so famous. He was born and stayed in the little village of Maillane in the Crau near Arles, deriving inspiration from the local peasants and their regional traditions, writing for them in a language they understood. His most famous epic poem is *Mireille*, a Tess of the D'Urbervilles of the Camargue, which was first published in 1859. It was subsequently turned into an opera, of which it has been said, "One should listen to *Mireille* as one would a Mass."

Mistral tried to write prose as close to the speech of the peasants as he could, preserving local expressions and rural imagery. He also produced a definitive Provençal–French dictionary, and his *Memoirs*, the most readable of his works today, are full of detail about Provençal life. Mistral was awarded the Nobel Prize in 1904 for his achievement in reviving a regional language as a literary medium. He is the only writer in a minority language ever to have been awarded the prize. Typically he decided to found the Musée Arlaten in Arles, one of France's most important regional collections, with his prize money. According to Mistral's wish the attendants wear Arlesien costume, and labels come in French and Provençal only.

While Mistral may have ultimately failed to revive the Provencal language he thus established a fashion for collections of regional memorabilia and a greater awareness of the value of local peasant traditions. ❑

LEFT: bust of Provença standard-be Frédéric Mi (1830–1914

Map pages 48–9

Mistral *(see opposite)*. The house where the poet lived from 1876 until his death in 1914 has been turned into a museum, the **Museon Mistral** (11 avenue Lamartine; closed Mon; entrance fee; tel: 04 90 95 74 06), containing his desk and gloves as he left them, many of his books, and portraits of him, his wife and friends. He is buried in the cemetery just down the street from his former home.

The D5 runs directly into **St-Rémy-de-Provence** ㉑, the mini-capital of the area. St-Rémy makes a fine base for any vacation in the Alpilles, especially for those wishing to avoid the greater bustle of Arles. The town is located right in the middle of the region, it possesses many attractions of its own and is, all-in-all, an extremely pleasant place to spend time.

St-Rémy is also the place to come for those interested in herbalism, for which it is the recognised centre. During the 1960s and 1970s, the number of *herboristes* in Provence declined, due to the growing popularity of chemical substitutes, but in recent years there has been a resurgence in the use of natural products, and there are now many charming small shops selling *herbes de provences*, soaps, oils and teas.

Herbs are only one aspect of St-Rémy's popularity. Like a large number of the larger towns in the Bouches-du-Rhône, at the heart of the (relatively) new city lies a rather older city built in a round and criss-crossed with narow stone streets. In St-Rémy, these streets are labelled with names in Provençal as well as French, and several of the houses have been turned into museums.

One old house that hasn't been converted but is still worth taking a look at, stands along the carriero di Barrio de l'Espitau. The building has long been boarded up, but an exterior plaque proclaims its significance: "Here was born, on the 14th of December in 1503, Michel de Nostradame, alias Nostradamus, astrologer."

The cavernous **Collegiale St-Martin** is less modest. The ceiling of this church is

ow:
vities,
tagnettes.

decorated with faded blue paint and a sprinkling of gold stars and lit by numerous stained-glass windows. What really catches the eye, however, is the enormous and renowned organ – that dominates the church's anterior.

Crossing behind the church leads you to the **Musée des Alpilles** (rue du Parage; closed Jan and Feb, otherwise open daily; entrance fee; tel: 04 90 92 68 24), arranged within the 16th-century mansion of Mistral de Mondragon. This ethnological museum contains scores of photographs, portraits, costumes and household objects linked to the surrounding region.

One room features the minerals mined within the Alpilles including bauxite, limestone and sandstone. The building, which extends over an old alley as a courtyard, is also remarkable.

Across the street stands the **Hôtel de Sade**. Constructed during the 15th and 16th centuries, this is now the **Centre d'Archéologie** (Archaeological Museum; Hôtel de Sade, rue du Parage; open daily; entrance fee; tel: 04 90 92 64 04), housing all the objects discovered at the nearby site of Glanum, from votive altars to pottery to bones.

Glanum ㉒ and **les Antiques** ㉓ lie just outside the city on the route de Baux. Once the site of a major Phocaean trading post, constructed beside a sacred spring, they are the town's top tourist attractions (open: daily; entrance fee; tel: 04 90 92 23 79; www.monuments-france.fr).

Les Antiques stands on the right-hand side of the road and comprises a commemorative arch and a mausoleum. The arch, situated across what was once the road connecting Spain to Italy, was built during the reign of Augustus to indicate the entrance to the city of Glanum. The mausoleum is a funereal monument on three levels that was dedicated to Caius and Lucius Caesar, the two grandsons of Augustus who died prematurely. The mausoleum has been particularly well preserved, and both it and the arch are amazing pieces of Roman stonework.

BELOW: herb bath oils from St-Rémy-de Provence.

Map
pages
148–9

Glanum is located just across the road. Originally Celto-Ligurian, a sanctuary city and then a flourishing point of commerce during the Gallo-Greek years and later Roman times, it was virtually destroyed by invaders in the 3rd century. Excavations continue to uncover archaeological treasures, and facsimile columns give scale and sense to the site.

Posted in between Glanum and the centre of town is the **Clinique de St-Paul**, where Van Gogh commited himself after slicing off his earlobe in Arles. The tiny cloisters of the medieval monastery, **St-Paul-de-Mausole**, which houses the clinic, can be visited, but the still-active rest home can not.

One pleasant way to spend a meditative afternoon in St-Rémy is fishing. Follow the avenue Antoine de la Salle, just down the road from the clinic, until you see the sign for le Lac on the chemin de Barrage. At its end lies the **Lac de Peiroou** (Lake Perioou, meaning "cauldron" in Provençal). The lake is reserved for fishing – you're not supposed to swim there – and behind it is a nice park for picnicking.

If you are feeling lazy on a hot afternoon, stroll up to the sandy square in front of the *syndicat d'initiative* (tourist information office) and you will find the spot where the locals gather daily to play *boules*.

Les Baux-de-Provence

When you're ready for a little change of scenery, take the D99 west and switch onto the D27 south. This perilous route climbs up into the peak of the Alpilles, overlooking the aptly named **Val d'Enfer** (Valley of Hell). Narrow stone cliffs cut into the winding road on one side, and on the other you will find a sheer drop. Keep both hands on the steering wheel, and pray you don't meet another car.

From the **Cave de Sarragon**, the eyrie peak dominated by les Baux comes into view. But first, before making the prerequisite tour of this Provence-style ghost town, stop in on the **Cathédrale d'Images** (Val d'Enfer, 13520 les Baux-de-

OW: Roman
ze on les
ques.

Provence; open daily Mar–Jan; entrance fee; tel: 04 90 54 38 65). Movie buffs will recognise the spot as the site of both Jean Cocteau's *Orpheus* and *Antigone*.

Even as you near the huge covered quarry-turned-theatre, the cool air of its interior envelops you. When you step inside its darkened caverns, cold blackness surrounds you. Then, as your eyes begin to adjust, you realize that continually changing slides are being projected in monumental sizes over the rocky crevasses of the walls.

Originally, the quarry belonged to the citadel of **les Baux-de-Provence** ㉔. Set on an imposing site way above rocky outcrops that tumble into deep valleys, the site of les Baux has been occupied for the past 5,000 years. Its fame, however, comes from the period between the years 1000 and 1400 when the bold and arrogant Lords of Baux made their presence felt throughout the region.

The feudal life of les Baux offers a fascinating paradox. Here, "amidst this chaos of monumental stones and impregnable fortresses, inhabited by men whose roughness was only matched by that of their suits of armour, the 'Respect of the Lady' and ritual adoration of her beauty was born." The patronage of the troubadours by these violent lords engendered the first "Court of Love", and much of France's literary tradition emerged from their bloody citadel.

Today, more than 1½ million tourists a year come to see where once the poets roamed and the lords raged, with July and August being close to unmanageable. Craft shops and ice-cream boutiques spill out of many of the old buildings. The impenetrable les Baux has become the ultimate in tourist traps.

The spot divides into two parts – the ancient city, containing the ruins of the feudal court, and the village, where some 60 people still live and the shops and galleries now stand. In winter, the number of inhabitants drops to about 40, and ice and snow ravage the exposed

BELOW: the heights of les Baux.

Map
n pages
148–9

peaks. Over the years, les Baux has become something of a retreat, but the number of year-round artisans is currently on a decline.

The village boasts several museums. The **Musée Yves Brayer** (Hôtel Porcelet, rue de l'Eglise; open daily; tel: 04 90 54 36 99) contains many of Brayer's oil paintings of the region. The **Fondation Louis Jou** (Hôtel Brion, Grande Rue; open daily, 8am–10pm, by appointment only; entrance fee; tel: 04 90 54 34 17) exhibits typographical presses, wood blocks and manuscripts.

Best-preserved of all the monuments in the old city is the **Eglise de St-Vincent**, which has a central nave dating back to the 12th century and stained glass that is a striking *mélange* of ancient and modern. Across the road is the lovely 17th-century **Chapelle des Pénitents Blancs**, decorated by Brayer. The apt theme of its mural, painted in 1974, is the shepherds of Provence, with an Alpilles Nativity. Finally in this little corner, cut directly into the rock face, is the **Galerie St-Vincent** with more modern paintings and some notable sculptures.

The **Tour de Brau**, which was built at the end of the 14th century, marks the entrance into the **Cité Morte** (Ancient City). A tour of the Cité Morte begins with the 12th-century **Chapelle de St-Blaise**. Beside the chapel lies a small modern cemetery filled with fragrant lavender.

Continue further up to the top of the ruins, where there is a round tower from which the Baux family must have surveyed the valley with watchful eyes. The view from this point is incredible. In the distance, the Alpilles sweep across the countryside. Pepper fields and olive groves, all fof which are framed by white stone outcrops, nestle below.

More of the Ancient City can be found along the northern ramparts. The energetic can climb them to attain even wider views or to investigate what is left of the 15th-century castle, the 10th-century keep and the Tour (tower) Paravelle. ❑

LOW: the
od life at
Oustau de
Baumanière.

Map on pages 148–9

THE CAMARGUE

This area, which lies within the Bouches-du-Rhône, is a birdwatcher's paradise, an equestrian's dream, a historian's treasure chest, a gourmet's delight, and a windsurfer's playground

The **Camargue** lies directly to the south of the Pays d'Arles and, although officially a part of the Bouches-du-Rhône, is very much in a world of its own. Almost triangular in shape, bordered to the west by the Petit-Rhône, which flows to the sea past Stes-Maries-de-la-Mer, and to the east by the Grand-Rhône, which runs down from Arles, its unusual natural environment has helped to shape its unique history.

Most of the region is marsh and lagoon, creating an ideal setting for one of France's greatest wildlife reserves. The area also provides a spiritual home for the country's gypsies, stages a national windsurfing championship, offers the joy of riding across beaches and salt plains, and provides the tourist with a range of historic castles and churches to visit.

At the same time the Camargue can turn into a tourist's nightmare. The celebrated horizons that inspired the Provençal poet Frédéric Mistral and the glorious light that fascinated Vincent van Gogh have also encouraged an onslaught of tourism, resulting in the construction of simulated-rustic hotels and brash campsites, leaving behind a pile of debris generated by summer holidaymakers.

Coping with tourism

To get the best from the area, which covers more than 800 sq. km (480 sq. miles), takes careful planning. It's advisable to bear two things in mind: firstly, that it is not always possible to wander off the main track without special permits; secondly, the multiplicity of attractions makes it exceptionally popular with tourists, particularly families with children, in July and August. During the high season, demand often exceeds both space and services available. Be warned, however: mosquitoes are quite a problem here and you should take precautions to protect yourself against them. Proposals to spray them are frowned upon since this would upset the ecology of the region. Creams, nets and plug-ins are probably the best deterrents.

Despite the growth of tourism, there is still much worth seeing in the Camargue and, with a little forethought, you can get around most of its downfalls. Any exploration of the region entails a certain amount of unavoidable zigzagging, due to the layout of the land, so some people may prefer to stay on its edge near Arles and visit during a series of day trips.

Once within the region, travellers will find themselves with a wide selection of ways to get around. The curious blend of marsh, swamp and salt plain, which have

LES GARDIANS

The Camargue cowboys *(gardians)* are a key element in the Provençal mystique, clinging passionately to their traditional way of life, herding the small black bulls destined for the arenas of Nîmes or Arles, and riding their fine white horses. Their costume – flat black hat, leather chaps, high leather boots, velvet jackets and cowboy cut shirts in Provençal fabric – is reminiscent of the American West, although the *gardians* insist that they predate American cowboys.

Many still live on *manades* (bull-breeding ranches), in the Camargue, in traditional cabins, low white houses with reed-thatched roofs and rounded north ends as a protection against the blasts of the mistral wind. If you enquire about the *manades* that offer horseriding or demonstrations, you will be able to see *gardians* at work, or they can be seen parading proudly on horseback before the bullfights and festivals in Arles and Nîmes.

CEDING ES: …ering bulls a bullfight. **…:** white …ses beside …*as.*

led to the establishment of numerous wildlife parks, means that one can either journey by boat, by jeep, on horseback or on a bicycle. Real nature lovers will probably find that some areas can best be discovered on foot.

Even if you decide only to spend a few days in the region, visits to two or three well-chosen spots can reveal an amazingly rich variety of wildlife. And the real appeal of the Camargue lies in its wildlife: wild white horses, black bulls, a great variety of birdlife, salt-water vegetation and swamps and lakes.

Getting to know the area

For a good introduction to the region, take the N570 west from Arles to the **Musée Camarguais** ㉕, located at **Mas du Pont du Rousty** (Stes-Maries-de-la-Mer; closed Tues; entrance fee; tel: 04 90 97 10 82). This sheep farm-cum-regional museum contains an exhibition illustrating the history and traditional way of life of the Camargue. Especially notable is the museum's coverage of the different terrains in the region, which explains how the wildlife of fresh-water marshes differs from that of the salt lagoons and from that of the coastal dykes. Such contrasts are central to the enduring allure of this fabulous region – don't be surprised, for example, to suddenly see a flock of pink flamingoes, inhabitants of the marsh, in full flight over an industrial salt plant.

For a hands-on look, take the signposted footpath that lies to the rear of the museum and leads to the beginning of the marshes. The walk will take you about an hour and give you a personal feel for these strange flatlands. At first, you will be struck by the croaking of frogs, then the colour of the flowers, which range from alofile plants to tamarisk and, during the warmer six months of the year, daisies, irises and asphodels. In addition, you will see a wide selection of birds: the curious black-winged stilts with their long pink legs, herons and all sorts of wading birds such as the ringed plovers.

BELOW: Camargue bulls.

Map
n pages
148–9

Towards St-Gilles

Once you've left the Mas du Pont du Rousty, continue west along the D570 towards **Albaron**. This route will take you past both paddy and wheat fields – land that has been recovered from the swamps over the past 40 years. En route, you will probably see numerous advertisements for roadside ranches, which are usually complete with wagon wheels and mock "western" frontage. Many of these ranches run pony-trekking and safari trips into the marshes. The trips can be for just an afternoon or a full day.

At Albaron, a right turn onto the D37 will lead you into **St-Gilles** ㉖, a busy little agricultural town, which is well worth visiting for the magnificent carvings on the western front of the town's 12th-century church – one of the masterpieces of Provence. Upon entering the structure, you will find a remarkable stone spiral staircase, which managed to survive extensive destruction during the Wars of Religion (1562–98).

OW: portal the church St-Gilles.

The Etang de Vaccarès

If you had taken a left-hand turn in Albaron onto the D37, you would have entered the **Rhône Delta**, home of the **Etang de Vaccarès**. Travelling in this direction will provide you with excellent views of pink flamingoes and other water fowl, even from a car. On foot, a perceptive eye should be able to spot beavers, turtle or lime-green tree frogs.

The famous black bulls of the Camargue also roam here, and sometimes (but not as often as postcards may have you believe) you will see a *gardian (see page 189)* astride his white horse.

Some say that the white horses of the Camargue are the descendants of the wild horses that populated prehistoric Gaul and are depicted in the ancient cave paintings at Lascaux. Others claim that the horses are either of North African origin or that they were first introduced from Tibet.

To get a closer look at the horses, you may want to check in at one of the Camargue's "ranches", where the *gardians* take

you out on horseback to visit the marshes. The *mas* belonging to Paul Ricard (of the apéritif fame) at **Méjanes** ㉗ is especially well publicised. Here, you will find an efficient trekking centre, and some particularly knowledgeable *gardians*, who work in the winter months as herdsmen.

If you choose to travel without a guide, remember that the lagoon is a protected area. Hunting, fishing and the picking of plants and flowers are all prohibited.

Motorists will find few alternative routes once in the area beside the lagoon. This shouldn't matter since the views over seascapes, sandbanks and lagoon as you follow the curve of the *étang* east are magnificent. Butterfly-lovers will be delighted to discover a rich variety of these lepidopterous insects here, including the Southern White Admiral, Swallowtails and Spanish Festoons.

Eventually, you will start to see powdery white hills and salt pans decorating the landscape. This southeastern corner of the Camargue, leading down to **Salin-de-Giraud** ㉘, is the French capital for salt production, and over half of the country's supply comes from here.

This area is also the gateway to the Camargue's beaches. After a long hot drive, few things are more refreshing than racing into the Mediterranean and then collapsing behind a sand dune for an afternoon's siesta. One word of caution, however, if you've parked your car out of sight. Sadly, the last few summers have witnessed a deplorable increase in thefts by seaside resorts. It's advisable to leave your car visibly empty and to keep any valuables with you.

Continue along the D36 to what becomes a much narrower track and you will reach the nudist beach, **Plage de Piémanson** *(see panel, below left)*. For the more modest, the **Plage d'Arles** *(see panel)* is located on the same stretch of coast.

A saintly city

If you are lucky, you may be able to find a private boat operator along one of these beaches who can take you directly over the sea to **Stes-Maries-de-la-Mer** ㉙. However, if you prefer to drive, return by the D36 to the D37 up to Albaron, then head back south on the other side of the Etang de Vaccarès along the D570. At twilight this journey is a bewitching experience, with the setting sun casting its colours over the lagoon.

During the Middle Ages Stes-Maries-de-la-Mer stood several kilometres inland, and even as recently as 100 years ago its outlying borders were still a good 200 metres (600 ft) from the sea. Today, however, it is a flourishing resort, right on the border of the water.

The encircling seas have also brought scores of eastern visitors over the centuries. The town owes its name to an early group of these: Mary Jacoby (sister of the Virgin Mary), Mary Magdalene, Mary Salome (mother of Apostles John and James), Martha and the miraculously resurrected Lazarus, along with their Egyptian servant Sarah.

According to legend, these early Christians had set out to sea from Palestine *circa* AD 40 in a small boat without sails.

LOCAL BEACHES

Anyone familiar with beaches along the Côte d'Azur may well wonder why the local authorities have bothered to make any distinction between "nudist" beaches, such as the Plage de Piémanson *(see picture, right)* and "normal" beaches, but they do. And, true enough, there is something startling about watching middle-aged couples barbecuing in the nude.

Most people, however, soon get used to it. Besides, playing boules in the nude is more than fashionable nowadays – it is positively hip.

If you don't feel up to baring all, you will find plenty of other sandy stretches without nudists along the same coastline. The Plage d'Arles will give you more chances to glimpse sea birds, such as the yellow-legged gulls, slender-billed gulls or the tern as it dives into the water for a fish. A fine breeze blows across these waters, making them particularly good for windsurfing.

RIGHT: nude *boules* at the Plage de Piémans

Map on pages 148–9

They were miraculously washed ashore, safe and sound, on this spot. In thanks, they built a chapel to the Virgin, and Mary Jacoby, Mary Salome and Sarah remained in the Camargue as evangelists.

After their deaths, the two Marys that had stayed in the Camargue and Sarah became the subject of pilgrimage. In the 9th century, the **Eglise de Notre-Dame-de-la-Mer** was built in place of the simple chapel that existed on that site and was fortified against invading Saracens. Excavations beneath this structure, begun in 1448 under the behest of "Good" King René, led to the discovery of a still-extant well and a spring filled with "the fragrances of sweet-scented bodies". The remains of the saints were uncovered in this same spot. Their tomb was placed in the church's **Chapelle de St-Michel**. The stones on which the bodies had rested are kept below in the crypt and have become "miracle" stones. They are said to have the power to cure sterility in women and to be able to heal painful eyes.

During the holiday season Stes-Maries-de-la-Mer is unquestionably a commercial resort. The town's busy pedestrian zones are lined with souvenir shops, and the many reasonably priced hotels and camping sites do well here. There are numerous places where you can rent horses and boats, swim or play tennis during the day, and at night some of the area's hottest clubs swing into action. Bullfights *(see page 197)* are held in the local arena.

A less strenuous attraction in Stes-Maries-de-la-Mer is the **Musée Baroncelli** (rue Victor Hugo; closed Tues and mid-Nov–Apr; tel: 04 90 97 87 60) is a funky little museum with material on bullfighting and Camargue traditions donated by Marquis Folco de Baroncelli-Javon, champion of the *gardians*. Stuffed flamingoes and other rare birds are also on show – not very politically correct but nevertheless quite fascinating.

If the bustle is starting to get to you, escape by booking a boat trip along the

Petit-Rhône. Go down to the landing stage near Baroncelli-Javon's tomb to join one of these excursions, which leave at regular intervals. Photographers will doubtless be thrilled by the action shots they can take of Camargue wildlife from the water, especially of the marsh birds. These boat trips also offer the opportunity to see the herds of bulls and horses running along the banks of the river.

If you would prefer to find some quiet beaches in the area and are willing to challenge weathered tracks off the main road, head west out of Stes-Maries-de-la-Mer. Along here you will be able to find a place to park. Leave your car and climb the sand dunes, and you should be rewarded with some empty spaces away from the crowds. Van Gogh, who was fascinated by the light in this region, painted his *Bâteaux de pêche de Stes-Maries (The boats of Stes-Maries)* on these beaches.

At certain times of year, stretches of the shore nearer to town can get very busy, however, so pick your resting place with care. Frédéric Mistral, who set the tragic end of his famous Provençal work *Mireille* (*Mireio* in Provençal) on these sandy shores, would no longer be able to write of it "no trees, no shade and not a soul".

Regional festivities

This part of the country is famed for its festivities. Even Sarah, the servant of the saints' after whom Stes-Maries-de-la-Mer is named, has her own cult following. Considered the patron saint of gypsies, she is remembered on 24 and 25 May each year with two special nights of celebration. Gypsies from all over the surrounding regions descend upon the town for horse-racing, bull-running and a variety of other festivities.

In the evenings, the spirit of the *fiesta* runs wild here, and the frenzied excitement of gypsy music and dancing fills the air. At the same time, during this period, Stes-Maries-de-la-Mer is a meeting place for the bullherders of the Camargue. In recent years, the festival has become a

BELOW: pink flamingoes – a familiar sight around the lagoons.

Map
n pages
148–9

major media event, attracting television teams, film crews, journalists and even some politicians.

Another day of celebration in the region comes on the last Sunday of October. This is the special feast day for Mary Salome, and it is commemorated by colourful processions around the church of Notre-Dame-de-la-Mer in Stes-Maries. During the high tourist season in summer, this church is extremely crowded. If you decide to battle with the crowds and visit it anyway, climb to the roof for a stunning panoramic view across the sand hills and down to the waves as they splash against the sunlit shore.

Birdwatchers' paradise

As you leave Stes-Maries by the D570 main road, you may want to stop at the information centre at **Ginès** ❸⓿. Here, an excellent exhibition gives information on the flora and fauna that are indigenous to the area and grow in the outlying land. Next door to the information centre is the **Parc Ornithologique de Pont de Gau** (Ornithological Park; route d'Arles, 4 km/2½ miles from Stes-Maries; open daily: Apr–Sept, 9am until nightfall; Oct–Mar, 10am–5pm; entrance fee; tel: 04 90 97 82 62), where you can see bird species of the region in aviaries and also follow birdwatching trails.

The Camargue is a great place for bird-watchers. Springtime is the ideal season to come spotting, as this is when the large variety of migrants visit the Camargue on their journey back north. The best time of the day to look for birds is generally in the early morning.

The Western Camargue

Continue north on the D38, then turn left onto the D58 and you will enter the plain of Aigues-Mortes. The drive along here will take you across a part of the Camargue that has changed little in decades. From time to time, you will spot an authentic *mas* – a single-storey cabin with a thatched, mistral-defying roof.

LOW:
ung gypsy.

The plain borders on a rich agricultural area that produces grapes and cereals. The tower, known as the **Tour Carbonnière** ㉛, at the end of the drive along the D58 will give you the chance to look out over these fields, to the foothills of the Cévennes in the northwest, the Petite Camargue in the east and across the salt flats of Aigues-Mortes to the south. Built as an outpost to the garrison of Aigues-Mortes during the time of the Crusades, the tower guards what once was the only route in and out of town.

The area around **Aigues-Mortes** ㉜ is made up of salty lagoons and water channels, where the Rhône meets the sea. The town itself was built amidst the marshes, salt flats and lagoons in 1241. It was named for its location (Aigues-Mortes means "dead waters") as it contrasted with the town of **Aigues-Vives** ("living waters") that lay in the hills about 20 km (12 miles) further north.

Today Aigues-Mortes is a very well-preserved medieval town that, architecturally, has changed little on a superficial level. The ramparts, which dominate the surrounding countryside, still remain intact. With a little imagination, it is possible to picture this town as the springboard from which King Louis IX (the future St Louis) launched the Seventh Crusade in order to liberate Jerusalem.

When photographed at twilight from the southwest, the **battlements** at Aigues-Mortes make a fabulous picture, as sharp-silhouetted shapes emphasise the strategic position of this curious medieval garrison town. If by now you have become adept at bird-spotting, climb up and take a look out over the battlements. It is not uncommon to see kestrels, marsh harriers and bee-eaters, typified by their blue, yellow and green plumage, as they somersault after tasty insects.

Once you've passed through the gateway, you will find a number of attractive narrow streets criss-crossing the town. They lead to the central square, which is overlooked by a statue of St Louis, the

BELOW: preparing for the *feria du cheval.*

Map
on pages
148–9

patron of the town who granted it its special rights and privileges.

Although you will find the square lined by cafés and restaurants, you can get a better meal by wandering down the adjacent and more secluded side streets. Look for a restaurant that specialises in local dishes such as *Gardiane de Taureaux* (a delicious beef stew cooked with olives) or local seafood dishes.

After dining, you may want to climb another tower, **Tour Constance**, and the town's ramparts, which provide an excellent overview of Aigues-Mortes. Look down to the northeast sector of the town, and you will see what originally was all one farm owned by the Knights of St-John until the Revolution.

The town has a population of 5,000 and, although its importance as a seaport has diminished, it is still a centre for salt production and vine growing. Visits to "Les Salins du Midi" (the Salt Marshes of the South) are organised in July and August on Wednesday and Friday afternoons by the tourist office, which stands in the central square.

The local wine, Listel, is grown commercially and is remarkable for being a *vin de sable*. This means that it is made from vines that grow directly out of the sand. The white is called *gris de gris* and the red is known as *rubis*. Several *caves* in the area offer free wine-tasting.

Local superstitions

The horses that play such an important part in the life of the Camargue have also been woven into one of legends that surround Aigues-Mortes. Young children are told that if they misbehave they will be dragged off by "Lou Drape", a horse that is supposed to hover over the ramparts of Aigues-Mortes at night. It is said that the horse's body can lengthen to carry away as many as 100 naughty children on its back into the marsh, where it will then devour them. Even today, legends and superstitions are an integral part of life in the Camargue *(see pages 61–5).* ❑

LOW: the
margue
afront.

BULLFIGHTING

The "course Camarguaise", in which the bull is chased but not killed, is the style of bullfighting practised all over Provence. The *course* began as a game with lions, dogs, bears and men chasing bulls and then evolved into a contest between human wits and the speed and weight of the animal. Now the real competition is between the *manades* (bull-breeders), who raise bulls, and the *raseteurs*, who take the animals on. The contest begins with the *abrivado*, when the competitors parade around the arena; the bulls then enter the ring. The raseteurs, dressed in white, try to snatch the *cocarde* (rosette) and *ficelles* (tassels) attached to the head of the bull, using a metal comb, called a *crochet*. The fighting season starts with the April feria and the gardian festival on May 1, when the Queen of Arles is crowned; it culminates at the beginning of July with the awarding of the coveted Cocarde d'Or prize.

Map
pages
202–3

ALPES-DE-HAUTE-PROVENCE

This area shows the rugged face of Provence. Tourism is just starting to take off, with visitors attracted by the vertiginous gorges, azure lakes and field upon field of gorgeous lavender

Perhaps Provence's least-known *département* and certainly the least densely populated, the **Alpes-de-Haute-Provence** seem at first glance to miss out on much that makes the rest of Provence so attractive. Bypassed by the main artery of communications down the Val du Rhône, this vast region lacks the beaches and glitz of the Côte, the gems of art and architecture of the Vaucluse and the fertile vineyards and perfect *villages perchés* of the Var.

Instead, the Alpes-de-Haute-Provence show a wild, rugged face. The turbulent sweep of the Durance River and the desolate flatlands of the Plateau de Valensole, brought to life in summer by countless rows of lavender bushes, dominate the western region. Steep gorges to the south rise to heady alpine heights as you move north and east. In between are beautiful lakes, bizarre rock formations and inaccessible mountainous terrain.

Rustic Provence

Simplicity and practicality characterise the region's architecture. Stark defensive citadels crown many towns, and villages are constructed to give maximum protection against the elements. The much-vaunted climate – balancing on a happy axis of Provençal warmth and cool alpine clarity – can turn to harshly low temperatures in winter.

Ask any local to sum up life in this *département*, and they are likely to give the same answer: *pauvre* (poor). Like its architecture, the region's cultural heritage is marked by simplicity and austerity. Until recently, the inaccessibility of much of the country meant that progress arrived slowly and ancient traditions endured. Life followed the rural rhythms of the movement of sheep herds (known as *transhumance*) and was characterised by constant battles against the elements.

A changing region

Nonetheless, there has been a surprising amount of migration in the Alpes-de-Haute-Provence since the late 19th century. In common with the rest of inland Provence, many villages here were practically abandoned in the later part of the 20th century, as locals moved south to work in the more wealthy areas around the coast.

Since the 1960s, the Alpes-de-Haute-Provence have changed beyond recognition. The Durance has been tamed by an elaborate system of dams, providing fertile ground for fruit cultivation along the valley, and the region is now served along its length by the A51 *autoroute*. New jobs have been created in hydroelectricity and at the Cadarache Nuclear Research Centre.

CEDING
ES: hardy
ne sheep.
: the
nd Canyon
/erdon.
HT:
nder fields.

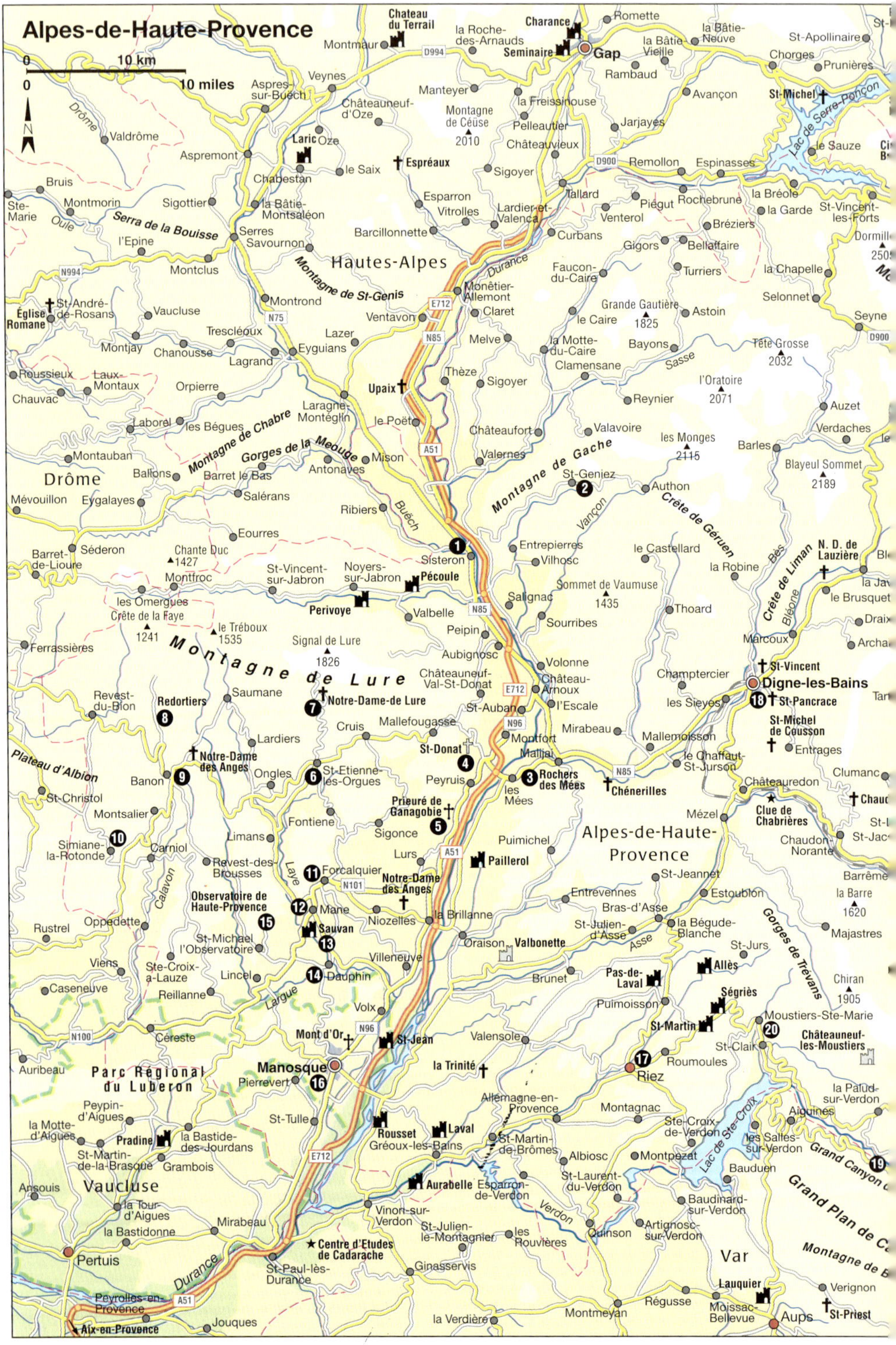

Alpes-de-Haute-Provence
0
10 km
0
10 miles
N
Chateau du Terrail
Montmaur
la Roche-des-Arnauds
Charance
Seminaire
Gap
Romette
la Bâtie-Neuve
la Bâtie-Vieille
St-Apollinaire
Chorges
Prunières
Rambaud
Veynes
Aspres-sur-Buëch
Manteyer
Châteauneuf-d'Oze
Montagne de Céüse
2010
la Freissinouse
Pelleautier
Jarjayes
Avançon
St-Michel
Lac de Serre-Ponçon
Drôme
Valdrôme
Laric
Oze
Châteauvieux
le Sauze
Aspremont
Espréaux
D900
Remollon
Espinasses
Bruis
Chabestan
le Saix
Sigoyer
Tallard
la Bréole
Ste-Marie
Montmorin
Sigottier
la Bâtie-Montsaléon
Esparron
Vitrolles
Lardier-et-Valença
Piégut
Venterol
Rochebrune
la Garde
St-Vincent-les-Forts
Oule
Serra de la Bouisse
Serres
Savournon
Barcillonnette
Curbans
Bréziers
l'Epine
Gigors
Bellaffaire
Montclus
Hautes-Alpes
Durance
Faucon-du-Caire
Turriers
la Chapelle
N994
Montagne de St-Genis
Monêtier-Allemont
Église Romane
St-André-de-Rosans
Montrond
Claret
Selonnet
Vaucluse
N75
Ventavon
E712
Grande Gautière
1825
le Caire
Astoin
Seyne
Trescléoux
Lazer
N85
Melve
la Motte-du-Caire
Bayons
D900
Montjay
Chanousse
Eyguians
Clamensane
Tête Grosse
2032
Lagrand
Sasse
Roussieux
Laux-Montaux
Thèze
Sigoyer
l'Oratoire
2071
Orpierre
Upaix
Chauvac
Reynier
Auzet
Laragne-Montéglin
le Poët
Laborel
les Bégues
Montagne de Chabre
Châteaufort
Valavoire
Verdaches
les Monges
2115
Barles
Gorges de la Meouge
Mison
A51
Valernes
Montauban
Antonaves
Montagne de Gache
Blayeul Sommet
2189
Ballons
Barret le Bas
Drôme
St-Geniez
Authon
Mévouillon
Eygalayes
Salérans
Vançon
Crête de Géruen
Ribiers
Buëch
Eourres
Entrepierres
Barret-de-Lioure
Séderon
Chante Duc
1427
Sisteron
Vilhosc
le Castellard
N. D. de Lauzière
Montfroc
St-Vincent-sur-Jabron
Noyers-sur-Jabron
Pécoule
la Robine
Bès
Crête de Liman
les Omergues
Sommet de Vaumuse
1435
le Brusquet
Crête de la Faye
1241
Perivoye
Salignac
Thoard
Bléone
Valbelle
N85
le Trébous
1535
Peipin
Sourribes
Ferrassières
Montagne de Lure
Signal de Lure
1826
Aubignosc
Marcoux
Châteauneuf-Val-St-Donat
Volonne
Champtercier
St-Vincent
Digne-les-Bains
Château-Arnoux
Revest-du-Bion
Redortiers
Saumane
E712
l'Escale
les Sieyès
St-Pancrace
Notre-Dame-de-Lure
St-Auban
Mirabeau
St-Michel de Cousson
Cruis
Mallefougasse
N96
Montfort
Mallemoisson
Lardiers
Malijai
Entrages
Plateau d'Albion
Notre-Dame des Anges
St-Donat
le Chaffaut-St-Jurson
N85
Banon
Ongles
St-Etienne-les-Orgues
Peyruis
Rochers des Mées
Clumanc
St-Christol
Chénerilles
Châteauredon
les Mées
Clue de Chabrières
Montsalier
Prieuré de Ganagobie
Mézel
Fontienne
Simiane-la-Rotonde
Limans
Sigonce
Puimichel
Alpes-de-Haute-Provence
Chaudon-Norante
Carniol
Lurs
A51
Paillerol
Revest-des-Brousses
Forcalquier
Barrême
Calavon
Laye
Notre-Dame des Anges
St-Jeannet
Observatoire de Haute-Provence
N101
Entrevennes
Estoublon
la Barre
1620
Mane
Bras-d'Asse
Rustrel
Oppedette
Niozelles
la Brillanne
St-Julien-d'Asse
la Bégude-Blanche
Majastres
St-Michel l'Observatoire
Sauvan
Oraison
Valbonette
Asse
Gorges de Trévans
St-Jurs
Viens
Ste-Croix-a-Lauze
Villeneuve
Allès
Chiran
1905
Lincel
Dauphin
Brunet
Pas-de-Laval
Caseneuve
Reillanne
Largue
Ségriès
Puimoisson
Volx
Moustiers-Ste-Marie
N100
Céreste
Mont d'Or
N96
St-Jean
Valensole
St-Martin
Châteauneuf-les-Moustiers
St-Clair
Auribeau
Parc Régional du Luberon
Manosque
la Trinité
Roumoules
Pierrevert
Riez
la Palud-sur-Verdon
Peypin-d'Aigues
Allemagne-en-Provence
Montagnac
Aiguines
la Motte-d'Aigues
St-Tulle
Rousset
Laval
Ste-Croix-de-Verdon
Pradine
la Bastide-des-Jourdans
St-Martin-de-Brômes
Lac de Ste-Croix
les Salles-sur-Verdon
Grand Canyon
St-Martin-de-la-Brasque
Grambois
Gréoux-les-Bains
Albiosc
Montpezat
E712
Bauduen
Ansouis
Vaucluse
Aurabelle
Esparron-de-Verdon
St-Laurent-du-Verdon
Grand Plan de C
la Tour-d'Aigues
Vinon-sur-Verdon
Verdon
Baudinard-sur-Verdon
Mirabeau
St-Julien-le-Montagnier
les Rouvières
Quinson
Artignosc-sur-Verdon
la Bastidonne
Centre d'Etudes de Cadarache
Montagne de B
Pertuis
Durance
St-Paul-lès-Durance
Ginasservis
Var
Lauquier
Verignon
Peyrolles-en-Provence
A51
Régusse
Moissac-Bellevue
Aups
St-Priest
Aix-en-Provence
Jouques
la Verdière
Montmeyan

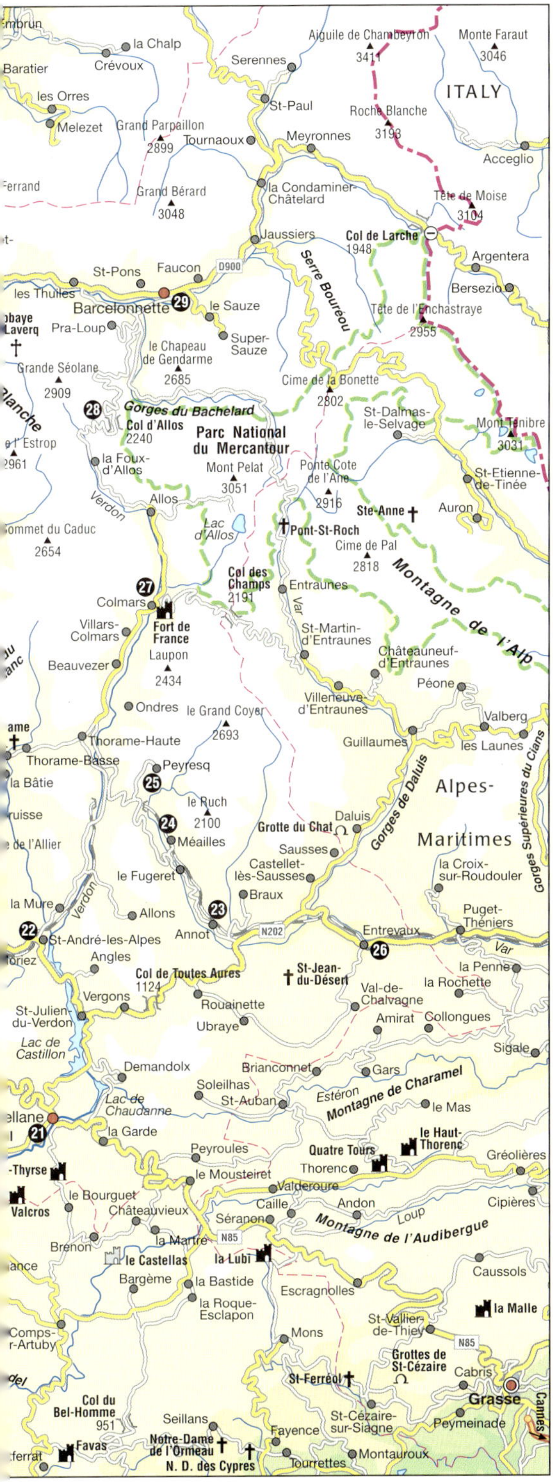

Tourism, although a good deal slower to develop here than in the more obviously enticing parts of Provence, has gained impetus in recent years. The spa towns of Digne-les-Bains and Gréoux-les-Bains both attract health-cure seekers, the northern alpine resorts lure skiers throughout the winter, and wind-surfers and hikers are attracted by the region's vast lakes and austere peaks.

The French press has devoted considerable space to the Alpes-de-Haute-Provence as the next French region to be "discovered". Wealthy Parisians now spend the summer in Manosque and increasing numbers of city-dwellers from Marseille buy holiday homes in the mountains here. The *pauvreté* (poverty) that has marked the lives of many of the *département's* inhabitants is still in evidence, but the impressive, singular beauty of the Alpes-de-Haute-Provence is increasingly attracting profitable new visitors.

Sisteron

The natural gateway to Provence, **Sisteron ❶**, hardly seems Provençal at all. This pretty, tidy town, dominated by a stark towering citadel, has a definite air of Dauphiné about it. Just to the north, the olive trees stop and, to all intents and purposes, you say goodbye to Provence.

Sisteron's setting – on the left bank of the Durance and looking across at the craggy **Rocher de la Baume** – is impressive. For centuries, people have passed through this strategically placed "gateway", lending it a feeling of lively, if not exactly cosmopolitan, activity. A bustling market, some light industry and a steady wave of tourists along the N85 maintain that atmosphere today.

In the past, such comings and goings brought Sisteron both good times and bad. Plague and typhus, carried by passing travellers and armies, decimated the population during the 14th, 17th and 18th centuries. Napoleon stopped here for lunch on a misty March day in 1815, when returning from exile on Elba. Still standing in the Rue Saunerie is the now-private **Bras d'Or** inn, owned at the time by the grandfather of the Sisteron novelist

Paul Arène (1843–96). A plaque commemorates the site where the imperial lunch was consumed.

Sisteron's most obvious crowd-puller, **La Citadelle** (open Mar–mid-Nov: open daily; entrance fee; tel: 04 92 61 27 57), the town's citadel, was originally built in the 13th century then redesigned by Henri IV's military engineer Jean Erard during the 16th. An impressive collection of keeps and dungeons, watchtowers and crenellated battlements stands on a massive rock topped by a small chapel.

The citadel's complex and fascinating history as a fortress and prison pales next to the blow dealt by our own age. On 15 August 1944, the Allies bombed it in an attempt to speed up the retreat of the German occupying army that had taken refuge there. More than 300 people died, and a quarter of Sisteron's fine medieval town was destroyed. Today the citadel provides an atmospheric setting for the Nuits de la Citadelle, Sisteron's summer festival of music, dance and theatre.

Fortunately, a good deal still remains of the **Vieille Ville** (old town) that sits huddled at the foot of the citadel rock. A mixture of modern boutiques and pleasant old-fashioned shops line its narrow streets, known here as *andrônes*, from the Latin word for "alleyway" or the Greek term for "between two houses", depending on which linguist you ask.

The bakers in the town sell the local speciality, *fougasse à l'anchois*, a delectable bread smeared with anchovies and sold by the kilo. Butchers display the locally celebrated Sisteron lamb, which is given a fragrant herbal flavour by the wild thyme and rosemary culled from pastures of the Haute Val du Durance (Upper Durance Valley).

Northeast of Sisteron, on the D3 in the direction of **St-Geniez** ❷, look out for a rock slab covered with Roman inscriptions. The **Pierre-Ecrite**, carved in the 5th century, records the conversion to Christianity of Claudius Dardanus, prefect of the Gauls. Tantalisingly, it mentions a

BELOW: the dam at Serre-Ponço

Map
pages
202–3

nearby "city of God", which was apparently founded by Claudius, though archaeologists have been unable to fix its exact setting.

For many centuries, the Durance was known as one of the "three scourges of Provence" (the *mistral* and the Parlement at Aix completed the triumvirate). In recent years, the river's unpredictable surges have been harnessed by a series of major dams beginning at **Serre-Ponçon** on the northernmost border of the *département*. Apple and pear orchards, planted since the 1960s on the newly irrigated alluvial plains, have brought a refreshing vigour to the once-ailing economy hereabouts. And hydro-electric power, nicknamed by locals *la houille blanche* (meaning "white coal"), has also brought added prosperity to the region.

Nonetheless, the Durance remains tortuous, complex and peppered with islets. It is one of the few rivers in Provence that contains more than a thin trickle of water in summer.

Limestone penitents

As the Durance snakes its way south and meets the Bléone arriving from the east, a sprawling collection of light industrial plants appears. Across the apex of the confluence, south of Château-Arnoux, the rocks known as **Rochers des Mées** ❸ stand eerily over miles of flat maize fields.

The village of les Mées itself does not tempt much, but the staggering "**Pénitents**", the name given to the curious row of limestone pinnacles outside it, do. The smooth, dolmen-shaped formations, some as high as 100 metres (330 ft), rise out of what seems like a dwarfed, stunted forest – some stand alone, some are clustered in groups – until they close ranks to form a single mini-*massif.*

The legends that surround these peaks have a sadness that echoes their lonely aspect. During the Arab invasions in the Middle Ages, a group of monks from the Montagne de Lure are said to have been attracted by the beauty of some Moorish girls. As the cowled, disgraced figures

ow:
vial plains,
ited with
t trees, in
north of the
artement.

were banished from the village, St Donatus turned them to stone, in punishment for their impropriety.

The religious theme continues on the opposite bank of the Durance, in the foothills of the **Montagne de Lure**. The ruins of the **Eglise de St-Donat** ❹, reached by the narrow D101, sit isolated in thick oak woods. Formerly the retreat of St Donatus, a 6th-century monk from Orléans, nowadays the church is in a sorry state, its floor covered with rubble and graffiti etched into its venerable stone. The eight mighty pillars that support its ancient vaulting and a faded-white apse, decorated with pale terracotta-coloured stars, hint at its former glory. This is one of Provence's few remaining examples of early medieval Romanesque architecture.

More obviously impressive is the nearby medieval **Prieuré de Ganagobie** ❺ (open Tues–Sun afternoons; guided tours available; free; tel: 04 92 68 00 04). Like St-Donat, this priory was in a dilapidated state until restoration work began on it in the 1960s. Now its principal attractions, other than the wonderful view of the Val du Durance to be had from its grounds, are its magnificent zigzag west portal and the stunning 12th-century mosaics, in red, black and white, that decorate the interior.

Alpine summits

The vast and forbidding Montagne de Lure is a continuation of the vine-rich Ventoux mountain range to the west; it is bordered by the Lubéron to the south. Its heights are reached via the little town of **St-Etienne-les-Orgues** ❻ that lies at its feet. The prosperity of this pretty village was traditionally based on medicinal remedies concocted from mountain herbs and sold by travelling pedlars.

A road lined with fir trees and, in summer, purple fields of lavender leads out of the village. Soon, the lavender stops, and the dense oak and fir forest of the mountain proper appears. Though seemingly deserted, this route becomes an animated pilgrims' way in August and September

BELOW: you goatherd wi one of her fl

Map
ı pages
202–3

each year, as locals continue the centuries-old tradition of pilgrimage to the isolated **Chapelle de Notre-Dame-de-Lure** ❼, located halfway to the summit.

Also founded by the reclusive St Donatus, Notre-Dame-de-Lure has none of the architectural distinction of the Eglise de St-Donat, but its setting is compensation enough. In summer, locals and tourists picnic in the shade of the lime trees that shelter the entrance to the church.

After Notre-Dame-de-Lure, the road to the summit rises in steep curves, edged in summer by seas of purple larkspur. The **Signal de Lure**, the mountain's summit (1,826 metres/5,990 ft) boasts an undistinguished *station de ski* and some of the most impressive panoramas to be found anywhere in Provence. Views of the Cévennes and Mt-Ventoux are interrupted only by the sight of soaring buzzards.

The wild isolation of the Lure inspired many of the novels of Jean Giono *(see box below right)*. Many have tried to locate Giono's settings, mostly without success. Nonetheless, it is widely believed that his fictional Aubignane is based on the ruined village of **Redortiers** ❽, just north of **Banon** ❾. Whether or not intimations of Giono appeal, it is worth making a visit to Banon to sample its renowned goat's cheese wrapped in chestnut leaves.

A 1980s' angle on Giono's literary theme is provided by the changes that have taken place in the beautiful, remote village of **Simiane-la-Rotonde** ❿. Simiane, dominated by the strange "rotunda" that gives the village its name, is today almost entirely composed of *maisons secondaires* (second homes). Outside the summer months, its closed shutters and deserted streets have much in common with the desolate ruins of Redortiers.

An unshaken heritage

No such cultural instability dogs the everyday life of one of the most appealing towns of the *département*, **Forcalquier** ⓫. The locals here happily welcome visitors in the summer but don't allow the brief

.OW:
t's cheese
n Banon.

JEAN GIONO

Writer Jean Giono (1895–1970) was a lifelong resident of Manosque *(see page 209)*. He was an ecologist and pacifist, imprisoned by the Nazis for his beliefs at the start of World War II, and by the French at the end because his philosophical love of nature had been twisted to support Nazi propaganda. He made his name with a series of novels on village life in the Alpes-de-Haute-Provence.

Giono's Provence has little in common with the sunny region of Pagnol or even Daudet. His main themes were the abandonment of the mountain villages, the destruction of the traditional patterns of rural life and the rough sensuality of man's communion with nature. In Manosque, visit the **Centre Jean Giono** (open Tues–Sat; entrance fee; tel: 04 92 70 54 54), featuring an exhibition on the writer, and his house, **Lou Parais** (montée des Vrais Richesses; tel: 04 92 87 73 03 to check opening times), north of the Old Town.

invasion to disrupt the rhythm of their prosperous lives. Forcalquier is at its best on Monday – the day of its wonderful weekly market. Countless stalls, groaning with local produce or stacked high with passable *objets artisanaux,* crowd the spacious **place du Bourguet** and the labyrinth of streets around it. The market acts as a magnet to people from the region who come to buy, sell or simply gossip in the pleasant marketplace cafés.

Forcalquier's air of independence has its roots in the 12th century, when the town was an independent state. During this period, the town served as the capital of Haute-Provence, making it a centre for culture and trade and a favourite residence of the counts of Provence.

The origin of the town's name, however, goes back much further. Situated on the Via Domitia, one of the three great Roman roads in Provence, Forcalquier is said to be derived from *furni calcarii*, Latin for the limestone kilns that the Romans hewed into the hillside.

Forcalquier boasts a clutch of fairly interesting sights, notably the **Couvent des Cordeliers**, a Franciscan convent, restored in the 1960s and now part privileged private housing, part visitable monument; the austere **Cathédrale de Notre Dame** on the main square; and the 19th-century **chapel** on the hill above the old town with a *table d'orientation* to help you identify the surrounding mountains.

The real flavour of Forcalquier, however, can be tasted more sharply simply by taking an aimless wander around the splendid alleyways of the **Vieille Ville** (Old Town). Almost every narrow street here is lined with fine stone doorways and arches that are decorated with chiselled plaques, scrolls and intricate relief.

Forcalquier seems to be a place where the exigencies of the 20th century have had to work hard to dislodge a firm historic anchor. However, preservation of the cultural heritage that emanates from Forcalquier has its official home a few miles south of the town.

BELOW: dus
at Montfuro

Map pages 02–3

The former priory, the **Prieuré de Salagon**, located just outside the village of **Mane** ⓬, has been converted into a major centre for local studies and research. As well as excellent permanent exhibitions covering local history and a botanical garden planted with the medicinal plants that once played a significant role in the region's economy, lectures are given throughout the summer on aspects of local rural life, architecture and customs.

Those with a taste for imposing country seats should combine a trip to Salagon and its priory with a visit to the **Château de Sauvan** ⓭, arguably the *département*'s finest 18th-century building. The Alpes-de-Haute-Provence is not known for its châteaux, and many are little more than small stately homes. Nonetheless, Sauvan possesses a classical elegance that merits its local title of "*Petit Trianon Provençal*".

Other delights in the region include the small hilltop village of **Dauphin** ⓮, the pretty series of *pigeonniers* in and around **Limans**, and the **Observatoire de Haute-Provence** ⓯ (open Wed only; guided tours available; entrance fee; tel: 04 92 70 64 00), which attracts astronomers from all over France.

Manosque

The town of **Manosque** ⓰ has an elegance and sense of refinement that sets it apart from the rest of the Alpes-de-Haute-Provence. Largely as a result of its position – a plum site on the Durance within easy reach of Forcalquier, the Montagne de Lure, the Plateau de Valensole and the Grand Canyon du Verdon – Manosque has become the principal economic axis of the *département*.

In the 1970s, Manosque was a sleepy town with a population of less than 5,000, but today that number has increased more than fourfold. Blossoming agriculture in the Val du Durance (Manosque is known for its yellow – as opposed to "white" – peaches), the proximity of the Cadarache nuclear research centre that has drawn scientists and their families to settle here, and

ow: inside Château ;auvan.

the relentless flow of tourists have combined to give Manosque an energetic air of modernity.

Fortunately, progress has not seeped fully into the bricks and mortar of the town, which remains essentially medieval in layout and character. Manosque covers a small hill above the Durance; "a tortoise shell in the grass" in the words of town's own Jean Giono *(see box, page 207).*

Two imposing stone archways, the tall crenellated **Porte Saunerie** and the **Porte Soubeyran**, stand guard at the entrance to the **Vieille Ville** (Old Town). These are linked by the town's main artery, the Grande Rue. Encircling old Manosque is a busy ring road that has replaced the town's ancient ramparts.

Stepping through either of the *portes* (gates) brings you into a pedestrian area of narrow streets, honey-coloured churches and fountain-filled squares. Outwardly, Manosque seems to have survived the onslaught of its astonishing growth, though the rows of chic modern shops and small pretty squares converted to parking areas jolt you back to the future.

Manosque *la Pudique* (the Modest), the nickname given to the town in the 16th century, seems rather inappropriate today. The name derives from a tale, almost certainly apocryphal, concerning a visit by François I. The young king showed more than a passing interest in the daughter of a local dignitary. To repel the king's advances and preserve her honour, the young girl promptly disfigured her face with sulphur.

The Plateau de Valensole

The sweep south from the Montagne de Lure, through Manosque, and west to the vast plains of Valensole and Puimoisson mark the boundaries of Giono's Provence. He called the wide, flat Plateau de Valensole his "magnificent friend". Today the **Plateau de Valensole** is France's principal centre of lavender cultivation, but this was not always the case. Lavender production is a 19th-century phenomenon, and the almond trees that blossom so

BELOW: alpi
peaks north
Digne-les-B

Map
pages
202–3

spectacularly on the plain in early spring are a much more ancient element of the economy. Summer is the time to see the Valensole in all its purple magnificence. On the cusp of July and into August, around the time of the harvest, the dusky violet rows stretch away to the horizon and the unmistakable odour fills the air.

The few villages that huddle on the plain, surviving the winter lashings of wind and hailstorms are for the most part unremarkable. The exception is **Riez ⓱**, which is notable for its four Corinthian columns – remains of a Roman temple of Apollo – standing alone in a field just outside the town. The ancient Merovingian baptistry is Riez's other great "sight". What is most appealing about the town, however, particularly in its old quarter, is a pleasing scruffiness and an attitude of *laissez-faire* that pervades the streets, making the people seem relaxed and welcoming. North of the old town is the **Musée Nature de Provence** (4 allée Louis Gardiol; closed Sun, Mon and public hols; entrance fee; tel: 04 92 77 82 80), which explains the geology of Provence with a good collection of fossils and minerals.

By contrast, **Digne-les-Bains ⓲**, the modern-day capital of the Alpes-de-Haute-Provence and last stop on the Train des Pignes, is not at all scruffy. A genteel spa town, it lies northeast of Riez in the imposing Pré-Alpes de Digne. It was here that Victor Hugo set the first chapters of *Les Misérables*.

However, Digne is not simply a town of fictional *malheureux*, rheumatics and departmental officials. The shady boulevard Gassendi tempts with the pleasant cafés along its length, and in early August Digne asserts its position as capital of the region with a boisterous festival and procession called the *Corso de la Lavande*.

Four days of revelry climax in a grand procession. An array of huge flower-bedecked floats, some modern in theme, some traditionally Provençal, glide down the main boulevard to uproarious applause, preceded by the town's sanitation depart-

OW: a
·tan monk
esidence at
Alexandra
·id-Néel
ndation.

LAVENDER

The fragrant lavender bush, otherwise known as *lavandula officinalis*, is one of Provence's main claims to fame, and the principal crop on the Plateau de Valensole. In summer, when the lavender bushes on the plateau are in full bloom, a gorgeous, evocative scent fills the air, and wooden trucks piled high with vast purple bunches lumber their way along the roads of the high plateau.

The botanical name *lavandula* comes from the Latin word *lavare* meaning "to wash", and the use of lavender as a strewing and bathing herb by the Romans is well documented. Not only does this wonderful herb have soothing and calming effects, it is also highly beneficial as a healing agent for burns, wounds, insect bites and stings. Lavender, or its more common hybrid "lavandin", is sold in towns and villages across Provence in every conceivable form from soap and essence to sachets of dried lavender.

ment trucks, which douse the streets with lavender water. Organised Dignois reserve their tables at the boulevard's cafés for lunch and a good view of the parade.

Those with no wish to take the waters, either of the thermal or lavender varieties, should head south towards the outskirts of town to Digne's **Alexandra David-Néel Foundation** (27 avenue Maréchal Juin; closed Mon; guided tours available; tel: 04 92 31 32 38). The woman after whom this cultural-centre-cum-museum is named was a Parisian adventurer who spent much of her life travelling in remote parts of Asia, including perilous trips to the forbidden Tibetan capital of Lhasa. Seduced by the beauty of the Alpes-de-Haute-Provence, which she called a "Himalayas for Liliputians", she bought a house in Digne in 1927 and named it *Samten Dzong*, meaning "the fortress of meditation." When she died in 1969, aged 101, David-Néel left the house and its contents to the city of Digne. The Foundation continues to attract visitors and Buddhist pilgrims.

Architecturally, Digne's greatest attraction is the Lombard-style **Cathédrale de Notre-Dame-du-Bourg**, north of the boulevard Gassendi on the outskirts of town. Look for the 13th-century portals in striking blue-and-white limestone. Digne also has a **Musée Municipal** (64 boulevard Gassendi; currently under renovation with re-opening scheduled for 2002; tel: 04 92 31 45 29), with paintings, local art, and the scientific instruments of the Digne-born astronomer, Pierre Gassendi.

Nearby is the well-ordered **Centre de Géologie** (open Apr–Oct: daily; Nov–Mar: Mon–Fri; tel: 04 92 36 70 70), signposted on the opposite bank of the Bléone, with a vast range of fossils and animal skeletons from prehistoric times.

The Grand Canyon du Verdon

Near the southern borders of the Alpes-de-Haute-Provence lies the *département*'s greatest natural site, the **Grand Canyon du Verdon** ⓳. Even if you see little else in the area, on no account miss this.

BELOW: on road to Ann

Map pages 202–3

First stop on the Canyon trail is **Moustiers-Ste-Marie** ⑳, where an astonishing backdrop of craggy cliffs provides a taste of the glories to come. Moustiers is an attractive small town perched on the edge of a ravine. High up behind the town, the two sides of the ravine seem held together by a massive chain that is around 220 metres (720 ft) long, and suspended from the chain is a man-sized metal star.

This curious piece of adornment has inspired poems by Provençal writers Frédéric Mistral and Jean Giono and all manner of speculation as to its origin. However, local historians have settled on the legend that it was placed there by a knight returning from the Crusades, in fulfilment of a religious vow. In any event, the present star dates only from 1957, when the mayor of Moustiers decided that the town's most famous piece of jewellery was due for a facelift.

More obviously visible is Moustiers's major claim to fame – its faïence. The narrow village streets are crammed to bursting with shops and studios producing this white-glazed decorative pottery.

Established in the late 17th century by Antoine Clérissy, the recipe for the white glaze was believed to have come via an Italian monk from Faenza. The industry prospered for the following 200 years, counting Madame de Pompadour among its customers. Changing fashions, however, brought about its decline during the 19th century, and the art was not revived until the mid-1920s.

Sadly, many of the items produced today have fallen prey to the depressing combination of high prices and low quality. Though it is still possible to seek out good examples from among the vast range available, perhaps more rewarding is a visit to the **Musée de la Faïence** (open Apr–Oct: daily except Tues; Nov–Mar: weekend afternoons only; tel: 04 92 74 61 64) in the Placette du Prieuré. Opposite the entrance to the museum, housed in a vaulted crypt, is the stunning three-tiered belfry of the Romanesque village church.

OW: ıstierware ı the Atelier Segriès. **HT:** autumn loustiers.

A fork in the road under 3 km (2 miles) south of Moustiers offers a choice of routes to the Grand Canyon du Verdon. Heading south, the road skirts the spectacular man-made **Lac de Ste-Croix**, an 11-km (7-mile) stretch of azure water created in the 1970s by the installation of a hydroelectric dam. The route then doglegs east to follow the southern ridge of the canyon, known as the **Corniche Sublime**. Alternatively, the old road to Castellane (the D952) snakes along the northern ridge, veering away from the canyon edge around halfway along its length.

Both routes have their virtues. Choosing the Corniche Sublime means consistently spectacular views, most notably those at the **Balcons de la Mescla**, where the Verdon converges with the smaller canyon formed by the Artuby River. The left bank has its own impressive *belvédère* (viewing point), the **Point Sublime**, a dizzy 180 metres (600 ft) above the river, and offers two chances to climb down to the Canyon floor, at Chalet de la Maline (branch off from the village of la Palud) and just east of the Point Sublime (follow signs for Couloir de Samson). Both routes require at least a half-day trip.

Statistics on the Grand Canyon only hint at its magnificence. Around 21 km (12½ miles) in length and 1,500 metres (5,000 ft) deep, the vertiginous limestone cliffs are gouged by the waters of the Verdon River, in turn glassy and crystalline or tumbling in white-water chaos. Colours are out of this world: jewelled emerald and turquoise contrast in autumn with the ochres and russets of surrounding deciduous trees.

In the early 20th century, the canyon was largely deserted, with only a few local peasants still eking out a meagre living as woodcutters. By the late 1940s, the touristic potential of the canyon was accelerated by the construction of the Corniche Sublime. Tourism has now moved in wholesale, and those in the know make great efforts to avoid the area completely during the month of August.

BELOW: quirky activi at one of th region's ma festivals.

Map pages 202–3

Nowhere are the crowds of summer visitors more oppressive than in **Castellane** ㉑. As in the case of Moustiers-Ste-Marie, proximity to the canyon has brought welcome prosperity to the locals of Castellane, at the expense of over-commercialisation. Queues of cars choke the town's narrow streets, beachballs and hiking paraphernalia fill its shops, and the native hospitality becomes, at times, understandably strained.

Seasonal demands aside, Castellane has a pleasing, if small, old quarter, lying to the north of the town's bustling hub, place Marcel-Sauvaire. Market days, on Wednesday and Saturday, enliven the town throughout the year, and the *Fête des Fétardiers*, held annually on 31 January, commemorates the lifting of a Huguenot siege in 1586.

The chapel of **Notre-Dame-du-Roc**, perched daringly on a high rocky outcrop, makes Castellane's skyline its most appealing feature. The town also has a museum of local crafts and traditions, the **Conservatoire des Arts et Traditions Populaires** (34 rue Nationale; open June–Sept: daily except Mon; Sept–June Wed only, or by appointment; entrance fee; tel: 04 92 83 71 80).

From Castillon to Rouaine

The Verdon River, so resplendently enclosed by the Grand Canyon in the south, keeps its luminous colour in its northern reaches. The **Lac de Castillon**, in the Vallée du Haut Verdon (Upper Verdon Valley), has much in common with its larger cousin, the **Lac de Ste-Croix**. Also man-made, it was created by a dam that was constructed and managed by Electricité de France. The dam was completed in 1947, making it the first of five built to harness the waters of the Verdon. Ste-Croix, completed in the 1960s, is the most recent.

The lakes that have resulted (Chaudanne, Ste-Croix, Castillon) perform the dual function of conserving precious water for this region of Provence and

ow: Ste-x de Verdon he Lac de Croix.

attracting tourism. Edging the Lac de Castillon, bizarre vertically grooved rock formations alternate with dazzling white sand spits that provide pleasant spots for swimming in summer.

In a valley of orchards and lavender fields at the head of the lake sits the small summer resort of **St-André-les-Alpes** ㉒, a haven for wind-surfers, hang-gliders, anglers and other *sportifs*. This small village has little to recommend it architecturally or historically but it is redeemed by the genuine hospitality of its population. In summer, the village somehow manages to find room for four times its normal number of inhabitants. Nonetheless, tourism has not left as deep a scar here as in Moustiers or Castellane. St-André's tiny station forms a stop on the route of the Train des Pignes. In addition, a *Belle Epoque* steam train, dating from 1909, rattles through on its way from Puget-Théniers to **Annot** ㉓ every Sunday in summer.

East of St-André, the route to the delightful little town of Annot leads through one of the numerous *cols* (high passes) that pepper this mountainous eastern side of the Alpes-de-Haute-Provence. Moving north and east, towards the "Grands Alpes" and the Alpes-Maritimes respectively, the *cols* increase in frequency and, at times, almost alarmingly in altitude. The **Col de Toutes Aures** (Pass of All Winds), however, is relative small-fry, at a mere 1,124 metres (3,688 ft) high. Towering over it is the massive **Pic de Chamatte** which, at 1,878 metres (6,160 ft), dwarfs even the Montagne de Lure in the west.

This is a richly forested landscape, which stands in marked contrast to the bleak beauty of the canyon region. Here, shaley precipitous slopes are cloaked with vast sweeps of dark evergreens parading down the steep cliff faces. Minuscule villages such as **Vergons** and **Rouaine**, which consist of little more than a handful of dry-stone houses protected by weathered shutters, prefigure the alpine experience to come.

BELOW: the historic tow of Entrevau

Map
ı pages
202–3

Annot and its environs

Set in the Val du Vaire **Annot** is typical of this area's dual aspect, being warmly Provençal yet markedly alpine. The town's wrought-iron balconies and stone *lavoirs* are as classically Provençal as anything found further south, but the majesty of the Alps leaves its mark in the pure clarity of the air and the steely grey waters of the numerous streams that tumble through the town.

During the winter months, Annot sleeps under thick coverings of snow – although the oldest populated centre in the area, Annot was unreachable by carriage as recently as 1830. In common with much of the rest of the Alpes-de-Haute-Provence, access was provided only by the network of mule tracks that crisscross the mountainous landscape.

For years the town has attracted painters. East of the sizeable main square, planted with a fine esplanade of ancient plane trees, the narrow streets of the picturesque **Vieille Ville** (Old Town) climb steeply in medieval formation. Vaulted archways and a predominance of carved stone lintels bearing their 17th and 18th-century dates of construction line the tall houses of the Grand Rue. At the top of the old town, the narrow streets converge on a pretty square with the parish church and surrounding houses painted in many different pastel hues.

The quaintly picturesque lure of Annot is not simply confined to its evocative old quarter. Just outside the town to the south is a vast cluster of massive rocks scattered far across the hillside. Known as the **Grès d'Annot**, these house-sized sandstone boulders seem to have been flung to earth from the cliff behind by an angry giant. Locals have built houses directly beside them, often using their sheer faces as an outside wall. Local legends, featuring troglodytes and primitive religions, surround them to this day.

Annot's local industry is based on two thriving factories, specialising in the production of biscuits and, more traditionally,

.OW:
›cher with
al meat
›cialities

meat products. The town is also a popular centre for summer excursions and, as with St-André, it is a stop on the route of the Train des Pignes.

Those with stout hearts and boots can follow the spectacular hiking trails into the nearby high-altitude **Val du Coulomp**. Alternatively, the Val du Vaire, running due north from Annot, is the setting of the typical mountain village of **Méailles** ㉔, perched high above the river. Located still further north is the ancient village of **Peyresq** ㉕, which was in ruins until 1955, when a group of Belgian students decided to transform it into a tiny but thriving cultural centre.

Entrevaux

Cross the drawbridge of the **Porte Royale** into the fairytale town of **Entrevaux** ㉖, and the 21st century seems to recede as if by magic. Situated on the eastern fringes of the Alpes-de-Haute-Provence and for centuries a frontier post defending Provence from Savoy, Entrevaux exudes a history more tangible than any town in the *département*. The town's 17th-century ramparts (the work of Louis XIV's masterful engineer, Vauban), turrets, drawbridges and a deep moat formed by the Var River cocoon the town. Cars are firmly relegated to the busy Nice road on the opposite bank of the river.

Like the ramparts, the majority of Entrevaux's houses, together with its cathedral church, date from the 17th century. A **citadel**, testimony to the town's key strategic position, is reached by an ascending path of nine zigzag ramps, a remarkable feat of engineering that took 50 years to complete.

As well as with its history, Entrevaux entices with cultural and folkloric events. In August there is a two-week music festival of 16th- and 17th-century music. The festival of John the Baptist, held annually on the weekend closest to 24 June, sees locals in traditional costume celebrating with a Mass, dancing and a procession to the isolated **Chapelle de St-Jean-du-**

BELOW: tend the flock.

Map pages 202–3

Désert, 7 km (4 miles) to the southwest. The popularity of the saint is such that similar festivals on a smaller scale are held concurrently in many of the small villages nearby, each with its procession to a chosen chapel "in the desert".

One delightful curiosity brings the visitor to Entrevaux back into the modern age. The minuscule **Musée de la Moto** (open Apr–Sept; tel: 04 93 79 12 70) is devoted entirely to the history of the automobile. Run by a former Grand Prix mechanic, it houses over 70 vehicles dating from 1905, all still in working order.

Entrevaux is also home to a thriving Association of Mycology and Applied Botany (Association Entrevalaise de Mycologie et de Botanique), which attracts mushroom experts from all over France in the autumn. Perhaps of greater interest to the casual visitor, however, is the tiny main square, **place St-Martin**, which features a pleasant café, a clutch of pretty chestnut trees and a butcher who dispenses the local speciality, *secca de boeuf*, a type of dried salt beef, which is delicious when eaten with olive oil and lemon juice.

.OW:
:eron.

Colmars

If Entrevaux seems uniquely untouched by the proximity of the Alps, **Colmars** 27, 30 km (18 miles) to the north, could hardly be more alpine. Colmars is a fortified town crowned by two massive medieval castles, and, like Entrevaux, a former frontier post between Provence and Savoy. There the similarity between the two towns ends, however.

Approaching Colmars along the attractive D908 from St-André, the sloping roofs of wooden alpine chalets seem a universe away from the dry-stone *bories* of the Lure or the long, low *mas* of the Var. Inside the well-preserved ramparts of the town, once again the work of the architect Vauban, the alpine feel only increases. Houses are constructed with tidy wooden balconies, known as *solerets* (sun traps), locals sport jaunty alpine caps that would not seem out of place in

Bavaria, and shop windows display amber bottles of *génépi* liqueur, made from alpine flowers. Only the small fountains and the geraniums that line the balconies in summer confirm that this is in fact part of Provence.

Colmar's name stems from Roman times when a temple to the god Mars was erected on the hill *(collis Martis)* that today forms the backdrop to the town. Of the two castles that dominate Colmar's skyline, the **Fort de Savoie** (open July–Aug: daily; Sept–June: visits by appointment only; guided tours obligatory; entrance fee; tel: 04 92 83 46 88) is the more imposing. Reached by a covered alleyway, the fort is a fine piece of 17th-century military engineering.

Sleepy in winter, Colmar's unspoilt charm and beautiful setting make it a popular centre for family holidays, particularly among residents of the major coastal cities. A *bravade*, more rooted in tradition than the celebrated St-Tropez version, takes place in June.

North of Colmars

Map on pag[e] 202–3

The French Alps proper lie hidden behind the **Col d'Allos** 28, 25 km (15 miles) north of Colmars, The high-altitude **Lac d'Allos**, ringed by snow-capped mountains and the breathtaking **Col de la Cayolle** (2,327 metres/7,635 ft) form stunning diversions along the route to the Alps, though they are frequently inaccessible in winter.

Barcelonette 29, squeezed into a narrow glacial valley surrounded by towering peaks and completely alpine in character, is the northernmost town in Provence. It owes its unlikely name to its 12th-century rulers, the counts of Barcelona, who originally christened the town Barcelona.

The Hispanic connection does not end there. Early in the 19th century, a period of migration to Mexico began, prompted by the success achieved by three local brothers who opened a textile shop there. Many locals followed, some of whom later returned to Barcelonette to build the incongruous Mexican-style villas for which the town is famous.

Less than a century ago, the villages of the Vallée de l'Ubaye remained spectacularly remote, ancient traditions persisted and locals spoke *le gavot*, an alpine version of Oc. The **Musée de la Vallée** (open Wed, Thur and Sat afternoons and daily in school holidays; entrance fee; tel: 04 92 81 27 15), on the avenue de la Libération, provides fascinating accounts of the region's chequered history.

Today, although the "Mexican connection" remains strong, with frequent cultural exchanges and shops selling Mexican artefacts, a new flavour has emerged to dominate the atmosphere and preoccupations of the town: skiing. From December to April the modern ski resorts of **Super-Sauze** and **Pra-Loup**, just south of Barcelonette, pack the Vallée de l'Ubaye with international tourists and bring a welcome upturn in local fortunes.

In many ways, the history of Barcelonette is the history of the Alpes-de-Haute-Provence in microcosm: poverty, migration, gradual prosperity. It is an evolution that continues today. ❑

LEFT: mount[…] wildflowers.
RIGHT: local […] of Entrevaux[…]

NCHOIS

Map
n pages
226–7

THE VAR

This densely forested region, the southernmost point of Provence, is home to Toulon, St-Tropez, numerous pretty hill-top villages and an imposing 12th-century Cistercian abbey

The Var is a palette of varied landscapes that connect the sea with the mountains and plains of the north. The forested *massifs* of Ste-Baume, Maures and Estérel dominating the southernmost section of the *département*, by the coast, give way to acres of vineyards in the centre of the region. Further north, substantial hills are studded with hill-top villages, waterfalls, caves and more vines. Here, in the least spoiled section of the *département*, the calm atmosphere contrasts markedly with the noise and frenzy of the coast.

The coastal area is a spectrum of sights and sounds: the cosmopolitan sprawl of Toulon, the wild beauty of the Iles d'Hyères, the gentility of summer resorts such as Bandol, Hyères and Sanary-sur-Mer and the glamour of St-Tropez.

Tourism is as much a major industry in the area as wine production. Many *visages pâles* (or "pale faces" – a local nickname for summer visitors) never venture north of the busy A8 *autoroute* that bisects the *département* from east to west. However, many restored farmhouses and elegant modern villas serve as summer homes in the hills from St-Tropez to Aups. In the central and upper Var alone, the number of *résidences secondaires* (second homes) is estimated at more than 25,000.

The inland areas offer many hidden delights to those who are prepared to explore beyond the *autoroute*: pretty squares dappled by the shade of plane trees, medieval architecture, endless light, craggy coves and fine beaches. As they say in Lorgues, "*Ici on vit vieux et heureux*" (Here you live a long and happy life).

Toulon

The *préfecture* (administrative capital) of the Var, **Toulon ❶**, is a major port and, as such, is not subject to the seasonal ebb and flow of population experienced by much of the rest of the *département*.

Clustered round a deep natural harbour and enclosed by a crescent of high hills, Toulon is France's leading naval base. Many tourists bypass it, however, as its fetid narrow alleyways and chaotic suburban sprawl offer little obvious enticement to the casual visitor. However, along with all the low-life trappings of a major seaport, Toulon has its own share of grand buildings, chic boutiques, lively fish-markets and cosmopolitan energy that is matched in Provence only by Marseille.

The main route through the city, the **boulevard de Strasbourg**, bisects the grid of tall apartment blocks, department stores and imposing administrative buildings that make up historic 19th-century Toulon. South of the **place Victor Hugo**,

ECEDING
ES:
Massif
Maures.
T: vegetable
rket, Toulon.
HT:
rway,
res.

Var
0 10 km
0 10 miles
N
Manosque
Sisteron
la Trinité
Riez
Pierrevert
Alpes-de-Haute-Provence
Allemagne-en-Provence
Montagnac
Lac de Ste-Croix
la Palud-sur-Verdon
Point Sublime
Aiguines
Trigance
St-Tulle
Rousset
Laval
Gréoux-les-Bains
St-Martin-de-Brômes
Albiosc
Ste-Croix-de-Verdon
Montpezat
les Salles-sur-Verdon
Grand Canyon du Verdon
Canyon de l'
A51
N96
Durance
Aurabelle
Esparron-de-Verdon
St-Laurent-du-Verdon
Bauduen
Baudinard-sur-Verdon
Grand Plan de Canjuers
Vinon-sur-Verdon
Verdon
Quinson
Artignosc-sur-Verdon
Mirabeau
E712
les Rouvières
Aix-en-Provence
St-Paul-lès-Durance
St-Julien-le-Montagnier
Montagne de Barjaude
Ginasservis
Lauquier
Verignon
Bouches-
Régusse
Moissac-Bellevue
St-Priest
Jouques
la Verdière
Montmeyan
Aups
26
Couan
Ampus
Rians
du-
Varages
Cormeil
Fabrègues
Taurenne
la Beaume
Gorges de Châteaudouble
Artigues
Esparron
Tavernes
Grottes
29
Tourtour
St-Martin
Barras
Fox-Amphoux
Villecroze
Rebouillon
Barjols
25
28
Sillans-la-Cascade
St-Jean
Salernes
27
Rhône
Montagne Ste-Victoire
Pontevès
les Salgues
Dragui
Rifforand
Flayosc
Brue-Auriac
Bois du Bessillon
Cotignac
30
31
St-Foy
Berne
le Général
Entrecasteaux
Puyloubier
Pourrières
Seillons-Source-d'Argens
Argens
Châteauvert
St-Antonin-du-Var
N. D. de Benva
Lorgues
Ollières
Montfort-sur-Argens
Carcès
N7
A8
Bras
Abbaye du Thoronet
32
la Martinette
Taradea
Pourcieux
Lac de Carcès
Mont Aurélien
24
Cauron
le Thoronet
Argens
Olympe 880
St-Maximin la-Ste-Baume
le Val
Vins-sur-Carami
la Plaine
St-Loup
Vidauba
Peynier
Trets
E80
Carami
Cabasse
le Vieux-Cannet
23
St-Jean-du-Puy
N7
Tourves
St-Pré
Brignoles
la Gayole
St-Julien
la Celle Abbaye
Var
A8
le Luc
22
St-Zacharie
N560
Rougiers
Camps-la-Source
le Cannet-des-Maures
Auriol
Nans-les-Pins
Flassans-sur-Issole
N97
la Ste-Baume
Massif de la Sainte-Baume
Besse-sur-Issole
St-Pilon 994
Mazaugues
Forcalqueiret
la Croix de Bontar
Plan-d'Aups
le Mourre d'Agnis 915
la Roquebrussanne
Ste-Anastasie-sur-Issole
Gonfaron
les Mayons
Garéoult
Néoules
Rocbaron
Carnoules
Servante
N. D. du Figuier
Pignans
Gémenos
Signes
Méounes-lès-Montrieux
Ste-Philomène
Puget-Ville
la Sauvette 779
Cuges-les-Pins
O.K. Corral (Parc d'attractions)
A57
Massif des Maures
Juhans
N8
Circuit du Castellet Paul Ricard
Chartreuse Montrieux-le-Jeune
Collobrières
Belgentier
Cuers
17
Chartreuse de la Verne
Marseille
Ste-Anne-du-Castellet
Gapeau
Pierrefeu-du-Var
Montaud
le Brulat
Solliès-Toucas
St-Guillaume
Arboretum
Ceyreste
le Castellet
Mont Caume 801
la Cadière-d'Azur
le Beausset
Solliès-Pont
St-Cyr-sur-Mer
Ste-Anne-d'Evenos
le Revest-les-Eaux
la Farlede
Bormes-les-Mimosas
9
St-Cla
les Lecques
les Baumelles
Evenos
A50
la Crau
la Londe-les-Maures
le Lavandou
le Gros Cerveau
la Valette-du-Var
2
Bandol
Ollioules
Toulon
1
la Garde
A570
Hyères
4
N98
Port-de-Miramar
Léoube
la Favi
Île de Bendor
Sanary-sur-Mer
3
la Moutonne
Port-Pothuau
Bénat
le Pradet
Carqueiranne
Ayguade-Ceinturon
Brégançon
Cap Bénat
Six-Fours-les-Plages
la Seyne-sur-Mer
la Garonne
Fort de la Colle-Noir
Cap de Brégançon
Cap Blanc
Grand Rouveau
les Sablettes
Fort de la Gavaresse
l'Almanarre
Hyères-Plage
Île des Embiez
le Brusc
St-Mandrier-sur-Mer
Rade d'Hyères
Presqu'île de St-Mandrier
Cap Cépet
Golfe de Giens
Etang des Pesquiers
la Capte
Îles
Notre-Dame-du-Mai
5
Presqu'île de Giens
Cap Sicié
Giens
la Tour-Fondue
Île de Bagaud
Pointe du Grand Langoustier
6
Porquerolles
Île de Porquerolles
Île de Port-Cr
Cap d'Arme
7

with its fine theatre and opera house, lies the seamier side of the city – a warren of narrow streets leading down to the **Vieille Ville** (Old Town) known locally as the *darse vieille*. Insalubrious bars rub shoulders with dingy restaurants, dispensing the Toulon version of *bouillabaisse* (made with potatoes in addition to fish) and North African specialities. Scruffy kids play football in the shadow of peeling tenements, and locals watch the world go by.

The *basse ville*, as the lower part of the town is known, isn't all sleaze, however, and is undergoing a huge restoration project. Small attractive squares (Puget, Trois Dauphine and Camille Ledeau) draw elegant locals and tourists to their designer shops and shaded cafés. Superb fish, vegetable and flower markets characterise mornings in the **cours Lafayette**. And the patchwork streets lead inexorably towards Toulon's *raison d'être*: the port.

Much of the *basse ville*'s bad press comes from the avenue de la République, a grubby roadway lined with concrete post-war architecture. Damage caused by Allied bombings and the German razing of the harbourfront "for reasons of hygiene" hasn't been well disguised.

Naval traditions

Historically, Toulon's era of major expansion occured in the 17th century, though the city was a base for the royal navy as early as 1487. Under the orders of Louis XIV, the arsenal was expanded and the city's fortifications enlarged. A century later, the city took the side of the English against the Revolutionary government and was promptly brought to heel by a young Napoleon. The English fleet was defeated in 1793, ensuring that the general's name would never be forgotten.

High on the list of Toulon's many visitable sights is the comprehensive **Musée Naval** (924 corniche Bonaparte; closed Mon, Jan and June; entrance fee; tel: 04 94 94 84 72), in Fort Balaguier along the western shore, which commemorates Napoleon's capture of Toulon. There is also the **Musée de la Marine** (place Monsenergue; closed Tues; tel: 04 94 02 02 01**),** housing ships' figureheads, model ships and marine-related paintings, and the **Musée du Vieux Toulon** (cours Lafayette; open Mon–Sat afternoons; free; tel: 04 94 62 11 07), which evokes Toulon's history. Note the figures by local sculptor, Pierre Puget, the *Atlantes*, on quai Cronstadt.

For an excellent overall view of Toulon, take the cable car ride at **Mont Faron**, just outside the city. From the top you will have a terrific bird's-eye view over the city itself, its satellite towns and the sea.

Calm resorts

To either side of the steamy cityscape of Toulon lie three attractive coastal resorts. Bandol and Sanary-sur-Mer to the west and Hyères to the east are not as lively or chic as St-Tropez and Cannes, but many visitors prefer them for that very reason.

Screened from the ravages of the mistral by an arc of wooded hills, **Bandol** ❷ has attracted numerous visitors to its sandy coves and pleasant promenades since the beginning of the 20th century. Among its more famous guests are the New Zealand author Katherine Mansfield (1888–1923), who wrote *Prelude* in the quayside Villa Pauline in 1916, and the celebrated Provençal actor Raimu.

Most modern-day visitors, a large proportion of them French, come for the town's three sandy beaches, lively harbour and air of calm sophistication. Another plus is Bandol's vineyards, which produce wines (particularly reds) that are rated as being among the best in Provence.

About 2 km (1 mile) off the coast of Bandol lies the tiny island of **Bendor**, which was enterprisingly transformed into a holiday village in the 1950s by the *pastis* magnate Paul Ricard. On the island is a hotel, a clutch of rather expensive cafés, a re-creation of a Provençal fishing village and Ricard's pride and joy – a museum devoted to the pleasures of alcohol. The grandly titled **Exposition Universelle des Vins et Spiritueux** (signposted from the ferry quay; open Apr–Sep: Thur–Tues; admission free; tel: 04 94 24 44 34), which contains over 8,000 bottles of wine

BELOW: Port Cros.

Map
n pages
226–7

and spirits from all over the world, plus a selection of glassware. Though the island has an air of artificiality, its shady paths, lined with mimosa and eucalyptus, and tiny sandy beach are reason enough for a visit.

Just 5 km (3 miles) from Bandol is the pretty pink-and-white resort of **Sanary-sur-Mer** ❸. Like Bandol, Sanary benefits from a sheltered position supplied by its backdrop of hills, known as the Gros Cerveau. A number of *pointus* (old fishing vessels) add spice to its attractive harbour.

Artists and writers began to flock to Sanary in the early 1930s, inspired by the presence there of the writer Aldous Huxley (1894–1963). They were soon joined by a group of German intellectuals, headed by Nobel Prize-winning writer Thomas Mann (1875–1955) and his novelist brother Heinrich (1871–1950), who fled to the town after Hitler's rise to power in 1933.

The nearby **Cap Sicié** peninsula makes for a worthwhile trip from Sanary. At its southern point, the **Chapelle de Notre-Dame-du-Mai** sits on a high clifftop that drops sharply towards the sea. The view from here takes in fjord-like *calanques (see page 155)* and the Iles d'Hyères.

To the east is **Hyères** ❹, the most substantial of the three major resorts that surround Toulon and, in many ways, the most interesting. Hyères was the first resort to be established on the Côte, setting a trend that spread rapidly east from the late 18th century onwards. The list of famous consumptives, or merely pleasure-seekers, drawn to its balmy winter climate reads like an international Who's Who: Queen Victoria, Tolstoy, Pauline Bonaparte, Aubrey Beardsley, Edith Wharton, etc. Robert Louis Stevenson, though desperately ill during his stay, wrote: "I was only happy once – that was at Hyères."

By the 1920s, however, medical opinion had switched its allegiance to the curative properties of mountain – rather than sea – air. This and the increasing popularity of the main section of the so-called Riviera to the east soon relegated Hyères to a distinctly unfashionable position.

LOW:
nary-sur-Mer.

In many ways, the town's lack of chic is now one of its most attractive qualities. Busy all year round, Hyères plays host to several sporting and cultural events (such as a sailing regatta and cartoon animation festival) and has a thriving agricultural economy (peaches and strawberries) independent of tourism. It is also famous for its flowers and palms, which add an exotic flavour to the town. The **Vieille Ville** (Old Town) is a small, appealing, medieval quarter, topped by a park and ruined 14th-century castle with the spacious, flagstoned **place Massillon** at its heart.

Modern Hyères has an elegant feel and some notable examples of neo-Moorish architecture. A 19th-century taste for things from the East (inspired by Napoleon's Egyptian campaign) led to the erection of **la Mauresque** (avenue Jean Natte) and **la Tunisienne** (avenue de Beauregard) in the 1870s. Minarets, Arab arches and tropical date palms add a taste of the exotic.

Outside the town lie the vestiges of ancient Hyères (called Olbia), once a main Phocaean and Roman port. Antiquities excavated from the site can be seen in the **Musée Municipal** (place Théodore Lefèbvre; open Mon, Wed– Fri; free; tel: 04 94 00 78 42).

The Iles d'Hyères

Jutting out into the sea, the **Presqu'île de Giens** ❺ is a joyless, flat peninsula composed of salt marshes and some good beaches surrounded by ugly campsites. Salt collection, a local industry since pre-Roman times, continues today at the Côte's only remaining productive marsh, the Marais Salins des Pesquiers.

The main reason for taking this uninspiring route is to catch a boat from **la Tour-Fondue** at the southeastern tip to the **Iles d'Hyères**. (Boats also sail from le Lavandou and Cavalaire.)

This group of three subtropical islands, nicknamed the **Iles d'Or** (Isles of Gold), is a haven of unspoilt natural beauty. On **Porquerolles** ❻, the largest and most accessible island, there is a small town with cafés and some fabulous beaches amidst dense vegetation. **Port-Cros** ❼, more rugged and mountainous, is one of only six designated national parks in France. The third, **Levant** ❽, is 90 percent inhabited by the French military and, therefore, mostly out of bounds. All that exists on Levant is a small nudist colony, founded in the 1930s and known as **Héliopolis**, which clings to the bare and dramatic western tip of the island.

Unless you're a naturist or a botanist, Porquerolles is probably the best choice for a visit. Its village, established as a small military base in the 19th century, is more colonial than Provençal in character. From here, you can hire bicycles to tour the eucalyptus- and pine-clad island – note that cars are not allowed. Major beauty spots include the lighthouse at the **Cap d'Arme** and one of the beaches, **Plage Notre-Dame**, which is also great for swimming.

On Port-Cros, the terrain is much more challenging, and strict rules against smoking and the lighting of fires must be observed. A small **tourist centre**, open in summer, provides maps and advice.

LEFT: the isla
of Porquerolle

Map
n pages
226–7

Perhaps the most rewarding walk (around two hours for the round-trip) takes you along the **Vallon de la Solitude**, which cuts across the southern end of the island. Divers can follow an underwater "path" to see the marine flora and fauna.

Bormes-les-Mimosas

Back on the mainland, a number of towns line the coastal road that leads to St-Tropez. This is not, strictly speaking, part of the Côte d'Azur, being too far away from the coast itself, but it's difficult to tell. The first stop here is fashionable **Bormes-les-Mimosas** ❾, a hill-top village with lovely views of the Iles d'Hyères and the sea. Some critics accuse Bormes of being over-prettified, but the village is certainly one of the jewels of Provence. - Bougainvillea, mimosa and eucalyptus (some of which were destroyed by the harsh winters of the late-20th century) make this the archetypal *village fleurie*.

The names of the picturesque narrow streets – Roumpi-Cuou (neck-breaker) and Plaine-des-Anes (donkey's sorrow) – suggest their steepness. Look out for the painted sundial on the **Eglise St-Trophime**, the fine medieval château at the top of the Old Town and the small **Musée d'Art et d'Histoire de Bormes** (103 rue Carnot; closed Tues and Sun afternoons; admission free; tel: 04 94 71 56 60) that contains some terracottas by Rodin as well as an exhibition on the Massif des Maures' Chartreuse de la Verne, a ruined 12th-century Carthusian monastery.

South of Bormes, linked to the exclusive promontory of Cap Bénat by a dyke, the **Fort de Brégançon**, the "Camp David" of the French president, sits proudly on its own islet. The fort cannot be visited.

The Massif des Maures

The **Massif des Maures**, a tract of deep forest, much of which is inaccessible, stretches roughly from Hyères to Fréjus and from the A8 *autoroute* down to the Mediterranean. The name comes from the Provençal word *maouro*, meaning dark.

LOW: la
uresque,
ères.

The Maures, together with the neighbouring Estérel *massif*, are components of the oldest geographical area in Provence. Schist rock, shot with sparkling mica, makes up the high hills and deep ravines of the massif. Cork oaks, Aleppo pines and chestnut trees form its dense vegetation.

The area was ruled by invading Arabs for more than 100 years, beginning in the early 9th century. Pillaging the countryside as far afield as Lake Constance, now bordered by Germany, Switzerland and Austria, their reign of terror lasted until 972 when Count Guillaume destroyed their bastion at la Garde-Freinet.

More recently, the area has been ravaged no less destructively by the constant plague of forest fires, which are sparked spontaneously or by pure human carelessness. The desiccated forests quickly transform into monstrous walls of flame, leaving nothing but charred scrub in their wake. More than a million acres of the Var have been destroyed during the last 50 years. Preventative measures, such as the creation of fire-break paths and radical pruning of vegetation have had some impact since their introduction, but the light aircraft of Canadair scooping water from the sea to douse flames remains a common sight. It is an annual battle that is still being fought.

The Massif des Maures is home to few towns of any size, though its wooded hills conceal the private estates and villas of the rich and sometimes famous. **La Garde-Freinet ⓾**, an ancient Arab stronghold and, in a sense, the capital of the Maures, is little more than a large village. Its traditional industry of cork production was a skill acquired from the Arabs during the 9th century. By 1846, the town produced more than 75 percent of France's bottle corks but, like many of the traditional industries, decline set in after the 1950s. Since the early 1980s, however, the industry has diversified into other uses of cork, and neatly stripped trunks of cork oaks line the *massif*'s serpentine roads and tracks.

BELOW: bar in la Garde-Freinet

Map
n pages
226–7

In the town, the only obvious evidence of cork production are the cork bowls and ornaments on sale to tourists in the pricey boutiques of the rue St-Jacques. St-Tropez chic has left its mark here, accelerating particularly in the last decade. Arty café loungers at the **Claire Fontaine**, epicentre of the village, are now more likely to read the trendy national newspaper *Libération* than the local *Var-Matin*. More down-to-earth locals congregate at the **Cercle des Travailleurs**, a bar on place Neuve, where local men drink *pastis* under the watchful eye of a splendid bust of Marianne. North of the village, a walk to the ruins of an Arab fortress, is rewarded with great views of the massif and the sea.

The rollercoaster road heading south from la Garde-Freinet cuts through the centre of the Maures to the St-Tropez peninsula. *En route* is the hill-top village of **Grimaud** ⓫, a maze of pretty streets peppered with bougainvillea and oleander. Wander along the rue des Templiers, for its medieval arcades, then head up to the ruined castle, which was destroyed on the orders of Cardinal Richelieu.

Cogolin ⓬, 3 km (1½ miles) to the south, is a small but lively town known for the manufacture of briar pipes and carpets. It is also an important producer of good-quality wines. Visits can be made to the pipe and carpet factories. You can also visit the **Musée Raimu** (open daily in summer; closed Sun mornings in winter; tel: 04 94 54 18 00), set up in memory of Pagnol's favourite actor,

St-Tropez and surroundings

Once on the peninsula, you won't be able to resist the pull of **St-Tropez** ⓭, enduringly connected with the French sex symbol Brigitte Bardot *(see page 93)*. The town (generally referred to simply as St-Trop) still features the most celebrities per capita of any spot on the Riviera. Its 6,000 permanent residents (many of whom rely on tourism for a considerable portion of their income) take the summer fashion show in their stride and understandingly tolerate the gatherings at the Senequier Restaurant along the port and dancing until dawn at the Caves du Roy.

The centre of St Tropez is the newly restored old port, its harbour packed full of glamorous yachts and lined with cafés from which you can watch them. To the west side is the **Musée de l'Annonciade** (place Gramont; closed Tues; entrance fee; tel: 04 94 97 04 01), which has a superb modern-art collection, featuring the work of many of the artists who visited and painted St-Tropez at the beginning of the 20th century, including Signac, Bonnard, Maillol and Dufy. There is also the **Musée Maritime** (Mont de la Citadelle; closed Tues; entrance fee; tel: 04 94 97 59 43), with everything you need to know about Mediterranean shipping.

The main attraction of St-Tropez, however, is its glorious beaches, fringed with restaurants, and packed with sun-bronzed bodies all summer long. Pampelonne is the most chic, with several kilometres of perfect sand, though it might be difficult to make this out in mid-summer.

Even at the height of the season one of the best places to see the real St-Tropez

LOW:
est at the
artreuse
la Verne.

is early morning on the the **place aux Lices**, where there is a fabulously colourful market, offering all the best produce of Provence.

If the town gets too much for you, from St-Tropez you can easily reach nearby pine forests or the vineyards on the adjacent peninsula. Another chic getaway is **Port Grimaud** ⓮, a modern town designed in the 1960s by the architect François Spoerry around a network of canals to resemble a contemporary Venice. Grimaud is now a seriously fashionable and expensive resort, built in traditional Provençal style, with plenty of space for boats to tie up right outside the houses.

Head inland to investigate two gorgeous *villages perchés*, **Gassin** ⓯ and **Ramatuelle** ⓰. Both have stunning views over the Golfe de St-Tropez and numerous tiny streets, some no more than an arm's length across. Between the two villages, on the highest point of the peninsula, are a group of ancient windmills, the **Moulins de Paillas**, and a superb panorama.

Collobrières to Ste-Maxime

While the eastern section of the Maures is tinged with the atmosphere of the Côte, the villages to the west remain largely unscathed. **Collobrières** ⓱, bisected by a small river, is shady and peaceful even in August. This town is famous for its *marrons glacés*, along with all manner of confections made from the local chestnuts. Unlike the nougat of Montélimar or the faïence of Moustiers, Collobrières keeps its most famous export well hidden, but a small shop attached to the main factory (the **Confiserie Azuréenne**) is a good source of chestnut delicacies.

Deep in the forest east of Collobrières is one of the real treasures of the Maures: the **Chartreuse de la Verne** ⓲ (closed Tues, religious feast days and Jan; entrance fee; tel: 04 94 43 45 41). Founded in the 18th century, the Carthusian Charterhouse suffered centuries of fires and Protestant attack. The majority of the still-existing buildings date from the 17th and 18th centuries, although the

BELOW: alon
the Côte d'O

Map
n pages
226–7

medieval cloisters and a sparsely restored monk's cell are evidence of more ancient origins. Various signs enjoining visitors to silence are a reminder that, after years of neglect, the Chartreuse is now occupied by nuns from the Order of Bethlehem.

Squeezed between the massifs of the Maures and Estérel are the major resorts of **Fréjus** ⓳ and **St-Raphaël** ⓴. For many years these towns were playgrounds for the rich, but today the choking traffic that pours through them during the summer has dissolved much of their appeal. Unfortunate high-rise developments have aggregated the two towns together into one urban mass that is overcrowded in the summer and grim in the winter.

Of the two, Fréjus, 3 km (1½ miles) inland, is certainly the more interesting, largely because it contains more vestiges of the Roman past that both towns share. The 2nd-century **Arènes** (amphitheatre) on rue Henri Vardon, although substantially damaged, is still in use as a setting for rock concerts and bullfights. In the centre of town stands the medieval **Cathédrale St-Léonce**, begun in the 10th century and bordered by fine 12th-century cloisters that feature a fantastical ceiling decorated with animals and chimera. Within the cathedral complex is an unmissable 5th-century **baptistry** (Cité Episcopale, 48 rue Fleury; open Apr–Sept: daily; Oct–Mar: closed Mon; entrance fee; tel: 04 94 51 26 30), one of the three most ancient in France, reached from an entrance on place Formigé.

Having devoted time to Fréjus's Roman and medieval attractions, it would be a shame to miss a couple of very un-Gallic curiosities nearby. A **Buddhist pagoda**, just off the N7 to Cannes, commemorates the death of 5,000 Vietnamese soldiers who perished in World War I. A prettily faded Sudanese **mosque** lies unprepossessingly in the middle of an army camp off the D4 to Bagnols.

St-Raphaël's rail terminus accounts for much of its liveliness, though it fell out of fashion as a tourist base some years

LOW:
bour front
St-Tropez.

ago. Around the mid-19th century, its attractions were much vaunted by the journalist Alphonse Karr, whose enthusiasm lured the likes of Dumas and Maupassant to winter here. Now, though less trendy, St-Raphaël has no lack of visitors, even if they're just here to lose a few francs at the rather hideous casino on the sea-front. The **Musée Archéologique** (place de la Vieille Eglise; closed Mon; entrance fee; tel: 04 94 19 25 75), next to the 12th-century Romanesque church of St-Pierre-des-Templiers, is probably the town's only worthwhile "sight". It contains a good collection of Roman amphorae and a display of underwater equipment.

Heading west along the Gulf of St-Tropez, **Ste-Maxime** ㉑ offers a taste of what St-Raphaël was like in the not-too-distant past. The archetypal Côte resort, its palm trees, promenades and parasols offer the classic *corniche* experience. Though suffering as much as its neighbours from accelerating suburban sprawl, Ste-Maxime's neat marina and relatively golden beaches are still undeniably attractive. When quayside strutting and café lounging loses its appeal, head just north to visit the **Musée du Phonographe et de la Musique Mécanique** (Museum of Sound and Mechanical Instruments; open Easter–Sept Wed–Sun; entrance fee; tel: 04 94 96 50 52), in the parc de St-Donat. It houses a wonderful collection of old phonographs, bizarre music boxes and an Art Nouveau dictaphone.

The Massif de l'Estérel

Highwaymen and sundry criminal types ruled the impenetrable reaches of the **Massif de l'Estérel** for many centuries. Separated from the neighbouring Massif des Maures by the Val d'Argens (Argens Valley), the Estérel is more sparse in vegetation – a result of the devastating forest fires that swept the area in recent decades. In addition, a disease has decimated the indigenous sea pines. However, you will still find this an appealingly wild region only steps from the glitter of the Côte.

BELOW: tiled kitchen in Salernes.

Map pages 226–7

The red porphyry rock of the Estérel tumbles down to the sea in a dramatic sweep of high hills and ravines. The coastal road, the **Corniche d'Or**, is one of the least crowded sections of the Côte, though the familiar pattern of private villas and large hotels blocking views and access to the sea can be terribly frustrating even here. Head to the section from Cap Roux to Anthéor for some welcome relief and to the inviting coves around Agay for swimming. Inland, those with an eye for a panorama should head for **Mont Vinaigre** (at 618 metres/ 2,027 ft, the highest point of the massif); for great sea views, make for the **Pic de l'Ours.**

The central Var

The central area of the Var is dominated by the fertile **Val d'Argens**, which runs horizontally across the *département*. To the south and north are the wooded, vine-covered hills that produce the majority of the *appellation d'origine controllée* (AOC) Côtes-de-Provence rosés and reds. To most tourists, however, the area is little more than a transport corridor *en route* to the Côte. **Le Luc** 22, where the *autoroute* and N7 intertwine, is a small market town which sadly has been overrun, like many of its neighbours, by the pressure of passing traffic. Its rich history as a Roman spa town and Protestant refuge can be traced in the local museum, the **Musée Historique du Centre Var** (open May–Oct Mon–Sat; tel: 04 94 60 70 20), housed in the 17th-century **Chapelle de Ste-Anne**. Look out, too, for le Luc's best-known landmark, a 16th-century hexagonal tower.

As well as its wine, olives and chestnuts, le Luc gained fame during the 1800s for the health-giving purity of its mineral water, *eau de Pioule*, which is still bottled at source on a small scale today. Perhaps less medically sound was le Luc's reputation two centuries earlier as the centre for what was considered to be the most effective cure for whooping cough. Provençal superstition maintained that children could be cured by being passed

…LOW: …hroom at Château …ntrecasteaux, …r Cotignac.

seven times under the belly of a donkey. Le Luc's donkey had such prestige that children from Draguignan and even Cannes were brought to suffer the ordeal.

Outside le Luc is **le Vieux Cannet** ㉓, one of the prettiest of the region's hill villages, clustered around an 11th-century church. Further west along the *autoroute* lies **St-Maximin-la-Ste-Baume** ㉔. Pilgrims have poured into this town since the 5th century to view one of the greatest of all Christian relics – the presumed bones of Mary Magdalene. After the so-called "Boat of Bethany" *(see page 192)* supposedly landed in the Camargue, its saintly crew dispersed to preach the word of God throughout Provence. Mary Magdalene is said to have made her way to the Massif de la Ste-Baume, where she lived in a cave for more than 30 years. She died in St-Maximin, where her remains were jealously guarded by the Cassianites.

In 1295 work began on the magnificent **Basilique Ste-Marie-Madeleine** (place des Prêcheurs; tel: 04 42 38 01 78) that now contains the relics. The basilica is considered to be one of the most impressive examples of Gothic architecture in Provence. Inside, a tiny blackened crypt, etched with centuries of grafitti, houses the relics. Visitors peer through iron bars to catch sight of the holy remains, wedged into a somewhat macabre gold setting.

The 19th-century writer Prosper Mérimée, in his role as inspector of monuments, dismissed St-Maximin as a dreary place and, excluding the basilica, it's tempting to share his view. But the **Vieille Ville** (Old Town) does have some notable medieval arcades in rue Colbert.

To the south of St-Maximin, in the ancient limestone mountain range of Ste-Baume, is the evocative, dank cave where Mary Magdalene is said to have spent those last years. Reaching its entrance involves a strenuous climb through dense forest. This forest, in particular the reaches lying below the holy cave, was a magic and sacred place to Ligurians, Gauls and Romans, and the towering

BELOW: wine country.

Map
n pages
226–7

beech trees and lush undergrowth still seem bewitchingly sylvan today.

Some 150 stone steps lead up from the shade of the forest to the cliffside cave. Inside the vast dark recess, which is now filled with altars and saintly effigies, the old stones drip water. A final effort will bring you to **St-Pilon**, which is almost the highest point of the *massif*. Mary Magdalene was said to have been lifted up to this peak by angels seven times a day during her years of cave-dwelling.

The northwest Var

North of the *autoroutes*, in the northwest corner of the Var is **Barjols** ㉕, dubbed the "Tivoli of Provence" – a small industrious town filled with streams, fountains and masses of peeling plane trees. What is reputedly the largest plane tree in France, measuring an impressive 12 metres (40 ft) in circumference, casts its shade over the most celebrated of Barjols's 25 fountains, the vast moss-covered "Champignon" (mushroom) fountain, next to the Hôtel de Ville (Town Hall) in the tiny place Capitaine Vincens.

Though the Tivoli tag attracts a good number of summer visitors, Barjols is in reality more of workaday town than a successful tourist trap. Its prosperity was originally based on its tanneries, the last of which closed in 1986. Barjols is still, however, known for the manufacture of the traditional Provençal instruments, the *galoubet* (a three-holed flute) and *tambourin* (a narrow drum), which are played simultaneously by a single musician.

Barjols's old quarter, known as "**Réal**", is being extensively renovated and, as such, is in a state of flux. Ancient cobwebbed hovels alternate with low medieval archways in the dusty alleyways around the former college **Chapelle de Notre-Dame-de-l'Assomption**. The chapel is all that remains of what was the most-favoured school for the children of the counts of Provence in the Middle Ages.

An undistinguished square located close to the chapel hides one of Barjols's best

ow:
fighters
the Massif
Maures.

treasures, the magnificent entrance to the **Maison des Postevès**, that dates back to the Renaissance.

Barjols's claim to fame rests largely on its Fête de St Marcel, which is arguably the most ancient and picturesque festival in Provence. Held on the weekend nearest to 16 January, the fête marks the town's victory over the rival village of Aups in securing the relics of St Marcel for its own chapel. The day that the relics arrived, in 1350, coincided with the long-standing pagan practice of sacrificing an ox for a village feast. Eventually, secular and Christian festivities were combined into a single ecstatic festival.

Nowadays, the festival consists of noisy processions to the sound of instruments including *galoubets* and *tambourines*, as a bust of St Marcel is paraded through the streets of the town. Every four years (2002, 2006, 2010 etc) an ox, decorated with garlands, is roasted on the place de la Roquière and then shared out among the hungry revellers.

From Aups to Thoronet

Between the empty northern expanses of the **Grand Plan de Canjuers**, a plain occupied by the French military, and the *autoroute* to the south lies a string of towns that come closest to representing the "authentic" Var.

Aups ㉖, situated on the fringes of the plain, is an access point for the Grand Canyon du Verdon (on the Var's northern border) and a busy market town. The town is crowned by a fine 16th-century clock-tower adorned with a sundial. Aups, and the northern part of the Var in general, has a strong tradition of republican resistance and it was the scene of many popular uprisings during the mid-19th century. The portal of the town's **Eglise de St-Pancrace** proudly bears the republican inscription: *Liberté, Egalité, Fraternité.*

Salernes ㉗, 10 km (6 miles) to the south, is a larger and more sprawling town than Aups, with one of the best markets in the area. Like Aups, the town of Salernes has been a centre of political

BELOW: tilemaker and son.

Map pages 26–7

resistance, especially in World War II. Above all, though, Salernes is known for being the most prolific tile-making town in the *département*. Around 15 factories still function today, many using traditional wood-fired kilns.

Salernes lacks the classic Provençal prettiness of many of the towns further east, but nearby are some unmissable gems of hill-top village architecture which are worth seeking out. Minuscule **Fox-Amphoux** 28 (pronounced "fox-amfoox" by the local Provençals) crouches on a high hill to the west, its pretty streets clustered round a Romanesque church.

More commercial, but even more spectacular, is **Tourtour** 29, "the village in the sky". A *mélange* of breathtaking views and medieval vaulted passageways, Tourtour keeps its appeal even in the crowded summer months. Sadly, its finest "monument" – two venerable elms planted in the main square to commemorate the birth of Louis XIV – recently fell prey to disease. They have been replaced by olive trees.

From **Cotignac** 30, a superb collection of 16th-century houses dominated by two ruined towers, the D50 snakes east to **Entrecasteaux** 31. The elegant **château** (contact the tourist office for information on guided tours; tel: 04 94 04 40 50), the centrepiece of this small village, was constructed for a local nobleman in the 1600s. Scandal ruined the family during the next century, when the residing *seigneur* shot his wife, and the château fell into disrepair. In 1974, however, it was bought by painter, soldier and adventurer Ian McGarvie-Munn, a larger-than-life Scotsman who married into the Ecuadorean political hierarchy. The family set about the castle's restoration, despite the death of McGarvie-Munn in 1981 and considerable local hostility.

South along the **Vallée de Bresque** (Bresque Valley) from Entrecasteaux, in the thick of the Darboussière forest, stands one of the most imposing sights in Provence: the 12th-century **Abbaye du Thoronet** 32 (open daily; entrance fee; no tourist visits

ow:
flutes
arjols.

on Sun from noon until 2pm; tel: 04 94 60 43 90; *see box below*). To reach it, travel 15 km (9 miles) southeast of Cotignac via Carcès on the D13/D279.

Draguignan

The only major inland town in the Var is **Draguignan** ❸❸, capital of the *département* until 1975, when it lost the title to Toulon. Its name recalls a dragon that was said to have terrorised the town in the 5th century. This mythical creature can be seen in stone crests on many of the town's medieval gateways and houses.

The small city's main attractions are in the tiny medieval quarter beyond the grid of 19th-century boulevards, designed by Baron Haussmann. The rue de la Juiverie still has the remains of a synagogue façade, a relic of the notable Jewish community that thrived here in the Middle Ages. Nearby is a fine clocktower built in 1663, with a wrought-iron campanile.

After the sure delights of Draguignan's bustling market days, head out of town for an eclectic collection of sights. Just to the northwest on the D955 is the mysterious stone monolith of the **Pierre de la Fée** ("fairy stone"), a vast slab of neolithic rock on three mighty stone legs. Following this road further north brings you to the verdant **Gorges de Châteaudouble**, a smaller version of the Verdon Gorges, cut by the River Nartuby. East of Draguignan, on the D59, is an **American military cemetery**, a legacy of the bitter fighting that raged around le Muy in August 1944.

The eastern Var

The villages of the eastern Var have much the same appeal as parts of the Alpes-Maritimes. **Fayence** ❸❹, the largest town in the area and a big hang-gliding centre, has little overt charm, but its satellite villages are among the prettiest in Provence.

The German artist Max Ernst (1891–1976) made **Seillans** ❸❺ his home, spending the last years of his life in a villa at the top of the village. An atmospheric place, Seillans tumbles down a sheer hillside in a mass of pink and ochre stone and steep cobbled streets. Its boundaries are marked by the hill-top château, and the shady place du Thouron at the lower end of the village. Cars are banned within the ramparts.

The town, its name derived from the "pot of boiling oil" they poured over the heads of unwelcome Arabs, is known for its perfume-making and flower cultivation, a thriving industry since 1884. In recent years, Seillans has instituted an annual flower festival, a suitably chic affair for this attractive and prosperous village. Visit the **Eglise de Notre-Dame-de-l'Ormeau**, moments away on the low road, for its stunning colourful altarpiece, carved from wood by an unknown 16th-century Italian artist.

Equally tempting, are the villages of **Bargemon**, west of Seillans, and **Mons** ❸❻ and **Bargème** ❸❼, north of Fayence. Mons has all the ingredients of a perfect Provençal village, plus a superb view of the Italian Alps, the Iles de Lérins and Corsica, from place St-Sebastien. Bargème, the highest village in the Var, perched on a peak of the **Montagne du Brouis**, is more spartan but splendidly isolated. ❑

ABBAYE DU THORONET

The austere simplicity of this 12th-century abbey may be enough to turn non-believers into believers. Thoronet is one of the Provençal trio of so-called "Cistercian sisters", together with the abbeys of Sénanque and Silvacane, which were all built during the 12th century to the ascetic precepts of the Cistercian Order. Only the play of light and shadow decorates the finely proportioned, simply designed chapel, cloisters and chapterhouse.

Neglected since before the French Revolution, the abbey was saved from ruin by Prosper Mérimée (1803–70), author of *Carmen* on which Bizet's celebrated opera was based, who urged its restoration during the 1840s. Although work continues still today, a new threat to the abbey has surfaced in recent decades. Bauxite mining, the lynchpin of the local economy, has destabilised the abbey's foundations.

Map on page 226–7

RIGHT: Statue of Liberty, St-C

Map pages 48–9

THE ALPES-MARITIMES

This area is characterised by high mountain plateaux, plunging gorges, clear sparkling rivers and, crowning some seemingly inaccessible craggy peaks, several justly celebrated hill-top villages

It would come as a surprise to many of the tourists who regularly fight for a deck chair on the French mediterranean coast to find that the Côte d'Azur has a peaceful back garden. Around 90 percent of the *département* of the **Alpes-Maritimes** remains undiscovered by tourists.

In the summer months, a combination of heat haze and smog along the overburdened Côte hides the *arrière-pays* (or back country). The rugged hills and snow-capped alpine peaks are only revealed during other seasons, affording a tempting peek at what the rest of the region has to offer.

The Vallée des Merveilles

Reaching this peaceful hinterland takes only a matter of minutes from the Côte d'Azur. The **Vallée des Merveilles** ❶ (Valley of Wonders) lies barely 70 km (40 miles) north of Nice, close to the Italian border. Its solitary population of ibex, goats and the occasional lynx are hidden from prying eyes by rugged mountains that shelter a remarkable display of prehistoric rock drawings.

Located just west of the Lac des Mèsches is the Minière de la Vallaure, an abandoned mine quarried from pre-Roman times to the 1930s. Early prospectors came in search of gold and silver but had to settle for copper, zinc, iron and lead instead. The Romans were beaten to the valley by Bronze-Age settlers who carved mysterious symbols on the polished rock, smoothed by glaciation.

These carvings were first recorded in the 17th century but were investigated only from 1879 by Clarence Bicknell, an English naturalist. Bicknell made it his life's work to chart the carvings and died in a valley refuge in 1918.

The rock carvings are similar to ones found in northern Italy, notably those in the Camerino Valley near Bergamo. However, the French carvings are exceptional in that they depict a race of shepherds rather than hunters. The scarcity of wild game in the region forced the Bronze-Age tribes to turn to agriculture and cattle-raising. Carvings of yokes, harnesses and tools depict a pastoral civilisation, and these primitive inscriptions served as territorial markers for the tribes in the area.

However, the drawings are also open to some less earth-bound interpretations. Anthropomorphic figures represent domestic animals and chief tribesmen but also dancers, devils, sorcerers and gods. Such magical totems are in keeping with Mt-Bégo's reputation as a sacred spot. Given the bleakness of the terrain, it is hardly surprising that the early shepherds

:EDING
:S: hill-top
e, Saorge.
:
d Alpes-
:imes.
r: the
ée des
;, la Turbie.

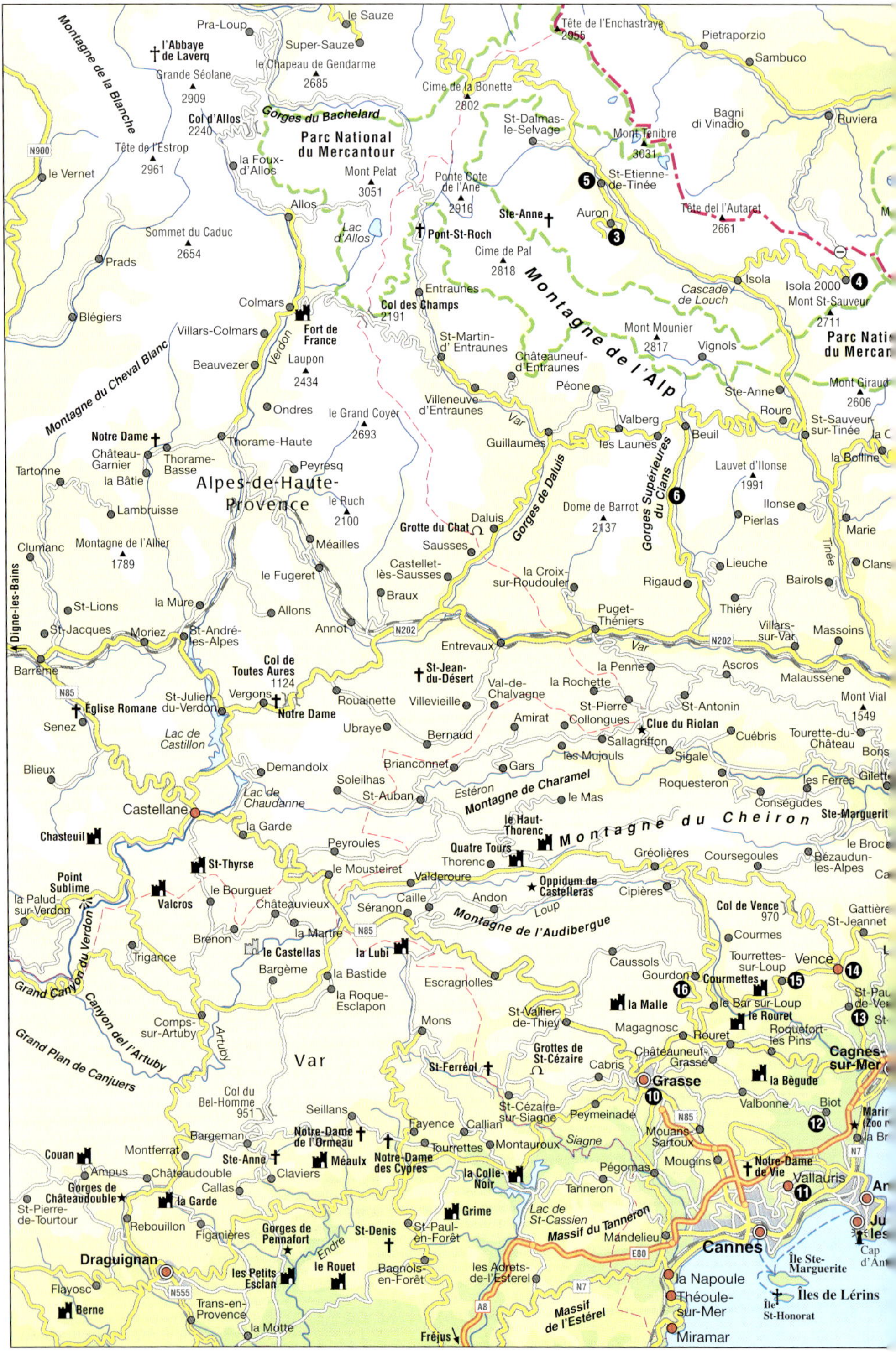
Montagne de la Blanche
Pra-Loup
le Sauze
Super-Sauze
l'Abbaye de Laverq
le Chapeau de Gendarme 2685
Grande Séolane 2909
Tête de l'Enchastraye 2955
Pietraporzio
Sambuco
Cime de la Bonette 2802
Col d'Allos 2240
Gorges du Bachelard
Parc National du Mercantour
St-Dalmas-le-Selvage
Bagni di Vinadio
Ruviera
N900
Tête de l'Estrop 2961
Mont Tenibre 3031
la Foux-d'Allos
le Vernet
Mont Pelat 3051
Ponte Cote de l'Ane 2916
St-Etienne-de-Tinée
Allos
Ste-Anne
Auron
Tête del l'Autaret 2661
Lac d'Allos
Pont-St-Roch
Sommet du Caduc 2654
Cime de Pal 2818
Prads
Montagne de l'Alp
Cascade de Louch
Isola
Isola 2000
Entraunes
Colmars
Col des Champs 2191
Mont St-Sauveur 2711
Blégiers
Fort de France
Mont Mounier 2817
Parc National du Mercantour
Villars-Colmars
St-Martin-d'Entraunes
Vignols
Beauvezer
Verdon
Laupon 2434
Châteauneuf-d'Entraunes
Montagne du Cheval Blanc
Péone
Ste-Anne
Mont Giraud 2606
Ondres
le Grand Coyer 2693
Villeneuve-d'Entraunes
Roure
Valberg
St-Sauveur-sur-Tinée
Var
Beuil
Notre Dame
Thorame-Haute
Guillaumes
les Launes
Château-Garnier
Thorame-Basse
la Bolline
Tartonne
la Bâtie
Peyresq
Lauvet d'Ilonse 1991
Alpes-de-Haute-Provence
Gorges de Daluis
Gorges Supérieures du Cians
Ilonse
le Ruch 2100
Dome de Barrot 2137
Lambruisse
Pierlas
Daluis
Grotte du Chat
Marie
Clumanc
Montagne de l'Allier 1789
Méailles
Sausses
Tinée
Lieuche
Clans
Castellet-lès-Sausses
la Croix-sur-Roudoule
Rigaud
Bairols
le Fugeret
Braux
Dignes-les-Bains
la Mure
Thiéry
St-Lions
Allons
Puget-Théniers
Annot
Villars-sur-Var
Massoins
St-Jacques
Moriez
St-André-les-Alpes
N202
Entrevaux
Var
Barrême
Col de Toutes Aures 1124
St-Jean-du-Désert
la Penne
Ascros
Malaussène
N85
la Rochette
Val-de-Chalvagne
St-Julien-du-Verdon
Vergons
Église Romane
Rouainette
Villevieille
St-Pierre
St-Antonin
Mont Vial 1549
Notre Dame
Amirat
Collongues
Clue du Riolan
Senez
Ubraye
Cuébris
Tourette-du-Château
Lac de Castillon
Bernaud
Sallagriffon
les Mujouls
Sigale
Bonson
Blieux
Demandolx
Brianconnet
Gars
Soleilhas
Roquesteron
les Ferres
Lac de Chaudanne
St-Auban
Estéron
Montagne de Charamel
le Mas
Conségudes
Castellane
le Haut-Thorenc
Montagne du Cheiron
Ste-Marguerite
la Garde
Chasteuil
Peyroules
Quatre Tours
le Broc
Gréolières
Coursegoules
Bézaudun-les-Alpes
St-Thyrse
Thorenc
Point Sublime
le Mousteiret
Valderoure
Oppidum de Castelleras
Cipières
le Bourguet
la Palud-sur-Verdon
Valcros
Caille
Andon
Col de Vence 970
Gattière
Châteauvieux
Séranon
Loup
Montagne de l'Audibergue
St-Jeannet
la Martre
N85
Courmes
Brenon
le Castellas
la Lubi
Tourrettes-sur-Loup
Vence
Trigance
Bargème
la Bastide
Caussols
Gourdon
Courmettes
Grand Canyon du Verdon
Escragnolles
la Roque-Esclapon
la Malle
le Bar sur-Loup
St-Paul-de-Vence
Canyon del l'Artuby
Comps-sur-Artuby
Mons
St-Vallier-de-Thiey
Magagnosc
le Rouret
Roquefort-les Pins
Rouret
Artuby
Grand Plan de Canjuers
Var
Grottes de St-Cézaire
Châteauneuf-Grasse
Cagnes-sur-Mer
St-Ferréol
Cabris
Grasse
la Bègude
Col du Bel-Homme 951
Seillans
St-Cézaire-sur-Siagne
Peymeinade
Valbonne
Biot
Fayence
Callian
N85
Mouans-Sartoux
Bargeman
Notre-Dame de l'Ormeau
Tourrettes
Montauroux
Siagne
Couan
Montferrat
Ste-Anne
Méaulx
Notre-Dame des Cypres
Mougins
N7
Ampus
Châteaudouble
Claviers
la Colle-Noir
Pégomas
Notre-Dame de Vie
Vallauris
Gorges de Châteaudouble
Callas
Tanneron
St-Pierre-de-Tourtour
la Garde
Grime
Lac de St-Cassien
Massif du Tanneron
Rebouillon
Figanières
Gorges de Pennafort
St-Denis
St-Paul-en-Forêt
Mandelieu
Cannes
Endre
E80
Draguignan
le Rouet
les Adrets-de-l'Esterel
Île Ste-Marguerite
Cap d'Antibes
les Petits Esclan
Bagnols-en-Forêt
la Napoule
Flayosc
N555
N7
Théoule-sur-Mer
Îles de Lérins
Île St-Honorat
Berne
Trans-en-Provence
A8
Massif de l'Estérel
la Motte
Fréjus
Miramar

looked heavenwards for help. Nowadays, as then, flocks of cows, sheep and goats graze by the lower lakes, especially at Fontanalbe. However, the abandoned stone farms and shepherds' bothies (outhouses) attest to the unprofitability of mountain farming.

The valley is accessible only on foot (although a few all-terrain vehicles are permitted), preferably only those hikers with limbs and lungs strong enough to endure a day or two of solid walking and with a stock of hiking gear to match.

There are no four-star hotels, luxury flats or villas with swimming pools here. If an overnight stay is necessary, the solid virtues of a mountain refuge will have to do. There are no buses or trains to hop on to if you get tired and no cafés in which to stop if you become thirsty. In many cases, there aren't even any paths, let alone signposts to look at if you lose your way.

For the less experienced hiker, a mountain guide is essential if you want to visit these parts, and the tourist office in **Tende** (tel: 04 93 04 73 71; *see page 263)* should be able to help with this. Hardened hikers, on the other hand, can probably make do with a more small-scale map.

The area between **Mt-Bégo** and the 2,934-metre (9,626-ft) **Montagne du Grand Capelet** makes for a good, if tough, hike, with several lakes on the way. There are mountain refuges on either end of this 60-km (40-mile) valley. If a thunderstorm strikes, don't panic – for the shepherds working in the valleys below more than 3,000 years ago, Mt-Bégo was like a temple, a place where sheep were sacrificed in an attempt to appease terrifying storms. In contemporary and less superstitious times, the mountain is simply seen as an effective lightning conductor.

Parc National du Mercantour

The Vallée des Merveilles is the centrepiece of the **Parc National du Mercantour** ❷, a huge national park that cloaks the northern edge of the Alpes-Maritimes. As a whole, it is rather less foreboding than the Vallée, but it is still a deserted mountain area and comes with the same warnings. Snow and ice are present from October until June, and the weather can change without warning or differ considerably from one valley to the next. Even in summer the local newspaper, *Nice-Matin*, is full of stories of hikers lost for days and of those found injured or even dead in the mountains. The locals and the officials at the *gendarmerie* (police station) will not laugh at people wearing heavy gear in summer, nor will they shrug at those asking about a mountain guide.

The Mercantour is the lifeblood of the Alpes-Maritimes. The sources of all the rivers that flow through the *département* can be found here – the Tinée, the Vésubie and, ironically, the Var. (After successive re-drawings of departmental boundaries the River Var is now located outside the *département* to which it gave its name.) Yet, for all its rigour, the Mercantour is now much more civilized than when it was the protected hunting ground of the kings of Italy.

Although the Comté de Nice was returned to France in 1860, the Mercantour remained an Italian enclave until 1946. After it was seceded, however, hunting was banned and the whole of the park became a nature reserve. Botanists now believe that more than half of the 4,000 or so species of wildflowers to be found in France grow in the Mercantour. Equally, of course, another reason for the survival of such natural treasures is the minimal impact that human civilisation has had on the region.

Ski country

Public transport in this area of Provence is scarce, making some form of private transport a necessity. Travel up the main road – the N202, nicknamed the Route d'Hiver des Alpes (Alpine Winter Route) – from the coastal town of St-Laurent-du-Var, and the reasons for the absence of public transport become clear. Nearer the

BELOW: ski chalet in Aur

Map on pages 248–9

coast, the highway on the eastern bank of the Var River is wide and straight, but as you gradually move inland it becomes narrower and starts to wind. Within 25 km (15 miles) you find yourself at the base of a gorge, one of the chief geological features of the *département*. These sheer valleys carved by torrents are the only way to reach the north.

From Plan-du-Var northwards, the N202 leads off into several smaller roads, following tributaries of the Var, which head down the narrow gorges and into the mountains to the skiing resorts. All are dead ends or circular routes that eventually return to the N202 as it heads west to the Lac de Castillon, in the neighbouring *département* of the Alpes-de-Haute-Provence. There is no way out of the north of the Alpes-Maritimes, which are blocked by mountains.

During the summer months, the N202 remains virtually deserted. In the winter, however, the 85 percent of the population of the Alpes-Maritimes that lives near the coast suddenly seems to acquire a taste for the wilderness of the *arrière-pays* (back country) The right bank of the Var becomes a fashionable artery on weekends as the Niçois head to the skiing resorts: Auron and Isola 2000 for the *sportif* in search of a conversation piece; **Valberg** and **Beuil** for the less pretentious or those more inclined to cross-country skiing.

Auron ❸ lines up a full range of slopes and trails for the inveterate skier, as does Isola 2000. However, modern chalets and flats are not what the back country is about. It may be fun for a while, but mountains that have had trees and rocks gouged out, with ski lifts dotting the pastures, are the inland equivalent of the concrete structures on the coast.

Isola 2000 ❹ has no history beyond skiing. It borrowed its name from the village below and added a then-futuristic-sounding number – actually the station's altitude in metres – to match the space-age architecture of the buildings. Isola seems lurid next to the charms of other more historic villages in the area that double up as ski resorts. Beuil, for example, was once the seat of the Grimaldi family. During the Middle Ages, it was also the capital of the region.

St-Etienne-de-Tinée

Head down the mountain from Auron into the old town of **St-Etienne-de-Tinée** ❺ and you rediscover rural France, with stone buildings and churches that enclose the most anonymous forms of artwork the region has to offer. The **Chapelle St-Sébastian** hides some of the frescoes that are the unsung treasures of the Alpes-Maritimes. They may be a far cry from the Picassos on the coast, but the artist was undoubtedly aware of their presence and value.

Most of the frescoes are hidden inside the simple stone churches found in villages all over the Alpes-Maritimes, such as the **Chapelle St-Antoine** in the village of **Cians**. Many were painted on ceilings and walls by artists whose names have not survived the five centuries that

ALPINE TRANSPORT

Some form of personal transport is essential to get around the Alpes-Maritimes, as public transport is poor, centred on coach routes to some of the larger towns and the skiing resorts. Only two railways run inland: one (four times daily) from Nice to Sospel, Breil, then on to Cuneo in Italy; the other, dubbed the Train des Pignes by the locals, goes from Nice to Digne four times a day, taking in many small villages en route.

Train travel inland is a commodity that, thankfully, has been neglected by the regional council. Soon after the first trains crossed the Massif de l'Estérel in 1863, the Côte d'Azur began to take on the crowded appearance that it thrives upon today. However, in the *arrière-pays* there are many ruined railway viaducts and stretches of disused track to testify to a different attitude. The most striking is the Pont du Loup, which straddles the southern edge of the Gorges du Loup.

their masterpieces have endured. Others are by figures whose fame has not gone beyond the art world, such as Louis Bréa, possibly because their work lacks the transportability of framed canvas.

The Gorges du Cians

The majority of spectacular sights in this region, however, have to be attributed to Mother Nature, most notably the **Gorges Supérieures du Cians** ❻, which are located on the way to the ski slopes at Beuil and Valberg. The gorges are formed of a deep red slate, which is a step away from the more typical Provençal narrow limestone rift valley. The mix of red from the slate and the green from the vegetation makes for a colourful contrast that does not abate even when the weather is dull.

From here the **Vallée de la Tinée** becomes disappointing, though the **Gorges de la Mescla** at its southern end have spectacular slabs of rock overhanging the road and the river.

The Vallée de la Vésubie

To revive one's enthusiasm for the area, the glorious **Vallée de la Vésubie** is on hand. Within easy reach of the coast, it takes you from a Mediterranean landscape (pines rooted on parched rock and dusty soil; olive trees) into a fresher Alpine scenery of tall dark-green pines, waterfalls near la Boréon and, at Roquebillière, green pastures.

Situated a few kilometres to the west of St-Martin-Vésubie is **Valdeblore** and a small skiing resort at **la Colmiane** ❼, complete with a few old chalets. Visitors like to call the area "Little Switzerland", which produces a quizzical look on the face of many of the locals – if only because the translation, "*Petit Suisse*", is a brand name for a type of cottage cheese. The name is, in fact, a very apt reminder that the region north of Nice formed part of the kingdom of Savoy for several centuries. The same kingdom covered what is now contained within the western half of Switzerland.

BELOW: hotel sign near Etienne-de-Tinée.

Map
n pages
248–9

The valley is rich in revolutionary history. Republican soldiers on their way south to Nice in 1793 were attacked here by a small local army, which used the area's geography to its advantage. They literally sneaked up behind the enemy and pushed them off the cliff face. The location of this minor setback to the French Republic is known as the Saut des Français, or "the Frenchmen's Leap".

The Vallée de la Vésubie is also lined by several crumbling and precarious mule tracks, which were once used by smugglers. One of the substances transported along the tracks was salt, brought in by traders from Italy anxious to avoid the *gabelle*, a tax on salt imposed shortly after the Revolution.

St-Martin-Vésubie ❽ offers cool respite as a mountaineering centre in the summer. This is a sleepy and unpretentious small town, disturbed only by the rush of water down a 1-metre wide (3-ft) canal that bears a distinct resemblance to an overgrown gutter. All its native inhabitants seem to have the rough and thick skin that goes along with decades spent in the mountains, yet they are unmistakably Mediterranean by dint of their robust, olive complexion.

In summer, they sit by and watch the hikers leave the Bureau des Guides de la Haute-Vésubie, generally on a trip into the nearby Mercantour. Their winter routine seems to change little, though much of the watching is done from behind closed windows (temperatures can be over 27°C/50°F colder than in the warm season). Summer for a Vésubian starts on 2 July, when a procession wends its way out of St-Martin carrying an 800-year-old wooden statue of Notre-Dame-de-Fenestre 12 km (7 miles) to the sanctuary at **Madone de Fenestre**. Winter begins when the procession makes the return journey in the third week of September.

Utelle, at the foot of the Vallée de la Vésubie, has a similar religious vocation. Its sanctuary, the **Madone d'Utelle** ❾, is on the hill above the village, at a height

LOW:
agers take
e to stop
d chat.

of 1,154 metres (3,786 ft). The view is impressive, taking in the whole of the south and west down to the coast. Looking north, up the valley, you can see the gradual rise of the mountains.

Grasse

The areas nearer the coast are already becoming more developed. The greater width of the lower valleys has allowed for the sprawling, ramshackle development of large towns such as **Grasse** ❿.

France's perfume capital (literature fans may recognise Grasse as the 18th-century setting for Patrick Süskind's excellent if gruesome novel, *Perfume*) is a town with a venerable past. Between 1138 and 1227 it was a free city, allied to Pisa and Genoa, and governed by a consulate, like the Italian republics. It became a bishopric in 1243 and remained so until 1791, becoming a focal point for local power. Its most famous cleric was the 15th-century Bishop Isnard de Grasse head of the monastery on the Iles de Lérins.

The town was annexed by the counts of Provence until 1481, when Provence was united with France. Grasse continued to trade with Italy, importing animal skins and selling linen and leather goods. Grasse leather was of high quality, typified by its greenish hue, caused by treating it with myrtle leaves. In the 16th century, the fashion for perfumed gloves (masking, along with pomanders and handkerchiefs, the undesirable smell of the populace) was introduced by Catherine de Medici. This encouraged the perfume industry in Grasse, but it was not until the 18th century that tanning and perfumery began to develop as separate trades.

On a still day, Grasse lives up to its reputation as a scent capital – a sweet aroma lingers in the air from the three large perfume factories dotted around the town. The perfumiers **Fragonard, Molinard** and **Galimard** offer guided tours for visitors, including the chance to create your own perfume, but much of the finely tuned creation of scents for Paris

BELOW: the Madone d'Utelle.

Map
n pages
248–9

couturiers is carried out in small unnoticed laboratories on the cours Honoré Cresp. Don't expect much antiquity beyond the huge copper vats used to distil perfume: their modern factories have to keep up with a cost-efficient 21st century.

History is provided at the **Musée Internationale de la Parfumerie** (8 place du cours Honoré Cresp; open June–Sept: daily; Oct–May: Wed–Sun; tel: 04 93 36 80 20), an elegant 18th-century mansion housing a wonderful display of antique perfume bottles. Best of all is the greenhouse garden of Mediterranean and subtropical perfumed plants.

Beyond perfume, Grasse is little more than a provincial town on a hill. The top of the hill, peppered with red villas surrounded by cypress trees, peering out occasionally at a panorama of Cannes, is the most affluent part of Grasse. Down below, in the darkened narrow alleyways is the **Vieille Ville** (Old Town).

Grasse suffers from faded glory; the days when it welcomed regular holiday visits from the British monarch, Queen Victoria, or Napoleon's sister, Pauline, are distant. The elegant cypress trees are confined to the gardens of the villas above and the remaining palms are somewhat scraggy. The casino is being rebuilt in a bid to recapture some of that swinging clientèle that made the Côte d'Azur a cliché.

To go with the lavender, mimosa and jasmine that grows on the surrounding terraced hills is the town's **Villa-Musée Fragonard** (23 boulevard Fragonard; June–Sept: daily; Oct–May: Wed–Sun; tel: 04 93 40 32 64). The perfumer Jean-Honoré Fragonard (1732–1806) was as torn between Paris and Grasse (his place of birth and death) as he was torn between the charms of several wealthy consorts. However, Grasse has managed to hold on to the elegant villa to which Fragonard retreated, which contains many of the artist's floral and voluptuous works, thanks to a series of paintings commissioned by Madame du Barry. They also possess the *oeuvres* of his less-renowned son and grandson.

All in all, this is not a town that shouts its interest at you. You have to find the hidden gems. On the south wall of the nave of the **Cathédrale Nôtre-Dame-de-Puy** hang three Rubens paintings: *The Crown of Thorns*, *The Crucifixion* and *St Helen in Exaltation of the Holy Cross*, painted in Rome in 1601. The **Musée de l'Histoire de Provence** (2 rue Mirabeau; June–Sept: daily; Oct–May: Wed–Sun; tel: 04 93 36 01 61), in a splendid 18th-century building, shows how the Provençals used to live.

Vallauris

The town of **Vallauris** ⓫, which owes its contemporary fame largely to its connection with artist Pablo Picasso (1881–1973), is a predominately residential town, hidden in a valley of its own barely 3 km (2 miles) from the sea. The mimosa on the surrounding hillsides struggles for a revival after having suffered some hard winters in the last decades. At least the orange groves survived, leaving some idea of the summer light that lured

HT:
· inside
Madone
elle.

Picasso away from the more arid inland sprawl of Mougins.

Ceramics have been the livelihood of Vallauris for more than four centuries, and unfortunately now the main shopping street is thick with tacky shops selling plates, bowls and other artefacts. Uphill, however, visitors can experience the more high-brow side of Vallauris, in the shape of the town's two prestigious museums, both of which are housed in the château on the the place de la Libération and feature numerous works by Picasso. The **Musée Nationale Picasso** (Château de Vallauris, closed Tues; entrance fee; tel: 04 93 64 16 05), with the masive *War and Peace* mural that the artist finished in 1952, is one. (Note that there is also a Musée Picasso, which is larger than this exhibition space, in Antibes.) Just outside the Château de Vallauris, note Picasso's bronze of a man holding a sheep, which he presented to the town in 1949.

Situated next door, the town's other museum, the **Musée Municipal/Musée de la Céramique** (Château de Vallauris; closed Tues; entrance fee; tel: 04 93 64 16 05) is devoted to *"l'art céramique"* and exhibits some of the ceramics that Picasso produced during his six years on the rue de Fournas. The Madoura Pottery, which is set a few yards away from the summer bustle on the main avenue Clemenceau, still retains the copyright to Picasso's ceramics – an arrangement that dates from the friendship between the artist and the workshop's owners, the Ramie family.

Biot

The artist Fernand Léger (1881–1955) adopted **Biot** ⓬, a *village perché* (perched, or hill-top, village) in a valley about 3 km (2 miles) from the sea, as his outpost. Shortly before his death, he bought the land that was later used by his wife, Nadia, to build a museum for his works. The **Musée National Fernand Léger** (chemin de Val de Pome; closed Tues; entrance fee; tel: 04 92 91 50 30)

BELOW: pott
in Vallauris.

Map
n pages
248–9

has a vast ceramic mosaic on the outside, and is the permanent home of nearly 400 of the artist's paintings, carpets, stained glass and ceramics.

The stark design of the Léger museum, the creation of a Niçois architect, stands out against the rusticity of Biot. The steep cobbled alleyways are lethal once the rain falls, causing the visitor to slip and slide with his precious cargo of Biot glass and pottery.

A brief look through one of the gaps between the ramparts shows yet another landscape for the Alpes-Maritimes. Its own private valley with a view reminiscent of Tuscany: cypress trees and the occasional goat wandering nonchalantly in between villas and swimming pools.

St-Paul-de-Vence

Further inland is **St-Paul-de-Vence** ⓭. Countless celebrities have chosen to live in the valleys below Vence and St-Paul – a cheaper alternative to the hills of expensive Cannes. The Mediterranean vegetation is still here, emphasised at times by the cultivated sprawl of cyclamen and primula in the gardens. The curious bright blue dots add to the impression of colour brought by the flowers in the spring and summer light, though the feeling dwindles somewhat when a more attentive glance reveals that they are swimming pools.

St-Paul is a larger version of Biot. Here, however, the emphasis is on artists' studios and medieval history rather than glass. There should be no fear of the cannon that menacingly points towards you at the entrance to the village; the favourite ammunition in one minor skirmish with the inhabitants of Vence was cherry stones. Nevertheless, the village had a more serious function through the centuries as a fortress guarding the entrance to the Var region.

Art has thrived in St-Paul for hundreds of years. The church houses paintings by Murillo and one by Tintoretto as well as works by other Italian masters.

.OW: asso's *omme mouton n with heep)* 'allauris.

Nevertheless, it wasn't until the 1920s that the village became known as a centre for art. The **Auberge de la Colombe d'Or** was a meeting place for a bevy of artists – including Picasso, Utrillo, Bonnard, Chagall, Modigliani, Soutine – who, as the tale goes, left their canvasses behind, sometimes to settle long-running accounts. Whatever the truth, the Colombe d'Or has now assembled its own priceless – and private – collection of paintings and its own ceramic mural by Léger. You have to dine or stay here, however – a delightful if pricey experience – in order to see the collection. It would be difficult, however, to rival the collection to be found further up the hill, at the **Fondation Maeght** *(see panel, below right)*.

Back in St-Paul, lesser mortals can at least sit opposite la Colombe d'Or at the **Café de la Paix**, which looks as if it provided the model for the French café in countless Hollywood productions. Amid all the contemporary richness and revelry, it is worth remembering that St-Paul's history is rather more harsh. When King François I built the ramparts of the village in the 16th century, he uprooted all the inhabitants and packed them off to live in nearby la Colle-sur-Loup.

Over 100 years later, new residents arrived in the form of the monks of the Ordre des Pénitents Blancs. The order, created by the Bishop of Grasse, lent its name to countless chapels and churches throughout the region. Mercifully, the monks, clad in hooded white gowns, no longer parade eerily through the streets to celebrate the Lord's Supper.

Vence

Modern-art fans should end their journey by making straight for **Vence** ⓮ and its **Chapelle du Rosaire** (468 avenue Henri Matisse; open July–Aug: daily; Sept–June: Tues and Thur; entrance fee; tel: 04 93 58 03 26). Designed by Henri Matisse (1869–1954) in 1951, the chapel is probably the most recent example of the kind of religious patronage that brought artists such as Michelangelo to decorate churches across Italy.

In design the chapel is typically Provençal and simple. Rows of lofty, narrow arches form the windows, and the tiled roof is dominated elegantly by a tall and thin wrought-iron cross. Overall it is strikingly pure and bright, with the only colour in its white interior brought by the stained-glass windows. Matisse called it his most satisfying work.

Vence is a large, lively with 21,000 inhabitants. Its origins date to the 5th century, and its turbulent history matches that of Entrevaux: Ligurians, Lombards, Romans, countless Christians and Saracens plus the Germans and Italians of World War II all passed through here. Some invaders caused destructions – the Lombards flattened Vence on the two occasions that they occupied it. The 15th-century walls of the **Vieille Ville** (old town) within the modern town, betray its former feudal vocation.

The historical instability of the town, however, has lent it curiosity value. The **Ancienne Cathédrale**, located in place

FONDATION MAEGHT

The Fondation Maeght (Monté des Trious; open dail entrance fee; tel: 04 93 32 81 63) is arguably the mos interesting of all the museums on the Côte d'Azur – on of the best art collections in the world in an exquisit setting. The building's brick-and-white-concrete exterio was designed by the Spanish architect José-Luis Ser who was heavily influenced by Le Corbusier, and is par nered by Miró sculptures dotted around the pine-shade garden. All the structural features were devised to pro mote an understanding of 20th-century art, and the arch tect worked directly with some of the artists, principal Miró and Chagall, to achieve this.

Aimé Maeght's position as an art dealer undoubted helped him in his efforts to assemble the collection b 1964. Few people can boast of having a Chagall with th personal dedication "à Aimé et Guigette (Marguerit Maeght". Fewer still could have had the friendship knowledge and money to integrate mosaics by Miró an Braque or a garden full of Giacomettis into the whole ar then continue collecting works of the following young generations. Some of the holdings are on loan to speci exhibitions from time to time, but the collection is so va that there is always something to replace them.

Map n pages 248–9

Clemenceau was built on the site of the Roman temple and mixes a patchwork of styles and eras. The cathedral possesses a simple baroque facade, some Byzantine stonework, Gothic windows, Roman tombs and a mosaic by Chagall. Indeed, Vence's religious offerings are as refreshing as the fountain in the place du Peyra and the bright atmosphere in the summer months.

Despite its popularity, the town retains a purer feeling of southern France, with its vegetable and fruit markets and the restaurants spilling into the squares.

Tourrettes-sur-Loup

In the southeastern corner of the Alpes-Maritimes is the attractive village of **Tourrettes-sur-Loup** ⓯, where geraniums flower on the stone walls throughout spring and summer. Here, simple methods are used to keep the tourist hordes at bay: traffic is allowed to pass through the village but it may not stop in its steep and narrow alleyways. This *village perché* overlooks the southeastern end of the Val du Loup, though the Loup river is a short distance further down through olive trees and, in spring, fields of violets.

The reason behind Tourrettes's relative emptiness, even in the height of summer, is probably just that it lives in the shadow of its more illustrious neighbours, Vence and St-Paul. Arts and crafts are carried out without the glare of renown, although with equal skill. The potters, painters and wood-carvers have to be sought out. Most such craftspeople welcome the public, but their only sign is normally the open door of a village house. Few attempt the external displays to be found in Vallauris or Biot.

The town's history is tranquil, as it attracted few of the attacks by invading Arabs or Lombards experienced by its other perched neighbours. Today, the only time the village ventures to cry its fame comes with the Fête des Violettes in March, a processional celebration of the flowers in the surrounding countryside.

LOW: buffet ntain at Fondation eght.

But March is still the low season as far as tourism is concerned, with only a trickle of outsiders making their way to the town for the festivities.

There are no ramparts, walls or battlements surrounding Tourrettes. The only war-like evocation comes with the 15th-century château, once the entrance to the village and now in the middle and occupied by the *mairie* (Town Hall). A belfry marks the archway that leads through to the cobbled hills of the old part of the village. The church stands in the main square and houses a Bréa triptych – an apt reminder that Tourette is on the edge of the *arrière-pays*.

The Gorges du Loup

Descending into the river valley at Pont-du-Loup, you find yourself at the mouth of the imposing **Gorges du Loup**, the nearest of the inland rift valleys to the southern coast. This valley is also one of the most spectacular in the region, with the torrential river scything its way through a deep gorge of grey rock and lush vegetation.

There are several waterfalls in this area *(see panel, below left)*, most notably the **Cascade de Courmes**, which is to be found halfway along the Gorges du Loup, and the smaller **Cascade des Desmoiselles**. Further up still are some nice spots for trout fishing. Trips in the river valley are punctuated by warning signs about sudden rises in the water level, depending on the workings of a small hydro-electric station upstream.

WATERFALLS

The Cascade de Courmes – a waterfall that drops about 50 metres (160 ft) into a pool by a roadside tunnel – is situated halfway along the Gorges du Loup. A path runs underneath the falls, but years of erosion and a covering of moss have made it slippery and treacherous. The start of the path is around 20 metres (65 ft) to the right of the water. Another path, which is for the agile only, as it involves a short scrambled climb, begins on the opposite side of the road by the tunnel entrance.

Heading north, the road crosses to the other side of the gorges. A glimpse of the river from the bridge that links the cliffs (be careful that you don't lean against a rickety barrier) bears witness to the link between the spectacular and the dangerous. Forty metres (130 ft) below, the Loup plunges through the rocks. A smaller waterfall, the Cascade des Desmoiselles, is located nearby.

Gourdon

If the term *village perché* needed a perfect example, it would find it in **Gourdon** ⓰. One whole side of the town teeters on the edge of a rocky cliff, a natural rampart obviating the need for any fortress walls to repel invaders. The feudal **Château de Gourdon** (open June–Sept: daily; Oct–May: closed Tues; entrance fee; tel: 04 93 09 68 02) was restored most recently during the 16th century. Inside you are treated to a display of all the charms of feudality: weaponry, a dungeon – complete with a bed, which apparently enabled the torturers' victims to rest in between sessions – and a small collection of medieval art and memorabilia. The château also contains a museum of naive art, which has an original painting by Douanier Rousseau (1844–1910).

The château is reached after a brief walk up into the village – cars are not allowed here. A few steps more allow you to run the gauntlet of the main street, lined with small shops full of crafts and postcards. The main square lies just down this way, with an anonymous and simple 11th-century church. But the view from the end of the square is Gourdon's real delight: the Val du Loup to the sea, the Massif de l'Estérel to the mouth of the Var, hills and valleys. Apart from defensive reasons, the *villages perchés* were placed as they were so as to have a clear line of sight to allied villages, to signal impending invasions.

The road from Gourdon, which is very narrow at the top and bottom, winds

Map
n pages
248–9

down to Grasse. Curiously, the middle section of the road widens into a large expanse of smooth pitch-black tarmac, though the road never takes on the kind of traffic that could warrant such an extension. In 1988, several villages around the Val du Loup began to voice concern at projects for a new *autoroute* running inland, ostensibly to relieve the load on the coastal motorway and to ease access to the Côte d'Azur. Controversy still surrounds the proposal.

Finding a straight stretch of road on the eastern side of the Var River, where the Alps spill down into the sea, is virtually impossible. Immediately behind Nice, a cluster of rocky hills surround **Mt-Chauve** (or "bald mountain"). The name was aptly chosen – vegetation stops dead partway up, leaving a bald patch at the top.

The "monk's head" is occupied by a disused fort with a 360-degree view. From here, the distance between villages appears short, and you may optimistically think of a quickly completed excursion through the dusty hills. However, you will find that the miles are often tripled as you slowly swing through a pitted series of hairpin turns from one commune to the next.

Contes

A Renaissance fountain set in the place Republicaine of **Contes** ⑰ offers some refreshment. And therein hangs a Provençal tale of how the God-fearing inhabitants of this small village tried to chase the devil away. The devil, being a thirsty soul, was known to quench his dry palate at the village fountain. The Contois conspired to capture him by smearing glue over the square, and he was banished from the town.

Contes is a rarity in that it is not situated at the top of a hillside but rather on a spur that juts out into the Vallée du Paillon. The château is found at the bottom of the village and it retains its Provençal name, Lou Castel.

LOW: ectacular ountain enery ar Utelle.

This area is more densely populated than the rest of the inner reaches of the *département*, as the villages within 25 km (15 miles) of Nice begin to assume the role of dormitories.

Coaraze

Few hamlets have stranger names than **Coaraze** ⓲, a derivation of the Provençal for *queue rasée*, or "shaved-off tail." Here, the devil appears anew. In search of a new home after his banishment from Contes, he entered this medieval village. The inhabitants once again took exception to his presence and this time captured him by his tail. He managed to struggle free, but his tail was ripped off in the process.

Despite its medieval setting, Coaraze has taken on an artistic zest that is more akin to the towns on the other side of the Var River. On the wall alongside the cobbled stairway leading up to the church are three ceramic sun-dials, one by Jean Cocteau (1889–1963), the eccentric writer, filmmaker and artist *(see Menton, pages 286–7).*

Situated on the edge of the village, the **Chapelle Bleue** furthers the strange mix. From the outside, the building appears to be no more than one of the interminable number of ageing chapels in the area. However, the inside has been well restored, with post-war frescoes decorating the walls. Everything, including the light through the stained-glass window, is blue, which is a reminder of the Côte d'Azur rare in these parts – here, the light rarely takes on the clarity for which the region is justly famous.

Peillon and Tende

Peillon ⓳ offers far more classical charms. It is medieval once again, a period of history that seems rather sombre and full of strife. Peillon is painfully thrust on to the jagged edge of a small mountainside, the houses clustered together in such a way that from a distance the village appears to be a castle,

BELOW: farmers' wives in Berthmont-les-Bains.

Map on pages 248–9

with the church standing proud in the middle like a turret. Located barely 15 km (9 miles) from the avenues of Nice, the little town has no streets, just alleyways and steps.

Heading northeast of Peillon, within easy reach of the international border, the Italian influence starts. **Tende** ⑳ remained under Italian rule for many decades – the town was handed back to France in 1947 after a plebiscite – but its inhabitants always professed to feel French. It looks Italian, however. The atmosphere is medieval, but not with the dismal stone walls of so many of the neighbouring villages.

Many houses have plastered walls, painted with matt colours that fade under the onslaught of the sun. Others use a green-hued schist, as befits an alpine area using local materials. Indeed, the style is more Romanesque, and each has a balcony and an overhanging roof.

Tende, like any self-respecting town in a predominantly Catholic region has a church. But it is a different type than its western neighbours, with a belfry shaped like two stacked barrels and a small roof. Built in the 15th century, green columns protect its doorway.

ELOW: aorge-style violi.

La Brigue and Saorge

La Brigue ㉑, which is only a brief excursion away from Tende, offers a similar history, as does the majority of the **Vallée de la Roya**. This valley, which runs south from Tende towards Breil, was retained by the Italians until October 1947, because it was the only link with the Mercantour and the hunting grounds of the king of Italy. The current border has been designated according to the water table. No tributaries cross the frontier on either side.

The isolated **Chapelle de Notre-Dame-des-Fontaines**, located near la Brigue, is worthy of note. Visits to the chapel are arranged through the tourist office in la Brigue's town hall (tel: 04 93 04 36 07). Note that if a visitor finds a chapel locked, the normal procedure – something that may shock guarded city dwellers – is to ask about the key at a nearby restaurant or *mairie*.

Saorge ㉒ is a spectacular sight. Squeezed onto a cliff face at the entrance of a gorge, it is the only town in the region to have lent its name to a gorge. It takes a trek on foot to reach the centre, through some of the steepest cobbled alleyways one could imagine in an urban, albeit small, area. Some people do still live here, but the young tend to be quick to move out. The contemporary exodus contrasts with ancient times, when it seemed like everyone was trying to invade the fortified village – unsuccessfully. Such was its reputation for impregnability that the town's potential invaders eventually all stopped trying.

The steepness does not rule out the existence of a Renaissance church, **St-Sauveur**, with an imposing altar of red and gold. Bear in mind that the church organ dates from the 19th century, and some poor mules had to carry it up the hill. Saorge has not forgotten the contribution the animals made (and still make) to life in the village. One of the village festivals is dedicated to St Eloi, patron saint of mules.

Visitors may complain about the steep alleyways but, for the Franciscan monks that dwell in the monastery, this all helps create a tranquil and serene atmosphere. The monastery rests in a small square at the top of the village, among a cluster of olive trees. Below it, the valley apparently has a good echo, a feature that allowed 20th-century soldiers to communicate with a nearby château from the ruined castle above. The Franciscans only returned to their home in 1969.

Breil and Sospel

By some quirk of administration and diplomacy in 1947, the frontier south of **Breil-sur-Roya** ㉓ was not arranged according to the border rules applied to the section further north. The Roya River flows happily through the Italian border and into the sea at Ventimiglia. So does the main road, and Breil offers visitors their last chance to turn off to head towards Sospel and Nice.

Breil produces olive oil and is the centre for a type of olive that is only found in the Alpes-Maritimes, the *cailletier*. Olive cultivation in this *département* is unusual in that the fruit are grown up to an altitude of 800 metres (2,600 ft), which is twice as high as they are cultivated anywhere else. Production of olive oil, however, is quite limited – to about 285 tonnes per year. Most of it is used to make high-quality cooking oil, and little of the production falls to industrial use. Breil itself lays claim to more than 40,000 olive trees and celebrates a lively grand Fête de l'Olive at harvest time, some time in October.

The town of Breil makes for a restful stop. The drama of Saorge is past, and here the urban centre lies on a flat expanse of valley, with the wide Roya running calmly through it.

Sospel ㉔ shares the tranquillity and the olive groves, if not the river. The

BELOW: dusk in winte over the Alpe Maritimes.

Map
n pages
248–9

Bevéra, a tributary of the Roya, runs through Sospel instead, leaving a series of islets around an old bridge. The bridge is an oddity, with a toll gate in the middle that was reconstructed following World War II, when it was destroyed in a bombing raid. North of the bridge is the oldest part of the town, a close cluster of buildings with wooden balconies. By the river there is still an old sheltered washing trough filled with water even at the height of summer.

The setting for Sospel is Italian: the valley with its olive groves, the rivers meeting at the town with their islets, the toll gate on the old bridge. The impression is reinforced on the southern side by the square around the church. Of no particular shape and bare, the town has a baroque church at one end. All the buildings are plastered and painted in weathered shades of orange, yellow, ochre or red, with contrasting green shutters. This is a style predominant in the east and all the way down through Italy, but which disappears just a few miles to the west. The trick here is to head south towards the coast at Menton, a town with similar architectural appeal. The road climbs to the **Col de Castillon** then winds interminably through a small dry valley.

Piène to Gorbio

Slightly northeast of Sospel, the village of **Piène** offers a reminder of how relatively underdeveloped this part of France remains. An Italianate square similar to Sospel but smaller, its unkempt buildings only escape tattiness by virtue of being baked by the sun. The church has a rather odd exterior, possessing a bell tower with strange pointed horns on all four corners. And tacked beneath the arch of the belfry is a modern-style clock. The rest of this dusty, deserted and humble village, however, seems to have missed modernity.

Some 20 km (12 miles) beyond the Castillon Pass, you drop below the motorway into the populous coastal resort of Menton *(see pages 286–7),*

LOW: villa
a Turbie.

Map on pag 248–

which comes as rather a shock after the tranquil villages of the interior. You might prefer to rise away from the coastal sprawl towards the sanctuary of villages such as **Castellar** ㉕. Moving further west, with the ridge overlooking the Mediterranean on your left, you pass simple hillside villages including **Ste-Agnès** ㉖ and **Gorbio** ㉗.

Here, within a few kilometres of one another stand two different worlds. To the south is the developed coast, peppered with villas and shops in between the pine trees. Just north is the simplicity, quietness and relative poverty of the back country.

La Turbie

Sitting on the edge of the overdeveloped world is **La Turbie** ㉘. Sometimes the town is caught in a swirl of clouds, lending a rather more sinister vein to the Roman ruin of the **Trophée des Alpes** (18 avenue Albert I; open Sept–Mar: daily except Mon; entrance fee; tel: 04 93 41 20 84). Set on the Grand Corniche (known as the Via Julia by the Romans and Napoleon's favourite way to Italy), the Trophée is the bait, and the Grande Corniche is the fishing line. The tourists reel themselves in.

LEFT: statue of Honoré Fragonard, Grasse

The Trophée des Alpes originally was presented as a reward by the Roman Senate to the Emperor Augustus for his successful campaign against the remaining rebellious tribes of Gaul. Only one side with four columns remains to bear witness to the imposing 50 metres (164 ft) the monument used to measure. This section was restored by archaeologists, using original stones, to a height of 32 metres (105 ft). Inscribed inside are tributes to Augustus and a list of the 44 conquered tribes. Adorning the Trophy's walls are quotes from Virgil and one from Dante's *Purgatory*.

Below the monument lies the **Eglise St-Michel**. This church is an 18th-century offering, with a domed top to the bell tower and a clock. Baroque styles use elaborate colour and decoration, and this one is no exception. Inside, the red marble is extensive, bordering on the gaudy, insolent style that might befit a film star's villa in St-Tropez.

The Grande Corniche is the highest of the three corniches that run parallel to the coast. Of them, it's also the longest route from Monaco to Nice, though not the slowest since heavy traffic clogs the coast road. The Moyenne Corniche is the quickest and probably the most stylish of the three routes. Alfred Hitchcock caught a bus here, as an extra in his 1955 film, *To Catch a Thief*. In that same movie, Cary Grant lived alongside the road, a retired cat burglar, residing in this part of the Côte d'Azur because he wanted to avoid the bustle of the coast and the big towns. Who could forget Grace Kelly – the beautiful Hollywood star and the epitome of elegance who was having a real-life romance at the time of filming in 1956 with Prince Rainier of Monaco – as she swooped along the curves of the Moyenne Corniche in her roadster? She died tragically following a car-accident on that same corniche in 1982. ❑

The Perfumes of Provence

The gentle climate, rich soil and cradle of mountains that protect Grasse from the north wind make it an ideal place for flower production almost all year round: golden mimosa in March; fragrant roses by early summer and jasmine in autumn. In addition, high above the town, the mountains are terraced with rows of purple lavender.

The perfume industry in Grasse originated with an immigrant group of Italian glovemakers in the 16th century. They discovered the wonderful scents of the flowers in the area and began perfuming their soft leather gloves, a favourite way to use perfume (along with pomanders and scented handkerchiefs) at a time when the odour of the general populace definitely required masking.

Demand for the floral perfumes steadily grew in the 18th and 19th centuries, and Grasse prospered as a perfume mecca. Local production of raw material declined, however, after World War II. Competition from countries such as Turkey, Egypt and Bulgaria, where labour costs are much lower than in France, proved decisive, and the gentle climate attracted many wealthy people to the area, pushing the price of land sky-high and causing acres to be sold off as building plots.

Today, Grasse is better known for improving raw materials imported from other countries. Nonetheless, you can still see vast mountains of rose petals, vats of mimosa or jonquils and spadefuls of violets and orange blossom just picked and waiting to be processed each morning.

The flowers must be picked early, when the oil is most concentrated, and delivered immediately. It takes vast quantities of blooms to produce the tiniest amounts of "absolute" (concentrated) perfume: around 750 kilos (1,650 lbs) of roses for just one kilo (2.2 lbs) of rose "absolute" and about 4,000 kilos (8,800 lbs) for one kilo of essential oil.

There are various different methods used to create the "absolutes" or essential oils that the perfumer mixes to create a fragrance. The oldest method is steam distillation, which is now used mainly for orange blossom. Water and flowers are boiled in a still, and the essential oils are extracted by steam.

Another ancient, though expensive method is *enfleurage*. The flowers are layered with a semi-solid mixture of lard, spread over glass sheets and stacked in wooden tiers. When the fat is fully impregnated with perfume, the scent is separated out by washing the *axonge* with alcohol. A more modern method is extraction by volatile solvents, leaving a final concentrate called the "absolute".

The highly trained perfumers or "noses" of Grasse can identify and classify hundreds of fragrances. In creating a fragrance, a perfumer is rather like a musician, using different "chords" of scent to blend together in harmony. The desired result is a complex perfume that will radiate around the body in a slow process of diffusion – what the French call "*sillage*". A good perfume may include hundreds of different ingredients to achieve the right balance, using powerful animal fixatives such as ambergris, civet and musk to capture the delicate, ephemeral fragrances of the Provençal hillsides. ❑

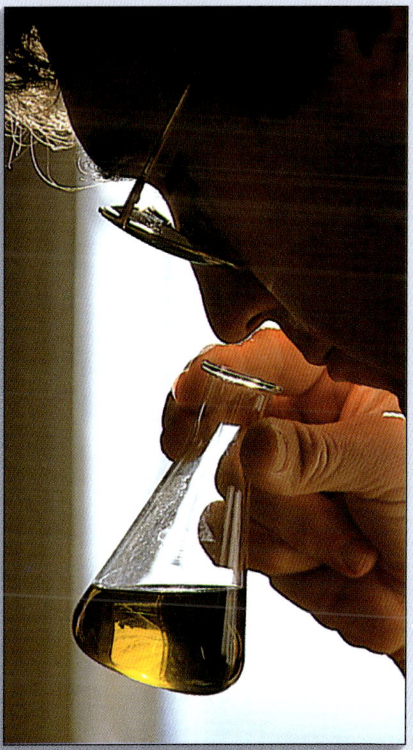

HT:
ose"
ork.

Map
ı pages
272–3

THE CÔTE D'AZUR

More than a century after France's southern coast established itself as a tourist hotspot, it remains a chic holiday destination. Lovely beaches, an artistic legacy and an unspoilt hinterland add to the allure

Officially, the Côte d'Azur – or French Riviera, as this fabled stretch of land is often dubbed – is contained within the *départements* of the Var (the western Côte) and the Alpes-Maritimes (the eastern Côte, from Miramar, just west of Cannes, to Menton). However, this strip is so frequently referred to as an area in its own right that a separate chapter is devoted to it here.

There is much debate as to the exact definition of the Côte and this chapter covers the stretch from St-Tropez to Menton. Some of the sites mentioned in this section have larger entries in other chapters in the book; cross-references are given where applicable.

Coining a phrase

The term "Côte d'Azur" was coined in 1887 by the French writer Stéphen Liégeard, who was inspired by the deep blue of the sea along the stretch of Mediterranean seaside that runs from St-Tropez to the Italian border. The name alone seems to excite the senses, and almost everyone, whether long-time residents on the Côte or fleeting visitors to the area, likes to boast familiarity with the territory.

The components of the Riviera myth – something that goes back to the second half of 19th century when this part of the world first became a popular holiday destination *(see pages 50–1)* – are easy enough to enumerate: Great Gatsby parties at private villas, with vast lawns sloping down to the deep blue sea at Cap Ferrat and the Cap d'Antibes; breaking the bank at the casino in Monte-Carlo, before returning to a luxurious suite at the Hôtel de Paris; getting a pass to the Cannes Film Festival each May and basking in the late-afternoon sun in Nice's Cimiez arena every July while listening to cool, laid-back jazz. The stories go on and on.

St-Tropez to la Napoule

Towards the western end of the Côte is **St-Tropez** ❶, referred to by the locals and those in the know as "San Trop"). Although the resort has been a place of inspiration to artists including Guy de Maupassant, Paul Signac, Henri Matisse and Raoul Dufy, it is probably most famous for its connections with the now-reclusive film siren Brigitte Bardot. There is an attractive old port, a few good museums and plenty of excellent beaches here. *(For the main entry on St-Tropez, see pages 233–4.)*

Situated north from St-Tropez, along the N98 coastal road, is the picturesque hilltop village of **Grimaud**, a former Arab stronghold. The name derives from Gibelin

**CEDING
ES:** view
Menton.
T: façades,
franche.
HT: palms
eaulieu-
Mer.

de Grimaldi, a knight who was granted lordship of this area in the 10th century. (Grimaldi is more familiar today, of course, as being the surname of the Monegasque royal family.) The village has gorgeous views and an attractive church.

Nearby is the canalled resort of **Port Grimaud**, a playground for the rich built during the 1960s thanks to the determination and according to the design of architect François Spoerry.

Continuing east, just across the Golfe de St-Tropez, is **Ste-Maxime** ❷, a small, low-key resort that often accommodates visitors who are unable to find space to stay in St-Tropez. Boats ferry visitors across the bay.

The next main resort heading east is **Fréjus** ❸, a major Roman heritage site. The city was founded by Julius Caesar in 49 BC on the Aurelian Way, which ran from Rome to Arles. Much of the Roman city was destroyed by Arab invaders during the 10th century but you can still see the Roman walls and the 2nd-century AD **Arènes** (amphitheatre; rue Henri Adon; open: Apr–Oct, Wed–Mon; Nov–March: mornings only), on the road to Brignoles, which was erected to house 10,000 spectators; the arena is now used for bullfights and summer theatre. Also of note is a tower in the western part of the **Porte des Gaules**, which formed part of the Roman ramparts and marked one end of a 40-km (25-mile) long aqueduct.

Fréjus also has an impressive cathedral, the **Cathédrale St-Léonce et Cloître** (place Formigé; open: Tues–Sun; tel: 04 94 51 26 30), the majority of which dates from the 12th century, although the baptistery goes back to the 5th century, making this one the oldest of its kind in France. The cathedral is home to the **Musée Archéologique** (opening times as above), containing excavated material from the locality.

Around 2 km (3 miles) south-east of Fréjus is the pretty seaside resort of **St-Raphaël** ❹. The town, which has a population of around 30,000, has a turbulent history involving the Romans, plundering

Map n pages 272–3

Arabs, 10th-century Lérins monks and, from the 13th century, the Knights Templar. In the 19th century Napoleon landed in St-Raphaël on his return from Egypt and this was also his departing point 14 years later when he was banished to Elba.

St-Raphaël's status as a fashionable resort is largely down to Alphonse Karr, chief editor of *Le Figaro* in the 19th century. Karr lived in Nice until he discovered St-Raphaël and encouraged his friends to follow him down the coast. Those that did include Alexandre Dumas, Guy de Maupassant, Hector Berlioz and Charles Gounod.

Continuing east, slightly west of Cannes, is **la Napoule**, which is in effect just a seafront extension of the Cannes satellite, Mandelieu. La Napoule possesses three sandy beaches, a leisure port and the **Château de la Napoule** (open Mar–Oct: Wed–Mon; afternoons only; entrance fee; tel: 04 93 49 95 05), an arts foundation set in a converted medieval castle filled with the idiosyncratic sculptures of American artist Henry Clews.

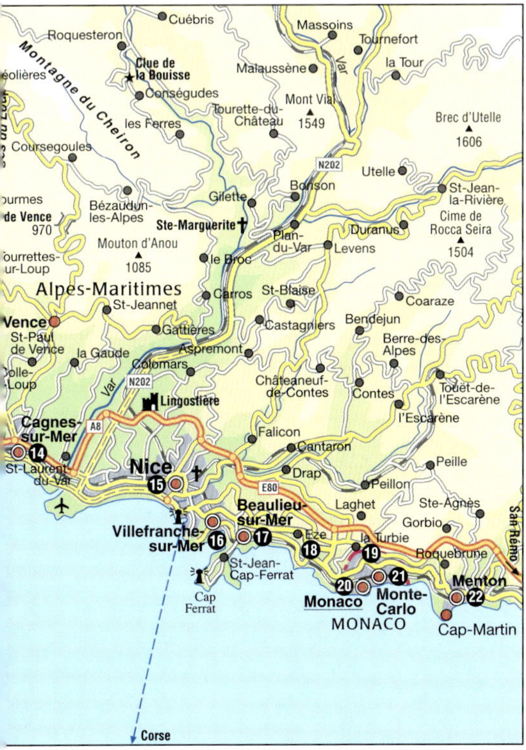

Cannes

Taking its name from the reeds *(les cannes)* in the marshes that used to surround the town, **Cannes** ❺ was first put on the map in 1834, when the then-British Chancellor, Lord Brougham, was forced to spend the winter here – his usual winter resting stop of Nice was out of bounds owing to an outbreak of cholera. Brougham was so taken with Cannes that he ordered a villa to be built there and thus started the trend of wintering in the town.

Cannes's status as an internationally recognised name, however, was cemented with the establishment of the town's annual film festival *(see pages 93–5)*. Although the first festival was due to be held in 1939, it was postponed owing to World War II; the inaugural festival was eventually held in 1946.

There is more to Cannes than its annual two-week event, however. The town is small and manageable and has a pleasant shopping street, the rue d'Antibes, which is lined with boutiques. Alongside the manicured beach there's an attractive beachfront, la Croisette, which is peppered with chic bars, many offering delightful views across the bay. At No. 1 la Croisette is the **Palais des Festivals et des Congrès**, which since 1983 has been home to the Film Festival (tours by arrangement only: Wed afternoons; tel: 04 93 39 24 53), a brutalist block of concrete, nicknamed the "Bunker" by locals.

In recent years, Cannes has used its film-circuit fame to market itself as a top venue for business conferences and other media gatherings, and the Palais is now in almost constant use, hosting more than 100 events a year.

Also on la Croisette are some of Cannes's grandest hotels, which pay homage to the resort's glamorous history. The oldest and most elaborate of these is the **Carlton**, with a wedding-cake façade that has barely changed since it was built in 1912. The pepper-pot cupolas at each end of the Carlton are said to be modelled on the breasts of la Belle Otero, a celebrated dancer and courtesan of the Art Deco period. Located further down the drag, at No. 73, is the Art Deco-style

Hôtel Martinez, built in 1929. Heading in the other direction, you come to the less attractive **Noga Hilton Hotel**, at No. 50. This concrete eyesore was built in 1992 on the site of the old Palais des Festivals, where Vadim launched Brigitte Bardot.

Beside, and virtually swamped by, the Hilton, is **la Malmaison**, the only surviving part of the original Grand Hotel, a 19th-century forerunner of today's seafront giants. The elegant building houses temporary art exhibitions (open: Wed–Mon; entrance fee; tel: 04 93 99 04 04).

The oldest part of Cannes is **le Suquet**, which still has secret alleys, passages and half-hidden *auberges* and bistros, especially on rue St Antoine. At the top of the hill is the **place de la Castre**, where you can enjoy commanding views along the shore in both directions and inland to the hill of la Californie.

Facing the place de la Castre is a 19th-century church, **Notre-Dame d'Espérance**. Behind the church are a castle and tower, which were built by Lérins monks in the 11th century to guard against Arab attack. Also here is the 12th-century Romanesque Chapelle Ste-Anne. The castle and chapel house the **Musée de la Castre** (closed Tues; entrance fee; tel: 04 93 38 55 26), which contains displays covering ethnology, archaeology, art of the region and musical instruments.

If you plan to hit the beach at Cannes during the high season it's wise to head for the water early because by mid-morning the sea will already be spilling over with bathers. Finding a parking spot can become an all-day event in peak season and during the Film Festival, when the town heaves with visitors.

Le Cannet

A short bus ride away from Cannes is **le Cannet ❻**, which was at one time a separate village from the former but has now been more or less engulfed by its bigger neighbour. Le Cannet is notable as the former home of the painter Pierre Bonnard, who lived in the Villa du Bosquet

BELOW: paln trees, Canne

Map
pages
272–3

from 1939 until his death in 1947. However, it's also worth visiting for its good-value restaurants, quirky narrow streets and musical evenings in summer.

Îles de Lérins

If you want to escape the crowds on the Côte, take a boat from the Gare Maritime beside the Palais des Festivals in Cannes and head for the delightful **Îles de Lérins**. **Ste-Marguerite** ❼, the larger of the islands, is home to the fortress that featured in Alexandre Dumas's *Man in the Iron Mask* – the mysterious prisoner was apparently held in the 17th-century **Fort Royal** (closed Tues; entrance fee; tel: 04 93 43 18 17) from 1687 to 1698.

The fort houses the **Musée de la Mer**, which displays artefacts salvaged from nearby wrecks, including a 1st-century Roman ship and a 10th-century Arab vessel. If you're looking for real seclusion, make your way away from the crowded port and you'll find quiet paths through the woods and rocky inlets for bathing.

At a mere 400 metres (1,300 ft) wide **St-Honorat** ❽, which is mainly covered by parasol pines, eucalyptus trees and cypresses, is the smaller of the two Lérins islands. It has an impressive ecclesiastical history, dating back to a monastery founded by St Honorat in the 5th century. For hundreds of years this island was a centre of religious life for the whole of Southern Europe and was so powerful that it owned much of the land along the Mediterranean coast, including Cannes.

At one time 3,700 monks lived here, and the island's monastery was responsible for the training of many important bishops, including Ireland's St Patrick. However, its wealth meant it was subject to constant raids from pirates, as well as papal corruption. In 1869 the island was bought by the Cistercians, who built a new monastery (open daily; closed for Sun services; entrance fee: June–Sept only) on the site of the old one. Only one ferry company serves the island, and as there are no restaurants here you are advised to bring a picnic.

ow:
seekers,
bes.

Mougins and Vallauris

Back on the mainland, north and inland of Cannes, is **Mougins ❾**, an upmarket getaway that is discreetly dotted with millionaires' mansions and several gourmet restaurants, including that of top chef Roger Vergé, the Michelin-starred Moulin de Mougins. The town is not only known for its culinary connections, however; this is a place with a history. There was a fort here in Ligurian times, and during the days of the Romans Mougins it was a staging post. During the Middle Ages the town overshadowed its neighbour, Cannes.

In the 1920s and 1930s, when it became the done thing to holiday on the Côte d'Azur, artists such as Cocteau and Man Ray came to Mougins, enticed by the attractive location near to the sea and the excellent quality of the light in the area. Picasso lived here from 1961 until his death in 1973. The town's connections with art are still reflected today in the number of art galleries here; for photography lovers there is the **Musée de la Photographie** (67 rue de l'Eglise; open: July and Aug: daily; Sept–Oct and Dec–Jun, Wed–Sun pm only; closed Nov; entrance fee; tel: 04 93 75 85 67), which has numerous photographs of Picasso as well as some works by master snapper Robert Doisneau.

Another town with strong connections with Picasso is **Vallauris ❿**, the next main stop south east of Mougins, around 3 km (2 miles) from the coast. *(For the main entry on Vallauris, see pages 255–6.)*

Juan-les-Pins to Villeneuve

Back on the coast is the indulgent party town of **Juan-les-Pins ⓫**, renowned for its clubs, expensive boutiques and casinos. The town's reputation for hedonism is well established – self-indulgent visitors including the F. Scott Fitzgeralds and other wealthy American socialites were swinging here as early as the 1920s. An international jazz festival was officially established in Juan-les-Pins in 1960 and this still takes place each year for 10 days at the end of July. For information on the

BELOW: Art Deco signage, Ni

Map
n pages
272–3

festival, tel: 04 92 90 53 00 or visit www.antibes-juanlespins.com.

The nearby **Cap d'Antibes** features the jet-setters' favourite, Hôtel de Cap-Eden Roc, and Bacon, a top fish restaurant *(see Where to Eat, Travel Tips)*. **La Garoupe**, the beach on the Cap d'Antibes that Gerald and Sarah Murphy used to rake clean every morning, is still *the* place to enjoy the sun.

Continuing east, you will come to **Antibes** ⓬ ("the city opposite" – a description that refers to Antibes's proximity to Nice). The resort has seafront ramparts, an old fort, tree-lined avenues and a splendid cobble-stoned **Vieille Ville** (Old Town) with a seductive array of markets. Picasso lived in the **Château Grimaldi** here for six months in the 1940s; the château now houses the **Musée Picasso** (Château Grimaldi, place Mariejol; open June–Sept; closed Mon; entrance fee; tel: 04 92 90 54 20), which features his celebrated work *Joie de Vivre (The Joy of Life)*. Another famous visitor to Antibes was Napoleon, who was imprisoned in Fort Carré.

Heading inland again, you'll reach the *village perché* of **Biot**, set 3 km (2 miles) from the coast and home to the **Musée National Fernand Léger** (chemin de Val de Pome; closed Tues; entrance fee; tel: 04 92 91 50 30). The museum contains around 400 paintings, carpets, stained glass and ceramics by Biot's greatest export, artist Fernand Léger (1881–1955), who adopted the town as his own. *(For the main entry on Biot, see pages 256–7.)*

East of Biot is the medieval village of **Villeneuve-Loubet** ⓭, located east of the river Loup, just off the N7. Above the village, which is characterized by steep narrow lanes and ancient buildings that resist gentrification, is an imposing château, which was restored in the 19th century and is now private property. Visitors may walk along the path round the castle walls, from where there are good views out to the Baie des Anges.

There are two museums of note in Villeneuve: the **Musée Militaire** and the **Fondation Auguste Escoffier**. The for-

.OW:
menade des
lais, Nice.

mer specialises in the two world wars and the colonial wars in French Indo-China (Vietnam) and Algeria. The **Fondation Escoffier** (Museum of Culinary Art), housed in the great chef's birthplace, is situated a few steps up the hill from the main square. Exhibits include Escoffier's hand-written recipe book and photographs of Dame Nelly Melba, for whom he invented the Peach Melba while he was chef at the London Carlton Hotel.

Cagnes-sur-Mer

Cagnes-sur-Mer ⓮ splits into three parts: the modern seaside resort of Cros-de-Cagnes, the modern town of Cagnes-sur-Mer, with its shops, public park and a good covered market (mornings only), and the old town of **Haut-de-Cagnes**, crowned by a 14th-century château.

The history of the town begins with the monks of Lérins, who founded an abbey at Saint-Véran in the 5th century; the abbey is now the site of the Hippodrome. By the 14th century Cagnes fell into the possession of the Grimaldi family and became subject to the constant turmoil of the Middle Ages. Cagnes has always depended on agriculture, notably olives, vines and flowers, for economic survival. By the 19th century, Mentonnais fishermen had settled on the coast, and the town developed between its coast and castle. Today Cagnes is a major artistic centre, a popular tourist destination and especially noted for its flower production – every spring the Exposition Internationale de Fleur takes over the town, the château and the Hippodrome.

Nice: the big olive

Nice ⓯ is the Côte's administrative capital. The city is arguably not as chic as neighbouring Monaco, as quaint as perched villages such as Eze, nor as celebrity-filled as St-Tropez. However, it is the Riviera's largest city (almost half of the area's one million people live in and around it) and has much to offer the visitor in the way of culture (some excellent art museums and a good theatre), an attractive Vieille Ville (Old Town), a lively night scene, some great beaches and a celebrated seafront.

Founded by the Greeks, Nice was first embraced by English lords and Russian aristocrats as a winter resort. The boom in bathing and summer tourism did not begin until the 1920s. Today, Nice combines a traditional Mediterranean-mellow lifestyle with a big push towards conventions (it is France's second-largest convention city after Paris) and high-tech business (income from which now rivals the Riviera's annual revenue from tourism).

The state-of-the-art Acropolis Convention Centre and the lavish Arenas business complex, opposite the airport that was itself built on reclaimed land and is now the second busiest in France, have forced inhabitants to re-adjust their priorities. The result: improved services, more hotels and restaurants, and an increasing number of offbeat and inviting activities.

Nice divides up neatly into old and new parts. **Vieux Nice** (Old Nice) is a maze of lively, narrow streets with tiny boutiques selling perfume and gifts, and a wealth of moderately priced restaurants featuring

LEFT: Hôtel Negresco, Nice.

Maps: Area 272 City 279

local specialities. The best way to discover the city is to wander through the **cours Saleya** Ⓐ, filled with antique stalls and flower markets and the centre of action in Old Nice. Early risers can hit the fish market on place St-François.

At the heart of Vieux Nice is the 17th-century **Cathédrale de Ste-Réparate** Ⓑ (open daily; free; tel: 04 93 62 34 40) on **place Rossetti**. The cathedral is named after the patron saint of Nice, a young virgin who was supposedly brought here in the 4th century from Israel in a boat decked out with flowers and pulled by angels. Her landing place is now known as the Baie des Anges (Angels' Bay). Another notable church, the gilt-decorated baroque **Chapelle de l'Annonciation** Ⓒ, dedicated to Saint Rita, is located nearby, at 1 rue de la Poissonnerie.

On the place du Palais de Justice, where a pottery, books and print market is held every Saturday, is Nice's imposing lawcourt, the **Palais de Justice** Ⓓ. On the far side of the square are pavement cafés, where you can while the time away. Northeast of the cathedral, at 15 rue Droite, is the **Palais Lascaris** Ⓔ (closed Mon; free; tel: 04 93 62 05 54), a grand building with a fine balustraded staircase and a notable decorative arts collection.

Located to the northeastern edge of the old town is the excellent **Musée d'Art Moderne et d'Art Contemporain** Ⓕ (MAMAC; open Wed–Mon; entrance fee; tel: 04 93 62 61 62), the spacious home of a large permanent exhibition of modern and contemporary art including work by the Nice School of Yves Klein (after whose work the colour "International Klein Blue" is named), Martial Raysse, César, Arman and Provence's clever wordsmith Ben *(see page 82)*. Some of the permanent works of sculpture are on display outside, notably several pieces by Niki de Saint Phalle. The museum also holds important changing exhibitions. Opposite is the city' main theatre.

At the southeastern edge of the old town is **le château**, the site of a pleasant park –

ironically the castle is no longer here. The park is hilly and there are excellent views from the top; if you don't want to walk, you can take a lift (open: daily 8am–6pm).

The sun usually sets late on Niçois summer nights, and the **promenade des Anglais** G, a palm-tree lined walkway that runs all the way along the seafront, is a delightful place to spend your evenings. The promenade is furnished with chairs, so you can either look at the waves on one side or the fashion parade and Nice's grand *Belle Époque* hotels on the other.

Two museums set along the western end of the promenade include the eclectic **Musée Masséna** H (65 rue de France; closed Mon and Nov; free; tel: 04 93 88 11 34), home to the work of several primitive Niçois painters and to Napoleon's coronation robe and death mask, and the **Musée des Beaux-Arts** I (33 avenue des Baumettes; closed Mon; entrance fee; tel: 04 92 15 28 28), a collection of artworks from the 17th century onwards including pieces by Sisley and Dufy.

Also on the promenade is the **Musée des Arts Asiatiques** (405 promenade des Anglais; closed Tues; entrance fee; tel: 04 92 29 37 00; www.arts-asiatiques.com), a collection of asian arts in spectacular building by Japanese architect Kenzo Tange.

Another museum well worth visiting in Nice is the **Musée National Message Biblique Marc-Chagall** J (avenue du Docteur Menard; closed Tues; entrance fee; tel: 04 93 53 87 20), dedicated exclusively to the work of this Russian-born artist. The **Musée Matisse** K (164 avenue des Arènes de Cimiez; closed Tues; entrance fee; tel: 04 93 81 08 08) is set further out of town, in a renovated 17th-century building, to the north of the Musée Chagall, via the boulevard Cimiez and the avenue de Flirey. The collection, which documents Matisse's career, life and influence, and the temporary exhibitions, are excellent and worth the trek out of town. The Cimiez cemetery, which is located next to the museum, is the site of a simple memorial to the painter.

BELOW: exot gardens of t Villa Ephrus de-Rothschi Cap Ferrat.

Maps:
Area 272
City 279

From Villefranche to la Turbie

The town of **Villefranche-sur-Mer** ⓰ was established in the 14th century as a customs-free port by Charles II d'Anjou; British and American ships still use its wonderful harbour, which is one of the deepest in the world. The town, complete with citadel, is well restored but not bijou, with an homogenous, medieval character.

Heading further east from Villefranche is **Cap Ferrat**, hideout of the seriously rich and famous. The **Fondation Ephrussi de Rothschild** (open daily; entrance fee) gives a hint of the champagne lifestyle, with 7 ha (17 acres) of exotic gardens spread along the crest of the Cap with gorgeous views on all sides – inhabitants often refer to the part of the coast between Nice and Monaco as "little Africa" in reference to its bougainvillea, palm trees and other vegetation. The pink-and-white *belle époque* villa was built to house the art collection of the Baroness Ephrussi de Rothschild (1964–1934) and includes an impressive range of 18th-century furniture, porcelain, carpets, and paintings, with ceilings specially designed to house her Tiepolo paintings.

On the other side of the Cap is **Beaulieu-sur-Mer** ⓱, which lays claim to the best climate on the coast, since it is protected from the north wind by a great rock face. Beaulieu is a popular retirement town, with many elegant rest homes and genteel hotels. It also has some of the best hotels on the Riviera and was where the British and Russian gentry used to spend their winters. Worth a visit is the **Villa Kerylos** (open daily; mid-Dec–mid-Feb: afternoons only; entrance fee), a complete reconstruction of a Greek villa with marble columns and cool courtyards open to the sea and sky, and housing a large collection of mosaics, frescoes and furniture.

East from Beaulieu and impaled on a rocky spike by the road, some 400 metres (1,300 ft) above the sea, is the village of **Eze** ⓲. On a clear day, Corsica is visible from the highest point. The German philosopher Friedrich Nietzsche is thought to have found the inspiration for his final book, *Thus spake Zarathustra*, while walking down a pathway to the sea here.

The entrance to Eze through a small, hidden archway comes after a short winding climb from the main road. Few other *villages perchés* command the popularity of Eze, and pushing through the narrow streets at the height of summer can be trying.

Eze's current prosperity belies its troubled past. For most of its history Eze has been nothing but a charred ruin: razed successively over several centuries, enslaved by Arabs, its citizens regularly tortured and burned. One undoubtedly flourishing aspect of the village is the **Jardin Exotique** (open daily; closed Sept–Feb; entrance fee), a fine collection of cacti and succulents. This garden was planted in 1950 around the ruins of the château, which had been dismantled under the orders of Louis XIV in 1706.

High up on the *grande corniche* coastal road beyond Eze there is a dramatic view of Monaco from the ruins of the Roman monument at **la Turbie** ⓳. The name la Turbie comes from the

HT: tropical dens, Eze.

Grimaldi Inc.

If Monaco is now referred to as Grimaldi Inc, it is thanks to the business acumen of the present ruler, Rainier III. The Grimaldi are Europe's oldest reigning family and the last constitutional autocrats. This old Ligurian family from Genoa was exiled during the medieval political struggle between Guelphs and Ghibellines. The Grimaldi clan found a new power base in Monaco in 1297 and have ruled there ever since. Legend has it that a woman wronged by Rainier I put a curse on the Grimaldi line, denying them lasting happiness.

Until the French Revolution, the princes lived on taxes levied on wine, lemons, tobacco, shipping and playing cards. Menton and Roquebrune formed part of Monaco until 1848 and their loss reduced Monaco's territory by 94 percent. However, the creation of Monte Carlo by Charles III delivered Monaco to grand tourism, which flourished until the reign of Louis II, Rainier III's grandfather. Rainier's mother, Princess Charlotte, was the fruit of Louis's liaison with a washerwoman he met in North Africa. Rainier III, educated in England and Switzerland, is the first prince to have been born in Monaco and the first full-time sovereign. After acceding to the throne in 1949, he set about running Monaco as a business empire, reducing its dependence on gambling.

Rainier's marriage in 1956 to the Hollywood star Grace Kelly injected a new glamour to Monaco, and her tragic death in a car accident in 1982 was a great blow. Grace's legacy lies in the Americanisation of Monaco, from the business ethos to the sophisticated social life, from the street names to the shopping malls. The Gallerie du Sporting is typical Monaco franglais, in keeping with Rainier's mixed marriage. The greatest crisis of his reign was in 1962, when Président de Gaulle, trying to stop French citizens settling in Monaco to avoid paying French taxes, sealed off Monaco's borders until Rainier conceded the issue. Still, except for unlucky French citizens, Monaco remains a tax haven.

However, the fortunes of the principality are far from secure. The possibility that Monaco may be dragged into the European Union presents a major threat, especially if EU nationals lose their tax-exempt status. In the 1990s there was a drop in tourism in Monaco, the casino business suffered disastrous losses and several financial scandals were uncovered.

Nor has the Grimaldi family escaped disaster. Princess Stephanie's sad trail of broken romances and failed careers has resulted in an unsuitable liaison with her bodyguard and her pursuit of a life in the circus with lover Franco Knie. Princess Caroline, the eldest, who assumed most of her mother's cultural duties after Grace's death, has not evaded the Grimaldi curse. In 1990 her second husband, Stefano Casiraghi, was killed while competing in the World Offshore Boat Race, leaving Caroline with three children and huge debts. In more recent years, Caroline's troubles have eased, however – in 1999 Caroline married Prince Ernst of Hanover and the couple now have a daughter together. Prince Albert, Rainier's heir apparent, shows no sign of marrying. Despite his playboy tastes, Albert has been perfectly groomed to inherit a $200-million fortune. ❑

LEFT: Prince Rainier III in younger day

Maps:
rea 272
ity 283

Latin *tropaea*, meaning trophy, and the village is named after the vast monument, la Trophée des Alpes, which was erected to commemorate the Emperor Augustus's mighty conquest of the 45 alpine tribes who had been attacking Romanised Gaul.

The monument, which when originally built was surmounted by a 6-metre (20-ft) statue of Augustus, was erected between 13 and 5 BC, probably using enslaved tribes as labour. The names of the tribes are inscribed on the monument, making them the longest intact Roman inscription to have survived.

Monaco

The Principality of Monaco, Europe's second-smallest independent country after the Vatican – its 186 ha (460 acres) make it smaller than New York's Central Park – is often considered a hotbed of gossip, intrigue and royal shenanigans. But don't go to Monaco expecting theatrics – even though columnists certainly spare no ink regaling readers with tales of high-spending gamblers breaking the bank at the casino (almost never), beautiful princesses dancing into the night (rare), the rich and not-always-famous frolicking on and in the Mediterranean (occasionally) and small apartments selling for big bucks (almost always).

More than 250,000 visitors flock to Monaco each year, and hundreds of day-trippers arrive in tour buses to look at the sights. The heavily touristed Monaco of today is more likely to include attendees at an insurance conference than gigolos and high rollers heading for the casino tables.

Contemporary Monaco, which has a population of around 32,000, is a more sedate playground in the sun than a scandalous one and it's also home to a serious business community. The streets can be safely walked at midnight, the omnipresent police force is usually more helpful than intimidating, the public services are exceptional and even the clubs are rarely raucous.

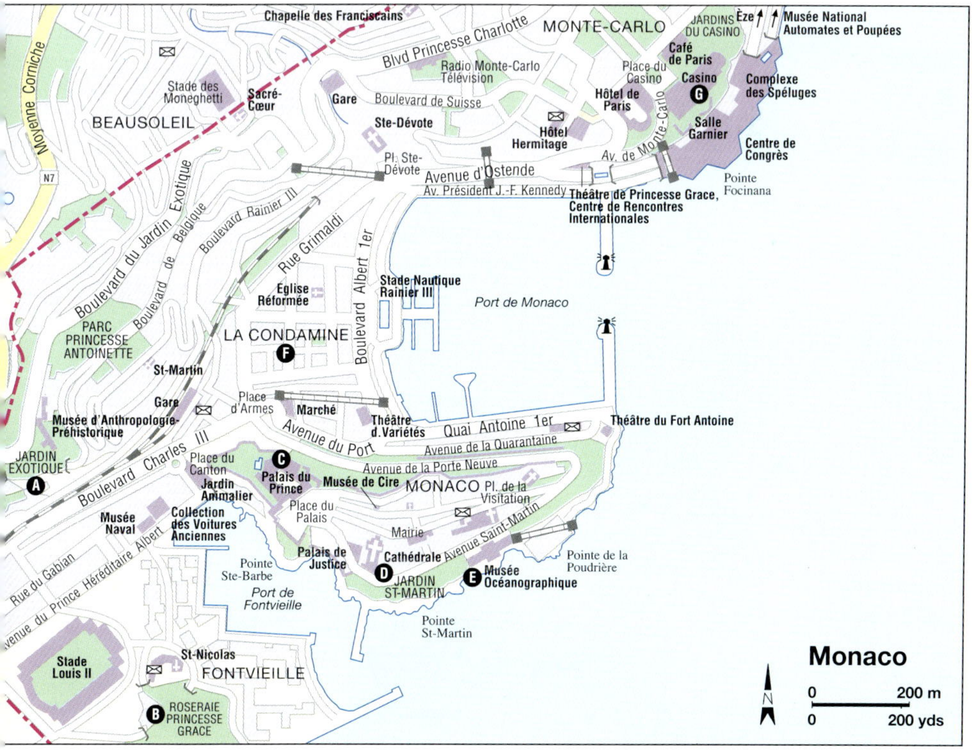

Monaco is ruled by Prince Rainier III, whose family, the Grimaldis, have been running the principality since 1297, when François Grimaldi sneaked in disguised as a Franciscan monk. Rainier shows little sign of wishing to relinquish power to his son, Prince Albert, who remains the Riviera's most sought-after bachelor and has been linked to a bevy of beauties including supermodel Claudia Schiffer.

Since her mother's tragic death in a car accident in 1982, a maturing Princess Caroline, who is now married to Prince Ernst of Hanover and the mother of four children, has assumed the role of being Monaco's most important cultural and social force. As the head of various organisations, including the Monte-Carlo Ballet and the Fondation Princess Grace, she is often seen performing official functions about town.

Monaco splits into two parts, the most southwesterly of which is the old part of the principality, the medieval **Monaco-Ville** ⓴. This part of town is also referred to as "the Rock", since it sits on a sheer-sided block of land, which juts around 800 metres (2,600 ft) into the sea.

Before you reach Monaco-Ville, you might like to take respite in two of the principality's green spaces: the **Jardin Exotique** Ⓐ (open daily; entrance fee; tel: 00377 93 30 33 65), an incredible feat of gardening high on a cliff and home to an impressive range of subtropical and tropical plants, located just off the boulevard of the same name, or the **Roseraie Princesse Grace** Ⓑ (Princess Grace Rose Garden), part of the Parc Paysager in the reclaimed Fontvieille district, which was laid out in honour of Princess Grace.

The "Rock" is the site of Prince Rainier's pink-tinted palace, the **Palais du Prince** Ⓒ (place du Palais; open Apr–Oct daily; entrance fee; tel: 00377 93 25 18 31), where there is a daily changing of the guard at 11.55am. It is also home to Monaco's Neo-Byzantine **Cathédrale** Ⓓ (4 rue Colonel Bellando del Caste; open daily), which was built in la Turbie stone

BELOW: Casir Monte-Carlo.

Maps:
Area 272
City 283

during the 19th century on the site of the 12th-century church of St-Nicolas. Princess Grace, the former American actress Grace Kelly who married Rainier in 1956, is entombed here, as are numerous other members of the Grimaldi line.

On the seafront is the majestic **Musée Océanographique** E (avenue St-Martin; open daily; entrance fee; tel: 00377 92 05 28 48), where visitors can see more than 90 tanks. **La Condamine** F is Monaco's harbour and the site of a daily food market. This area is particularly popular with artists – Arman and Sosno number among those who have studios here.

Heading northeast, you will reach **Monte-Carlo** 21, the glitziest district in the principality. Here, you can visit architect Charles Garnier's chocolate-box **Casino** G (place du Casino; open: noon until late; tel: 00377 92 16 23 00, 00377 92 16 23 67, box office), constructed during the late 19th century and a wash of pastel colours, gilt, cherubs and other elaborate rococo trimmings. Opera and ballet are performed in the overtly decorative Salle Garnier.

If you really want to partake of the myth that is Monaco, blow the budget in the **place du Casino** and on the **avenue des Beaux Arts**, only 150 metres (500 ft) long, at such luxury boutiques as Cartier, Bulgari, Buccelati and Ribolzi. Want to spend a fortune before you go to the casino? The Louis XV Restaurant on the ground floor at the Hôtel de Paris, which überchef Alain Ducasse has wondrously transformed into the Riviera's culinary hotspot since it opened in May 1987, is worth its weight in gold.

A final stop before you head northeast and away from Monaco might be the **Musée National Automates et Poupées** (Museum of Dolls and Automata; open daily; entrance fee; tel: 00377 93 30 91 26), located near to the Casino, at 17 avenue Princesse Grace. The museum is home to more than 400 dolls, an impressive collection of 18th- and 19th-century dolls' houses and various automata.

LOW:
ng-glider
ove Monaco.

Menton: lemon capital

Sheltered by mountains, **Menton** ㉒ basks in an enchanted setting with 300 days of sun a year. In this tropical greenhouse, Mexican and North African vegetation flourishes in a climate at least two degrees centigrade warmer than that of Nice. In the 19th century, Menton was more renowned as a winter sanatorium than as a hot-house, and Royal visitors such as Queen Victoria and Edward VII helped the town to acquire a reputation as the most aristocratic and anglophile of all the resorts on the Riviera.

Nowadays the dowager-like image has softened, and Menton is cosy rather than genteel, anglophile rather than aristocratic. However, even this image is passé, since Menton has more young people than any other Riviera town. Certainly, the presence of Italian executives and trippers has revived the town, especially since the joining of Menton with Ventimiglia in 1993, as the European Union's first joint urban community, when frontier posts, municipal and business activities were combined.

Originally Genovese, Menton became part of the Principality of Monaco in 1346 and by and large remained a Grimaldi possession until 1860. However, the Grimaldi astutely placed Menton under the protection of the rising political powers, a form of opportunism still practised by the present Monégasque rulers. In succession, Menton became a Spanish, French and Sardinian protectorate. Given such a cosmopolitan past, it is hardly surprising that Menton can feel so delightfully foreign.

In 1848 Menton rebelled against high Monégasque taxes on oil and fruit. Along with Roquebrune, the town declared itself a republic but this was shortlived and in 1861 Monaco sold both towns to France. This coincided with the start of grand tourism, and Menton was one of the first health resorts to benefit, thanks to the good publicity generated by Dr Bennet. The English doctor promoted Menton's mild climate as perfect for invalids and as a result British and Germans flocked to winter there.

BELOW: cathedral, Monaco.

Map
n pages
272–3

Menton has much to offer today's visitors, including a casino, nightclubs, marinas and sandy beaches. The town hosts an impressive array of cultural events: concerts (notably the Chamber Music Festival, created by the Hungarian André Borocz in the mid-20th century), museums, exhibitions, a theatre season from November to April, the Lemon Festival in February, flower festivals throughout the year, festive evenings in the **Parc du Pian**, a circle of poets and the Katherine Mansfield Prize, awarded for the best novel (the New Zealand-born author spent some time in Menton *circa* 1900).

Surrealism fans will be interested to learn that the room used to conduct marriage ceremonies in Menton's **Hôtel de Ville** (Town Hall), the *salle des mariages,* was decorated with murals by Jean Cocteau in the 1950s. In fact, the town is a heaven for Cocteau *aficionados*: in a small 17th-century fort on Quai Monléon, by the harbour, is the **Musée Jean Cocteau** (closed Tues; entrance fee; tel: 04 93 57 72 30).

The **rue St Michel**, with its orange trees, is a popular pedestrian shopping zone; below it is the lovely **place aux Herbes** and the covered market, next to the **place du Marché** with its flower stalls.

At the western end of the town is the 18th-century pink-and-white **Palais Carnolès**, the former summer residence of the Monaco royal family; its **Musée des Beaux Arts** (3 avenue de la Madone; free; closed Tues; tel: 04 93 35 49 71) is worth a visit both for its collection and its enticing gardens, the **Jardin des Agrumes**, where around 400 gloriously scented lemon trees grow.

From this point on the Côte, you're very close to Italy and the attractive town of Ventimiglia just over the border. For a stark contrast to the glitz of the coast, head north, into the thick of Provence's alluring hinterland and the tranquil Alpes-Maritimes. Or maybe – just maybe – the pull of the coast will prove so strong that you'll decide to stay here a while. Or at least return for a repeat visit. ❑

LOW: cteau's lle des riages", nton.

INSIGHT GUIDES

Travel Tips

INSIGHT GUIDE
NEW YORK CITY
INSIGHT POCKET
INSIGHT GUIDES
The world's largest collection of visual travel guides
Welcome to The Insight Guides Website
Africa & The Middle East
Click here for details of how to advertise on this site
or click on the relevant map for useful travel information
IRAN
IRAQ
KUWAIT
SYRIA
LEBANON
ISRAEL
JORDAN
SAUDI ARABIA
EGYPT
TUNISIA
LIBYA
CHAD
INSIGHT COMPACT
BRITTANY
Back
Forward
Home
Reload
Images
Open
Print
Find
Stop
Netscape
Yahoo!
Net Search
Personal
News
Weather
Mail
CHOOSE YOUR DESTI
Go to ..
Africa
BUYING OUR BOOKS
NOTICE BOARD
ABOUT INSIGHT
INSIGHT & DISCOVERY
INSIGHT
TRAVEL DICTIONARY
GERMAN

Probably the most important
TRAVEL TIP you will ever receive
Before you travel abroad, make sure that you and your family are protected from diseases that can cause serious health problems.
For instance, you can pick up hepatitis A which infects 10 million people worldwide every year (it's not just a disease of poorer countries) simply through consuming contaminated food or water!
What's more, in many countries if you have an accident needing medical treatment, or even dental treatment, you could also be at risk of infection from hepatitis B which is 100 times more infectious than AIDS, and can lead to liver cancer.
The good news is, you can be protectec by vaccination against these and other serious diseases, such as typhoid, meningitis an yellow fever.
Travel safely! Check with your doctor a least 8 weeks before you go, to discover whether or not you need protection.
Consult your doctor before you go... not when you return
SB
SmithKline Beecham
VACCINES
Produced as a service to public health

CONTENTS

Getting Acquainted

The Place

Situation: Provence is located in the southeastern corner of France. It is bordered to the west by the Rhône River, to the north by the Baronnies Range and the Hautes-Alpes, to the east by Italy and to the south by the Mediterranean. The landscape is widely varied – from seaside cliffs and sandy beaches to dry wide plains and salt marshes, to opulent Alpine reaches and jagged limestone mountains.
Area: Around 30,000 sq. km (11,500 sq. miles).
Population: 4.5 million for the entire Provence-Alpes-Côte d'Azur region. Marseille 800,500; Nice 342,000; Avignon 87,000.
Language: French is the official language but Provençal and, in the Nice area, Nissart are also spoken.
Religion: Predominantly Catholic, with a small percentage of Protestants, Muslims and Jews.
Telephone code: The international code for France is 0033. For Monaco, tel: 00377 plus an eight-figure number.
Time zone: France is one hour ahead of Greenwich Mean Time.

Climate

Provence and its Côte d'Azur are renowned for their sunshine. Each year there are typically more than 300 sunny days a year and less than 800 mm (31½ inches) of rain. When it does rain, however, it pours. Average temperatures range from 45°F (7°C) in winter to 76°F (24°C) in summer. Winters are usually mild and sunny, and summers are typically hot and dry, with long days.

Weather Information

For weather information in English, tel: 08 36 70 12 34. For local forecasts in Provence, dial 08 36 68 02 04. On Minitel, go to 3615 METEO. On the web visit: www.meteo.fr.

Temperatures are always given in celsius (centigrade). To convert to fahrenheit, see below:

0°C = 2°F	20°C = 68°F
10°C = 50°F	25°C = 77°F
15°C = 59°F	30°C = 86°F

Climate varies between the high country and low country. However, the whole region experiences the sporadic virulence of the legendary northwest wind, the mistral, during the late autumn to early spring. There have also been violent storms in the area in recent years, causing major floods and damage.

Government

Provence is one of the 22 separate regions that make up France and it comprises six of the country's 96 *départements*. The capital of the region is Marseille – France's largest seaport and second largest city, with a population of almost 1 million. The six Provençal *départements* are: the Alpes-de-Haute-Provence, Alpes-Maritimes, Bouches-du-Rhône, Hautes Alpes, Var and the Vaucluse. The Bouches-du-Rhône is home to the Camargue, an area that is often referred to as a region in its own right.

Each *département* is divided into disparately sized *communes*, with a district council controlling a town, village or group of villages under the direction of the local mayor.

Each French *département* is identified by an individual number, which is used as a convenient reference for administrative purposes, for example it forms the first two digits of the postcode in any address and the last two figures on vehicle licence plates. The number for Provence and the Côte d'Azur is 04.

Economy

For centuries, Provence's economy has been agriculturally based, producing a lion's share of the country's fruits, vegetables, herbs, olive oil, rice, lamb, etc. Many of these products are, in turn, used in such local industries as soapmaking. Provence also has vital interests in fishing and oil refineries. Since the early 1900s, the economy has been overwhelmingly assisted by a growth in tourism, and the region now receives around 25 million visitors a year.

Currency

The euro was introduced as the official French currency in January 1999, with euro (€) notes and coins coming into everyday use in January 2002. These replace the previous currency, the French franc (FF).

Public Holidays

Banks, post offices and public offices close on public holidays.

Who controls what

Until the late 20th century, France was ruled largely by central government. However, the Paris-appointed *préfets* lost much of their power in the 1980s, when the individual *départements* gained their own directly elected assemblies, giving them far more financial and administrative autonomy. The role of the *préfet* is now more advisory than executive, and the préfecture is based in the principal town of each *département*. *Communes* are responsible for most local planning and environmental matters; tourism and culture are mostly dealt with at regional level, while the state controls education, the health service and security.

US Credit Phone Cards

If you want to use a US credit phone card, dial the company's access number *(see below)*, then 01, then the country code.

• Sprint	00 0087
• AT&T	00 0011
• MCI	00 00 19

Food shops, in particular *boulangeries* (bread shops), remain open, even on Christmas Day. It is common practice, if a public holiday falls on a Thursday or Tuesday, for French businesses to *faire le pont* (literally, "bridge the gap") and take the Friday or Monday as a holiday as well.

Details of closures should be posted outside banks, etc. a few days before the event but it is easy to be caught out, especially on days such as 15 August (Assumption), which is the climax of the summer and the biggest holiday of the year. While the shops may be shut, there will almost certainly be a *fête* in every town and village. Note that foreign embassies and consulates observe French public holidays as well as their own.

Public holidays are as follows:

- **1 January**: New Year's Day (Nouvel an)
- **March/April**: Easter Monday (Lundi de Pâques)
- **1 May**: Labour Day (Fête du Travail)
- **May**: Ascension Day (Ascension), on a Thursday 40 days after Easter
- **8 May**: Victory Day (Fête de la Libération) to commemorate the end of World War II
- **May/June**: Pentecost (Pentecôte), 10 days after Ascension.
- **14 July**: Bastille Day (Quatorze Juillet)
- **15 August**: Assumption Day (Fête de la Assomption)
- **1 November**: All Saints' Day (Toussaint)
- **11 November**: Armistice Day (Fête de l'Armistice)
- **25 December**: Christmas Day (Noël)

Weights and Measures

The metric system is used in France for all weights and measures, although you may encounter old-fashioned terms such as *livre* (about 1 pound in weight or 500 grammes) in smaller shops and markets. As a kilometre is five-eighths of a mile, a handy reckoning whilst travelling is to remember that 80 kilometres is the same as 50 miles, thus 40 kilometres equals 25 miles.

Electricity and Gas

The electric current is generally 220/230 volts. It alternates at 50 cycles, not at 60 cycles as in the US, so Americans will need a transformer for shavers, travel irons, hairdryers, etc. Gas and electricity are supplied by the state-owned EDF-GDF (Electricité de France-Gaz de France). If you suffer a power failure or gas leaks, contact the service number in the local *annuaire* (telephone directory).

Many rural areas do not have mains gas supplies, and Butane gas is therefore used for cooking and heating water. New bottles of gas are available from local shops and garages – note that you should exchange the empty one for a full bottle. Electricity in rural areas occasionally fails, so ensure that you have candles or torches, computer back-up and surge control. During thunder storms it is always advisable to disconnect computers and modems.

Planning the Trip

Visas and Passports

To visit France, you need a valid passport, and all visitors to France require a visa except for citizens of EU countries. Citizens of the US, Canada, Australia or New Zealand do not need a visa for stays of up to three months. As regulations such as this can be subject to change, or if you are in any doubt about how long you can stay or what documentation you require, you can always check with the French

Customs

You may take any quantity of goods into France from another EU country as long as they are for personal use and provided that you can prove that tax has been paid on them in the country of origin. Customs officials still have the right to question visitors.

Quantities accepted as being for personal use are as follows:

- up to 800 cigarettes, 400 small cigars, 200 cigars or 1kg loose tobacco.
- 10 litres of spirits (more than 22 percent alcohol), 90 litres of wine (under 22 percent alcohol) or 110 litres of beer.

For goods from outside the EU, recommended quantities are:

- 200 cigarettes or 100 small cigars, 50 cigars or 250g loose tobacco
- 1 litre of spirits (over 22 percent alcohol) and 2 litres of wine and beer (under 22 percent alcohol)
- 50g perfume.

Visitors may also carry up to €7,500 in currency.

consulate in your country. If you intend to stay in France for more than 90 days, you should apply for a *carte de séjour*.

Money Matters

French banks usually open 9am–5pm Mon–Fri (some close for lunch noon–1.30pm); some banks also open on Saturday. All banks are closed on public holidays, sometimes from noon on the day prior to the bank holiday. All banks have foreign exchange counters. Commission rates vary between banks. Most banks accept travellers' cheques, but Eurocheques are no longer accepted, due to widespread fraud.

CREDIT CARDS AND CASH MACHINES

You will find that most major international credit cards are accepted in France (Visa, Cirrus and Maestro are very common), although American Express is sometimes not welcome due to high charges to the retailer.

Cards issued by French banks are fitted with security microchips *(puces)*. When you pay with a French card, the latter is slotted into a card reader and you must then key in your PIN number to authorise the transaction; with a UK or US card, however, you may be asked for a signature rather than a PIN number. There are sometimes problems when you present cards that have magnetic strips, issued by UK or US banks, and your card might be rejected. The French Tourist Office recommends that you explain that your card has a magnetic strip rather than a chip and that the retailer should telephone your bank for confirmation of this. In French, this translates as: *"Les cartes internationales ne sont pas des cartes à puce, mais à bande magnetique. Ma carte est valable et je vous serais reconnaisant d'en demander la confirmation auprès de votre banque ou de votre centre de traitement."*

You can withdraw money from bank and post office automatic cash machines using cards from foreign banks using your PIN number, as long as the card and machine show either a Visa or Cirrus symbol.

Tipping

You do not usually need to add service to a **restaurant** bill in France. A charge of 10 percent is added automatically as part of the bill. (To be sure, check it says *"Service compris"* on the menu, or ask *"Est-ce que le service est compris?")*

Taxis also include service charges. Doormen, porters, guides, hairdressers, etc., are usually given a tip of €1.5. Note that in bars and cafés you pay less at the counter than if you sit at a table. It's normal to leave a little small change as a tip.

What to Bring

You should be able to buy anything you need in France. Pharmacies offer a wide range of drugs, medical supplies and toiletries, along with expert advice, but you should bring any prescription drugs you might need. A second pair of spectacles or contact lenses is recommended. (Note that drivers are required by law to carry a spare pair of glasses.) Sunscreen and anti-mosquito products are advisable in summer. Remember to bring an adaptor if you have electrical equipment *(see page 291)*.

The clothing you bring depends on your destination and when you travel; you will only need to really dress up for chic restaurants in the cities or casinos. Don't be too casual, however; be prepared to dress for dinner after a day at the beach. Dress appropriately for visiting churches; a scarf or shirt are always useful cover-ups. Most sports equipment can be hired but you should bring personal gear such as walking boots with you.

In the larger cities you will find English-language newspapers and magazines and English bookshops, but elsewhere you will need your own reading matter. Ensure that you have up-to-date local guides, phrase books and maps, though these items are increasingly available in supermarkets. Electronic translators can be really useful. Don't forget essentials such as your passport, driving licence, insurance documentation, special passes, emergency credit card numbers, etc.

Tourist Information

Every town and city, and almost every small village has its own **office de tourisme**, sometimes also referred to as the "maison" or "bureau de tourisme", or the "syndicat d'initiative". These are usually located on or near the main square, and sometimes also at main stations, and they can invariably be relied upon to supply the best-available map of the locality as well as information about restaurants, accommodation, sights and events.

Tourist office staff should be able to give you impartial advice or point you to the piles of free advertising leaflets, which are left by hotels, shops, museums and the like. Note that – especially in small places – these offices often close at midday, and some may not open again in the afternoon.

For more in-depth information you may need to buy a book in a local shop. If there is no tourist office in a town you can get a wide range of help and information from the local *mairie* (town hall).

REGIONAL TOURIST OFFICES

Comité Regional du Tourisme de Provence-Alpes-Côte d'Azur
Les Docks
Atrium 10.5, BP 46214
10 place de la Joliette
13567 Marseille
Cedex 2

Tel: 04 91 56 47 00
Fax: 04 91 56 47 01
www.cr-paca.fr
Details of city/town tourist offices are also available from here.
Comité Regional du Tourisme Riviera Cote d'Azur
55 promenade des Anglais
BP 602, 06011 Nice
Tel: 04 93 37 78 78
Fax: 04 93 86 01 06
www.crt-riviera.fr
Office de tourisme et des congrès de la Principauté de Monaco
2a boulevard des Moulins
9800 Monaco
Tel: 00377 92 16 61 16
Fax 00377 92 16 60 00
www.monaco-congres.com

MAISONS DE FRANCE

UK:
French Government Tourist Office
178 Piccadilly
London W1V 0AL
Tel: 0891-244 123
Fax: 020 7493 6594
Email: piccadilly@mdlf.demon.co.uk
www.franceguide.com
This tourist office incorporates the French Travel Centre, which gives information on France and sells books and guides.
USA:
French Government Tourist Office
444 Madison Avenue
New York NY 10022
Tel: 410 286 8310
Fax: 212 838 7855
www.franceguide.com
Canada:
French Government Tourist Office
1981 Avenue Mcgill College
No 490
Montreal
Quebec
Tel: 514 876 9881
Fax: 877 520 8400
Australia:
Level 22, 25 Bligh Street
Sydney, NSW 2000
Tel: 02 9231 5244
Ireland:
10 Suffolk Street
Dublin
Tel: 1679 0813
Fax: 679 0814

PROVENCE ON THE WEB

- provence.web.fr

Lists villages, hotels, restaurants and gives links to all the main towns and cities in Provence.

- www.visitprovence.com

French government tourism website. Information in French and English on sights, tours, specialist walks, hotels and restaurants plus essential practical information.

- www.provence-beyond.com

English-language website with details on lesser-known places. Personally tailored tours may be arranged.

- www.riviera-reporter.com

Local English-language magazine site with archive of articles on a variety of practical and political subjects and links to other relevant government and advice sites.

- www.cr-languedocroussillon.fr

French government tourist site offering an overview of sights, hotels, etc., plus brochures on-line and links to other web pages.

- luberon-news.com

Newspaper site offering links to restaurants and hotels, plus a variety of local information on shopping, markets, property, events, museums and sports.

- www.crt-riviera.fr

French government web page with local tourist information on sites, hotels, museums, transport, etc.

- www.sncf.fr

French Railways website; timetables and booking on-line.

Getting There

BY AIR

From the UK

There is an increasing number of low-cost flights to the region. **Go** (tel: 0802 838 383. www.go-fly.com) now fly to Nice from Stansted and Bristol. **Easyjet** (UK, tel: 0870 6000 000; Nice, tel: 04 93 21 48 33; www.easyjet.com) fly to Nice from Luton and Liverpool. **Ryanair** (UK, tel: 0870 1569 569; www.ryanair.com) have two daily low-cost flights from Stansted to Nîmes. **Buzz** fly Stansted to Marseille (UK, tel: 0870 240 7070 www.buzzaway.com).

Main airports

Nice
Tel: 04 93 21 30 30; 08 36 69 55 55 (recorded flight times)
www.nice.aeroport.fr
Nice International Airport, located 7 km (4 miles) west of the city centre, is the second largest in France. Although the majority of flights arrive and depart from terminal 1, Air France (flights to and from Paris), Air Liberté and AOM use terminal 2.
Marseille-Provence
Tel: 04 42 14 14 14
www.marseille.aeroport.fr
Situated in Marignane, 20 km (12 miles) northwest of the city centre.

Air France (UK, tel: 0845 0845 111; US: 1-800 237 2747; France 08 02 80 28 02; www.airfrance.com) fly from Paris to Nice, Marseille, Avignon and Nîmes. **British Airways** (UK, tel: 0345 222111; US: 1-800 247 9297; France: 08 02 80 29 02; www.britishairways.com) operate flights to Marseille and Montpellier from Gatwick, and flights to Nice from Heathrow and Manchester.

British Midland (UK, tel: 0870 607 0555; France: 08 00 05 01 42; www.britishmidland.com) fly to Nice from Heathrow and East Midlands Airport.

From the US

Delta (US, tel: 1-800 241 4141; France: 08 00 35 40 80; www.delta.air.com) have a daily flight from JFK–New York to Nice, and another to Lyon, 200 km (124 miles) north of Avignon. Otherwise flights from the US go via Paris.

To reach Provence from Paris, **Air Inter** (France, tel: 08 02 80 28 02) runs hourly *navettes* (shuttle flights) from Orly to Marseille, Nice, Avignon and Nîmes. **TAT** (France, tel: 08 03 80 58 05) flies from Paris to Toulon-Hyères. **Air Liberté** (France, tel: 08 03 09 09 09) fly from Paris Orly to Nice. **AOM French Airlines** (France, tel: 08 03 00 12 34) have flights from Paris Orly to Nice, Marseille and Toulon-Hyères.

BY TRAIN

The TGV high-speed track has now reached Marseille, reducing the journey time from Paris Gare de Lyon to only around 4 hours. There are between 10 and 12 TGVs per day from Paris to Marseille, 9 per day to Nice (journey time approx. 6 hours 30 minutes) and 15 a day to Avignon (approx. 3 hours 30 mins). All these stations connect with the local train network *(see Getting Around, page 301)*.

International trains connect with Spain, Italy, Switzerland, Germany and the Benelux countries. From the UK, Eurostar trains run to Lille and Paris Gare du Nord.

Sleepers

A comfortable way to get to the south is by overnight sleeper. The cheapest alternative is the *couchette*, which has six beds per carriage. The *voiture-lit* – a carriage for up to three people – is more private. You can travel first and second class in both types of carriage. Reservations must be made well in advance.

Tickets

In the UK tickets for journeys in France can be booked from any National Rail station or the International Rail Centre at Victoria Station (tel: 020 7834 2345). Otherwise visit the Rail Europe Travel Shop (179 Piccadilly, tel: 0870 584 8848) or book on-line at www.raileurope.co.uk or www.sncf.fr. For journeys on the TGV you must book in advance. Remember that before you get on the train you have to date-stamp your ticket in the orange *composteur* machine at the station, marked: *"compostez votre billet"* ("stamp your ticket"). The telephone number for SNCF central reservations and information is 08 36 35 35 35 (open 7am–10pm daily). Reservations by telephone or Minitel (3615 SNCF) have to be collected and paid for within 48 hours.

Bicyles on Trains

If you are travelling long distance by train, your bicycle must be transported separately and it must be registered and insured. Bicycles can be delivered to your destination but this may take several days. On the Eurostar you must check your bike in at least 24 hours before you travel.

Discounts and Passes

A variety of passes and discounts are available within France. A **Eurodomino** pass allows unlimited travel on France's rail network for 3 to 8 days within one month, but it must be bought before travelling to France. Discounted rates are available to children aged 4–11, or young people aged 12–25.

There are a number of good discounts and passes available to US visitors, including the **Eurailpass**, **Flexipass** and **Saver Pass**. These may be bought in the US before you travel. Tel: 1-212-308 3103 (for information) and 1-800 223 636 (for reservations).

BY FERRY

Since the Channel Tunnel opened, ferry services have become increasingly competitive, so it's worth shopping around for discounts and special offers. The following companies operate across the English Channel to various ports and all of these firms carry cars as well as foot passengers:

Brittany Ferries

This firm offers sailings from Portsmouth to Caen, and Poole to Cherbourg (during the summer only), and St-Malo. The Brittany Centre, Wharf Road, Portsmouth PO2 8RU; tel: 0870 536 0360; www.brittany-ferries.com.

P&O Ferries

P&O sail from Portsmouth to Cherbourg, St-Malo and le Havre, and also operate the short sea route from Dover to Calais. Channel House, Channel View Road, Dover CT17 9TJ; tel: 0870 242 4999; www.poef.com.

Hoverspeed

Hoverspeed Fast Ferries operates a Superseacat service from Newhaven to Dieppe crossing in 2 hours. International Hoverport, Dover CT17 9TG; tel: 0870 524 0241; www.hoverspeed.co.uk.

Alternative Routes

You could also travel by ferry to Northern Spain. **Brittany Ferries** go to Santander from Plymouth and **P&O** ferries go from Portsmouth to Bilbao; tel: 0870 242 4999.

BY BUS

The cheapest way to get to Provence is by bus, although this does entail a long journey. **Eurolines** (UK, tel: 01582 404511, France, tel: 08 36 69 52 52) run regular services from London to Avignon, Marseille and Nice.

For local bus information see Getting Around, page 301.

The Channel Tunnel

There are fast, frequent **Eurostar** rail services between London (Waterloo), Lille (2 hours) and Paris (Gare du Nord – 3 hours), from where there are connecting trains to Provence. Call 01233 617577 for enquiries. **Le Shuttle** takes cars and their passengers from Folkestone to Calais on a drive-on-drive-off system. The journey time through the tunnel is about 35 minutes and you do not need to book. Le Shuttle runs 24 hours a day, all year round, with a service at least once an hour through the night. Enquiries in UK, tel: 0990 353535.

BY CAR

If you don't mind a long drive, and want to have a car to tour when you get to Provence, then driving from the UK is a good option. There are potential overnight stops in many lovely places along the way, which can be incorporated in the holiday. However, note that during the

French summer holidays in July and August – particularly around 15 August, which is the main national holiday of the summer – the roads get very busy. Look for the small green **BIS** (Bison Futé) signs, which indicate scenic diversionary routes.

Road distances to the South are as follows:

- Calais–Nice: 1167 km (725 miles)
- Caen–Nice 1161 km (721 miles)
- Dieppe–Avignon: 854 km (531 miles)
- Calais–Avignon: 965 km (600 miles)

The fastest route to Provence is from Calais via Paris and the A6 Autoroute du Soleil to Lyon and the Rhône Valley. Alternatively you could go via the *autoroute* through the Massif Central, the A10-A71-A75 via Bourges and Clermont-Ferrand, which offers spectacular scenery. All *autoroutes* have *péage* toll-booths, where payment may be made in cash or by credit card. Tolls can work out fairly expensive on long journeys; a trip from Calais to Nice, for example, would cost around €75.

MOTORAIL

Motorail is a luxury way to travel, transporting your car by train from Calais or Paris and allowing you to sleep overnight in the train instead of driving. You must book a *couchette* to travel by Motorail, and this can prove fairly expensive for a number of people. The total price for car and family can be as much as €1,200, depending on the season. For UK bookings, contact **Rail Europe** (tel: 0870 584 8848).

CAR HIRE

Car hire is extremely expensive in France, mainly due to high VAT (TVA) rates. Sometimes fly-drive packages, or arranging car hire in advance can work out slightly cheaper than hiring once you arrive. Fly-drive packages are available from most airlines and SNCF run a train/car rental scheme.

To hire a car you need to be aged at least 25 years old and you must have held a driving licence for at least a year. Some hire companies will accept drivers aged between 21 and 24, but you may have to pay a supplement of between €7.5 and €15 per day. You will need to show your driving licence and passport. It is a good idea to check in advance that you know what to do in case of an accident or breakdown.

The bigger hire companies offer the best deals for weekly car hire – expect to pay about €245 a week for a small car with insurance and 1,700 km (1,056 miles) included. You can also sometimes find good weekend deals usually from Friday evening to Monday morning. Watch out for cheaper companies that may balance a low hire cost with high charges in the event of damage to the vehicle.

Car-Hire Companies

Ada Central Reservations
Tel: 01 55 46 19 99

Avis
Tel: 01 55 38 68 60

Budget
Tel: 08 00 10 00 01

Europcar
Tel: 08 03 352 352

Hertz
Tel: 01 39 38 38 38

Tour Operators

Allez France
Tel: 0800 731 2929
Gastronomic holidays

Alternative Travel Group
Tel: 01865 315 678
Visits to wine estates

Ace Study Tours
Tel: 01223 835 055
Cultural tours

Arblaster and Clarke
Tel: 01730 893 344
Wine tours

Bike Tours
Tel: 01225 480130

Cox and Kings
Tel: 020 7873 5005
Botanical tours

Erna Low Consultants
Tel: 020 7584 2841
Spa holidays

French Life
Kerry Street
Horsforth
Leeds LS18 4AW
Tel: 08704 448 877
Email: info@frenchlife.co.uk
www.frenchlife.co.uk
French holiday experts, specialising in gîte accommodation (villas and cottages). Also organise hotel and apartment holidays.

Headwater Holidays
Tel: 01606 813 333
Walking holidays

Limosa Holidays
Tel: 01263 578 143
Birdwatching

LSG Theme Holidays
Tel: 01509 231713
Language, painting and walking trips

Prospect
Tel: 020 7486 5705
Music and art tours

VFB Holidays
Tel: 01242 240 339
Skiing and walking holidays

Hitchhiking

Hitchhiking *(faire l'autostop)* is more common in France than in the UK. The safest way to arrange a lift is through a hitchhiking agency, such as Allô-Stop. You pay an agency fee and then a small fee per kilometre, which goes directly to the driver. Contact the agency well in advance to arrange a conveninet lift. Avignon, Marseille and Nice are all popular destinations.

Allô-Stop
8 rue Rochambeau
Paris
Tel: 01 53 20 42 42
Open 9am–6.30pm, Mon–Fri; 9am–1pm, 2–6pm Sat.

Language Courses

There are numerous language courses and study tours available in Provence and the Côte d'Azur. For further details, contact: **Central Bureau for Educational Visits and Exchanges**, Seymour Mews House, Seymour Mews, London WIH 9PE, tel: 020 7486 5101.

Centre des Échanges Internationaux, 1 rue Jolzen, Paris 75006; tel: 01 40 51 11 71. A non-profit making organisation that organises sporting and cultural holidays and educational tours for 15- to 30-year-olds.
Alliance Français, 101 boulevard Raspail, Paris; tel: 01 45 44 38 28. A highly regarded, non-profit-making French language school with centres across France. Runs beginners' and specialist courses.

Business Travellers

The most important thing to know about doing business in France, and especially the south, is that people always prefer to meet in person. You will often be expected to go and see someone, even to discuss something that could easily be dealt with over the phone.

Most major banks can refer you to lawyers, accountants and tax consultants, and several US and British banks provide expatriate services, in Paris and locally. Chambres de Commerce et d'Industrie provide local details, and a calendar of trade fairs is available from the **Chambre de Commerce et d'Industrie de Paris**, 27 avenue de Friedland; tel: 01 42 89 70 00; fax: 01 42 89 78 68.

Business Information

BFM on 96.4 FM is a business radio station. **Les Echos** gives stock quotes on the website www.lesechos.com. Minitel service 3615 CD has real-time stock quotes. Business directories **Kompass France** and **Kompass Régional** also give company details and detailed French market profiles on 3617 KOMPASS. **The French Company Handbook** lists all companies in the 120 Index of the Paris Bourse, published by the International Herald Tribune (tel: 01 41 43 93 00) or from Paul Baker Publishing, 37 Lambton Rd, London SW20 OLW; tel: 020 8946 0590.

Travellers with Disabilities

It is not particularly easy for disabled visitors to travel in Provence and access to some sites can be a problem. (Even if it is claimed that hotels, restaurants, museums, monuments and other places have access for disabled people, it's always wise to check beforehand exactly what is meant by this – they may accommodate wheelchair users but not have accessible toilets, for example.) Small villages with steep streets and inaccessible cliff-top castles, can be exceptionally difficult to negotiate with a wheelchair. Bigger cities are sometimes better equipped with facilities but this is not always the case. The best approach is to check out your route as much as possible in advance. Disabled parking is available in most places – it is indicated with a blue wheelchair sign. The international orange disabled parking disk scheme is recognised in France. To hire a wheelchair or other equipment enquire at the local pharmacy.

TRANSPORT

Le Shuttle (tel in UK: 0990 353 353) – the Channel tunnel car-on-a-train service – allows disabled passengers to stay in their vehicle. **Eurostar** trains (UK special requests, tel: 020 7928 0660) give wheelchair passengers first-class travel for second-class fares.

Most ferry companies offer facilities for disabled travellers if they are contacted in advance of travel. Reduced tolls are charged on *autoroutes* to those people travelling in a vehicle fitted to accommodate the disabled.

AUTOROUTE GUIDE

An *autoroute* guide for disabled travellers *(Guides des Autoroutes à l'usage des Personnes à Mobilité Réduite)* is available free from the Ministère des Transports, Direction des Routes, Service du Contrôle des Autoroutes, La Défense, 92055 Cedex, Paris; tel: 01 40 81 21 22.

TAXIS

If you are disabled, a French taxi driver cannot refuse to take you. The driver must help you into the vehicle and agree to transport a guide dog for a blind passenger.

ACCOMMODATION

Gîtes Accessible à Tous lists gîte accommodation that is equipped for the disabled. It is available from: **Maison de Gîtes de France**, 59 rue St-Lazare, 75009 Paris; tel: 01 49 70 75 85; fax: 01 42 81 28 53.
A guide produced by the **French Federation of Camping and Caravanning** (Fédération de Camping-Caravanning) indicates which camp sites have facilities for disabled campers. It is obtainable from Deneway Guides, Chesil Lodge, West Bexington, Dorchester DT2 9DG; tel: 01308 897 809. The **Michelin Green Guide – Camping/Caravanning France** lists sites with facilities for the disabled. The **Association des Paralysés** publishes **Où Ferons Nous Étapes?**, which lists accommodation suitable for handicapped travellers. The Association is based at 22 rue du Père Guérain, Paris 75013; tel: 01 44 16 83 83.

Health Care

There are no unusual health hazards in Provence and along the Côte d'Azur, but it is still advisable to go prepared nonetheless.
EU nationals staying in France are entitled to use the French Social Security system, which refunds up to 70 percent of medical expenses (but sometimes less than this, eg. for dental treatment).

To claim a refund, British nationals should obtain form E111 before leaving the UK (or E112 for those already in treatment). This

Help Lines and Emergency Numbers

SOS Médecins,
tel: 04 93 85 01 01
Nice Médecins,
tel: 04 93 52 42 42
Alcoholics Anonymous, South of France, tel: 04 93 82 91 10
SIDA Information Service, tel: 08 00 84 08 00. Confidential information on Aids in French (note that some counsellors are bilingual). Open 24-hours daily.
Medical emergencies: for an **ambulance**, tel: 15; you can also call the **Service d'Aide Médicale d'Urgence** (SAMU), which exists in the majority of cities and large towns; for numbers, see the front of telephone directories.

form is open-ended, so you do not need a new one every time you travel abroad.

If you do undergo treatment while in France, the doctor will give you a prescription and a *feuille de soins* (statement of treatment). The medication will carry *vignettes* (stickers) that you must stick onto your *feuille de soins*. Send this, the prescription and your E111 form to the local Caisse Primaire d'Assurance Maladie (look in the telephone directory under "Sécurité Sociale"). Note that some refunds can take longer than a month to come through.

Nationals of non-EU countries are well advised to take out insurance before leaving home. Consultations and prescriptions have to be paid for in full in France and are reimbursed, in part, on receipt of a completed *fiche* (form).

The International Association for Medical Assistance to Travellers (IAMAT) is a non-profit-making organisation that anyone can join free of charge (a donation is requested). Benefits include a membership card (entitling the bearer to services at fixed IAMAT rates by participating physicians) and a traveller clinical record (a passport-sized record completed by the member's own doctor prior to travel). A list of English-speaking IAMAT doctors on call 24-hours a day is published for members. The contact details for IAMAT in the US and Canada are as follows:

US:
417 Center Street
Lewiston
NY 14092
Tel: 716-754 4883

Canada:
1287 St Claire Ave
W. Toronto M6E 1B9
Tel: 416-652 0137 and:
40 Regal Road
Guelph
Ontario, N1K 1B5
Tel: 519-836 0102

PHARMACIES

Pharmacies in France are good, but expensive, and many toiletries are cheaper in supermarkets. The staff in pharmacies are well qualified, however, and should be able to advise on many minor ailments; they may help with minor wounds and other basic medical services. All pharmacies can be identified by a neon green cross, Most open from 9am or 10am to 7pm or 8pm. If the pharmacy is closed there will be a sign giving details of a "pharmacy de garde", which will offer a night-time service. If you can't find a pharmacy, consult the Gendarmerie (police station).

OPTICIANS

Bring a note of your prescription in case you need to replace your glasses in an emergency. Drivers are required by law to carry a spare pair of glasses in the car.

HOSPITALS

For a complete list of hospitals consult the *Pages Blanches* telephone directory under "Hôpital Assistance Publique".

Practical Tips

Embassies and Consulates

You should find a list of embassies and consulates in *Pages Jaunes (*the French equivalent of *Yellow Pages)* under "Ambassades et Consulats". You should go to the consulate for general enquiries or problems with passports or visas; the staff there will be able to advise whether you need to consult the Embassy in Paris, or a local honorary consul. Call before going along to your consulate or Embassy, in case an appointment is necessary. The following may take you through to a recorded message with details of emergency numbers.

EMBASSIES AND CONSULATES IN PARIS

Australia
4 rue Jean-Rey, tel: 01 40 59 33 00. Métro: Bir-Hakeim. Open: 9am–6pm (visas: 9.15am–12.15pm) Mon–Fri.
UK
35 rue du Faubourg-St-Honoré, tel: 01 44 51 31 00. Métro: Concorde. Open: 9.30am–1pm, 2.30–6pm Mon–Fri. Consulate: 16 rue d'Anjou, tel: 01 44 51 33 01. Open: 2.30–5.30pm Mon–Fri.
Canada
35 avenue Montaigne, tel: 01 44 43 29 00. Métro: Franklin D. Roosevelt. Open: 9am–noon, 2–5pm Mon–Fri. Visas: 37 avenue Montaigne, tel: 01 44 43 29 16. Open 8.30–11am Mon–Fri.
Ireland
12 avenue Foch. Consulate: 4 rue Rude, tel: 01 44 17 67 00. Métro: Charles de Gaulle-Etoile. Open: 9.30am–noon Mon–Fri; by phone 9.30am–1pm, 2.30–5.30pm Mon–Fri.

New Zealand
7 rue Léonard de Vinci, tel: 01 45 00 24 11. Métro: Victor-Hugo. Open: 9am–1pm Mon–Fri.
US
2 avenue Gabriel, tel: 01 43 12 22 22. Métro: Concorde. Open: 9am–6pm Mon–Fri, by appointment. Consulate (visas): 2 rue St-Florentin, tel: 01 43 12 22 22. Métro: Concorde. Open: 8.45– 11am Mon–Fri. Passport service: 9am–3pm.

CONSULATES IN PROVENCE

Britain
24 avenue Prado, 13006 Marseille. Tel: 04 91 15 72 10; fax 04 01 37 47 06.
US
- 12 boulevard Paul Peytral, 13286 Marseille. Tel: 04 91 54 92 00.
- 31 rue du Marechal Joffre, 06000 Nice. Tel: 04 93 88 89 55.

Canada
10 rue Lamartine, 06000 Nice. Tel: 04 93 92 93 22.
Ireland
152 boulevard J.F. Kennedy, 06160 Cap d'Antibes. Tel: 04 93 61 50 63; fax 04 93 67 96 08.

Emergencies

In the case of a serious accident or medical emergency, telephone the **Police** (17) or the **Sapeurs-Pompiers** (18). Though primarily a Fire Brigade, the latter is a group of trained paramedics, and both they and the police have medical back-up and work in close contact with **SAMU** (the French ambulance service). In rural areas the local taxi service often doubles as an ambulance, so it is worth getting their number, from the tourist office or *mairie* (town hall).

Emergency Numbers

Most of the following services operate 24-hours daily.
Police 17
Fire (Sapeurs-Pompiers) 18
Ambulance (SAMU) 15

Security and Crime

France is a civilised country and you should be just as safe there as at home if you take the usual sensible precautions with your personal possessions. In cities, watch out for pickpockets, and be careful on trains, especially at night.

If you lose your credit card, notify the authorities immediately on the following numbers: **Visa/Carte Bleue**, tel: 08 36 69 08 80; **Diner's Club**, tel: 01 49 06 17 17; **American Express**, tel: 01 47 77 72 00; **Master Card**, tel: 01 45 67 84 84.

Lost Property

To report a crime or loss of belongings, go to the local police station *(gendarmerie* or *commisariat de police)*. Telephone numbers can be found at the front of local telephone directories. In an emergency, call 17. If you lose your passport, you should report it firstly to the police and then to the nearest consulate. If, for any reason, you are detained by the police, ask to call the nearest consulate to ask a member of the staff to help you.

Toilets

Anyone may use the toilet in a bar or café whether they are a customer or not, unless there is a sign specifying that this is not allowed. (Ask for *les toilettes* or *le WC*, which is pronounced vay-say). Public toilets vary considerably, and many are still old-fashioned squat toilets. Men and women sometimes use the same facilities.

Opening Hours

The sacred lunch hour is still largely observed in the South of France, which means that most shops and offices close at midday and do not re-open until 2pm or even 2.30pm. **Hypermarkets** *(grands surfaces)* usually remain open through lunch and normally until 7pm or 8pm in the evening.

Museums

Except in July and August most **museums** close for lunch from noon to 2pm; they also close on certain public holidays, notably 1 Jan, 1 May and 25 Dec. Municipal museums are usually closed on Monday, while national museums close on Tuesday. Most monuments and museums in France charge a modest entrance fee. This is indicated with the opening times (in brackets) in the Places section of this book.

Many shops also close in the morning or all day on Monday or Wednesday.

Opening hours for **food shops** and **DIY shops** are generally 8.30am to 1pm and 2.30pm until 7pm. **Boulangeries** (bakers) are open daily (but Sunday mornings only), though those in small villages may have a closing day. The usual hours are 9am to 7pm (with a break for lunch from noon until 2 or 3pm), though some may open earlier. Most shops close on Sunday but most **bureaux de tabac** – good places to buy stamps and cigarettes – and **maisons de la presse** (for newspapers, magazines, etc.) usually open on Sunday mornings. **Banks** tend to open 9am–noon and 1.30–5pm Mon–Fri, although these times can vary *(see also page 292)*.

Petrol stations usually open at 8.30am and close for lunch from noon–2pm or 2.30pm; most close at about 9pm except on motorways. Supermarket petrol stations may stay open for credit card sales only.

Public offices usually open from 8.30am–noon, and 2–6pm. ***Mairies*** (town halls) also tend to close for lunch and in smaller places they may only open in the morning, typically from 9am–noon.

Travelling with Pets

Animal quarantine laws have been revised so that it is possible to re-enter Britain with your pet without it having to go through quarantine. Conditions are stringent, however, with tough health requirements and restricted points of entry.

For further details you should contact the Ministry of Agriculture, or the French consulate if you are abroad. Once you are in continental Europe, you will only need a valid vaccination certificate to travel between countries with your pet.

Newspapers and Magazines

The French press is very regional. Popular papers in the south include *Nice Matin*, *La Provence*, *Var-Matin*, *Le Dauphiné Vaucluse*, and *La Marseillaise*. Foreign newspapers are widely available in the centre of the major towns, at train stations, airports and Maisons de la Presse. The local English-language magazine *Riviera Reporter* is good for regional information and politics.

Postal Services

Post Offices (PTTs) open Mon–Fri 9am–noon and 2–6pm, Sat 9am–noon. In large towns they may not close for lunch, but in small villages, they may only be open for a short time in the morning.

Before you start queuing check that the you are at the right counter; in larger post offices, each counter has specific services. If you only want **stamps**, look for the sign, *"Timbres"*. Standard-weight letters within France and most of the EU require a €0.5 stamp.

You can also buy stamps at tobacconists *(bureaux de tabac)* and some shops selling postcards. Large post offices and *maisons de la presse* (newsagents) also offer **fax** and **photocopying** services; many supermarkets also have coin-operated photocopiers. **Minitel** *(see page 300)* is being replaced by the Internet and is not always now available in post offices.

POSTE RESTANTE

Mail can be kept *poste restante* at a post office, addressed to Poste Restante, Poste Centrale (for the main post office), then the town postcode and name. A small fee will be charged and you will need to show your passport to collect your mail.

URGENT MAIL

Urgent post can be sent *par exprès*. The Chronopost system is also fast but is expensive. However, packages weighing up to 25g are guaranteed delivery within 24 hours.

Telephones

French telephone numbers are all 10 figures, always written – and spoken – in sets of two, eg 04 04 04 04 04. Regional telephone numbers are prefixed as follows: Paris, Île de France region 01; Northwest 02; Northeast 03; Southeast and Corsica 04, and Southwest 05. When dialling from outside France, omit the initial zero. If you want numbers to be given singly rather than in pairs, ask for them *"chiffre par chiffre"*.

PUBLIC PHONES

You should be able to find telephone boxes *(cabines publiques)* in every sizeable village. Card phones are now more usual than coin-operated phones – you can buy phone cards *(télécartes)* from post offices, stationers, railway stations, some cafés and *bureaux de tabac*.

Some cafés, shops or restaurants have **metred phones** but these may cost more than public phone boxes. If you need to make a phone call in a small village with no public phone, look out for a blue *téléphone publique* plaque on a house. The proprietor is officially appointed to allow you to use the phone and charge the normal rate for the call.

PHONE DIRECTORIES

You can find telephone directories *(annuaires)* in all post offices and in most cafés. *Pages Blanches* (White Pages) lists people and businesses alphabetically, while *Pages Jaunes* (Yellow Pages) lists businesses and services. Both are also now available on the Internet at:

- www.pagesjaunes.fr
- www.pagesblanches.fr

INTERNATIONAL CALLS

To make an international call dial 00 followed by the country's international call number. This can be found in the front of the *Pages Jaunes* section of the phone directory or on the information panel in a telephone box. For US credit phone-card numbers, *see page 291*.

REVERSE-CHARGE CALLS

You cannot make a reverse-charge call (call collect) within France but you can make such a call to countries that will accept them. To do so, go through the operator and ask to make a PCV (pronounced "pay-say-vay") call. Telephone calls can only be received at call boxes displaying the blue bell sign.

FREE CALLS

Numéros verts (literally "green numbers") are free numbers, usually beginning with 08. To dial

Telephoning Abroad

To make an international call, lift the receiver, insert your money or card, dial 00, then dial the country code, followed by the area code (omitting the area code prefix 0) and the number.

International dialling codes:
UK 44
US 1
Canada 1
Ireland 353
Australia 61

from a public telephone you still need to insert a card or money first. Any coins used will be returned immediately after your call, and your card will not be debited for the amount.

MINITEL

Minitel, a computer-based videotext information service that is linked to the telephone and found in most homes, cafés and hotels, is the precursor of the Internet in France. Post-offices have the Minitel as a telephone directory (on 3611) and information resource. However, it is now being superseded by the Internet. To use the Minitel for information key in 3611, wait for the beep, and press *connexion*. Type in the name and address you want, and press *Envoi* ("send").

MOBILE PHONES

If you are using a British-based mobile in France, dial as if you are a local subscriber. To call from one British phone to another use the international code even if you are both in France.

TV and Radio

TELEVISION

France has six terrestrial TV channels. **TF1**, the largest, has been privatised since 1987, and features movies, game shows, dubbed soaps, audience debates and the main news at 8pm.

France 2 is a state-owned station showing a mix of game shows, documentaries and cultural chat.

F3R is more heavyweight than the first two channels and shows local news, sports, excellent wildlife documentaries and a late-night Sunday Cinema, Minuit, which features classic films in the original language (VO for *version originale*). It also has a news and documentary programme, "Continentales", which is broadcast five days a week with news broadcasts from around Europe in the original language with French subtitles.

Canal+ offers a roster of satellite and cable subscription channels with recent movies (sometimes original language) and exclusive sport.

Arte is an excellent Franco-German hybrid, specialising in intelligent arts coverage and films in the original language. From 5.45am–7pm Arte's wavelength is shared with the educational channel, **La Cinquième**.

M6 is a daytime channel with a base of music videos plus magazine programmes such as Culture Pub.

Any suitably connected television can supplement these channels with a range of internationally broadcast satellite stations.

RADIO

There should be a French radio station to suit your taste. The following is just a selection of what is available (all wavelengths are given in MHz):

87.8 France Inter. A state-run, middle-of-the-road channel offering music and international news.

90.9 Chante France. French song.

91.7–92.1 France Musique. Another state-run channel, this time offering classical music and jazz.

93.5–93.9 France Culture. A high-brow state culture station with the stress on literature, poetry, history, cinema and music.

96.4 BFM. Business and economics news. Wall Street information is given in English every evening.

98.2 Radio FG. Gay station with music and lonely hearts.

101.5 Radio Nova. Funky station serving a mix of hip hop, trip hop, world music and jazz.

104.3 RTL. The most popular French station, providing a mix of music and talk programmes.

104.7 Europe 1. News, press reviews and sports.

105.5 France Info. Tune in for 24-hour news, economic updates and sports news.

BBC World Service. This can be received in France on shortwave between 6.195 and 12.095 MHz.

Getting Around

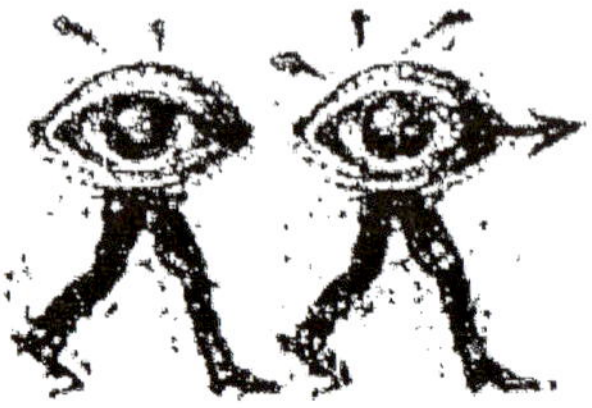

Although it is possible to get around Provence by train and bus, a car (or, if you're energetic, a bicycle) is essential if you want to explore the region independently. Bus and train services are adequate between towns and cities but there may only be one bus a day – and sometimes no buses at all – to small villages. There is a good train service along the coast, and a number of small mountain train services.

It is pleasant to drive inland, but traffic on the coast can be highly congested in summer. It's worth remembering that the hallowed French lunch break is still widely observed, so this is a good time to travel. French school holidays last through July and August, and the roads are at their worst around 15 August, a major national holiday.

Maps

A first essential for touring is a good map. The large-format **Michelin** atlases or sheet maps are good for driving. For walking or cycling, **IGN** (Institute Géographique National) maps are invaluable. The Top 100 (1:100,000, 1 cm to 1 km) and Top 50 (1:50,000, 2 cm to 1 km) maps have all roads and most footpaths marked. For greater detail, go for

Useful Websites

- www.sncf.fr (timetables and on-line booking for French Railways)
- www.britrail.co.uk
- www.eurostar.co.uk
- www.raileurope.com (European rail journeys on-line)
- www.iti.fr (route planner)
- www.autoroutes.fr (motorway news)

the IGN blue series 1:25,000 maps. Town plans are often given away free at local tourist offices. Most good bookshops should have a range of maps, but they may cost less in hypermarkets or service stations.

World Leisure Marketing, 11 Newmarket Court, Derby, DE24 8NW; tel: 0800 838080, fax: 01332 573399 is the IGN agent for the UK and offers a mail order service. Other stockists of French maps in the UK include: **Stanfords** International Map Centre, 12–14 Long Acre, Covent Garden, London WC2E 9LP; tel: 020 7730 1354 and **The Travel Bookshop**, 13 Blenheim Crescent, London W11 2EE; tel: 020 7229 5260.

By Bus

Details of routes and timetables are generally available free of charge from tourist offices and bus stations *(gares routières)*. Both places should also give details of coach tours and sightseeing excursions.

By Train

There is a reasonably good SNCF rail network in the South of France, especially in the Val du Rhône and along the coast. You can buy regional rail maps and timetables from *tabacs* and pick up free local timetables from railway stations *(gares SNCF)*. Services range from the high-speed **TGV** lines, which stop only at main stations, to the local **Omnibus** services, which stop at every station. Out-of-town stations usually (but not always) have a connecting *navette* (shuttle bus) to the town centre. Sometimes the SNCF runs a connecting bus service (indicated as "Autocar" in timetables) to stations where the train no longer stops or along disused lines; rail tickets and passes are valid on these routes.

The overland **Metrazur** line runs along the Côte d'Azur, stopping at all stations between Marseille and Ventimiglia. Two scenic mountain lines depart from Nice: the Roya valley line via Sospel and the privately operated Train des Pignes, which runs up the Var Valley to Digne-les-Bains. Information on services is available from railway stations.

If you intend to travel extensively by train it may be worth obtaining a rail pass before leaving home *(see Getting There, page 294)*. Before buying any tickets in France check on any discounts available. Children under 4 years old travel free, those from 4 to 12 may travel for half-fare. People travelling in groups of six or more can also obtain discounts (20–40 percent depending on numbers). *For further information on train travel, see page 294.*

By Car

British, US, Canadian and Australian licences are all valid in France. You should always carry your vehicle's registration document and valid insurance (minimum: third party; a green card, available from your insurance firm, is recommended). Additional insurance cover, in some cases including a "home-return" service, is offered by a number of organisations including the British and American Automobile Associations and Europ-Assistance, Sussex House, Perrymount Road, Haywards Heath, RH16 1DN; tel: 0144 411 999 or 442 211.

Another useful address is FFAC (Fédération Français des Automobiles Club et des Usagers de la Route), 8 place de la Concorde, 75008 Paris; tel: 01 53 30 89 30; fax: 01 53 30 89 29. This group assists with breakdowns and co-ordinates with non-French automobile clubs.

French Roads

Motorways (*Autoroutes*) are designated "A" roads, National Highways (*Routes Nationales*) "N" or "RN" roads. Local roads are known as "D" routes.

SPEED LIMITS

Speed limits are as follows, unless otherwise indicated: 130 kph (80 mph) on motorways; 110 kph (68 mph) on dual carriageways; 90 kph (56 mph) on other roads, except in towns where the limit is 50 kph (30 mph). There is a minimum limit of 80 kph (50 mph) on the outside lane of motorways in daylight with good visibility and on level ground. Speed limits are 20 kph (12 mph) less on motorways in wet weather. On-the-spot fines can be levied for speeding; on toll roads, the time is printed on the ticket you take at your entry point and can thus be checked and a fine imposed on exit.

RULES OF THE ROAD

Drivers should follow the rules of the road and always drive sensibly. Heavy on-the-spot fines are given for traffic offences such as speeding, and drivers can be stopped and breathalysed during spot checks.

Note the following:

- Drive on the right.
- The minimum age for driving in France is 18. Foreigners may not drive on a provisional licence.

Priority for Drivers

Nowadays, traffic on major roads normally has priority, with traffic being halted on minor approach roads by means of one of the following signs.

- ***Cédez le passage*** – give way
- ***Vous n'avez pas la priorité*** – you do not have right of way
- ***Passage protégé*** – no right of way.

However, care should be taken in smaller towns and in rural areas where there may not be any road markings, in which case you will be expected to give way to traffic coming from the right.

If an oncoming driver flashes their headlights it is to indicate that he or she has priority – not the other way around.

A yellow diamond sign indicates that you have priority; the diamond sign with a diagonal black line indicates you do not have priority.

- Full or dipped headlights must be used in poor visibility and at night; sidelights are not sufficient unless the car is stationary. Beams must be adjusted for right-hand-drive vehicles, but yellow tints are not compulsory.
- The use of seat belts (front and rear if fitted) and crash helmets for motorcyclists is compulsory.
- Children under 10 are not allowed to ride in the front seat unless the car has a rear-facing safety seat or it does not have a rear seat.
- Carry a red warning triangle to place 50 metres (165 ft) behind the car in case of a breakdown or accident (strongly advised, and compulsory if towing a caravan).

In an accident or emergency, call the police (dial 17) or use the free emergency telephones (every 2 km/1 mile) on motorways. If another driver is involved, lock your car and go together to call the police. It is useful to carry an European Accident Statement Form (obtainable from your insurance company), which will simplify matters in the event of an accident.

FUEL

Unleaded petrol *(essence sans plomb)* is widely available in France. Leaded petrol is no longer available but there is a substitute unleaded petrol for leaded fuel vehicles. A map showing the location of filling stations is available from main tourist offices. Petrol is generally cheapest at hypermarkets and most expensive on motorways.

Motocycles and Mopeds

Rules of the road are largely the same for two-wheeled riders as for car drivers. The minimum age for driving machines over 80cc is 18. Nationality plates (eg GB stickers) must be shown, and it is compulsory to wear crash helmets. Dipped headlights must be used at all times, and children under 14 may not be carried as passengers.

Cycling

Local tourist offices keep information on hire facilities. Bikes *(vélos)* are usually available from hire cycle shops; French Railways (SNCF) also hire them from several stations in the region – conveniently, you do not always have to return the bike to the station that you hired it from. Bikes can be carried free of charge on buses and on some slow trains *(Autotrains)*; on faster trains you will have to pay a supplement.

On Foot

France has a network of footpaths, called *Grande Randonnées*, which are well signposted and offer good facilities for walkers en route. The paths are classified with a "GR" number and there are countless opportunities for exploring on foot, following a long route, or on one of the shorter circular tours. The IGN Blue Series maps at a scale of 1:25,000 are excellent for walkers. Contact the **Centre d'Information Sentiers et Randonnée**, 64 rue Gergovie, 75014 Paris; tel: 01 45 45 31 02, or tourist offices for details of local clubs and events.

For information on walking holidays, see page 323.

Taxis

Taxis are normally available at railway stations and official taxi ranks in city centres. Outside the cities check telephone directories or local notice boards for taxi firms.

Nice

Centrale de Taxi
Tel: 04 93 13 78 78
There are 29 taxi ranks in the city but you can also hail them in the street. Pay by the kilometre.

Marseille

Eurotaxi
Tel: 04 91 02 20 20; 04 91 97 12 12 (drivers who speak foreign languages). There are eight ranks in Marseille and you can hail taxis in the street.

Where to Stay

There is a vast range of accommodation in Provence, including deluxe city hotels and seafront palaces, country villas and *gîtes*, campsites, and a wide range of small town hotels, country *auberges* and *chambres d'hôtes*. In the summer months (between mid-July and mid-August, when the French head south *en masse*) it is wise to book ahead, especially around the coastal regions; if you visit outside the peak holiday period, however, you should find accommodation without too many difficulties. Note that some hotels in the more remote areas may close between November and February, and most campsites will be closed during the winter.

Hotels

All hotels in France conform to national standards and carry star ratings, which are set down by the Ministry of Tourism, according to their degree of comfort and amenities. Prices, which are charged per room not per person, range from as little as €30 for a double room in an unclassified hotel (ie. its standards are not sufficient to warrant a single star, but it is likely to be clean, cheap and cheerful), to around €90 for the cheapest double room in a four-star luxury hotel.

Useful Websites

- www.chatotel.com (chateaux and independant hotels)
- www.fuaj.org (youth hostels)
- www.relaischateaux.fr
- www.campingfrance.com
- www.gites-de-france.fr

Gîtes

Rural *gîtes* provide a good way to appreciate a holiday in the French countryside, with accommodation ranging from simple farms to grand châteaux. All *gîtes* are set up with the help of government grants, aimed at restoring rural properties, and they are regularly inspected by the Relais Départemental (the county office of the national federation) and given an *"épi"* (ear of corn) classification. Prices average €180–280 per week in August for a 2–4 person gîte.

Gîtes are self-catering, and you should check what you need to bring with you in the way of utensils, bedding etc before travelling. Some *gîtes* are fairly remote, and you will need your own transport to reach them. *Gite* owners will be able to advise about shopping facilities in the neighbourhood, local sights and activities and bicycle hire etc.

Brittany Ferries are the UK agents for Gîtes de France; bookings can be made through: The Brittany Centre, Wharf Rd, Portsmouth PO2 8RU; tel: 0870 5360 360. The list of *gîtes* in the Brittany Ferries brochure is only a selection of those available.

In France, contact the **Maison de Gîtes de France**, 59 rue St Lazare, 75009 Paris; tel: 01 49 70 75 85; fax: 01 42 81 28 53. The Gîtes de France brochure *Gîtes Accessible à Tous* lists *gîte* accommodation with disabled access and services. You can also investigate *gîtes* on the web at www.gites-de-france.com.

Hotels are required by law to display their menus outside, and details of room prices should be visible either outside or in the reception, as well as on the back of bedroom doors. Note that it is possible for a hotel to have a one-star rating, with a two-star restaurant.

When booking a room you should normally be shown it before you agree to take it, so don't hesitate to ask to do so. Supplements may be charged for an additional bed or a cot *(lit bébé)*. You may be asked when booking if you wish to dine, particularly if the hotel is busy – and you should confirm that the hotel's restaurant is open (many are closed out of season on Sunday or Monday evenings).

Lists of hotels can be obtained from the French Government Tourist office in your country or from regional or local tourist offices in France. If you just want an overnight stop to break a journey, you may find clean, modern, basic chains such as Formule 1 handy.

LOGIS DE FRANCE

Logis de France is France's biggest hotel group, with over 5,000 private hotels in small towns and the French countryside. Most of these hotels are one- or two-star and they vary greatly in facilities, atmosphere and level of service. Contact the **Fédération Nationale des Logis et Auberges de France**, 83 avenue d'Italie, 75013 Paris; tel: 01 45 84 70 00, or the French Government Tourist office for a Logis de France handbook (free of charge to personal callers).

Bed-and-Breakfasts

Bed-and-breakfast *(chambre d'hôte)* accommodation is fairly widely available in private houses, often on working farms, whose owners are members of the Fédération Nationale des Gîtes Ruraux de France. Bookings can be made for an overnight stop or a longer stay. Breakfast is included in the price, and evening meals, which are usually made with local produce and very good value, are often also available.

Welcome Guides Bed and Breakfast in France, lists B&Bs including châteaux. UK booking service: tel: 01491 578803; fax: 01491 410806. www.bedbreak.com.

If you don't wish to book in advance, you can always just look out for signs along the road (usually most common in the country) offering *chambres d'hôtes*. You shouldn't have too many difficulties finding a bed out-of-season and you may be surprised by the good value of the simple farm food and accommodation on offer.

Châteaux Guides

Various guides can be obtained from the French Tourist Office. These include **Châteaux & Hotels de France** (hotels and bed-and-breakfasts in private châteaux) and **Relais du Silence** (hotels in châteaux or grand houses in peaceful settings). For the latter, you can also visit: www.silencehotel.com.

Camping

French campsites *(les campings)*, many of which are run by local councils, can often be remarkably comfortable and well appointed. Prices range from €5 to around €15 per night for a family of four, with a car, caravan or tent. On the coast during high season the campsites can extremely crowded. Although camping rough *(camping sauvage)* is generally not permitted, it may be worth asking the owner of the land for permission if there is nowhere official to pitch up nearby. Fire is an ever-present risk in the region, so be particularly careful when cooking.

Campsites are graded from one-star (minimal comfort, water points, showers and sinks) to four-star luxury sites, which allow more space for each pitch and offer above-average facilities. The majority of sites are two-star. Sites that are designated *Aire naturelle de camping* and *Camping à la Ferme* tend to be cheaper and have fewer services than standard sites.

The *Guide Officiel* of the French Federation of Camping and Caravanning (FFCC), available from French Government Tourist Offices, lists 11,600 sites nationwide and indicates which sites have facilities for disabled campers. The useful *Michelin Green Guide: Camping/Caravanning France* also lists sites with facilities for the disabled.

Reservation Services

Canvas Holidays
Tel: 01383 644000
Fax: 01203 422010
Select Site Reservations
Tel: 01873 859876
Fax: 01873 859544
Avis Car Away (camping cars)
Tel: 01 47 49 80 40
Fax: 01 47 49 80 50
www.aviscaraway.com

Youth Hostels

To stay in most youth hostels *(auberges de jeunesse)* you need to be a member of the International Youth Hostel Association (YHA) or the Fédération Unie des Auberges de Jeunesse, which is affiliated to the International Youth Hostel Federation. For more information, contact: **Fédération Unie des Auberges de Jeunesse** (FUAJ), 27 rue Pajol, 75018 Paris, tel: 01 44 89 87 27; fax: 01 44 89 87 10. **Youth Hostel Association**, Trevelyan House, 8 St Stephens Hill, St Albans, Herts, AL1 2DY, tel: 01727 855215.

Gîtes d'Etapes

Gîte d'Étape offer very basic accommodation for walkers or cyclists, often in remote mountain areas; expect communal accommodation, bunk beds, shared bathrooms etc. You will need to make reservations, especially in busy periods. *Gîte de neige, gîte de pêche* and *gîte équestre* offer similar facilities.

Mountain refuges *(refuges)* offer similar accommodation and may also be able to provide drinks and meals. Many refuges are open from June–September only and they should always be booked in advance. Prices vary from €5 to €15 per person. Lists of refuges are available from local tourist offices.

To book youth hostels while in France, call: 0044 1629 581418. For the American Youth Hostelling International, contact: PO Box 37613, Dept USA, Washington DC 20013/7613, tel: 0202 783 6161.

Bon Weekend en Villes

This excellent-value tourist office promotion has been running for ten years, offering two nights (either Fri–Sat or Sat–Sun) for the price of one. Towns include Aix-en-Provence, Nîmes, Marseille, Arles and Draguignan. The offer is usually valid between November and March, although it is available throughout the year in some towns. You need to book at least eight days in advance. Contact the French Government Tourist Office *(see page 293)* for further details.

Hotel Listings

Hotels are listed by *département*, according to the chapters is this book, and thereafter by place, then hotel name, in alphabetical order.

THE VAUCLUSE

Avignon

Auberge de Cassagne
450 allée de Cassagne
Le Pontet-Avignon
Tel: 04 90 31 04 18
Fax: 04 90 32 25 09
This extremely upmarket hotel – a member of the Relais du Silence and Châteaux et Hôtels de France groups – is located around 8 km (5 miles) from the centre of Avignon, providing a veritable refuge from the buzz of the city. The chalet-style rooms are furnished in the regional style and are well equipped with all mod cons. Facilities include a sauna, exercise room and a lovely pool, set among exotic vegetation. There's a top-quality, if expensive, restaurant, where excellent breakfasts are served. A haven. **$$$**
La Ferme
Chemin des Bois
Île de la Barthelasse
Tel: 04 90 82 57 53
Fax: 04 90 27 15 47
A beautiful farm in a peaceful spot on an island yet within easy reach of the city centre. Pleasant rooms, a pool and fresh, simple cuisine. **$$**
Hôtel de Blauvac
11 rue de la Bancasse
Tel: 04 90 86 34 11
Fax: 04 90 86 27 41
A 17th-century hotel in a quiet setting with a friendly atmosphere. Large rooms at decent rates. **$$**
Hôtel Europe
12 place Crillon
Tel: 04 90 14 76 76
The Europe, which is favoured by celebrity types, is probably Avignon's best hotel. Once a coaching inn, it is mentioned in many early travellers' accounts. It's conveniently situated, extremely quiet, elegant and comfortable. **$$$**
Hôtel de Garlande
20 rue Galante
Tel: 04 90 85 08 85
Fax: 04 90 27 16 58
Email:
hotel.garland@avignon-et.provence.com
Located in Avignon's lovely Vieille Ville, by the place St-Didier, this hotel with 12 rooms is comfortable and reasonably priced. **$$**
Hôtel Mignon
12 rue Joseph Vernet
Tel: 04 90 82 17 30
Fax: 04 90 85 78 46
This sweet little hotel with 15 rooms is surprisingly adequate for its category and price. It's not luxurious, but the location is central and the bathrooms sparkle. **$**
Hôtel de la Mirande
4 place de la Mirande
Tel: 04 90 85 93 93
Fax: 04 90 86 26 85
La Mirande, which is tucked behind the Palais des Papes, was a cardinals' residence during the 14th century and has been a hotel since the 18th. Nowadays, it offers modern-day comfort combined with beautiful period décor. **$$$**
Hôtel Saint-George
12 traverse de l'Etoile
Tel: 04 90 88 54 34
This clean, good-value hotel is located outside the ramparts on the road to Marseille. Friendly staff. **$**

Mercure Cité des Papes
1 rue Jean Vilar
Tel: 04 90 80 93 00
Fax: 04 90 80 93 01
If you are determined to stay next door to the lovely Palais in Avignon, consider the 73-roomed Cité des Papes. Be sure to request one of the quiet back rooms with palatial views. Other rooms overlook the place de l'Horloge. No restaurant. **$$**

Carpentras

Le Fiacre
153 rue Vigne
Tel: 04 90 63 03 15
Fax: 04 90 60 49 73
An interesting old townhouse and an excellent choice if you want to stay somewhere central. **$–$$**

Châteauneuf-du-Pape

La Garbure
3 rue Joseph-Ducos
Tel: 04 90 83 75 08
Fax: 04 90 83 52 34
A simple townhouse on the main street, with comfortable rooms and good regional cuisine. **$$**

Nîmes

L'Hacienda
Chemin du *mas* de Brignon
Marguerittes
Tel: 04 66 75 02 25
Fax: 04 66 75 45 58
Country villa with pool and gardens set among the vineyards and olive groves outside town. Rooms with private terraces. Good cuisine. **$$**

Orange

Glacier
46 cours Aristide Briand
Tel: 04 90 34 02 01
Fax: 04 90 51 13 80
A straightforward hotel in a good location on the edge of the old town. Very friendly staff. No restaurant. **$$**

Hôtel Arènes
Place des Langes
Tel: 04 90 11 40 40
Fax: 04 90 11 40 45
A great central hotel on a traquil square. Good restaurant. **$$**

Sault

Hostellerie du Val de Sault
Ancien chemin de Sault
Tel: 04 90 64 01 41
Fax: 04 90 64 12 74
Email: valdesault@aol.com
This is an elevated modern hotel with gardens and a swimming pool looking out onto Mont-Ventoux. There are rooms with terraces, and the cuisine served is typical of the region and tasty. **$$–$$$**

Vaison-la-Romaine

Hostellerie le Beffroi
Rue de l'Evêché
Tel: 04 90 36 04 71
Fax: 04 90 36 24 78
Le Beffroi is a delightful 16th-century hostelry with period décor and a restaurant offering good cuisine. The views from here are excellent. **$$**

Villeneuve-lès-Avignon

Hôtel–Restaurant La Magnaneraie
37 rue Camp de Bataille
Tel: 04 90 15 92 00
Fax: 04 90 25 46 37
Email: magnaneraie@gulliver.fr
If you're having trouble finding somewhere to stay in Avignon (sometimes a problem during the summer festival), you could consider staying in Villeneuve. This hotel, which is quiet and handily situated, is housed in a 15th-century building in a garden with ponds, palms and ancient oaks. More contemporary facilities include a swimming pool and tennis courts; you can also hire bicycles from here. The rooms are furnished in a style that is contemporary with the building, and the dining room is decorated with frescoes. **$$$**

THE BOUCHES-DU-RHÔNE

Aix-en-Provence

Hôtel des Augustins
3 rue de la Masse
Tel: 04 42 27 28 59
Fax: 04 42 26 74 87
The Hôtel des Augustins is housed in a building that was an Augustine convent until the French Revolution of 1789. It became a hotel in the 1890s. Conveniently located near to the cours Mirabeau, this place has comfortable rooms and a very imposing reception area. **$$**

Price Ranges

The ranges given, which are intended to be guides to prices only, are quoted per double room. Breakfast is not normally included, and credit cards are accepted unless otherwise stated.
$ = under €50
$$ = €50–115
$$$ = more than €115

Grand Hôtel Nègre Coste
33 cours Mirabeau
Tel: 04 42 27 74 22
A magnificent old hotel set on Aix's elegant main street. Lovely views. **$$**

Le Manoir
8 rue d'Entrecasteaux
Tel: 04 42 26 27 20
A comfortable old-style hotel where you can breakfast in the 14th-century cloister. **$$**

Hôtel Mascotte
Avenue de la Cible
Tel: 04 42 37 58 58
Fax: 04 42 37 58 59
Located around 10 minutes by bus away from the city centre, this is a standard business hotel, offering 93 rooms. There's a lovely big pool outside and a hotel restaurant and bar. Conference facilities. **$$**

Le Pigonnet
5 avenue du Pigonnet
Tel: 04 42 59 02 90
A luxurious old country house-style hotel, in a park in central Aix. **$$$**

Hôtel des Quatre Dauphins
54 rue Roux Alpheron
Tel: 04 42 38 16 39
Fax: 04 42 38 60 19
The Quatre Dauphins, which is located near to the fountain of the same name, is inexpensive but not without character and comfort. There is no hotel restaurant but that is hardly a problem in this central part of town. 12 rooms. **$**

Arles

Grand Hôtel Nord-Pinus
Place du Forum
Tel: 04 90 93 44 44
A luxury hotel. The bar, "La Corrida", becomes packed with *matadors* and their retinues when fights take place. Great Art Deco brasserie. **$$$**

Price Ranges

The ranges given, which are intended to be guides to prices only, are quoted per double room. Breakfast is not normally included, and credit cards are accepted unless otherwise stated.
$ = under €50
$$ = €50–115
$$$ = more than €115

Hôtel d'Arlatan
26 rue du Sauvage
Tel: 04 90 93 56 66
Fax: 04 90 49 68 45
Email: hotel-arlaten@provnet.fr
A very popular hotel and a member of the Châteaux and Hôtels de France group. It has a pool, an enclosed garden and a scattering of Roman archeological remains. 34 rooms and 7 suites. **$$–$$$**

Hôtel Calendal
22 Place Pomme
Tel: 04 90 96 11 89
Good rooms and a shady garden in a good location behind the Arena. **$$**

Hôtel du Cloître
16 rue du Cloître
Tel: 04 90 96 29 50
Fax: 04 90 96 02 88
Within Arles, you won't find a more conveniently located, pleasantly run and well-priced hotel with traditional Provençal décor. Good location on a narrow street near the Roman Théâtre Antique. **$$**

Hôtel du Forum
Place du Forum
Tel: 04 90 93 48 95
The Forum lacks the style of the Grand Hôtel Nord-Pinus *(see page 305)* but it is still comfortable and has the advantage of a swimming pool in a secluded courtyard. **$$**

Hôtel de Musée
11 rue du Grand Prieuré
Tel: 04 90 93 88 88
A 17th-century mansion tucked away on a winding street, with a pretty courtyard for breakfast. **$$**

Les Baux-de-Provence

L'Oustau de Baumaniere
Route d'Arles
Tel: 04 90 54 33 07
Fax: 04 90 54 40 46
This is a superbly renovated old farmhouse near les Baux, with a magnificent view and celebrated restaurant. **$$$**

Cassis

Hôtel Liautaud
2 rue Victor-Hugo
Tel: 04 42 01 75 37
Fax: 04 42 01 12 08
Book well in advance and you should find this waterfront hotel a reasonably priced and accommodating place to stay. No restaurant. 39 rooms. **$$**

Fontvieille

Hôtel Peireiro
36 avenue des Baux
Tel: 04 90 54 76 10
Fax: 04 90 54 62 60
Hotel with 43 rooms, a lovely veranda, pool and mini-golf. **$$**

Marseille

Hôtel Le Corbusier
280 boulevard Michelet
Tel: 04 91 16 78 00
Fax: 04 91 16 78 28
Architecture fans might like to check in at this hotel on the 7th floor of Le Corbusier's Cité Radieuse. Basic but iconic. **$–$$**

Novotel Vieux-Port
36 boulevard Charles Livon
Tel: 04 96 11 42 11
Fax: 04 96 11 42 20
Email: ho911@accor-hotels.com
This elegant hotel right on the old harbour has balconies offering wonderful views over the yachts and fishing boats moored in the harbour. The Novotel is within easy walking distance of many of Marseille's major attractions and it has a small pool and several restaurants. 90 rooms. **$$$**

Sofitel Vieux Port
36 boulevard Charles Livon
Tel: 04 91 15 59 00
Fax: 04 91 15 59 50
This modern, comfortable hotel, is very handy for sightseeing around the old port. **$$**

St-Maximin-la-Ste-Baume

Hôtellerie du Couvent Royal
Place Jean-Salusse
Tel: 04 94 86 55 66
Very reasonable rates at this beautiful, former convent, next to the Basilica. Some rooms offer simple, monastic peace, while others overlook the cloisters and have more modern amenities. **$$**

St-Rémy-de-Provence

Hotel des Arts
30 boulevard Victor Hugo
Tel: 04 90 92 08 50
A reasonably priced hotel on St-Rémy's central boulevard with an art gallery, a terrace with a bar and a good restaurant. **$$**

THE CAMARGUE

Le Sambuc

Le Mas de Peint
13200 le Sambuc
Tel: 04 90 97 20 62
Fax: 04 90 97 22 20
Email: peint@avignon.pacwan.net
This *mas* (country house) offers the full rural Camargue experience including delicious Provençal meals *à la table d'hôte* (by reservation only) and bulls and horses outside. **$$$**

Stes-Maries-de-la-Mer

Hotel Camille
13 avenue de la Plage
Tel: 04 90 97 80 26
This hotel offers very reasonable rates for the Camargue, especially for somewhere with views of the sea. No frills but friendly. **$–$$**

THE ALPES-DE-HAUTE-PROVENCE

Castellane

Hotel de Commerce
18 place Marcel Sauvaire
Tel: 04 92 83 61 00
Fax: 04 92 83 72 82
Reasonably priced rooms but most notable is the excellent restaurant managed by a former student of Alain Ducasse. **$$**

Digne-les-Bains

Château de Trigance
Trigance
Tel: 04 94 76 91 18
Fax: 04 94 85 68 99

A member of the Relais and Château group, this 10th-century castle is lovely place to stay in the hill-top village of Digne. Good restaurant (booking advised). **$$$**

Hôtel Coin Fleuri
9 boulevard Victor Hugo
Tel: 04 92 31 04 51
Fax: 04 92 32 55 75
Visitors on a modest budget will find Digne's 15-roomed Coin Fleuri a pleasant option. This hotel has bright, practical rooms and several dining rooms. **$**

Hôtel le Grand Paris
19 boulevard Thiers
Tel: 04 92 31 11 15
Fax: 04 92 32 32 82
Le Grand Paris, a 17th-century former convent with an old-fashioned ambience, is the place to stay in Digne if you have both discerning taste and a large wallet. The restaurant is excellent and there's a stylish health centre. 24 rooms and 4 suites. **$$–$$$**

Garde

Auberge du Teillon
Route Napoleon
Tel: 04 92 83 60 88
Fax: 04 92 83 14 08
A small *auberge* offering reasonably priced, basic rooms and excellent cuisine (booking essential). **$–$$**

Gordes

Domaine de l'Enclose
Route de Sénanque
Tel: 04 90 72 71 00
Fax: 04 90 72 03 03
A little hamlet arrangement in a park with terraced gardens (ground floor rooms have their own garden) and views out over the Vaucluse. Imaginative seasonal cuisine for residents only. Other facilities include baby-sitting. **$$$**

La Bastide de Gordes
Route de Combe
Tel: 04 90 72 12 12
Fax: 04 90 72 05 20
A fine Renaissance building on the ramparts with elegant rooms, wonderful views and many modern facilities including a solarium and sauna. Visits to local vineyards can be arranged. 29 rooms and 2 suites. **$$–$$$**

Manosque

Francois 1èr
18 rue Guilhempierre
Tel: 04 92 72 07 99
Fax: 04 92 87 54 85
A quiet, friendly two-star hotel. **$$**

Moustiers Ste-Marie

La Bonne Auberge
Le Village
Tel: 04 92 74 6618
Fax: 04 92 74 65 11
A reasonable, mid-range hotel. **$$**

Sauze

Hôtel Pyjama
Super-Sauze
Tel: 04 92 81 12 00
Fax: 04 92 81 03 16
Ski buffs should make for this homely winter sports hotel. Geared for the snow seeker, it is also open in summer (20 Dec–20 May and mid-Jun–mid-Sept). Some rooms have mezzanines to accommodate families. There is no restaurant but breakfast is served at all hours. 10 rooms and studios. **$$**

THE VAR

Aiguebelle

Beau Soleil
Aiguebelle
Tel: 04 94 05 84 55
Fax: 04 94 05 70 89
Reasonably priced hotel where the rooms have balconies and you can dine under the plane trees. **$$**

Les Roches
1 avenue des trois Dauphin
Tel: 04 94 71 05 07
Fax: 04 94 71 08 40
Set on the cliffs with fabulous sea-views, a luxurious modern hotel tastefully decorated and furnished. Private beach, freshwater swimming pool. Closed in winter. **$$$**

Bandol

Hôtel Bel Ombra
Rue la Fontaine
Tel: 04 94 29 40 90
Fax: 04 94 25 01 11
Email: belmonbra@wanadoo.fr
A very reasonable hotel in popular seaside resort. Restaurant for residents only. 20 rooms. **$$**

Master Ker-Mocotte
Rue Raimu
Tel: 04 94 29 46 53
Fax: 04 94 32 53 54
The sea-perched Ker-Mocotte with its private beach and pool was once home to the Provençal-born movie star Raimu. 19 rooms. **$$$**

Barjols

Hôtel Pont d'Or
Route St-Maximin
Tel: 04 94 77 05 23
Fax: 04 94 77 09 95
The Pont d'Or is a pleasant, modest and well-kept country *auberge*. 15 rooms. **$**

Draguignan

Hôtel du Parc
21 boulevard de la Liberté
Tel: 04 98 10 14 50
Fax: 04 98 10 14 55
Email: hotelduparc@provence-verdon.com
An ordinary but reliable 20-roomed hotel outside the old town. No restaurant. **$$**

Fréjus

Aréna
145 boulevard Général de Gaulle
Tel: 04 94 17 09 40
Fax: 04 94 52 01 52
Situated in the old town with a swimming pool, Aréna has a nice garden and an excellent restaurant serving regional specialities. **$$**

Sable et Soleil
158 rue Paul Aréne
Tel: 04 94 51 08 70
Fax: 04 94 33 49 12
Email: guyduale@free.fr
This hotel, which offers plain but adequate rooms at a reasonable price, is set in a 1950s' building under pine trees. No restaurant. **$**

Grimaud

La Boulangerie
Route de Collobrières
Tel: 04 94 43 23 16
Fax: 04 94 43 38 27
A small, comfortable, friendly hotel situated in the quiet of the Massif des Maures. Amenities include a pool and tennis courts. **$$**

Hostellerie du Coteau Fleurie
Place des Pénitents
Tel: 04 90 43 20 17

Price Ranges

The ranges given, which are intended to be guides to prices only, are quoted per double room. Breakfast is not normally included, and credit cards are accepted unless otherwise stated.
$ = under €50
$$ = €50–115
$$$ = more than €115

Fax: 04 90 43 33 42
Email: coteaufleuri@wanadoo.fr
A 1930s' inn on the outskirts of town with views over the vineyards. The restaurant serves traditional Provençal cuisine. **$$**

Hyères

Hôtel du Soleil
2 rue du Remparts
Tel: 04 94 65 16 26
Fax: 04 94 35 46 00
Email: soleil@hotel-du-soleil.fr
Near the Parc St-Bernard, a friendly, quiet hotel with a small terrace. **$$**

Île de Porquerolles

Mas du Langoustier
Tel: 04 94 58 30 09
Fax: 04 94 58 36 02
Email: langoustier@compuserve.com
A luxurious establishment in an old Provençal *mas* surrounded by exotic gardens. Fabulous restaurant. Full-board only. **$$$**

Île de Port Cros

Le Manoir
Tel: 04 94 05 90 52
Fax: 04 94 05 90 89
There's a tropical ambience at le Manoir, a colonial-style family home with a large garden. The rooms are cosy and some have balconies. **$$$**

Ramatuelle

Le Baou
Avenue Gustave Etienne
Tel: 04 94 79 20 48
Fax: 04 94 79 28 36
Email: hostellerie.lebaou@wanadoo.fr
Good-sized modern rooms with balconies and delightful views. **$$$**
La Ferme d'Augustin
Plage de Tahiti
Tel: 04 94 55 97 00
Fax: 04 94 97 40 30
An old farm with a rustic atmosphere and furniture to match. There's also a lovely Mediterranean garden. All rooms with seaview. **$$**

Sanary-sur-Mer

Hôtel Tour
24 quai General de Gaulle
Tel: 04 94 74 10 10
Fax: 04 94 74 69 49
Located right next to the Saracen tower with most rooms overlooking the port. 24 rooms. **$$**

St-Raphaël

Bleu Marine
Port Santa-Lucia
Tel: 04 94 95 31 31
Fax: 04 94 82 21 46
The restored Bleu Marine has a pool and great views of the port. Some rooms have balconies and there is a good restaurant. **$$**
Golf de Valescure
Avenue des Golfs
Tel: 04 94 52 85 00
Fax: 04 94 82 41 88
A new traditional-style *mas* surrounded by pine trees, rooms with terraces and an elegant club house. **$$**

St-Tropez

Bastide de St-Tropez
Route des Carles
Tel: 04 94 55 82 55
Fax: 04 94 97 21 71
Email: bst@wanadoo.fr
This place, set in the heart of the vineyards, is the height of luxury. Some of rooms and suites have private gardens and jacuzzis. **$$$**
Hôtel Byblos
Avenue Paul Signac
Tel: 04 94 56 68 00
Fax: 04 94 56 68 01
Email: saint-tropez@byblos.com
A huge legendary glamorous hotel that is still popular with the Johnny Halliday eternal rocker set. **$$$**
Lou Cagnard
18 avenue P. Roussel
Tel: 04 94 97 04 24
Fax: 04 94 97 09 44
A very reasonably priced hotel located near the port, with a pretty courtyard. No credit cards. **$$**
La Ponche
3 rue des Remparts
Tel: 04 94 97 02 53
Fax: 04 94 97 78 61
This hotel, which has a great restaurant, was originally a row of fishermen's cottages in the old town. A favourite of Picasso's. **$$$**
Résidence de la Pinède
Plage de la Bouillabaisse
Tel: 04 94 55 91 00
Fax: 04 94 97 73 64
Email: Residence.pinede@wanadoo.fr
Set on the Bouillabaisse beach, under the pine trees, this Relais and Châteaux hotel has been refurbished to provide comfortable rooms and suites. **$$$**
Le Yaca
1 boulevard d'Aumale
Tel: 04 94 55 81 00
Fax: 04 94 97 58 50
Email: hotel-le-yaca@wanadoo.fr
An attractive old Provençal residence that has been tastefully refurbished. Accommodation is built around a pool and gardens. **$$$**

Seillans

Hôtel des Deux Rocs
Place Font d'Amont
Tel: 04 94 76 87 32
Fax: 04 94 76 88 68
This converted 18th-century manor house is set in a lovely spot above the town and is complete with restaurant, terrace and outdoor fountain. 14 rooms. **$$**

Toulon

Le Grand Hôtel Dauphinée
10 rue Berthelot
Tel: 04 94 92 20 28
For a hotel in such a central location in the Old Town, this place offers good value. Friendly staff. **$$**
La résidence de Cap Brune
Chemin de l'aviateur Gayraud
Tel: 04 94 41 29 46
This lovely big white villa is situated up above Toulon. It is surrounded by trees and has a swimming pool but no restaurant. **$$$**

Tourtour

Bastide de Tourtour
Route de Flayosc
83690 Tourtour

Tel: 04 94 10 54 20
Fax: 04 94 70 54 90
This 25-roomed hotel, set in a park with views over the Var, is a member of the Châteaux and Hôtels de France group and is probably the most expensive, palatial place in the region. Facilities include a heated pool, jacuzzi and billiard room. **$$$**

Le Mas l'Acacia
Route d'Aups
Tel: 04 94 70 53 84
This *mas* offers bed and breakfast just outside the village of Tourtour. It's a lovely place with a swimming pool and wonderful views. **$–$$**

Villecroze

Auberge des Lavandes
Place Général de Gaulle
Tel: 04 94 70 76 00
A small *auberge* in the picturesque village of Villecroze, with a good restaurant and well-priced rooms. **$$**

THE ALPES-MARITIMES

Biot

Hôtel des Arcades
Place des Arcades
Tel: 04 93 65 01 04
Fax: 04 93 65 01 05
A 15th-century mansion offering accommodation that combines antique furniture with modern convenience. The restaurant is also an art gallery, and meals and rooms are reasonably priced. **$$**

Grasse

La Bastide Saint-Antoine
48 avenue Henri Dunant
Tel: 04 93 70 94 94
Fax: 04 93 70 94 95
Email: info@jacques-chibois.com
The 18th-century Bastide has beautiful gardens, wonderful views of the mountains and sea, a pool and regular art exhibitions. It's best known for its restaurant owned by the acclaimed M. Chibois. **$$$**

Hôtel des Parfums
Rue Eugène Charabot
Tel: 04 92 42 35 35
Fax 04 93 36 35 48
Basic, moderately priced rooms with gorgeous views. Facilities include a jacuzzi and fitness room. **$$**

Peillon

Auberge de la Madone
Tel: 04 93 79 91 17
Fax: 04 93 79 99 36
Email: c.millo@club-internet.fr
Located at the gates of the hill-top village of Peillon, this *auberge* offers a flowery terrace with a wonderful view, a fairly expensive restaurant and gorgeous rooms fitted with antique furniture. **$$**

Sospel

Hôtel des Étrangers
9 boulevard de Verdun
Tel: 04 93 04 00 09
Fax: 04 93 04 12 31
Email: sospel@ifrance.com
This hotel has a pool on site, English is spoken, and the proprietor is an expert on local history. **$$**

St-Paul-de-Vence

La Colombe d'Or
Place des Ormeaux
Tel: 04 93 32 80 02
Fax: 04 93 32 77 78
The 16-roomed Colombe d'Or was once frequented by unknown, penniless artists who persuaded the original owner, Paul Roux, to accept their paintings in payment for meals and board. Works by Miro, Picasso, Modigliani, Matisse and Chagall can now be viewed by guests of the hotel and restaurant. **$$$**

Mas d'Artigny
Route de la Colle
Tel: 04 93 32 84 54
Fax: 04 93 32 95 36
Email: contact@mas-artigny.com
Set in the woods between St-Paul and la Colle. Splendid views of the sea and the mountains. **$$**

Tende

Le Prieuré
St-Dalmas-sur-Tende
Tel: 04 93 04 75 70
Fax: 04 93 04 71 58
Email: contact@leprieure.org
Three-star hotel with good restaurant in lovely valley. Organises summer trips to Vallée des Merveilles. **$**

Utelle

Bellevue
06450 Lantosque
Tel/fax: 04 93 03 17 19
A quiet, family hotel that is open in July and August, with stunning views and a swimming pool. Credit cards: Carte Bleu only. **$**

Vence

Château du Domaine St-Martin
Route de Coursegoules
Tel: 04 93 58 02 02
Fax: 04 93 24 08 91
Email: st-martin@webstore.fr
True luxury set on the hills above Vence, with a magnificent view of the coast. Extensive grounds and a swimming-pool. A member of the Relais et Châteaux group. **$$$**

La Closerie des Genêts
4 impasse M. Maurel
Tel/fax: 04 93 58 78 50
Hotel with comfortable, if chintzy, rooms. Good restaurant. **$–$$**

La Villa Roseraie
14 avenue Henri Giraud
Tel: 04 93 58 02 20
Fax: 04 93 58 99 31
This pretty villa, which dates from *circa* 1900, has a lovely garden, swimming pool and rooms decorated with Provençal fabrics. No restaurant. 14 rooms. **$$**

THE CÔTE D'AZUR

Antibes

Relais du Postillon
8 rue Championnet
Tel: 04 93 34 20 77
Fax: 04 93 34 61 24
Email: postillon@atsat.com
It's hard to find a bargain in high season on the Côte d'Azur, but the 15-roomed Relais du Postillon in the old town of Antibes comes pretty close. It's pleasant enough and has a good restaurant. The only drawback is that it's not right by the sea. **$$**

Beaulieu-sur-Mer

Hôtel Frisia
2 boulevard E. Gauthier
Tel: 04 93 01 01 04
Fax: 04 93 01 31 92
Email: info@club-internet.com
Set across from the port in Beaulieu-sur-Mer, this hotel has a solarium on the roof and some lovely rooms with terraces. No hotel restaurant. Good value. **$$–$$$**

La Réserve de Beaulieu
5 boulevard Leclerc
Tel: 04 93 01 00 01
Fax: 04 93 01 28 99
Email: reserve@wanadoo.fr
A luxurious late 19th-century villa, situated in a lovely spot on the coast. Facilities include a private beach and harbour and a swimming-pool in the garden. **$$$**

Cagnes-sur-Mer

Hôtel Beau Rivage
39 boulevard de la Plage
Tel: 04 93 20 16 09
The Beau Rivage is a more down-to-earth choice by the sea than the Cagnard. Some rooms have balconies and seaviews. **$$**

Le Cagnard
45 rue Sous-Barri
Tel: 04 93 20 73 21
Fax: 04 93 22 06 39
Email: resa@le-cagnard.com
A 14th-century residence on the ramparts offering rooms with character and an unusual dining-room, where you may sample the chef's highly rated specialities. 20 rooms and 5 suites. **$$$**

Cannes

Carlton Intercontinental
58 boulevard de la Croisette
Tel: 04 93 06 40 06
Fax: 04 93 06 40 25
Email: cannes@interconti.com
Cannes' world-famous waterfront luxury hotel and still a magnet for the rich and famous. The rooms and lobby have been completely renovated and are now more splendid than ever. Health centre and casino on the top floor. **$$$**

Martinez
73 boulevard de la Croisette
Tel: 04,92 98 77 00
Fax: 04 93 38 97 90
Email: martinez@concorde-hotels.com
An Art Deco palace with three restaurants, most notably the Palme d'Or. This is where the stars love to stay during the festival. **$$$**

Sofitel-Mediteranée
2 boulevard Jean Hibert
Tel: 04 92 99 73 00
Fax: 04 92 99 73 29
Standing on the tip of the Croisette, this first-class luxury and business hotel, which is rather akin to a grand country home, has beautifully appointed rooms looking out over the sea. There's a rooftop pool and restaurant, and the service here is excellent and courteous. **$$$**

Splendid
4 rue Félix Faure
Tel: 04 97 06 22 22
Fax: 04 93 99 55 02
Email: hotel.splendid@wanadoo.fr
A 19th-century mansion with a homely atmosphere but no restaurant. **$$**

Cap d'Antibes

Grand Hôtel du Cap
Boulevard Kennedy
Tel: 04 93 61 39 01
Fax: 04 93 67 76 04
Email: Edenroc-hotel@wanadoo.fr
Set on the water's edge in wooded grounds. The refurbished rooms are very comfortable. Heated sea-water pool and tennis courts. **$$$**

Eze

Château de la Chèvre d'Or
Rue de Barri
Tel: 04 92 10 66 66
Fax: 04 93 41 06 72
Staying here is an unforgettable experience. The 28-roomed hotel combines a warm provincial elegance with Riviera élan, and the four-star restaurant has magnificent views of the coast from Nice to Monaco.**$$$**

Château Eza
Rue de la Pise
Tel: 04 93 41 12 24
Fax: 04 93 41 16 64
Email: chateza@webstore.fr
Accessible only on foot (baggage may be carried up by donkey), this 400-year-old castle is perched on top of the cliff and overlooks 250 km (160 miles) of coast. Gorgeously decorated rooms with antique furniture, some with fireplaces. **$$$**

Juan-Les-Pins

Belles Rives
Boulevard Edouard-Baudoin
Tel: 04 93 61 02 79
Fax: 04 93 67 43 51
Email: info@bellesrives.com
Close enough to town to enjoy the lively atmosphere, yet sufficiently far away from the noise and crowds. The Belles Rives has retained all the attraction of the stylish Art Deco period, when it was the home of Zelda and F. Scott Fitzgerald. **$$$**

Garden Beach Hotel
15–17 boulevard Baudoin
Tel: 04 92 93 57 57
Fax: 04 92 93 57 56
Email: contct@lemeridien-juanlespins.com
Located on the site of the former casino, right in the centre of town. A pleasant terrace overlooks the bay. **$$$**

Juan Beach
5 rue de l'Oratoire
Tel: 04 93 61 02 89
Fax: 04 93 61 16 63
Email: juan.beach@atsat.com
Reasonable rates in this old family house with simple rooms. Summer dining in a flowery garden. **$$**

Nice

Hôtel Beau Rivage
24 rue Saint Francois-de-Paule
Tel: 04 92 47 82 82
Fax: 04 92 47 82 83
Email: nicebeaurivage@new-hotel.com
The 118-roomed Beau Rivage – handily located in the old town – is a modernised 1930s' hotel with a private beach. Matisse had an apartment here, and Nietzsche and Chekhov are counted amongst other famous past visitors. **$$$**

Grimaldi
15 rue Grimaldi
Tel: 04 93 16 00 24
Fax: 04 93 87 00 24
Email: zesse@le-grimaldi.com
A lovely little bed and breakfast, with all rooms beautifully furnished using different fabrics. **$$**

Hôtel Négresco
37 promenade des Anglais
Tel: 04 93 16 64 00
Fax: 04 93 88 35 68
Email: direction@hotel-negresco.com
The last vestige of Nice's era of splendour at the end of the 19th century. The dome dominates the coastline of the Baie des Anges. The rooms are decorated with furniture from the 16th and 18th centuries, and priceless paintings and tapestries. Fabulous. **$$$**

Price Ranges

The ranges given, which are intended to be guides to prices only, are quoted per double room. Breakfast is not normally included, and credit cards are accepted unless otherwise stated.
$ = under €50
$$ = €50–115
$$$ = more than €115

La Pérouse
11 quai Rauba-Capéu
Tel: 04 93 62 34 63
Fax: 04 93 62 59 41
Email: lp@hroy.com
At the east end of the promenade des Anglais, conveniently situated between the old town and the port. The rooms have splendid views of the Baie des Anges. Pool. **$$$**

Sofitel Splendid
50 boulevard Victor Hugo
Tel: 04 93 16 41 00
Fax: 04 93 16 42 70
Email: info@splendid-nice.com
The Sofitel Splendid is located close to the city centre, just a stone's throw from the sea and the hotel's private beach. 113 rooms and 14 suites. **$$$**

Hôtel Windsor
11 rue Dalpozzo
Tel: 04 93 88 59 35
Fax: 04 93 88 94 57
Email: windsor@webstore.fr
A gorgeous exotic garden, complete with aviary and tropical birds, surrounds the swimming pool at the side of this hotel. The 57 rooms are comfortable and have stylish touches such as Burberry shampoo sachets; several of the rooms are individually decorated by contemporary artists, including Ben, and a Moroccan-style hammam on the top floor adds to the originality. The hotel is in a good location, just a 5-minute walk from the promenade des Anglais, and the staff are very friendly. Stylish leather-seated bar. Piano *soirées* on certain evenings. **$$**

Menton

Chambord
6 avenue Boyer
Tel: 04 93 35 94 19
Fax: 04 93 41 30 55
Email: hotel-chambord@wanadoo.fr
Three-star hotel near the promenade du Soleil. No restaurant. **$$**

Hôtel les Ambassadeurs
3 rue Partouneaux
Tel: 04 93 28 75 75
Fax: 04 93 35 62 32
Email: ambassadeurs-menton@wanadoo.fr
Pure Riviera style from the early 1900s. Pink, green and bronze splendour amongst the palms and magnolias. 47 rooms. **$$$**

Hôtel de Londres
15 avenue Carnot
Tel: 04 93 35 74 62
A small central hotel that is popular during the lemon festival. **$$**

Monaco

Abela Hotel
23 avenue des Papalins
Fontvieille
Tel: 00377 92 05 90 00
Fax: 00377 92 05 91 67
Set a little way out of the centre, in the Fontvieille area of Monaco, this is nonetheless a comfortable modern hotel. It overlooks the new harbour and has lovely views. **$$**

Hôtel Helvetia
1 bis rue Grimaldi
Monte-Carlo
Tel: 00377 93 30 21 71
Fax: 00377 92 16 70 51
For those with slim purses there is the unremarkable but comfortable and friendly Helvetia, situated within easy reach of the port. **$$**

Hôtel Hermitage
Square Beaumarchais
Tel: 00377 92 16 40 00
Fax: 00377 92 16 38 52
Beautiful Edwardian architecture, spacious comfortable rooms. Facilities include a swimming pool and fitness centre. **$$$**

Hôtel de Paris
Place du Casino
Monte-Carlo
Tel: 00377 92 16 30 00
Fax: 00377 92 16 69 10
Email: hp@hbm.mc
The celebrated Hôtel de Paris, located by the Casioo and one of the three hotels owned by the Grimaldi-run Société Bains de Mer, is the most magnificent and glamorous place to stay in Monaco. Past celebrity visitors are far too numerous to name. **$$$**

Mougins

Le Moulin de Mougins
Notre Dame de Vie
Tel: 04 93 75 78 24
Fax: 04 93 90 18 55
Email: mougins@relaischateau.fr
An old mill restored by celebrated chef Roger Vergé with three rooms, a couple of apartments overlooking the garden and a gourmet restaurant *(see page 316)*. **$$$**

Les Muscadins
18 boulevard Courteline
Tel: 04 93 90 00 43
Fax: 04 92 92 88 23
Email: muscadins@alcyonis.fr
On the edge of the village, an attractive hotel with a good view of the Bay of Cannes. Only 8 bedrooms, each different, all nicely furnished and decorated. **$$$**

St-Jean Cap Ferrat

Brise Marine
58 avenue Jean Mermoz
Tel: 04 93 76 04 36
Fax: 04 93 76 11 49
Email: info@hotel-brisemarine.com
A small hotel in an attractive terraced garden. Some of the rooms overlook the sea. **$$**

Grand Hôtel du Cap Ferrat
71 boulevard Général de Gaulle
Tel: 04 93 76 50 50
Fax: 04 93 76 04 52
Email: marketing@grand-hotel-cap-ferrat.com
This is a magnificently situated, luxurious palace with a park, flowery gardens, a sea-side swimming pool and a private funicular to the beach. 44 rooms and 9 suites. **$$$**

La Voile d'Or
Yachting Harbour
Tel: 04 93 01 13 13
Fax: 04 93 76 11 17
Email: reservation@lavoildor.fr
An Italian villa situated in a lovely garden overlooking the yachting harbour. Rooms of all sizes are available and all are attractively decorated. Amenities include two swimming pools. **$$$**

Where to Eat

Eating Out

One of the great pleasures of visiting Provence is its glorious food, and wherever you go you will find a wide variety of different restaurants from simple *auberges* to the great classics.

Many hotels have their own restaurants, and some restaurants also have rooms to rent. The following selection includes good regional restaurants with typical local dishes as well as some of the great stars of French cuisine.

In the regions it is always worth seeking out typical local restaurants and sampling the specialities of the area. Increasingly, the regional produce is itself the focus of the great chefs who compete in their stylish treatment of peasant food and traditional dishes *(see Provençal Cuisine, pages 69–73)*.

Dining Habits

It is essential to be aware of dining hours in Provence. Most people stop for *le midi*, and often lunch will start as early as midday. By one o'clock it may be almost too late to lunch in some places, and you may not be served at all beyond 2pm. Evening meals are usually at 8pm and in smaller or country places you may not be served dinner after 9pm.

At the height of the season, or if you have a particular place in mind, it's wise to reserve in advance. Restaurants often have outdoor tables for fine weather, even in towns and cities, where you may find yourself sitting on the pavement or in an inner courtyard.

The French eat cheese before dessert – they think that it is bizarre to switch from eating savoury food for the main course, to a sweet dessert and then back to something savoury in the form of cheese. You will almost always be given bread with your meal. Water, which should be fine to drink, will be supplied if you ask for it.

You will find that wine lists often reflect the region and the restaurateur will usually be delighted to advise you as to which wine to choose. All restaurants offer a *vin de pays* by the carafe *(pichet)* or *demi-carafe* and this is almost always good value and perfectly drinkable.

Restaurant Listings

Restaurants are grouped according to *département*, following the chapters in this book, and then alphabetically according to location.

THE VAUCLUSE

Avignon

La Fourchette
17 rue Racine
Tel: 04 90 85 20 93
A great place to eat for modern bistro-style food with a Provençal touch. The menu of the day is always affordable. Reserve. **$$**

Hiély
5 rue République
Tel: 04 90 86 17 07
Avignon's temple of gastronomy is famed for its classic cuisine shaped by the best regional ingredients and complemented by a great wine list. Booking essential. Normally closed 18 Jun–4 July and Mon and Tues, except in July. **$$**

Restaurant La Mirande
4 place de la Mirande
Tel: 04 90 85 93 93
Fax: 04 90 86 26 85
Daniel Herbert, a former student of master-chef Alain Ducasse, has elevated this hotel's restaurant to the top place to eat in Avignon. Dine in the garden in summer. **$$**

Rose au Petit Bedon
70 rue Joseph-Vernet
Tel: 04 90 82 33 98
Provençal specialities are served at this Avignon favourite. Possibly not for slimmers – the name means "little paunch". Closed Sunday. **$**

La Tache d'Encre
22 rue des Teinturiers
Tel: 04 90 86 34 84
A café-theatre with live music at weekends and a reliably good *plat du jour* for lunch. Teinturiers is one of the most interesting streets in Avignon and a key spot for the alternative theatre in the summer. **$**

Bonnieux

Le Fournil
5 place Carnot
Tel: 04 90 75 83 62
A bistro in a former bakery, serving excellent, low-key, good-value Provençal cuisine. **$**

L'Isle-sur-la-Sorgue

Le Mas de Cure Bourse
Route de Caumont
RD25
Tel: 04 90 38 16 58
Delicious traditional Provençal meals in a cosy, restored *mas*. **$$**

La Prevote
4 rue Jean-Jacques
L'Isle sur la Sorgue
Tel: 04 90 38 57 29
Reservations are essential at this popular place, a former mill serving imaginative local dishes. **$$**

Lourmarin

Le Fenière
Just south of Lourmarin, on the D945
Tel: 04 90 68 11 79
One of France's top female chefs, Reine Sammut offers inventive cuisine with seafood, pasta or Sicilian-style roast lamb. **$$–$$$**

Price Ranges

The price ranges given, which are intended as guides only, cover the cost of the average set meal *(menu)* per person, not including wine or coffee. Note that *menu* prices at lunchtime are often half the price of the evening meal. Credit cards are accepted unless otherwise indicated.

$	menus up to €20
$$	menus up to €45
$$$	menus over €45

Le Moulin de Lourmarin
Rue du Temple
Tel: 04 90 68 06 69
An old mill just outside Lourmarin, where chef Edouard Loubet uses fresh herbs and vegetables from his garden to accompany such specialities as Sisteron lamb. Creative dishes using classic Provençal ingredients. **$$–$$$**

Monieux

Les Lavandes
Rue Nesque
Tel: 04 90 64 05 08
There is a spectacular view from les Lavandes, and the charm of the place is enhanced by the many riders – this is good riding country – who dine here, tying their horses in the square by to the restaurant. Advisable to phone in advance. **$$**

Monteux

Le Saule Pleureur
Le Pont des Vaches
Route d'Avignon
Tel: 04 90 62 01 35
This little restaurant well deserves the reputation that keeps guests coming out of their way to dine here. **$$**

Nîmes

Au Flan Coco
31 rue de Mûrier d'Espagne
Tel: 04 66 21 84 81
A lovely little restaurant serving fresh market food. Quaint terrace. **$**

Orange

Le Yaca
Place Sylvian
Tel: 04 90 34 70 03
Tasty dishes are offered at a good price in attractive beamed surroundings. **$**

Séguret

Le Mesclun
Rue des Poternes
Tel: 04 90 46 93 43
At Le Mesclun you can sit on the tranquil dining terrace and choose your wine by pointing to the vineyard where the grapes for that particular bottle are grown. The portions are lavish and the desserts are simply irresistible. **$$**

Villeneuve-lès-Avignon

Hostellerie la Magnaneraie
Rue de Camp de Bataille
Tel: 04 90 25 11 11
Even if you don't choose to stay at the hotel, you can still enjoy a feast on its lovely shaded porch. **$$**

THE BOUCHES-DU-RHONE

Aix-en-Provence

Le Clos de la Violette
10 avenue de la Violette
Tel: 04 42 23 30 71
Chef Jean-Marc Banzo offers light and healthy Provençal cuisine and some exceptional desserts. Dine in the garden under the chestnut trees. **$$$**

Côté Cour
19 cours Mirabeau
Tel: 04 42 93 12 51
A beautifully designed and fashionable restaurant. Classic Provençal cooking is accompanied by an interesting wine list. **$$**

Le Gibassier
46 rue Espariat
Tel: 04 42 27 53 54
Late-night *boulangerie* (bakery). Insomniacs will appreciate their 2am–1pm and 2–8pm hours. **$**

Arles

L'Affenage
4 rue Moliere
Tel: 04 90 96 07 67
Rustic old Coaching House serving classic Provençal meals. Start with a choice from the buffet, followed by a heartier dishes such as duck confit with cabbage. **$–$$**

Brasserie Nord Pinus
14 place du Forum
Tel: 04 90 93 44 44
An elegant grand-style *brasserie*, which belongs to the hotel that was frequented by Cocteau and Picasso. Summery regional cuisine. **$$**

Le Pistou
30 bis rond point des Arènes
Tel: 04 90 18 20 92
A small restaurant under the vaults opposite the amphitheatre, serving reasonably priced, tasty meals. **$**

El Quinto Torro
12 rue de la Liberté
Tel: 04 90 49 62 29
Plenty of atmosphere in this *bodega*-style restaurant with a bullfighting theme. Wood-fire grilled steaks and excellent salads. **$**

Les Baux-de-Provence

L'Oustau de Baumanière
Val d'Enfer
13520 les Baux-de-Provence
Tel: 04 90 54 33 07
Chef André Charial carefully mixes the classical and the regional with delicious results in one of France's best restaurants. Vegetarians are taken seriously here: the *ballade dans notre jardin* is a seven-course menu of vegetables from the restaurant's own gardens. **$$$**

Beaureceuil

Le Relais St-Victoire
N7 and D58 from Aix
Tel: 04 42 66 94 98
This highly rated restaurant is set in a homely *mas* at the foot of Mont Ste-Victoire, where chef René Jugy-Berges offers classic cuisine inspired by regional produce. **$$$**

Cassis

Le Jardin d'Emile
23 avenue Amiral Ganteaume
Tel: 04 42 01 80 55
This hotel-restaurant, situated in a garden next to the city walls, serves what is perhaps the best Provençal cuisine in Cassis. **$–$$**

La Presqu'île
Route de Port-Miou
Tel: 04 42 01 03 77
This place offers great views of the cliffs in Cassis. The menu is pretty special, although some might consider it pretentious. **$$**

Fontvieille

La Regalido
Rue Frédéric Mistral
Tel: 04 90 97 60 22
La Regalido is set in a restored olive-oil mill, which is brightly decorated with flowers. A culinary and aesthetic treat. **$$$**

Marseille

Les Arsenaulx
Restaurant-Salon de Thé
25 cours d'Estienne d'Orves
Tel: 04 91 59 80 30

Price Ranges

The price ranges given, which are intended as guides only, cover the cost of the average set meal *(menu)* per person, not including wine or coffee. Note that *menu* prices at lunchtime are often half the price of the evening meal. Credit cards are accepted unless otherwise indicated.

$ menus up to €20
$$ menus up to €45
$$$ menus over €45

This restaurant-cum-tea room is imaginatively located within an ancient stone arsenal that is adjoined to a bookstore and tea house. Much of the fare on the excellent and inspired menu is fresh fish. Not wildly expensive and a real find. **$$**

L'Epuisette
Vallon des Auffes
Tel: 04 91 52 17 82
The fresh fish here, served on an open terrace, makes a nice alternative to *bouillabaisse*. **$$**

Chez Fonfon
140 vallon des Auffes
Tel: 04 91 52 14 38
A good fish restaurant situated near the edge of the lively Marseillaise port. **$$**

Le Miramar
12 quai du Port
Tel: 04 91 91 10 40
Le Miramar is most celebrated for its *bouillabaisse*, which is very elegantly served, albeit for a hefty price. Always telephone ahead, since the dish takes hours to prepare. **$$$**

Une Table au Sud
2 quai du Port
Tel: 04 91 90 63 53
Lionel Levy, formerly with top chef Alain Ducasse in Paris, offers exquisite cuisine at fair prices in this popular restaurant on the first floor of the Café la Samaritaine. Fricassé of squid, roast pigeon with fennel hearts, country ham and *confit de tomates* are all recommended. Good views over the port. **$–$$**

St-Rémy-de-Provence

La Maison Jaune
15 rue Carnot
Tel: 04 90 92 56 14
Classic Provençal dishes such as roast pigeon with *aioli*, and the restaurant has a terrace upstairs. **$–$$**

THE CAMARGUE

Aigues Mortes

La Camargue
19 rue Republique
Tel: 04 66 53 86 88
A good local restaurant with an inner courtyard. $$

Mondragon

La Beaugravière
Rte N7
Tel: 04 90 40 91 01
A Provençal house with a rustic dining room, a shady terrace and classic cuisine. When truffles are in season they are definitely the restaurant's speciality. **$–$$**

La Paradou

Le Bistro du Paradou
Ave de la Vallée des Baux
Tel: 04 90 54 32 70
A genuine country café, with one daily meal, one price and a real homespun atmosphere. The cuisine is Provençal and the Friday *aioli* is famed. **$$**

THE ALPES-DE-HAUTE-PROVENCE

Barcelonette

La Mangeoire
Place 4-Vents
Tel: 04 92 81 01 61
La Mangeoire – a vaulted dining-room located in a 17th-century former stable – is a popular place with a lovely large terrace under the trees. **$$**

Digne-les-Bains

Le Grand Paris
19 boulevard Thiers
Tel: 04 92 31 11 15
Serves regional dishes that have been critically acclaimed. **$$**

Manosque

Hostellerie de la Fuste
Route D4
La Fuste Manosque
Tel: 04 92 72 05 95
If you're after something special, reserve a table for an all-out meal at the beautiful Hostellerie de la Fuste just outside Manosque. A real find. **$$**

Moustiers-Ste-Marie

Les Santons de Moustiers
Place de l'Eglise
Tel: 04 92 74 66 48
Reserve a table here for a pleasant meal on a special occasion. **$$**

La Bastide de Moustiers
D952 south of Moustiers-Ste-Marie
Tel: 04 92 70 47 47
This is a recently established Alain Ducasse restaurant set in a country inn. Hearty and stylish Provençal meals. **$$**

THE VAR

Aups

Le Yucca
3 rue Foch
Tel: 04 94 70 12 11
For a change from Provençal cuisine, try a Mexican-style barbecue in the garden of this restaurant. If you do want Provençal dishes, try the regional truffles served with ravioli. **$**

Restaurant Rules

It is now law in France to have separate eating areas for smokers and non-smokers. Unfortunately, this has to be one of the most commonly flouted laws in existence, and many French still puff constantly during a meal.

Menus must be displayed by law outside any establishment. Most places will offer a *prix-fixe* menu – a set meal at a particular price, sometimes including wine. Otherwise you order separate items from *la Carte*. Eating the set menu is nearly always the best value, unless you really only want one dish.

Bandol

Le Bérard
La Cadière
Avenue Gabriel Péri
Tel: 04 94 90 11 43
This former convent in the heart of the vineyards serves gourmet regionally inspired dishes. **$$$**

L'Oulivo
19 rue des Tonnoliers
Tel: 04 94 29 81 79
For simple, inexpensive but good Provençal fare in the old town. **$**

La Bayorre

La Colombe
663 route de Toulon
Tel: 04 94 65 02 15
Booking is advised for this cheerful and popular restaurant. **$$**

Brignoles

L'Hostellerie de l'Abbaye de la Celle
Place du general de Gaule
La Celle
Tel: 04 98 05 14 14
Chef Benoit Witz is more than capable at the healm of this restaurant that was established by Ducasse and Bruno. Provençal cuisine with that certain *je ne sais quoi* is served at fairly reasonable prices in the vaulted dining-room of this 18th-century abbey near Brignoles. **$$**

Cotignac

La Fontaine
27 cours Gambetta
Tel: 04 94 04 79 13
Eat lunch on La Fontaine's busy terrace after the Tuesday market or dine late on summer evenings. **$–$$**

Draguignan

Les Milles Colonnes
2 place aux Herbes
Tel: 04 94 68 52 58
This brasserie-cum-internet café in the old town serves dishes based around fresh local produce. It's shut in the evenings in late summer but is a good place for lunch. **$**

Flayosc

L'Oustaou
5 place Brémond
Tel: 04 94 70 42 69
A Provençal *mas* with a good-value, well-regarded restaurant serving regional dishes. Note the collection of artefacts from the 1920s and 1930s in the little dining-room and watch the world go by from the terrace that overlooks the central square. **$–$$**

La Garde-Freinet

La Faucado
RN 83310
Tel: 04 94 43 60 41
Good regional cuisine is served on a beautiful open-air terrace. Traditional décor. **$$**

Gassin

Auberge la Verdoyante
866 chemin de Coste Brigade
Tel: 04 94 56 16 23
Fax : 04 94 56 43 10
A small *auberge* situated fairly close to the sea, offering good-quality meals. Specialities include rabbit in garlic and *tarte du chocolat*. Don't be confused by the name – you can only dine, but not stay, here. **$**

Le Micocoulier
Place des Barrys
Tel: 04 94 56 14 01
Delicious Provençal cuisine with a touch of the Italian. **$$**

Villa de Belieu
Domaines de Bertaud-Belieu
Tel: 04 94 56 40 56
This villa is well worth a visit for its beautiful setting in a wine *domaine*. Four excellent menus are available. **$$**

Giens

Bistro de Marius
1 place Massilon
Tel: 04 94 35 88 38
Provençal seafood dishes are served in this bistro in the heart of the old town. A good place to come for tasty traditional *bouillabaise*. **$–$$**

Hyères

Potinière
27 avenue de la Mediterannée
Tel: 04 94 00 51 60
Excellent-value tasty seafood cuisine is served in the hotel's restaurant, which overlooks la Gavine port. **$**

Credit Cards

Increasingly most restaurants take credit cards in France. Visa is very common, but American Express is sometimes unpopular as restaurants incur hefty charges by accepting it. In this listing, credit cards are accepted unless otherwise indicated. Debit cards featuring the Cirrus or Maestro signs are widely accepted in France.

Île de Porquerolles

Restaurant l'Olivier
Le Mas du Langoustier
Tel: 04 94 58 30 09
Take the ferry for a special meal at this hotel's gourmet restaurant. Top food and impeccable, friendly service. Great fish soup, sea bass and exquisite desserts. **$$$**

Lorgues

Chez Bruno
Route de Vidauban
Tel: 04 94 85 93 93
Expect extremely rich menus based around truffles and *foie gras* at this beautifully situated and extremely popular restaurant that draws its customers from far and wide. **$$$**

St-Raphaël

Pastorel
54 rue de la Liberté
Tel: 04 94 95 02 36
Good traditional food with a Provençal touch. **$$**

St-Tropez

La Bouillabaise
Place de la Bouillabaise
Tel: 04 94 97 54 00
Simple Provençal cuisine with an Italian influence is served here. Recommended food, great service and a lovely terrace. **$$**

La Cascade
5 rue de l'Eglise
Tel: 04 94 54 83 46
La Cascade offers a lively atmosphere and spicy Caribbean specialities. **$$**

Lei Mouscardins
Tour du Portalet
Tel: 04 94 97 29 00

Chef Laurent Tarridec serves light seasonal dishes with a regional flavour, at this popular quayside restaurant. **$$–$$$**

L'Olivier
Route des Carles
Tel: 04 94 97 58 16
A country-house restaurant with garden and pool, serving elegant cuisine based on the flavours of Provence. **$$**

Le Relais des Caves du Roy
Hôtel Byblos
Avenue Foch
Tel: 04 94 56 68 20
Superb Provençal dishes make this one of St-Tropez's finest dining spots. The hotel is popular with the rich and famous and you may find a holidaying celebrity eating next to you. **$$$**

Tour du Portalet
St-Tropez
Tel: 04 94 97 29 00
Fashionable quayside dining with a seasonal menu of carefully prepared and original fish and vegetable dishes. **$$**

Toulon

Le Nautique
Carré du Port
Quai Constadt
Tel: 04 94 93 49 88
An inexpensive brasserie by the sea, where you can watch the boats go by as you eat. **$**

Tourtour

Les Chênes Verts
Route de Villecroze
Tel: 04 90 70 55 06
Reservations are essential at this highly rated restaurant where the chef Paul Balade presents the very best of seasonal Provençal dishes. Delicious specialities including *sanglier* (wild boar), truffles, *cèpes* (mushrooms) and artichoke are all given his expert and reliable touch. **$$–$$$**

Villecroze

Auberge des Lavandes
Place Generale de Gaule
Tel: 04 94 70 76 00
A reasonably priced, friendly restaurant where pasta dishes and regional specialities are served. **$**

THE ALPES-MARITIMES

Biot

Les Arcades
16 place des Arcades
Tel: 04 93 65 01 04
Classical Provençal cuisine in the dining room of a 15th-century house, which doubles as an art gallery. **$$**

Auberge du Jarrier
30 passage de la Bourgade
Tel: 04 93 65 11 68
Comfortable old *auberge* serving elegant French cuisine with a Mediterranean flavour. **$$**

Les Terraillers
11 route du Chemin Neuf
Tel: 04 93 65 01 59
An elegant restaurant just outside the village in a beautiful vaulted cellar. Attractive terrace in summer. Closed: Nov and Wed. **$$**

Breil-sur-Roya

Castel du Roy
Route de Tende
Tel: 04 93 04 43 66
Lovely riverside restaurant with tranquil, tree-shaded terrace serving specialities of the region. Credit cards: Visa. **$**

La Brigue

Le Mirval
Rue St-Vincent Ferrier
Tel: 04 93 04 63 71
This, the most delightful restaurant in la Brigue, is situated outside village, by the river. Specialities include trout, spinach ravioli and game. Open Apr–Nov only. **$**

Grasse

La Bastide St-Antoine
48 avenue Henri Dunant
Tel: 04 93 70 94 94
Difficult to find but well worth the search, this restaurant situated in an old olive grove outside Grasse is fashionable for its wonderful, good-value gourmet menu. Truffles and mushrooms are both house specialities. **$$**

Mougins

L'Amandier
Place du Commandant Lamy
Tel: 04 93 90 00 91
Masterchef Roger Vergé's second restaurant *(see Moulin de Mougins, below)*, in the old village. **$$$**

Le Bistrot de Mougins
Place du Village
Tel: 04 93 75 78 34
The Bistrot de Mougins is set in a beautiful vaulted stone cellar and serves excellent Provençal cuisine. **$$**

La Ferme de Mougins
10 avenue Saint Basile
Tel: 04 93 90 03 74
A Provençal residence built of stone, set in an idyllic garden. **$$**

Le Feu-Follet
Place de la Mairie
Tel: 04 93 90 15 78
Located next door to Le Relais *(see below)* but with food at much less frightening prices. Reserve a few days ahead. **$$**

Moulin de Mougins
Quartier Notre-Dame de Vie
Tel: 04 93 75 78 24
Roger Vergé, the chef at the Moulin de Mougins, is the most influential of all the great chefs of the Côte d'Azur. A visit to his restaurant to sample his *cusine du soleil* is certainly to be cherished. In summer, be sure to reserve at least two or three weeks in advance. **$$$**

Le Relais à Mougins
Place de la Mairie
Tel: 04 93 90 03 47
Fax: 04 93 75 72 83
Chef André Surmain creates new dishes with traditional ingredients. Dine on the terrace overlooking the square. In summer, reserve at least 10 days ahead. **$–$$**

Price Ranges

The price ranges given, which are intended as guides only, cover the cost of the average set meal *(menu)* per person, not including wine or coffee. Note that *menu* prices at lunchtime are often half the price of the evening meal. Credit cards are accepted unless otherwise indicated.

$ menus up to €20
$$ menus up to €45
$$$ menus over €45

Peillon

Auberge de la Madone
L'Escarène
Tel: 04 03 79 91 17
Come here for a well-prepared, unpretentious dining experience at reasonable prices. **$$**

St-Paul de Vence

La Colombe d'Or
1 place du Général de Gaulle
Tel: 04 93 32 80 02
The dining room at La Colombe d'Or is hung with the works of Matisse, Picasso, Léger, Delaunay and others, and the terrace must arguably be the most beautiful one in the region. **$$$**

Couleur Pourpre
7 rempart Ouest
Tel: 04 93 32 60 14
Well situated in the old town, this popular restaurant has intimate dining rooms on four levels. **$$**

Le Saint-Paul
86 rue Grande
This is a 16th-century mansion-hotel where chef Frédéric Buzet offers excellent regional cuisine with a modern approach. **$$$**

Tourrettes Sur Loup

Chez Grand'Mère
Place Mirabeau
Tel: 04 93 59 33 34
Popular for North African dishes and meats grilled on the open fire. Reservations are recommended. **$**

Le Petit Manoir
21 Grand Rue
Tel: 04 93 24 19 19
Elegant place serving fine cuisine. **$$**

Vence

Restaurant Jacques Maximin
689 chemin de la Gaude
Tel: 04 93 58 90 75
An exotic garden setting where this legendary French chef to produce both classic and unusual dishes, drawing on the best produce of the region. **$$$**

THE CÔTE D'AZUR

Antibes

Auberge Provençale
Place Nationale
Tel: 04 93 34 13 24
Attractive dining-room and beautiful courtyard in summer. **$**

Bacon
Boulevard Bacon
Cap d'Antibes
Tel: 04 93 61 50 02
A local institution where seafood is concerned. Reserve a week ahead and ask for a table with a view. **$$$**

La Bonne Auberge
RN 7
Near Antibes
Tel: 04 93 33 36 65
La Bonne Auberge is one of the best restaurants in the area. Excellent, if expensive, food. **$$$**

Casa Pablo
1 rue de la Touraque
Tel: 04 93 34 21 54
An unpretentious, pretty restaurant near the ramparts. **$**

Don Juan
17 rue Thuret
Tel: 04 93 34 58 63
Excellent service and tasty, reasonably priced pizzas, Italian and Provençal dishes. **$**

Les Vieux Murs
Avenue Admiral-de-Grasse
Tel: 04 93 34 06 73
A great and fairly reasonably priced meal can be had whilst sitting comfortably alongside the ancient sea wall. **$$**

Beaulieu-sur-Mer

Le Metropole
15 boulevard Leclerc
Tel: 04 93 01 00 08
Fish specialities in a discreetly luxurious setting. **$$$**

La Réserve
5 boulevard Leclerc
Tel: 04 93 01 00 01
Excellent cuisine in an elegant Renaissance-inspired setting. Emphasis on fish dishes. **$$$**

Restaurant Le Portofino
4 quai Whitechurch
Tel: 04 93 01 29 27
The excellent *soupe de poisson* is a bargain. Be sure to order the day before if you can, since it is made freshly for you. **$**

Cagnes-sur-Mer

Le Cagnard
Rue du Pontis Long
Haut-de-Cagnes
Tel: 04 93 20 73 21
The cuisine at Le Cagnard is elegant and beautifully presented. Lovely dining room in what was once the 14th-century castle's guardroom. **$$$**

Local Wines

There are some excellent wines produced in the South of France, many of which are available at very affordable prices. Good reds include Châteauneuf-du-Pape, Gigondas and Rasteau; almost as good are the reds of Costières de Nîmes and Côte du Ventoux. Tavel and Bandol both produce good rosés, and Bandol and Cassis are very good whites, especially for fish.

The French are fiercely proud of their wines and keen to educate visitors about their production. Across the region you will find roadside signs offering visits to cellars open for tours, tastings and the sale of wine.

French wines are graded according to their quality and this must be shown on the label. The grades are as follows:

- *Vin de table*: usually cheap everyday table wine that is of varying quality.
- *Vin de pays*: local wine.
- VDQS (*vin délimité de qualité supérieure*): wine from a specific area that is higher quality than *vin de table*.
- AOC (*appellation d'origine controlée*): Good-quality wine from a specific area or château where strict controls are imposed on the amount of wine produced each year.
- *Mis en bouteille au château*: bottled at the vineyard. Also indicated by the words, *récoltant* or *producteur* around the cap.
- *Négociant*: a wine that has been bought by a dealer and usually bottled away from the estate. However, this is not necessarily to the detriment of the wine; there are many top *négociants* in business today.

Cafés

Although there has sadly been a significant decline in the number of French cafés in recent years, they nevertheless remain a French institution and especially good for morning coffee, reading the newspaper, drinks or snack meals. In smaller towns and villages cafés are very much the centre of local life. Note that if you drink at the bar it is usually cheaper than sitting at a table.

Entre Cour et Jardin
102 montée de la Bourgade
Tel: 04 93 20 72 27
This lovely restaurant, which is tucked away in a side street, has a friendly atmosphere and features two art exhibitions a year in its courtyard. **$$**

La Table d'Yves
85 montée de la Bourgade
Haute-de-Cagnes
Tel: 04 93 20 33 33
Hearty Provençal dishes, good fish soup, pasta and excellent lamb, in a gorgeous village setting. **$$**

Cannes

La Côte
Carlton Intercontinental Hotel
58 boulevard de la Croisette
Tel: 04 93 06 40 23
Excellent – if expensive – cuisine is served in the exquisitely elegant dining room of this Cannes' institution. **$$$**

La Mère Besson
13 rue des Frères Pradignac
Tel: 04 92 18 03 58
Just the place for a taste of traditional Provence along the Riviera. No lunch from June to Sept. Closed: Sun. **$**

Neat
11 square Merimée
Tel: 04 93 99 29 19
Fax: 04 93 68 84 48
The only English chef, so far, to earn a Michelin star, Richard Neat serves excellent modern French cuisine at his highly rated, vaulted restaurant. Good location, only a short distance from the Palais des Festivals. **$$–$$$**

La Palme d'Or
Hôtel Martinez
73 boulevard de la Croisette
Tel: 04 92 98 74 14
Imaginative gastronomic cuisine with a taste of the Mediterranean. One of Cannes' top restaurants, with a view of the Bay and the Îsles de Lérins. **$$$**

Le Pizza
Quai St-Pierre
Tel: 04 93 29 22 56
Serves the best flame-oven-cooked pizza in Cannes – maybe even anywhere. The diminutive proprietors, with classically "Italian" temperaments, offer a wide variety of Italian favourites at very good prices. **$**

Le Royal Gray
Hôtel Gray d'Albion
38 rue des Serbes
Tel: 04 92 99 79 60
Top cook Jacques Chibois has been voted chef of the year numerous times, and this is widely recognised as being the best restaurant in Cannes. **$$**

Villa de Lys
Majestic Hotel
14 boulevard de la Croisette
Tel: 04 92 98 77 00
Chef Bruno Oger is one of the region's rising stars. He serves good traditional fare along with Oriental-inspired offerings in this hotel restaurant. **$$**

Eze

Château de la Chèvre d'Or
Moyenne Corniche Rue du Barri
Tel: 04 92 10 66 66
Light, traditional cuisine in a medieval castle with superb sea views. Closed: Wed. **$$$**

Château Eza
Rue de la Pise
Tel: 04 93 41 12 24
Spectacular former residence of the Prince of Sweden, suspended high above the sea. **$$$**

Price Ranges

The price ranges given, which are intended as guides only, cover the cost of the average set meal *(menu)* per person, not including wine or coffee. Note that *menu* prices at lunchtime are often half the price of the evening meal. Credit cards are accepted unless otherwise indicated.

$ menus up to €20
$$ menus up to €45
$$$ menus over €45

Juan-Les-Pins

Belles Rives
Boulevard Baudointel
Tel: 04 93 61 02 79
The Belles Rives is an elegant hotel and restaurant situated right on the water's edge. Book fans will love the fact that this was once the residence of the writer F. Scott Fitzgerald. **$$**

La Terrasse
La Pinède
Avenue Gallice
Tel: 04 93 61 20 37
Recognised as one of the region's best restaurants, with a palm-shaded terrace. **$$$**

Mandelieu–La-Napoule

L'Oasis
Rue Jean-Honoré-Carle
Tel: 04 93 49 95 52
Long-established restaurant serving classic cuisine with an original touch. **$$–$$$**

Menton

Le Lion D'Or
7 rue des Marins
Tel: 04 93 35 74 67
This good-value local favourite serves great fish straight from the sea. **$$**

Monaco

Bar et Beouf
Avenue Princesse Grace
Monte-Carlo
Tel: 00377 92 16 60 60
An Alain Ducasse establishment where protegé Didier Elena offers exquisite cuisine in a hip Philippe Starck-designed interior. **$$$**

Le Café de Paris
Place du Casino
Tel: 00377 92 16 20 20
Completely renovated in 1920s' style, this place deserves to be visited as one of the sights of Monte-Carlo. **$$**

Louis XV
Hôtel de Paris
Place Monte-Carlo
Monte-Carlo
Tel: 00377 92 16 38 40
The flagship of the Ducasse empire, the glittering restaurant in the Hôtel de Paris serves Mediterannean cuisine on a glamorous terrace overlooking the Casino. **$$$**
Polpetta
2 rue Paradis
Tel: 00377 93 50 67 84
Hearty Italian food that offers perhaps the best value for money in Monaco. Credit cards: Visa. **$**

For Mougins, see page 316

Nice

Auberge de Bellet
St-Roman de Bellet
Tel: 04 93 37 92 51
In Nice's most famous vineyard of the same name. Vintage wines and delicacies such as lobster, pigeon, and garlic stew. **$$**
Le Chantecler
Hôtel Négresco
37 promenade des Anglais
Tel: 04 93 16 64 00
Nice's finest restaurant, in the Négresco hotel. Elegant cuisine with a hearty Mediterranean touch, created by celebrated chef Alain Lorca, typical of a new generation of Provençal chefs who bring an original light twist to the region's delicacies. Great seafood and vegetable dishes with a stylish regional flavour. **$$–$$$**
Le Comptoir
20 rue Saint-François-de-Paule
Tel: 04 93 92 08 80
A 1930s-style bar and restaurant, excellent for late-night dining. **$**
La Merenda
4 rue Terasse
An unpretentious bistro in the old town with terrific regional food, such as stuffed courgette flowers, stockfish soup, and pesto. They don't have a phone, so you have to go in person to book ahead. **$$**
Nissa-Socca
5 rue Ste-Réparate
Tel: 04 93 80 18 35
Popular and unpretentious, serving Niçois specialities such as fresh pasta and vegetable fritters. Excellent value. Arrive early or be prepared to wait. Closed: Sun and Mon lunchtimes. Note: credit cards are not accepted. **$**
La Petite Maison
11 rue St-Francois de Paule
Tel: 04 93 85 71 53
A former grocer's shop, this restaurant serves Niçoise cuisine and is extremely popular with the locals. **$$**
Le Safari
1 cours Saleya
Tel: 04 93 80 18 44
A large café with outside tables in flower market street. Try the *bagna cauda*, a hot anchovy dip with raw vegetables. **$**
La Saleya
11 cours Saleya
Tel: 04 93 62 29 62
A trendy brasserie, set in Nice's flower market. A great place to stop and watch the world go by. **$**

St-Jean Cap Ferrat

Le Provençal
2 avenue Denis Semeria
Tel: 04 93 76 03 97
Imaginative, gastronomic cuisine with a Mediterranean flavour. Closed: Sun. **$$**
La Voile d'Or
Yachting harbour
Tel: 04 93 01 13 13
The high prices here are justified by the idyllic setting overlooking the pretty harbour and by the exquisite cuisine. Closed: Nov–Mar. **$$$**

For St-Raphaël, see page 315
For St-Tropez, see page 315–16

Tipping

Most restaurant bills include a service charge, and this is generally indicated at the foot of the menu. If in doubt, ask: *Est-ce que le service est compris?* It is common to leave a small extra tip for the waiter if the service has been good. Remember to address waiters as *Monsieur*, never as *garçon*; waitresses should be called *Mademoiselle* or *Madame* according to age.

Culture

What's On

Provence is now an established cultural destination, especially in the summer, when world-class festivals of music, theatre and dance are staged here. Avignon is famous for its theatre festival, Cannes is world renowned for film and there is also the opera festival of Orange and the jazz festivals of Nice and Juans-les-Pins. Traditional festivals abound, where everything from bullfights and flowers to garlic and lemons is celebrated.

Provence has a magnificent legacy of art and there are many major art museums in the region. There are also many smaller museums and galleries offering a variety of art and crafts. In larger towns such as Marseille, Nice, Avignon, Aix, Arles, Cannes or Monte-Carlo you will find opera, theatre and cinema venues.

Museums

Most museums charge an entrance fee but they are often free or half-price on Sunday. As a rule, national museums are closed on Tuesday, while municipal museums shut on Monday. Opening times vary. Most museums close for a long lunch break, noon–2pm or noon–2.30pm, although major sites are often open continuously, especially in summer.

DIARY OF EVENTS

January

Cannes: Midem (International Disc and Music Publishing Festival)

Menton: Theatre season
Monaco: Monte-Carlo Rally; International Circus Festival
Nice: Festival of Birds

February
Isola 2000: Snow Carnival
Menton: International Lemon Festival
Nice: Carnival and Battle of Flowers

March
Antibes: Café Theatre Festival
Grasse: Carnival
Monte-Carlo: Mancas (music festival); Spring Arts Festival (until end April)
Arles: Féria Pascale

April
Cannes: MIP-TV (TV festival)
Roquebrune-Cap-Martin: Procession to the castle on Good Friday
Monte-Carlo: Biennial of Sculpture (odd-numbered years, until end Sept). Monte-Carlo Tennis Open

May
Cannes: Film Festival
Fréjus: Fleuriades – flower festival
Grasse: Expo Roses – rose show
Monaco: Grand Prix
Nice: May Festival and International Youth Folk Festival; Art Jonction International
St-Tropez: *Bravades* festival
Cavaillon: Ascension day Parade
Stes-Maries de la Mer: Pélerinage de Mai. France's biggest gypsy festival

June
Antibes: International Young Soloist Festival
Cannes: International Cabaret-theatre Festival
Fréjus: Arênes de l'Automobile: exhibition of collector's cars
France: Fête de la Musique
Monte-Carlo: St-Jean folk festival
Nice: Sacred Music Festival
Roquebrune-Cap-Martin: Theatre Festival
Nîmes: Féria de Pentecôte
Vaucluse: Fête de la Vigne et du Vin
Tarascon: Fête de la Tarasque
Uzès: Foire à l'Ail (garlic fair)

July
Aix-en-Provence: Festival d'Art Lyrique; Festival de Danse à Aix
Antibes: International Jazz Festival; Musiques au Coeur opera festival
Arles: Rencontres Internationales de la Photographie (until mid-Aug)
Arles: Suds à Arles. World-music festival (until mid-Aug)
Avignon: Festival d'Avignon theatre festival (until mid-Aug)
France: Bastille Day (14 July)
Fréjus: Forum des Arts et de la Musique: concerts, dance, theatre
Golfe Juan: Jean Marais Festival (theatre and music)
Grasse: International Festival of Military Music
L'Isle-sur-la-Sorgue: Festival de la Sorgue (until mid-Aug)
Monte-Carlo: Season of concerts in the courtyard of the Palais du Prince; Fireworks Festival and the Monaco carnival
Nice: International Folk Festival; "Grande Parade du Jazz"
Orange: Les Chorégies lyric opera (until mid-Aug)
Uzès: Nuits musicales d'Uzès (until mid-Aug)
Vallauris: Biennale de céramique (Pottery Festival, July–Oct)
Vence: Classical concerts in the cathedral and open-air
Villefranche-sur-Mer: Venetian Fête

August
Antibes: International Fireworks
Arles: Rencontres Internationales de la Photographie (until mid-Aug)
Arles: Suds à Arles. World-music festival (until mid-Aug)
Avignon: Festival d'Avignon theatre festival (until mid-Aug)
Brignoles: Festival de jazz
Fréjus: Fête du Raisin – wine-tasting and feasting
Grasse: Festival of Jasmine
L'Isle-sur-la-Sorgue: Festival de la Sorgue (until mid-Aug)
Menton: International Chamber Music Festival
Monte-Carlo: Feast of St-Roman
Orange: Les Chorégies lyric opera (until mid-Aug)
Roquebrune-Cap-Martin: Costumed procession to the castle
Uzès: Nuits musicales d'Uzès
St-Rémy: Féria Provençale
Vallauris: Biennale de céramique contemporaine (Pottery Festival, July–Oct)

September
Arles: Fêtes des Prémices du Riz
France: Journées du Patrimoine. Third weekend in September, throughout France, when historic monuments and official buildings are open to the public for free.
St-Tropez: grape-picking festival
Vallauris: Biennale de céramique contemporaine (Pottery Festival, July–Oct)

October
Monte-Carlo: Season of Symphony Concerts
Vallauris: Biennale de céramique contemporaine (Pottery Festival, July–Oct)

November
Arles: Salon International des Santonniers
Cannes: Festival International de la Danse
Monte-Carlo: 19 November, National Holiday: parades, ceremonies and spectacles (fireworks the previous evening)

December
Fréjus: Foire aux Santons: Provençal craftsmen exhibit *santons* (small clay figures of saints used for religious purposes)

Further Information and Tickets

For details on exhibitions and concerts contact local tourist offices *(see pages 292–3)*. The booklet *Terre de Festivals* (from main tourist offices and online at www.festival.cr-paca.fr) covers summer arts festivals in the Provence-Alpes-Côtes d'Azur region. Festival tickets for performances in Avignon and Orange, etc., can often be bought directly at Offices de Tourisme or at branches of the music and books chain FNAC (www.fnac.fr) and Virgin, or via France Billet (tel: 04 42 31 31 31).

Nightlife

What's On

In smaller towns and villages in Provence there is usually little going on at night unless a festival is taking place. In most places, however, cafés and bars stay open all day, often until the early hours of the morning, so there is usually somewhere to go for a drink in the evening. If festivities are happening, however, these will probably continue well late into the night, so don't expect to get a good night's sleep if you are staying in a town-centre hotel.

In the larger cities there is likely to be a variety of bars and clubs. The Côte d'Azur is famed for its nightlife, in particular the legendary casinos, which nowadays often also incorporate nightclubs, cabarets or restaurants. The following is a selection of recommended venues in the major towns in the region.

For details of particular events, see Festivals *(pages 319–20)*, or enquire at local tourist offices, and check local papers and magazines for listings. *César*, a weekly listings magazine is distributed free in the Gard, Vaucluse and Bouches du Rhône *départements*.

AIX-EN-PROVENCE

Cité du Livre
8–10 rue des Allumettes
Tel: 04 42 25 98 65
Multi-disciplinary arts centre with annual literary festival.

Théâtre des Ateliers
29 place Miollis
Tel: 04 42 38 10 45
Contemporary theatre.

Hot Brass
Route d'Eguilles
Tel: 04 42 21 05 57
Live jazz.

Le Richelm
24 rue de la Verrerie
Tel: 04 42 23 49 29
Bar-club with dance floor.

ANTIBES

La Siesta
Pont de la Brague
Tel: 04 93 33 31 31
Restaurant, bar, casino and club.

ARLES

Les Arènes d'Arles
Tel: 04 90 96 03 70
Bullfights, concerts and films.

Théâtre de la Calade
Le Grenier à Sel
49 quai de la Roquette
Tel: 04 90 93 05 23
Arles' main theatre company.

Cargo de Nuit
7 avenue Sadi-Carnot
Tel: 04 90 49 55 99
World music and jazz.

Poisson Banane
6 rue du Forum
Tel: 04 90 96 02 58
Jazz bar with restaurant and terrace.

AVIGNON

Théâtre Municipal
20 place de l'Horloge
Tel: 04 9082 2344
Main permanent theatre in Avignon. Stages official festival productions in July.

Théâtre des Carmes
6 place des Carmes
Tel: 04 90 82 20 47
Avignon's oldest theatre company, based in a restored Gothic cloister.

Cyberdrome
68 rue Guillaume-Puy
Tel: 04 90 16 05 15
Fifteen computers for Internet access, plus an alcohol-free bar with music.

L'Hélicon
23 rue Bancasse
Tel: 04 90 16 03 99
Traditional French *chanson* performed by guest stars or the owner himself at the piano, plus good-value menus.

Utopia
4 rue des Escaliers Sainte-Anne
Tel: 04 90 27 04 96
Avignon's main *version-originale* (original-language) cinema with a lovely bohemian bistro and café.

Café In et Off
5 place du Palais
Tel: 04 90 85 48 95
Favourite festival meeting place with terrace tables offering a good view of the Palais des Papes.

Le Bokao's
9 bis quai Saint-Lazare
Tel: 04 90 82 47 55
Big trendy dance club.

L'Esclave
12 rue du Limas
Tel: 04 90 85 14 51
Predominantly gay clientele. Popular during the summer theatre festival.

CANNES

Jimmy's
Palais des Festivals
Tel: 04 92 98 78 00
Fashionable disco.

Les Coulisses
29 rue de Commandant André
Tel: 04 92 99 17 17
Fashionable nightclub, especially popular during film festival.

Le Queens
48 boulevard de la Republique
Tel: 04 93 90 25 58
Big, funky club popular with locals and festival goers.

Zanzibar
85 rue Félix Faure
Tel: 04 93 39 30 75
Established gay bar and club.

Carlton Casino Club
Carlton Intercontinental
58 la Croisette
Tel: 04 92 99 51 00
Open: every day 4pm–4am.
Also has restaurants, piano bar and disco.

Juan-Les-Pins
Le J's
Avenue Georges Gallice
Tel: 04 93 67 22 74
Nightclub.

Whisky à Gogo
La Pinède
Tel: 04 93 61 26 40
Nightclub.

MARSEILLE

Cité de la Musique
4 rue Bernard Dubois
Tel: 04 91 39 28 28
Variety of musical concerts.
Théâtre du Gymnase
4 rue du Théâtre-Français
Tel: 04 91 24 35 35
Restored theatre that puts on innovative theatre.
Opéra Municipal
2 rue Molière
Tel: 04 91 55 14 99
Opera and classical music.
Le Trolleybus
24 quai de Rive Neuve
Tel: 04 91 54 30 45
Huge club offering techno, salsa and jazz.
The New Cancan
3 rue Senac-de-Meilhan
Tel: 04 91 48 59 76
The most popular gay club in Marseille.
L'Intermediaire
63 place Jean-Jaurès
Tel: 04 91 47 01 25
Jazz, blues and rock as well as traditional southern French music.

MONTE-CARLO

Théatre du Fort Saint-Antoine
Avenue de la Quarantaine
Tel: 00377 9325 6612)
Theatre-in-the-round for summer night concerts.
Le Cabaret du Casino
Place du Casino
Tel: 00377 92 16 36 36
Classic French cabaret.
La Rascasse
Quai Antoine
Tel: 00377 93 25 56 90
All-night pub with an outdoor terrace and a restaurant. Plays jazz and rock.
Le Sporting Club
Avenue Princesse Grace
Tel: 00377 92 16 22 77
Fashionable Euro-trash rendezvous.

NICE

Opéra de Nice
4 rue St-François-de-Paule
Tel: 04 92 17 40 40
Classic venue for symphony, ballet and opera.
Théâtre de Nice
Promenade des Arts
Tel: 04 93 13 90 90
French and foreign classics and contemporary work.
Cinématheque de Nice
3 esplanade Kennedy
Tel: 04 92 04 06 66
Recent films in their original language with subtitles.
Le Bar des Oiseaux
5 rue Saint-Vincent
Tel: 04 93 80 27 33
A bizarre combination of live bands and live birds.
Blue Boy Enterprise
9 rue Spinetta
Tel: 04 93 44 68 24
All-night gay club with drag shows.
Dizzy Club
26 quai Lunel
Tel: 04 93 26 54 79
Piano-bar and dancing.
Casino de Monte-Carlo
Place du Casino
Tel: 00377 92 16 23 00
The original and still the most famous casino on the Côte d'Azur. Formal dress is required. Open: all year: main salon from noon, private rooms from 3pm. Also has a separate cabaret and several restaurants.

ST-TROPEZ

Les Caves du Roy
Hôtel Byblos
Place des Lices
Tel: 04 94 97 16 02
Legendary club in Hôtel Byblos, still a favourite of Johnny Halliday.
Le Papagayo
Résidence du Port
Tel: 04 94 97 07 56.
Long the place to spot famous faces.
Le VIP Room
Residences du Nouveau Port
Tel: 04 94 97 14 70
St Tropez's latest and most fashionable club.

Sport

What's on Offer

Provence has a huge range of sports and activites to choose from. The mountains and river valleys offer walking, riding, cycling and climbing, river-rafting and canoeing, and, in the winter months, skiing. Golf is very popular, as is tennis, and even quite small villages often have tennis courts, though you may have to become a temporary member to use them. (Enquire at the local tourist office or *mairie*, the town hall, which will also provide details of all other local sporting activities.)

On the coast the sea is usually warm enough to swim in from June to September, and almost every town will have a municipal pool, though it may only be open in school holidays. You could just lounge on the beach, but even beach bums can indulge in surfing windsurfing and waterskiing. Antibes and Cannes are major water-sports centres, and the Îles des Lérins, the Îles de Hyères and the Calanques offer some of the best diving in the Mediterranean. For detailed listings pick up the *Watersports Côte d'Azur* brochure from main tourist offices or go to www.france-nautisme.com. General information on sports and activities can be picked up at local tourist offices, or national organisations. Many UK travel firms offer holidays tailored to specific activities.

Participant Sports

WATER SPORTS

Although it is not necessary to be a millionaire and member of the most fashionable yacht club to enjoy the pleasures of the sea, if you wish to

Cycling

Cycling is a wonderful way to enjoy Provence *(see page 294 for advice on transporting your own bike)*. If you don't have you own bike, you can rent cycles locally, from bike shops, or youth hostels *(see page 302)*. You could consider a package cycling holiday, with accommodation booked in advance and your luggage transported for you.

The IGN 906 Cycling France map gives details of routes, clubs and places to stay *(see pages 300–1)*. Information is also available from: **The Touring Department Cyclists Touring Club**, Cotterell House, 69 Meadrow, Godalming, Surrey GU7 3HS. Tel: 01483-417217. Their service to members includes competitive cycle and travel insurance, free detailed touring itineraries and general information sheets about France, whilst their tours brochure lists trips to the region, organised by members. The club's French counterpart, **Fédération Française de Cyclotourisme**, is at 8 rue Jean-Marie-Jégo, 75013 Paris. Tel: 01 44 16 88 88.

hire a luxury yacht for a week's cruise, being a millionaire might just help. You certainly need some money to enjoy several of the Côte's most exclusive beaches. In fact, only 70 percent of the beaches along the Côte d'Azur are open to the public; the rest – nearly 150 beaches – are privately owned (usually by hotels) and an entrance fee is charged to access them.

However, most private beaches have a good range of equipment for hire: dinghies, catamarans, surfing and water-skiing equipment, etc. To hire a boat, or a yacht, for a day or longer, all you need really do is stroll around the pleasure ports of the resorts and ask. Another source of information is the local *syndicat d'initiative* or tourist offices *(see pages 292–3)*.

Sailing and Windsurfing

Comité Regional de Voile Côte d'Azur
Espace Antibes
2208 route de Grasse
06600 Antibes
Tel: 04 93 74 77 05
Cannes
Station Voile
9 rue Esprit Violet
Cannes
Tel: 04 92 18 88 87

Scuba Diving

Fédération Française d'Etudes et de Sports Sous-Marins
24 quai Rive-Neuve
13007 Marseille
Tel: 04 91 33 99 31
Fax: 04 91 54 77 43

Canoeing and Kayaking

Fédération Française de Canoe-Kayak et des Sports associés en Eau-Vive
87 quai de la Marne
94340 Joinville-le-Pont
Tel: 01 45 11 08 50
Fax: 01 48 86 13 25
Ligue Régionale Alpes-Provence
14 avenue Vincent Auriol
30200 Bagnols-sur-Ceze
Tel: 04 66 89 47 71

Fishing

Here you have a choice of sea- or freshwater-fishing. The season opens around the second Saturday in March. For freshwater-fishing you will need to be affiliated to an association. For general information and addresses of local fishing associations contact:
Conseil Superieur de la Pêche
134 avenue de Malakoff
75016 Paris
Tel: 01 45 01 20 20

Climbing

Provence offers many opportunities for climbers. You can find guides for day outings or clubs that will organise beginners' courses.
For further information contact:
Club Alpin Français
14 avenue Mirabeau
Nice
Tel: 04 93 53 37 95

Golf

Provence has many excellent golf courses, and the good weather in the region means golf can be played all year round. Most clubs offer lessons with resident experts.
Fédération Française de Golfe
68 rue Anatole France
Le Vallois, Perret 92306
Tel: 01 41 49 77 00
Fax: 01 41 49 77 01

Horseriding

Horseriding and ponytrekking are popular activities in Provence, with Centres Equestres (Equestrian Centres) all over the region, in rural areas, the mountains, less

Walking Holidays

Walking holidays are an increasingly popular way to enjoy Provence, especially in the mountains. Ensure you are suitably equipped with water, and warm clothing and good boots. There is an excellent network of signposted footpaths, (*sentiers de grand randonée*; long-distance footpaths) in the region but make sure that you also have a good map *(see pages 300–1)*. Local tourist offices or ramblers' organisations may put on guided walks of local sights, plants or wildlife. For local information contact the relevant tourist office, or **Fédération Française de Randonnée Pédestre**, 14 rue Riquet, 75009 Paris. Tel: 01 44 89 93 90; fax: 01 40 35 85 48. You could also contact the **Comité Départemental de la Randonnée Pédestre**, 4 avenue de Verdun, Cagnes-sur-Mer. Tel/fax: 04 93 20 74 73.

inhabited parts of the coast, and especially in the Camargue.
For further information, contact:
Ligue Régionale de Provence de Sports Equestres
298 avenue du club Hippique
13090 Aix-en-Provence
Tel: 04 42 20 88 02

Spectator Sports

WATER-SPORTS EVENTS

There are all kinds of professional sailing and other watersport events for spectators to watch, with most of the major competitions taking place at Mandelieu-la-Napoule, just west of Cannes, including the **Grand Prix de la Corniche d'Or** (April), "**Les Vieilles Ecoutes**" (July), the **International Rowing Regatta** (August) and the **Grand Prix de la Ville** (October). Other events are the **International Marathon** in the Baie des Anges, Nice in April, the **Transgolfe Windsurf Regatta** in St-Tropez in July and the **Royal Regattas** in September in Cannes to coincide with the **International Pleasure Boat Festival**; there is also a **Boat Show** at Beaulieu-sur-Mer in May.

GRAND PRIX

Probably the most famous event in the whole region is the prestigious **Monte-Carlo Car Rally**, held in January. First staged in 1911, this road trial continues to attract the top names in the sport. Another lesser-known rally is held in November at St-Tropez: the 20-km (12-mile) **Rolls-Royce Rally**. The other big motoring event is the **Monte-Carlo Grand Prix** in May, one of the most decisive contests in the competition for the world motor racing championship.

TENNIS AND GOLF TOURNAMENTS

April is the time for the **International Tennis Championships** in Monte-Carlo, the **Monte-Carlo Open**, which is complemented by another "open", this time the **Golf Tournament**, which takes place in early July. Another golfing event is the **Professional Golf Open** at Mougins (Cannes), held every April.

HORSERACING EVENTS

The major horseracing venue is the **Côte d'Azur Hippodrome** at Cagnes-sur-Mer, where meetings are held during the day from December to May and in the evenings in July and August. One of its major events takes place in February. There is also an international show-jumping competiton in Cannes during May. Hyères is popular for racing, and meetings are held at the Hippodrome there during the spring and autumn. Fréjus hosts a horse show in June.

Skiing

The Maritime Alps are very popular for skiing and there are several large resorts in that area, such as Auron, Valberg and Isola 2000. They are only a few hours from the coast and at certain seasons you could combine the beach and skiing in one day. For details, contact:
Fédération Française de Ski
50 avenue des Marquisats
74000 Annecy
Tel: 04 50 51 40 34
www.ffs.fr
Club Alpin Français
14 rue Mirabeau, Nice
Tel: 93 62 59 99

Downhill Skiing
Auron: Office du Tourisme
Tel: 04 93 23 02 66
Isola 2000: Office du Tourisme
Tel: 04 93 23 15 15

Cross-Country Skiing
Val Casterino
Tel: 93 04 73 71
Le Boréon
St-Martin-de-Vésubie
Tel: 04 93 03 33 77

Children

Travelling with Children

Sightseeing with children is only likely to be difficult in steep hill villages, which can be very difficult to negotiate with a pushchair. Many conventional museums may not be of interest to them but there is a wide range of educational attractions that will appeal to children, such as specialised zoos.

A wide range of activities can be found to suit children of all ages from riding and cycling to river-bathing, rambling through the countryside and exploring castles. Most towns and villages have swimming pools, tennis courts and playgrounds.

The beach and the sea are the easiest way to amuse children, and private beach concessions with sun-loungers and parasols are the easiest of all – just book your parasol close to the shore and watch the kids build sandcastles. Inflatables are often provided and there are sometimes also bouncy castles.

Many seaside resorts have children's clubs on the beach, where for a fee children can be left for a few hours to take part in organised sports and fun events. When hiring a car, be sure to book any baby seats in advance, although larger hire companies do usually have a few ready to go.

HOTELS AND RESTAURANTS

Most hotels have family rooms so that children do not have to be separated from their parents, and a cot *(lit bébé)* can often be provided for a small supplement, although it is a good idea to double-check this in advance.

Eating out is easy, especially during the day, as all but the poshest restaurants welcome young children: just choose one with a terrace and they can run around while you have another glass of wine. Many restaurants offer a children's menu or will split a *prix-fixe* menu between two children or even give you an extra plate to share your own meal.

SHOPPING

French shops are well provided with all child necessities. Disposable nappies *(couches à jeter)* are easy to find, and French baby food is often of gourmet standard, especially the puréed artichoke – though watch out for added sugar.

HOLIDAY CENTRES

It is quite common in France, as in the US, for children to spend at least part of their summer vacation at a holiday centre. For information, contact the tourist office *(see pages 292–3)* or the Loisirs Accueil service in individual *départements*.

Shopping

Shopping Areas

Over the years the powers-that-be in most major French towns have made the sensible decision to keep the town centre for small boutiques and individual shops. Many of these areas are pedestrianised and rather attractive, although beware as some cars ignore the *voie piétonnée* signs. Large supermarkets, hypermarkets, furniture stores and DIY outlets are grouped on the outskirts of the town, mostly designated as a *Centre Commercial*. This laudable intent is, however, somewhat marred by the horrendous design of some of these centres – groups of garish functional buildings that make the town's outskirts very unattractive. In the case of Nice, for example, there are vast hypermarkets, out by the airport to the west of the town.

Centres Commercials are fine for bulk shopping, self-catering or finding a selection of wine to take home at reasonable prices, but otherwise the town centres are usually far more characterful. It is here that you will find the individual souvenirs that give a taste of the region, alongside the beautifully dressed windows of delicatessens and *pâtisseries*.

What to Buy

You should have no trouble finding wonderful gifts and mementos to take home from Provence, without having to spend a lot of money. The best things to buy are local crafts or products, for which the Provençals are so famous. Among these are: *santons* (little figures from clay or sometimes dough used together to create a nativity scene); pottery; faïence (fine ceramics decorated with opaque glazes); brightly coloured fabrics (the Souleiado stores carry the most famous examples, but they are also the most costly); hand-woven baskets; and toiletries made with local herbs such as lavender. You might just want to pick up a bottle of lavender essence, a little bag of fresh *Herbes de Provence* (usually a blend of dried herbs including thyme, sage, tarragon, rosemary, chervil and sometimes even lavender) and bottles of delicately coloured olive oil.

Some towns are inextricably linked with particular products, such as the wonderful handblown glass from Biot, the perfumes from Grasse or soap *(savon)* from Marseille, herbs from St Rémy-de-Provence or earthenware in Vallauris. The same goes for certain regions: honey is linked with the Alpes-Maritimes and Alpes-de-Haute-Provence; olive oil and *santons* with the Bouches-du-Rhône; and leather products are typical of the Camargue and the Alpes-de-Haute-Provence. And, if you're on the Côte d'Azur – well, there really is no better place to buy a bikini.

Buying Direct

Across the region you may be tempted by signs by the side of the road for *dégustations* (tastings). A large number of wine producers and farmers will invite you to try their

Tax Refunds (detaxes)

A refund (average 13 per cent) on value-added tax (TVA) can be claimed by non-EU visitors if they spend over €180 in any one shop. The shop will supply a *detaxe* form and you will need to have it stamped by customs when you leave the country. You send a stamped copy back to the shop, which will refund the tax, either by bank transfer or by putting money onto your credit card. *Detaxe* does not cover food, drink, antiques or works of art.

Size Conversion Chart

WOMEN

France	UK	US
38	10 (30")	8
40	12 (32")	10
42	14 (34")	12
44	16 (36")	14
46	18 (38")	16
48	20 (40")	18

MEN

France	UK	US
32	32	42
34	34	44
36	35	46
38	36	48
40	37	51
42	38	54

wines and other produce with an eye to selling you a case, or maybe a few jars of pâté. This is a good way to try before you buy and sometimes includes a visit to a wine cellar.

Sometimes farm produce is more expensive to buy this way than in the supermarkets – but do not forget that it is home-produced, not factory-processed, and should be extremely fresh.

Complaints

If you have a complaint about any purchase, return it to the shop you bought it from as soon as possible. In the case of any serious dispute, contact the Direction Départementale de la Concurrence et de la Consommation et de la Répression des Fraudes.

Markets

If there is one thing that symbolises Provence more than anything else, it is probably the open-air market. After cafés, these markets are usually the centre of social activity for the locals, as well as where the Provençal cook obtains the multitude of fresh ingredients that make up the region's rightly celebrated cuisine.

Vendors of locally produced vegetables, fruit, herbs, cheese, sausage, meat, honey, flowers, soaps, lavender essence and fresh-baked breads set up their stands at daybreak. In addition, some towns have a *marché au brocante* (literally meaning "junk market"), offering a range of items, from valuable antiques to brand-new wares (often clothing and shoes) to bric-a-brac. If you want to get to know Provence, you should visit one of the markets listed below.

THE VAUCLUSE

Apt: Sat.
Avignon: main market: daily; Produce and flea market: Sat and Sun am.
Bollène: Mon
Cavaillon: Mon
Châteaneuf-du-Pape: Fri
Gordes: Tues
Isle-sur-Sorgue: antiques and flea market: Sat and Sun
Roussillon: Wed
Vaison-la-Romaine: Tues

THE BOUCHES-DU-RHÔNE

Aix-en-Provence: main market: daily; flower market: Mon, Wed, Fri, Sun
Arles: Wed, Sat
Barbentane: Wed
Cassis: Wed, Fri
Fontvieille: Mon, Fri
Jouques: Wed afternoon, Sun
La Ciotat: daily
Maillane: Thur
Marseille: daily
St-Etienne-du-Grès: daily
Stes-Maries-de-la-Mer: Mon, Thur
St-Rémy–de-Provence: Wed, Sat
Salon-de-Provence: Wed, Fri
Tarascon: Tues

Market Etiquette

In a market all goods have to be marked with the price by law. Prices are usually by the kilo or by the *pièce*, that is, each item priced individually. Usually the stall holder *(marchand)* will select the goods for you. Sometimes there is a serve-yourself system – observe everyone else to see whether this is the case or not. With some foods, you may be offered a taste to try first; *un goûter*. Here are a few useful words:

bag	*le sac*
basket	*le panier*
flavour	*le parfum*
organic	*la biologique*
tasting	*la dégustation*

THE ALPES-DE-HAUTE-PROVENCE

Barcelonette: Wed, Sat
Castellane: Wed, Sat
Colmars-les-Alps: Tues
Digne: Wed, Thur, Sat
Forcalquier: Mon
Manosque: Sat
Moustiers: Fri
Sisteron: Wed, Sat

THE VAR

Bormes-les-Mimosas: Wed
Colobrières: Sun
Draguinan: daily.
Fayence: Thur, Sat
Hyères: flea market (place Massillon) – most mornings.
Le Lavandou: Thur
Salernes: Sun
Sanary-sur-Mer: Wed
Toulon: daily

THE ALPES-MARITIMES

Grasse: Tues
Vence: Tues, Fri
St-Etienne-de-Tinée: Fri, Sun.
St-Jeannet: Thur
Sospel: Thur
Tende: Wed
Vallauris: Wed, Sun

THE CÔTE D'AZUR

Antibes: daily except Mon and Fri
Cannes: daily except Mon
Menton: daily;
Nice: daily except Mon
St-Tropez: Tues, Sat

Language

The French Language

French is the native language of over 90 million people and the acquired language of 180 million. It is a Romance language descended from the Latin spoken by the Roman conquerors of Gaul. It still carries the reputation of being the most cultured language in the world and, for what it's worth, the most beautiful. People often tell stories about the impatience of the French towards foreigners not blessed with fluency in their language. In general, however, if you try to communicate with them in French, they will help.

Since much of the English vocabulary is related to French, thanks to the Norman Conquest of 1066, travellers will often recognise many cognates: words such as *hôtel* and *bagages* hardly need translation. Watch out, however, for misleading "false friends" (*see page 328*).

Words and Phrases

What is your name? *Comment vous appelez-vous?*
My name is... *Je m'appelle...*
Do you speak English? *Parlez-vous anglais?*
I am English/American *Je suis anglais(e)/américain(e)*
I don't understand *Je ne comprends pas*
Please speak more slowly *Parlez plus lentement, s'il vous plaît*
Can you help me? *Voulez-vous m'aider?*
I'm looking for... *Je cherche*
Where is...? *Où est...?*
How much is it? *C'est combien?*
I'm sorry *Excusez-moi/Pardon*
I don't know *Je ne sais pas*
No problem *Pas de problème*
Have a good day! *Bonne journée!*
That's it *C'est ça*
Here it is *Voici*
There it is *Voilà*
Let's go *On y va. Allons-y*
See you tomorrow *A demain*
See you soon *A bientôt*
Show me the word in the book *Montrez-moi le mot dans le livre*
yes *oui*
no *non*
please *s'il vous/te plaît*
thank you *merci*
(very much) *(beaucoup)*
you're welcome *de rien*
excuse me *excusez-moi*
hello *bonjour*
OK *d'accord*
goodbye *au revoir*
good evening *bonsoir*
here *ici*
there *là*
today *aujourd'hui*
yesterday *hier*
tomorrow *demain*
now *maintenant*
later *plus tard*
this morning *ce matin*
this afternoon *cet après-midi*
this evening *ce soir*

The Alphabet

Learning the pronunciation of the French alphabet is a good idea. In particular, learn how to spell out your name.
a=ah, **b**=bay, **c**=say, **d**=day **e**=uh, **f**=ef, **g**=zhay, **h**=ash, **i**=ee, **j**=zhee, **k**=ka, **l**=el, **m**=em, **n** =en, **o**=oh, **p**=pay, **q**=kew, **r**=ehr, **s**=ess, **t**=tay, **u**=ew, **v**=vay, **w**=dooblah vay, **x**-=eex, **y** ee grek, **z**=zed

On Arrival

I want to get off at...
Je voudrais descendre à...
Is there a bus to...?
Est-ce qui'il y a un bus pour ...?
What street is this? *A quelle rue sommes-nous?*
Which line do I take for...? *Quelle ligne dois-je prendre pour...?*
How far is...?
A quelle distance se trouve...?
Validate your ticket
Compostez votre billet
airport *l'aéroport*
train station *la gare (SNCF)*
bus station *la gare routière*
Métro stop *la station de Métro*
bus *l'autobus, le car*
bus stop *l'arrêt*
platform *le quai*
ticket *le billet*
return ticket *aller-retour*
hitchhiking *l'autostop*
toilets *les toilettes/les WC*
This is the hotel address
Voici l'adresse de l'hôtel
I'd like a (single/double) room...
Je voudrais une chambre (pour une/deux personnes) ...

Basic Rules

Even if you speak no French at all, it is worth trying to master a few simple phrases. The fact that you have made an effort is likely to get you a better response. More and more French people like practising their English on visitors, especially waiters in the cafés and restaurants and the younger generation. Pronunciation is the key; French-speakers will not understand if you get it very wrong. Remember to **emphasise each syllable**, but not to pronounce the last consonant of a word as a rule (this includes the plural "s") and always to drop your "h"s.

Whether to use "**vous**" or "**tu**" is a vexed question; increasingly the familiar form of "tu" is used by many people. However it is better to be too formal, and use "vous" if in doubt. It is very important to be polite; always address people as **Madame** or **Monsieur**, and address them by their surnames until you are confident first names are acceptable. When entering a shop always say, "Bonjour Monsieur/ Madame," and "Merci, au revoir," when leaving.

....with shower *avec douche*
....with a bath *avec salle de bain*
....with a view *avec vue*
Does that include breakfast? *Le prix comprend-il le petit déjeuner?*
May I see the room? *Je peux voir la chambre?*
washbasin *le lavabo*
bed *le lit*
key *la cléf*
elevator *l'ascenseur*
air-conditioned *climatisé*

On the Road

Where is the spare wheel? *Où est la roue de secours?*
Where is the nearest garage? *Où est le garage le plus proche?*
Our car has broken down *Notre voiture est en panne*
I want to have my car repaired *Je veux faire réparer ma voiture*
It's not your right of way *Vous n'avez pas la priorité*
I think I must have put diesel in the car by mistake *Je crois que j'ai mis du gasoil dans la voiture par erreur*
the road to... *la route pour...*
left *gauche*
right *droite*
straight on *tout droit*
far *loin*
near *près d'ici*
opposite *en face*
beside *à côté de*
car-park *parking*
over there *là-bas*
at the end *au bout*
on foot *à pied*
by car *en voiture*
town map *le plan*
road map *la carte*
street *la rue*
square *la place*
give way *céder le passage*
dead end *impasse*
no parking *stationnement interdit*
motorway *l'autoroute*
toll *le péage*
speed limit *la limitation de vitesse*
petrol *l'essence*
unleaded *sans plomb*
diesel *le gasoil*
water/oil *l'eau/l'huile*
puncture *un pneu de crevé*
bulb *l'ampoule*
wipers *les essuies-glace*

Shopping

Where is the nearest bank (post office)? *Où est la banque/Poste la plus proche?*
I'd like to buy *Je voudrais acheter*
How much is it? *C'est combien?*
Do you take credit cards? *Est-ce que vous acceptez les cartes de crédit?*
I'm just looking *Je regarde seulement*
Have you got...? *Avez-vous...?*
I'll take it *Je le prends*
I'll take this one/that one *Je prends celui-ci/celui-là*
What size is it? *C'est de quelle taille?*
Anything else? *Et avec ça?*
size (clothes) *la taille*
size (shoes) *la pointure*
cheap *bon marché*
expensive *cher*
enough *assez*
too much *trop*
a piece *un morceau de*
each *la pièce (eg ananas, €0.5 la pièce)*

False Friends

False friends are words that look like English words but mean something different.
le car motorcoach, also railway carriage
le conducteur bus driver
la monnaie change (coins)
l'argent money/silver
ça marche can sometimes mean walk, but is usually used to mean working (the TV, the car, etc.) or going well
actuel "present time" (*la situation actuelle* the present situation)
rester to stay
location hiring/renting
personne person or nobody, according to context
le médecin doctor

bill *la note/le reçu*
chemist *la pharmacie*
bakery *la boulangerie*
bookshop *la librairie*
library *la bibliothèque*
department store *le grand magasin*
delicatessen *la charcuterie/le traiteur*
fishmonger's *la poissonerie*
grocery *l'alimentation/l'épicerie*
tobacconist *bureau de tabac (can also sell stamps and newspapers)*
markets *le marché*
supermarket *le supermarché*
junk shop *la brocante*

Sightseeing

town *la ville*
old town *la vieille ville*
abbey *l'abbaye*
cathedral *la cathédrale*
church *l'église*
keep *le donjon*
mansion *l'hôtel*
hospital *l'hôpital*
town hall *l'hôtel de ville/la mairie*
nave *la nef*
stained-glass window *le vitrail*
staircase *l'escalier*
tower *la tour (la Tour Eiffel)*
walk *le tour*
country house/castle *le château*
Gothic *gothique*
Roman *romain*

Numbers

0 *zéro*
1 *un, une*
2 *deux*
3 *trois*
4 *quatre*
5 *cinq*
6 *six*
7 *sept*
8 *huit*
9 *neuf*
10 *dix*
11 *onze*
12 *douze*
13 *treize*
14 *quatorze*
15 *quinze*
16 *seize*
17 *dix-sept*
18 *dix-huit*
19 *dix-neuf*
20 *vingt*
21 *vingt-et-un*
30 *trente*
40 *quarante*
50 *cinquante*
60 *soixante*
70 *soixante-dix*
80 *quatre-vingts*
90 *quatre-vingt-dix*
100 *cent*
1000 *mille*
1,000,000 *un million*

- *The number 1 is often written like an upside down V, and the number 7 is always crossed.*

Romanesque *roman*
museum *la musée*
art gallery *la galerie*
exhibition *l'exposition*
tourist *l'office de*
information *tourisme/le*
office *syndicat d'initiative*
free *gratuit*
open *ouvert*
closed *fermé*
every day *tous les jours*
all year *toute l'année*
all day *toute la journée*
swimming pool *la piscine*
to book *réserver*

Dining Out

Table d'hôte (the "host's table") is one set menu served at a set price. **Prix fixe** is a fixed price menu. **A la carte** means dishes from the menu are charged separately.

breakfast *le petit déjeuner*
lunch *le déjeuner*
dinner *le dîner*
meal *le repas*
first course *l'entrée/les hors d'oeuvre*
main course *le plat principal*
drink included *boisson compris*
wine list *la carte des vins*
the bill *l'addition*
fork *la fourchette*
knife *le coûteau*
spoon *la cuillère*
plate *l'assiette*

Table Talk

I am a vegetarian *Je suis végétarien(ne)*
I am on a diet *Je suis au régime*
What do you recommend? *Que'est-ce que vous recommandez?*
Do you have local specialities? *Avez-vous des spécialités locales?*
I'd like to order *Je voudrais commander*
That is not what I ordered *Ce n'est pas ce que j'ai commandé*
Is service included? *Est-ce que le service est compris?*
May I have more wine? *Encore du vin, s'il vous plaît?*
Enjoy your meal *Bon appétit!*

glass *le verre*
ashtray *le cendrier*

Breakfast and Snacks

beurre **butter**
confiture **jam**
crêpe **pancake**
croque-monsieur **ham-and-cheese toasted sandwich**
croque-madame **ham-and-cheese toasted sandwich with a fried egg on top**
galette **type of pancake/cake**
oeufs **eggs**
oeufs à la coque **boiled eggs**
oeufs au bacon **bacon and eggs**
oeufs au jambon **ham and eggs**
oeufs sur le plat **fried eggs**
oeufs brouillés **scrambled eggs**
pain **bread**
pan bagna **bread roll stuffed with salad Niçoise**
petits pains **rolls**
poivre **pepper**
quiche **tart of eggs and cream with various fillings**
quiche lorraine **quiche with bacon**
sucre **sugar**
tartine **bread with butter**

Starters

An *amuse-bouche*, *amuse-gueule* or appetizer is something to "amuse the mouth", served before the first course

anchoïade **sauce of olive oil, anchovies and garlic, served with raw vegetables**
assiette anglaise **cold meats**
potage **soup**
rillettes **rich fatty paste of shredded duck, rabbit or pork**
tapenade **spread of olives and anchovies**
pissaladière **Provençal pizza with onions, olives and anchovies**

Viande/Meat

bleu **rare**
à point **medium**
bien cuit **well done**
grillé **grilled**
agneau **lamb**
andouille/andouillette **tripe sausage**
bifteck **steak**
boudin **sausage**
boudin noir **black pudding**
boudin blanc **white pudding (chicken or veal)**

Slang

métro, boulot, dodo nine-to-five syndrome
branché trendy (literally "connected")
C'est du cinéma It's very unlikely
une copine/un copain friend/chum/girlfriend/boyfriend
un ami friend but ***mon ami***, boyfriend; also ***mon copain***
un truc thing, "whatsit"
pas mal, not bad, good-looking

blanquette **stew of veal, lamb or chicken with a creamy egg sauce**
boeuf à la mode **beef in red wine with carrots, mushroom and onions**
...à la bordelaise **beef with red wine and shallots**
...à la Bourguignonne **cooked in red wine, onions and mushrooms**
brochette **kebab**
caille **quail**
canard **duck**
carbonnade **casserole of beef, beer and onions**
carré d'agneau cassoulet **rack of lamb stew with beans, sausages, pork and duck, from southwest France**
cervelle **brains (food)**
bacon and sausages
confit **duck or goose preserved in its own fat**
contre-filet **cut of sirloin steak**
coq au vin **chicken in red wine**
côte d'agneau **lamb chop**
boeuf en daube **beef stew with red wine, onions and tomatoes**
dinde **turkey**
entrecôte **beef rib steak**
escargot **snail**
faisan **pheasant**
farci **stuffed**
faux-filet **sirloin**
feuilleté **puff pastry**
foie **liver**
foie de veau **calf's liver**
foie gras **goose or duck liver pâté**
gardiane **rich beef stew with olives and garlic, from the Camargue**
cuisses de grenouille **frog's legs**
grillade **grilled meat**
hachis **minced meat**
jambon **ham**
lapin **rabbit**
lardons **small pieces of bacon**

magret de canard **breast of duck**
moelle **beef bone marrow**
mouton navarin **stew of lamb prepared with onions, carrots and turnips**
oie **goose**
perdrix **partridge**
petit-gris **small snails**
pieds de cochon **pig's trotters**
pintade **guinea fowl**
Pipérade **Basque dish of eggs, ham, peppers, onion**
porc **pork**
pot-au-feu **casserole of beef and vegetables**
poulet **chicken**
poussin **young chicken**
rognons **kidneys**
rôti **roast**
sanglier **wild boar**
saucisse **fresh sausage**
saucisson **salami**
veau **veal**

Emergencies

Help! *Au secours!*
Stop! *Arrêtez!*
Call a doctor *Appelez un médecin*
Call an ambulance *Appelez une ambulance*
Call the police *Appelez la police*
Call the fire brigade *Appelez les pompiers*
Where is the nearest telephone? *Où est le téléphone le plus proche?*
Where is the nearest hospital? *Où est l'hôpital le plus proche?*
I am sick *Je suis malade*
I have lost my passport/purse *J'ai perdu mon passeport/porte-monnaie*

Poissons/Fish

Armoricaine **made with white wine, tomatoes, butter and cognac**
anchois **anchovies**
anguille **eel**
bar (or *loup*) **sea bass**
barbue **brill**
belon **Brittany oyster**
Bercy **sauce made with fish stock, butter, white wine and shallots**
bigorneau **sea snail**
bouillabaisse **traditional Provençal fish soup, served with grated cheese, garlic croutons and *rouille*, a spicy sauce**
brandade **salt-cod purée**
cabillaud **cod**
calmars **squid**
colin **hake**
coquillage **shellfish**
coquilles St-Jacques **scallops**
crevette **shrimp**
daurade **sea bream**
flétan **halibut**
fruits de mer **seafood**
hareng **herring**
homard **lobster**
huître **oyster**
langoustine **large prawn**
limande **lemon sole**
lotte **monkfish**
morue **salt cod**
moule **mussel**
moules marinières **mussels in white wine and onions**
raie **skate**
saumon **salmon**
thon **tuna**
truite **trout**

Légumes/Vegetables

ail **garlic**
artichaut **artichoke**
asperge **asparagus**
aubergine **aubergine (eggplant)**
avocat **avocado**
bolets **boletus mushrooms**
céleri **grated celery**
rémoulade **with mayonnaise**
champignon **mushroom**
cèpes **cèpe mushrooms**
chanterelles **wild mushrooms**
cornichon **gherkin**
courgette **courgette (zucchini)**
chips **potato crisps**
chou **cabbage**
chou-fleur **cauliflower**
concombre **cucumber**
cru **raw**
crudités **raw vegetables**
épinard **spinach**
frites **chips, French fries**
gratin dauphinois **sliced potatoes baked with cream**
haricot **dried bean**
haricots verts **green beans**
lentilles **lentils**
maïs **corn**
mange-tout **mange-tout (snow pea)**
mesclun **mixed leaf salad**
navet **turnip**
noix **nut, walnut**
noisette **hazelnut**

Forms of Address

Garçon is the word for waiter but it should never be used directly, as this is considered impolite; say *Monsieur* or *Mademoiselle/Madame* (depending on how old the waitress is) to attract his or her attention.

oignon **onion**
panais **parsnip**
persil **parsley**
pignon **pine nut**
poireau **leek**
pois **pea**
poivron **bell pepper**
pomme de terre **potato**
radis **radis**
roquette **arugula, rocket**
ratatouille **tradition Provençal vegetable stew made from aubergines, courgettes, tomatoes, peppers and olive oil**
riz **rice**
salade Niçoise **egg, tuna, olives, onions and tomato salad**
salade verte **green salad**
truffe **truffle**

Fruits/Fruit

ananas **pineapple**
cavaillon **fragrant sweet melon from Cavaillon in Provence**
cerise **cherry**
citron **lemon**
citron vert **lime**
figue **fig**
fraise **strawberry**
framboise **raspberry**
groseille **redcurrant**
mangue **mango**
mirabelle **yellow plum**
pamplemousse **grapefruit**
pêche **peach**
poire **pear**
pomme **apple**
raisin **grape**
prune **plum**
pruneau **prune**
Reine claude **greengage**

Sauces/Sauces

aioli **garlic mayonnaise**
béarnaise **sauce of egg, butter, wine and herbs**
forestière **with mushrooms and bacon**

hollandaise **egg, butter and lemon sauce**
lyonnaise **with onions**
meunière **fried fish with butter, lemon and parsley sauce**
meurette **red wine sauce**
Mornay **sauce of cream, egg and cheese**
Parmentier **served with potatoes**
paysan **rustic style, ingredients depend on the region**
pistou **Provençal sauce of basil, garlic and olive oil; vegetable soup with pistou sauce**
provençale **sauce of tomatoes, garlic and olive oil**
papillotte **cooked in paper**

Dessert/Puddings

Belle Hélène **fruit with ice-cream and chocolate sauce**
clafoutis **baked pudding of batter and cherries**
coulis **purée of fruit or vegetables**
gâteau **cake**
île flottante **meringue in custard**
crème anglaise **custard**
pêche melba **peaches with ice-cream and raspberry sauce**
tarte tatin **upside-down tart of caramelised apples**
crème caramel **caramelised egg custard**

On the Telephone

How do I make an outside call? *Comment est-ce que je téléphone à l'exterieur?*
I want to make an international (local) call *Je voudrais une communication pour l'étranger (une communication locale)*
What is the dialling code? *Quel est l'indicatif?*
I'd like an alarm call for 8 tomorrow morning *Je voudrais être réveillé à huit heures demain martin*
Who's calling? *C'est qui à l'appareil?*
Hold on, please *Ne quittez pas s'il vous plaît*
The line is busy *La ligne est occupée*
I must have dialled the wrong number *J'ai dû faire un faux numéro*

crème Chantilly **whipped cream**
fromage **cheese**
chèvre **goat's cheese**

In a Café

If you sit at the bar *(le comptoir* or, more colloquial, *le zinc)*, drinks will be cheaper than if you sit at a table; your drink will cost even more if you sit on the outside terrace. It's normal practise to settle the bill when you leave – the waiter may leave a slip of paper on the table to keep track of what you've eaten or drunk.

Boissons/Drinks

coffee *café*
...with milk or cream *au lait or crème*
...decaffeinated *déca/décaféiné*
...black/espresso *express/noir*
...American filtered coffee *filtre*
large milky coffee *grand crème*
small milky coffee *petit crème*
tea *thé*
...herb infusion *tisane*
...camomile *verveine*
hot chocolate *chocolat chaud*
milk *lait*
mineral water *eau minérale*
fizzy *gazeux*
non-fizzy *non-gazeux*
fizzy lemonade *limonade*
fresh lemon juice served with sugar *citron pressé*
freshly squeezed orange juice *orange pressé*
full (eg full cream milk) *entier*
fresh or cold *frais, fraîche*
beer *bière*
...bottled *en bouteille*
...on tap *à la pression*
pre-dinner drink *apéritif*
white wine with *cassis*, a black-currant liqueur *kir*
***kir* with champagne** *kir royale*
with ice *avec des glaçons*
neat *sec*
red *rouge*
white *blanc*
rose *rosé*
dry *brut*
sweet *doux*
sparkling wine *crémant*
house wine *vin de maison*
local wine *vin de pays*

Days and Months

Days of the week, seasons and months are not capitalised in French.

- **Days of the week**
  Monday *lundi*
  Tuesday *mardi*
  Wednesday *mercredi*
  Thursday *jeudi*
  Friday *vendredi*
  Saturday *samedi*
  Sunday *dimanche*
- **Seasons**
  spring *le printemps*
  summer *l'été*
  autumn *l'automne*
  winter *l'hiver*
- **Months**
  January *janvier*
  February *février*
  March *mars*
  April *avril*
  May *mai*
  June *juin*
  July *juillet*
  August *août*
  September *septembre*
  October *octobre*
  November *novembre*
  December *décembre*
- **Saying the date**
  20th October 2002, *le vingt octobre, deux mille deux*

Where is this wine from? *De quelle région vient ce vin?*
pitcher *carafe/pichet*
...of water/wine *d'eau/de vin*
half litre *demi-carafe*
quarter litre *quart*
mixed *panaché*
after-dinner drink *digestif*
brandy from the Armagnac region of France *Armagnac*
Normandy apple brandy *calvados*
cheers! *santé!*
hangover *gueule de bois*

Time

At what time? *A quelle heure?*
When? *Quand?*
What time is it? *Quelle heure est-il?*
- *Note that the French generally use the 24-hour clock.*

Further Reading

Art and Architecture

France: A History in Art by Bradley Smith (Doubleday, 1984). The history of France through the eyes of artists.

The French Farmhouse by Elsie Burch Donald (Little Brown, 1992). Regional architectural vernacular styles analysed in detail.

A History of Architecture in France by T.W. West (University of London Press, 1969). Useful light introduction to the subject.

A History in Art by Bradley Smith (Doubleday, 1984). The history of France through the eyes of artists.

Inventing the French Riviera by Mary Blume (Thames & Hudson, 1992). Excellent account of the *emigré* Riviera.

Letters of Van Gogh, ed. Ronald de Leeuw (Penguin, 1997). Correspondence revealing a subtle side of the celebrated Dutch painter.

A Life of Picasso. Vols I and II by John Richardson (Cape, 1996).***The Sorcerer's Apprentice: Picasso, Provence and Douglas Cooper*** by John Richardson (Cape, 1999). Wonderful gossipy personal account from Picasso's biographer.

The Unknown Matisse by Hilary Spurling (Knopf, 1998). Well-researched biography of the great French painter.

Fiction

The Avignon Quintet by Lawrence Durrell (Faber, 1992). Classic travel writing from Durrell. Provence and other regions, 1974–85.

Baie des Anges by Max Gallo (Bouquins, 3 vols). Crime, corruption and the establishment of Nice by the English and the Italians.

Bonjour Tristesse by Françoise Sagan. (Penguin, 1998). The story of a teenager and her father, living the hedonistic Riviera life. Things turn sour when the father remarries.

Chocolat by Joanne Harris (Transworld, 1999). A stranger opens a chocolate shop in a rural French village during Lent, causing havoc in the community. 1999 Whitbread Book of the Year and a successful film starring Juliette Binoche and Johnny Depp.

The Count of Monte Cristo by Alexandre Dumas (Various editions). Gripping account of prison life and revenge at the Château d'If, near Marseille.

The Horseman on the Roof by Jean Giono (Harvil, 1995). Provence in the 1830s. Another film starring Juliette Binoche.

Letters from My Windmill by Alphonse Daudet (Penguin, out of print). Classic tales of 19th-century Provence from Daudet's windmill near Fontvielle.

Living Well is the Best Revenge by Calvin Tomkin (Random House, 1998). Portrait of members of a circle of artists during the Roaring Twenties.

The Man Who Planted Trees by Jean Giono (Harvill, 1992). The obsessive Elzéard Bouffier plants more than 100 acorns every day for 30 years in an attempt to regenerate a dead region.

The Water of the Hills: Jean de Florette and ***Manon of the Springs*** by Marcel Pagnol (Picador, 1982). Peasant struggles over the water supply in rural Provence. The two volumes that inspired the award-winning films starring husband-and-wife team Daniel Auteil and Emmanuelle Béart.

***Memoirs* by** Frédéric Mistral, translated by George Wickes. (Alyscamps Press, 1984). Memories of Provençal Nobel-prize winner.

Perfume by Patrick Süskind (Picador, 1989). Sinister but gripping tale of an 18th-century Grasse perfumer.

The Rock Pool by Cyril Connolly (Persea, 1996).

Tender is the Night by F. Scott Fitzgerald (Penguin, 1999). Glamorous Americans living out the eternal Riviera myth on the South French coast.

Travels in the South of France by Stendhal, translated by Elisabeth Abbott (Calder and Boyars, 1971). The author's account of the joys and frustrations of travelling in the region in the 19th century.

A Year in Provence by Peter Mayle (Penguin, 2000). Light-hearted and enjoyable, if somewhat clichéed, account of Mayle's first 12 months in a new home near Maillane.

Food and Wine

Flavours of France by Alain Ducasse (Artisan, 1998). Recipes from the Provençal masterchef.

The Food Lover's Guide to France by Patricia Wells (Workman, 1988). Regional dishes, restaurant recommendations, shops and markets from the food critic of *International Herald Tribune*.

A Table in Provence by Leslie Forbes (Webb & Bower). Recipes and more.

Touring in Wine Country: Provence ed. Hugh Johnson (Mitchell Beazley, 1993). Tours of the Provençal vineyards accompanied by attractive maps and informative text.

Wine Atlas of France by Hubrecht Duijker (Mitchell Beazley, London, 1997). Well-illustrated atlas, concentrating on wine and vineyards, but also supplementary information on history, architecture and culture.

History

The Albigensian Crusade by Jonathan Sumption (Faber & Faber, 1978). Accessible blow-by-blow account of the demise of the Cathars.

The Cambridge Illustrated History of France by Colin Jones (Cambridge University Press, 1994). An excellent overview of French history in general, in which the quality of the illustrations matches that of the text.

A Holiday History of France by Ronald Hamilton (The Hogarth Press, 1985). An illustrated guide to history and architecture designed to be taken along on a trip.

The Hundred Years' War Vol 1: Trial by Battle by Jonathan Sumption (Faber & Faber, 1999). The first in a series of books documenting the war.

The Identity of France by Fernand Braudel (Collins, 1988 and 1990). An arresting historical analysis, weaving major events with everyday life, by one of France's most brilliant historians.

A Traveller's History of France by Robert Cole (The Windrush Press, London, 1994). A succinct history of the main historical events in France. Slim volume that makes useful background reading.

Literature Studies

The New Oxford Companion to French Literature ed. Peter France (Oxford University Press, 1995). Standard reference work superseding ***The Oxford Companion to French Literature*** by Sir Paul Harvey and J.E. Heseltine (Oxford University Press, 1959).

Traveller's Literary Companion to France by John Edmondson (In Print, 1997). Gazetteer of places with literary associations, including detailed book lists and biographies.

Modern France

France in the New Century by John Ardagh (Penguin, 2000). Good overview of contemporary France by a recognised expert.

France Today edited by J.E. Flower (Hodder, London, 1993). Essays on contemporary France.

The French by Theodore Zeldin (Random House, New York, 1983). Irreverent, penetrating analysis of the French character.

On the Brink, the Trouble with France by Jonathan Fenby (Little Brown 1998). Controversial, personal and witty account of French politics and life today.

Wildlife

The Alpine Flowers of Britain and Europe by C. Grey-Wilson & M. Blamey (Collins, 2001). Comprehensive reference book.

The Birds of Britain and Europe by Hermann Heinzel, Richard Fitter and John Parslow (Collins, 1972). Brief descriptions of all species likely to be seen and light enough to carry in a bag.

Wild Flowers of the Mediterranean by I. & P. Schonfelder (Collins, 1984). Over 1,000 species described and hundreds of photographs.

Wildlife Travelling Companion France by Bob Gibbons and Paul Davies (The Crowood Press, 1992). Region-by-region rundown of the best nature-watching places.

Other Insight Guides

The 450 titles published by the award-winning Insight Guides include comprehensive coverage of French destinations.

Insight Guides

Other **Insight Guides** to France include *Alsace, Brittany, Burgundy, Corsica, France, French Riviera, Loire Valley, Paris, Normandy* and *Southwest France.*

Pocket Guides

Insight Pocket Guides, containing personal recommendations and a large fold-out map, cover *Alsace, Brittany, Corsica, The Loire Valley, Paris* and *The French Riviera.*

Compact Guides

Insight Compact Guides, fact-packed easy-reference guides, cover *Brittany, Burgundy, Paris* and *Normandy.*

Fleximaps

Insight Fleximaps, including Fleximap Paris, combine durability with accurate, up-to-date information.

Feedback

We do our best to ensure the information in our books is as accurate and up-to-date as possible. The books are updated on a regular basis, using local contacts, who painstakingly add, amend and correct as required. However, some mistakes and omissions are inevitable and we are ultimately reliant on our readers to put us in the picture.

We would welcome your feedback on any details related to your experiences using the book "on the road". Maybe we recommended a hotel that you liked (or another that you didn't), as well as interesting new attractions, or facts and figures you have found out about the country itself. The more details you can give us (particularly with regard to addresses, e-mails and telephone numbers), the better.

We will acknowledge all contributions, and we'll offer an Insight Guide to the best letters received.

Please write to us at:
Insight Guides
PO Box 7910
London SE1 1WE
United Kingdom

Or send an e-mail to:
insight@apaguide.demon.co.uk

ART & PHOTO CREDITS

AKG London 33, 46, 79, 80, 81, 83
Frank Broekhuizen 10/11
Robert Capa/Magnum 76
Imperial War Museum 49
Catherine Karnow back cover left, centre & bottom, back flap top, 1, 2/3, 4/5, 4L, 5, 6/7, 12/13, 16/17, 18, 19, 20, 21, 22/23, 27, 28, 32, 34, 35, 36, 37, 38, 39, 40, 41, 43, 44, 45, 53, 54, 55, 58/59, 60, 61, 62, 63, 64, 65, 66/67, 68, 69, 70, 71, 84, 85, 86, 98/99, 100/101, 102/103, 108/109, 118, 120, 121, 122, 123, 124 L/R, 125, 126, 128, 130, 131, 134, 135, 138, 139, 140, 141, 142, 143L/R, 144/145, 152, 153, 154, 155, 157, 162, 164, 165, 166, 167L/R, 158, 159, 160, 161, 172, 174, 175, 177, 178, 179, 180, 182, 183, 184, 185, 186/187, 188, 193, 194, 195, 196, 197, 198/199, 204, 205, 206, 207, 208, 209, 210, 211, 212, 213L/R, 214, 215, 216, 217, 218, 219, 220, 221, 222/223, 230, 231, 232, 233, 234, 235, 236, 237, 238, 239, 240, 241, 243, 244/245, 246, 247, 250, 252, 253, 254, 255, 256, 257, 259, 261, 262, 263, 264, 265, 267, 268/269, 270, 271, 284, 285
Cannes Film Festival Press Office 94
Christian Lacroix Haute-Couture 176
National Gallery of Art 74/75, 78
Rex Features 90/91, 92, 95, 119
Anne Roston 42, 87, 88, 89
Bill Wassman/Apa back cover top right, spine top & centre, back flap bottom, front flap top & bottom, 2 bottom, 4R, 8/9, 14, 24, 25, 26, 29, 30, 31, 52, 72, 77, 82, 93, 104, 110, 111, 114, 115, 127, 132, 136, 137, 146, 147, 150, 158, 159L/R, 160, 161, 181, 190, 191, 200, 201, 224, 228, 229, 278, 280, 281, 286, 287, 288
Marcus Wilson-Smith back cover top right, 56, 57, 73, 117, 129, 133, 163, 225, 266, 274, 275, 276, 277

Map Production Stephen Ramsay

INSIGHT GUIDE
Provence

Cartographic Editor **Zoë Goodwin**
Production **Linton Donaldson**
Design Consultant **Carlotta Junger**
Picture Research **Hilary Genin, Natasha Babaian**

Index

Numbers in italics refer to photographs

a

g

h

m

n

"I was first drawn to the Insight Guides by the excellent "Nepal" volume. I can think of no book which so effectively captures the essence of a country. Out of these pages leaped the Nepal I know – the captivating charm of a people and their culture. I've since discovered and enjoyed the entire Insight Guide series. Each volume deals with a country in the same sensitive depth, which is nowhere more evident than in the superb photography."

Sir Edmund Hillary

Travellers with true insight rely on Columbus for all their travel insurance needs.
If you are a frequent traveller who takes 2 or more trips a year, you can benefit substantially from our annual multi-trip policy. You can also buy on-line with total confidence and receive your policy certificate by email within minutes!
✓ 3-365 day cover
✓ single trip
✓ annual multi-trip
✓ short breaks
✓ summer holidays
✓ safaris
✓ sports/activities
and much more...
TM
COLUMBUS DIRECT
One specialist you can trust
www.columbusdirect.com
020 7375 0011
17 DEVONSHIRE SQUARE, LONDON. 2 MINS FROM LIVERPOOL ST STATION